SEVEN SEAS ENTER[TAINMENT]

Nameless Asterism

story and art by
KINA KOBAYASHI

TRANSLATION
Jenny McKeon

ADAPTATION
Lora Gray

LETTERING AND RETOUCH
Ray Steeves

COVER DESIGN
Nicky Lim

PROOFREADER
Danielle King

ASSISTANT EDITOR
Jenn Grunigen

PRODUCTION ASSISTANT
CK Russell

PRODUCTION MANAGER
Lissa Pattillo

EDITOR-IN-CHIEF
Adam Arnold

PUBLISHER
Jason DeAngelis

Translation ©2017 by SQUARE ENIX CO., LTD.

Seven Seas books may be purchased in bulk for promotional, educational, or
business use. Please contact your local bookseller or the Macmillan Corporate
and Premium Sales Department at 1-800-221-7945, extension 5442, or by
e-mail at MacmillanSpecialMarkets@macmillan.com.

Seven Seas and the Seven Seas logo are trademarks of
Seven Seas Entertainment, LLC. All rights reserved.

ISBN: 978-1-626927-44-5

Printed in Canada

First Printing: January 2018

10 9 8 7 6 5 4 3 2 1

FOLLOW US ONLINE: www.gomanga.com

READING DIRECTIONS

This book reads from *right to left*, Japanese style.
If this is your first time reading manga, you start
reading from the top right panel on each page and
take it from there. If you get lost, just follow the
numbered diagram here. It may seem backwards at
first, but you'll get the hang of it! Have fun!!

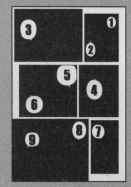

SPECIAL THANKS

Editor: Nakagawa Ken-sama

Asistant: Norita-sama

Everyone who was involved
in the making of this book...

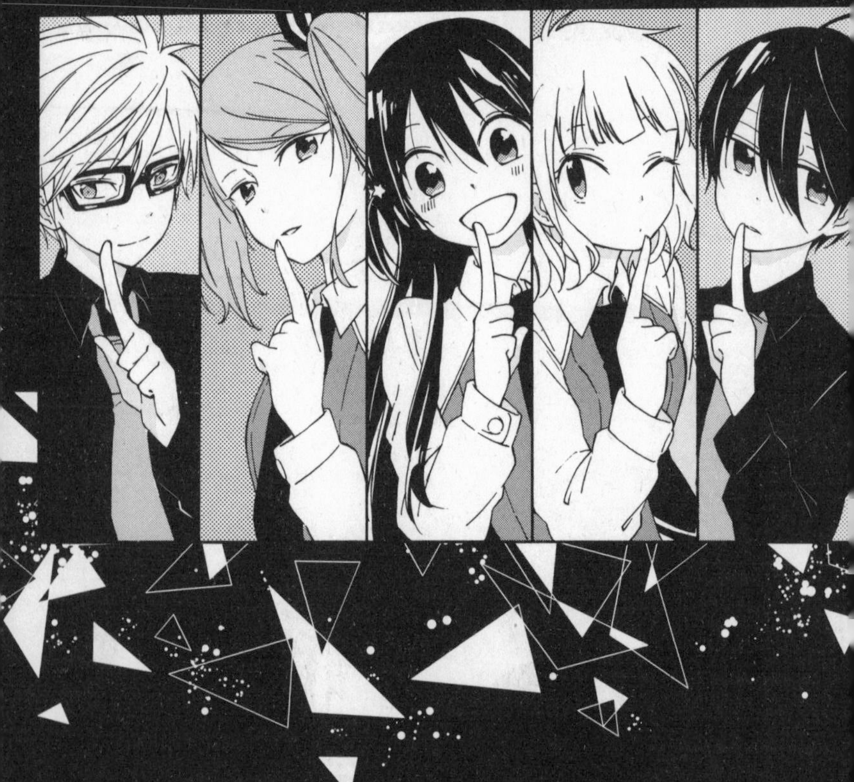

...and all of the readers.

Chapter 1

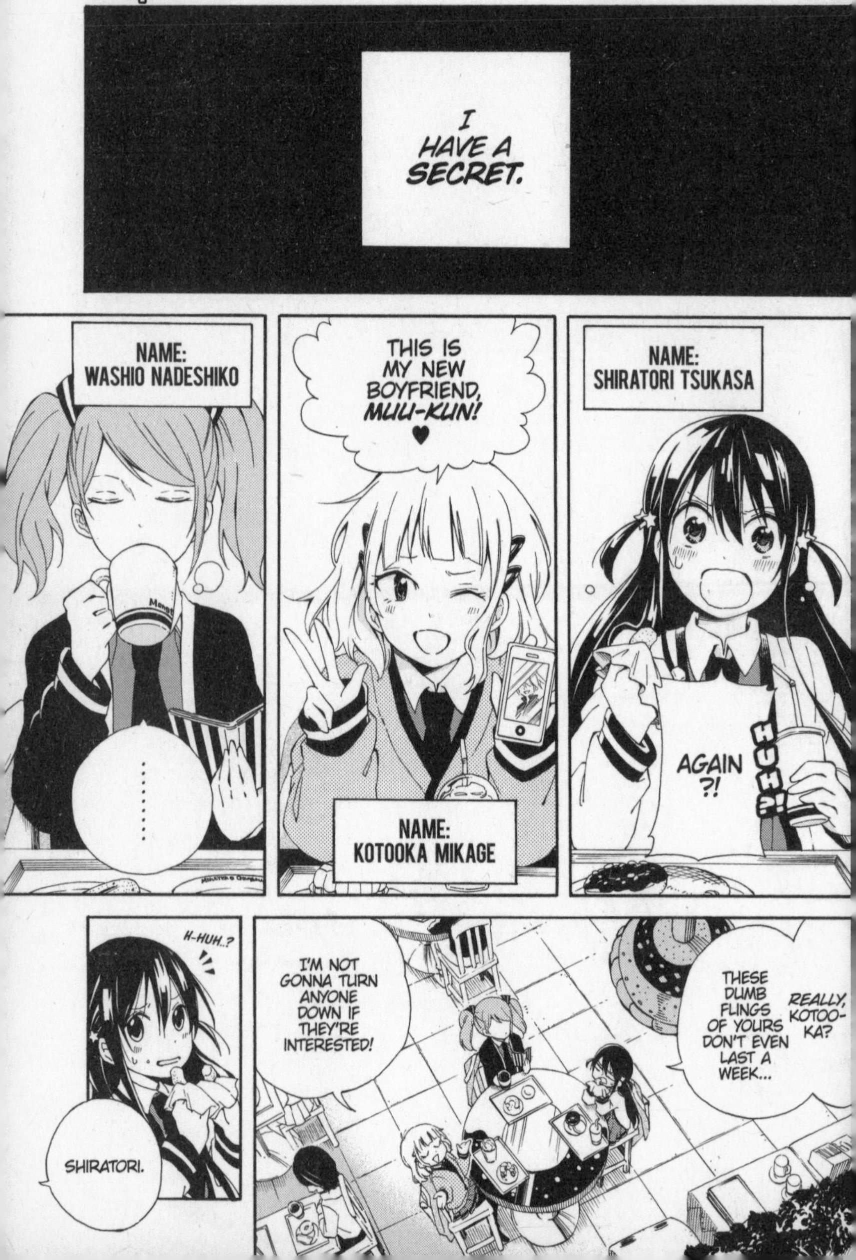

I HAVE A SECRET.
NAME: SHIRATORI TSUKASA
HUH?!
AGAIN?!
THIS IS MY NEW BOYFRIEND, MUU-KUN! ♥
NAME: KOTOOKA MIKAGE
NAME: WASHIO NADESHIKO
....
REALLY, KOTOO-KA?
THESE DUMB FLINGS OF YOURS DON'T EVEN LAST A WEEK...
I'M NOT GONNA TURN ANYONE DOWN IF THEY'RE INTERESTED!
H-HUH..?
SHIRATORI.

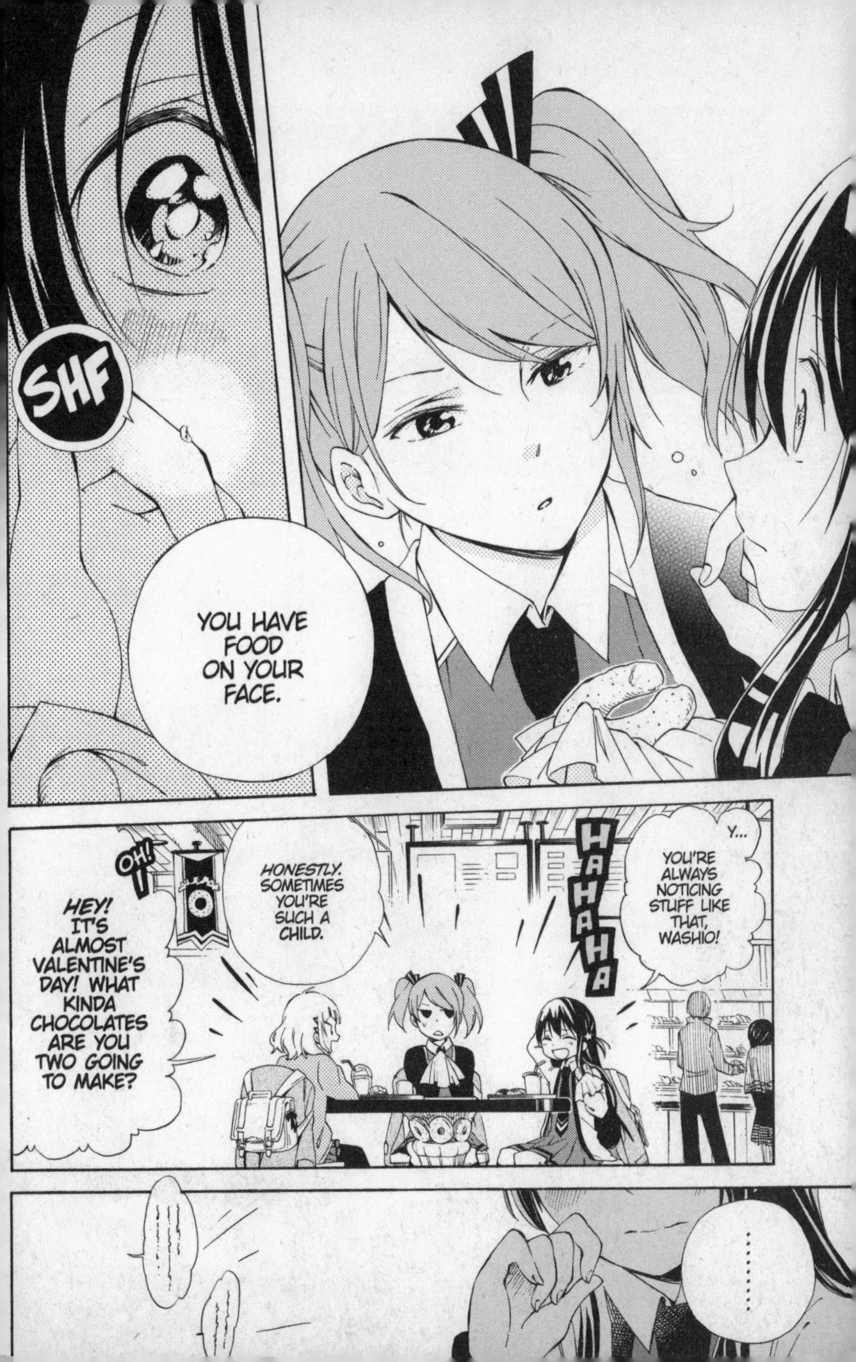
SHF
YOU HAVE FOOD ON YOUR FACE.
Y... YOU'RE ALWAYS NOTICING STUFF LIKE THAT, WASHIO!
HAHAHA
HONESTLY. SOMETIMES YOU'RE SUCH A CHILD.
OH!
HEY! IT'S ALMOST VALENTINE'S DAY! WHAT KINDA CHOCOLATES ARE YOU TWO GOING TO MAKE?
......
......
......

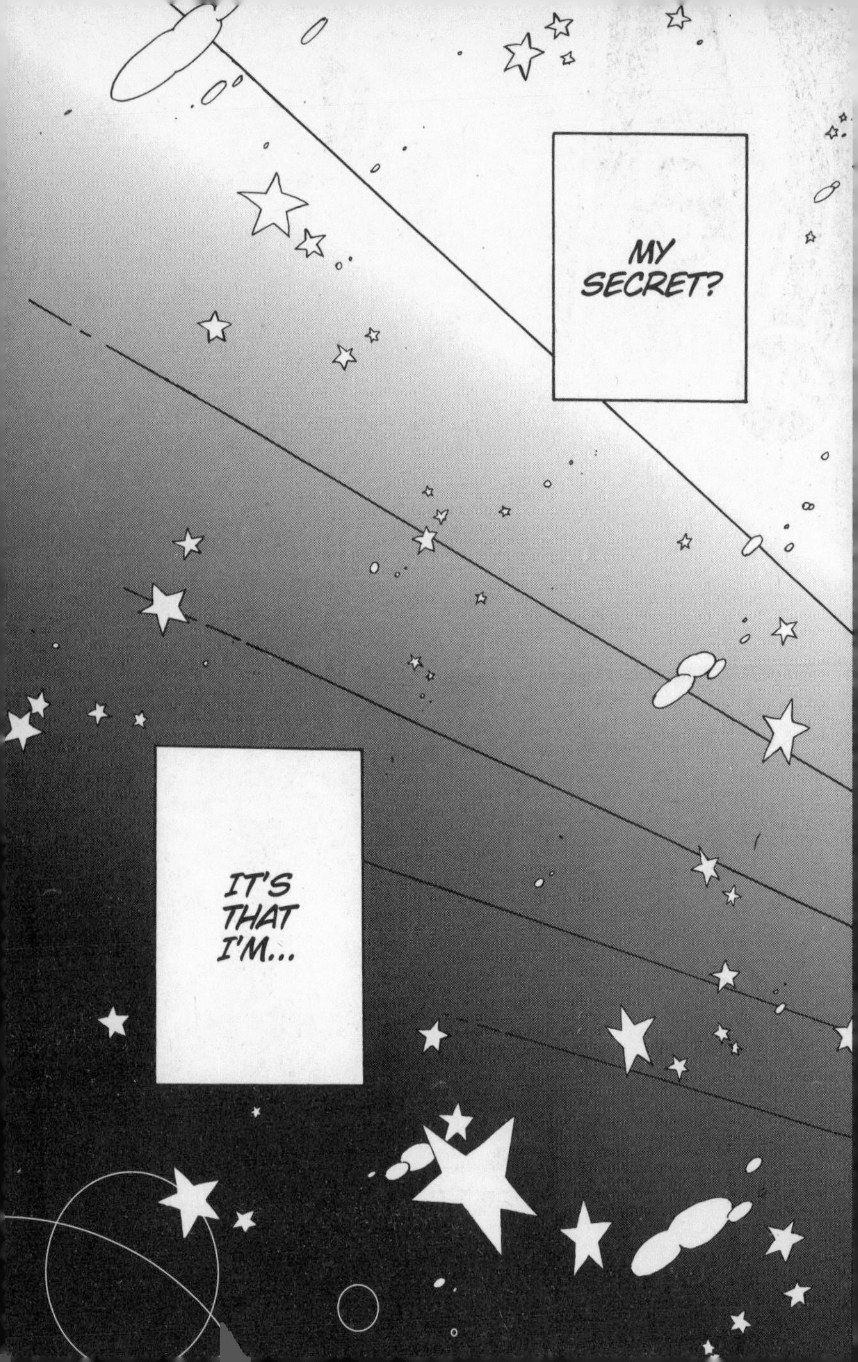
MY SECRET?
IT'S THAT I'M...

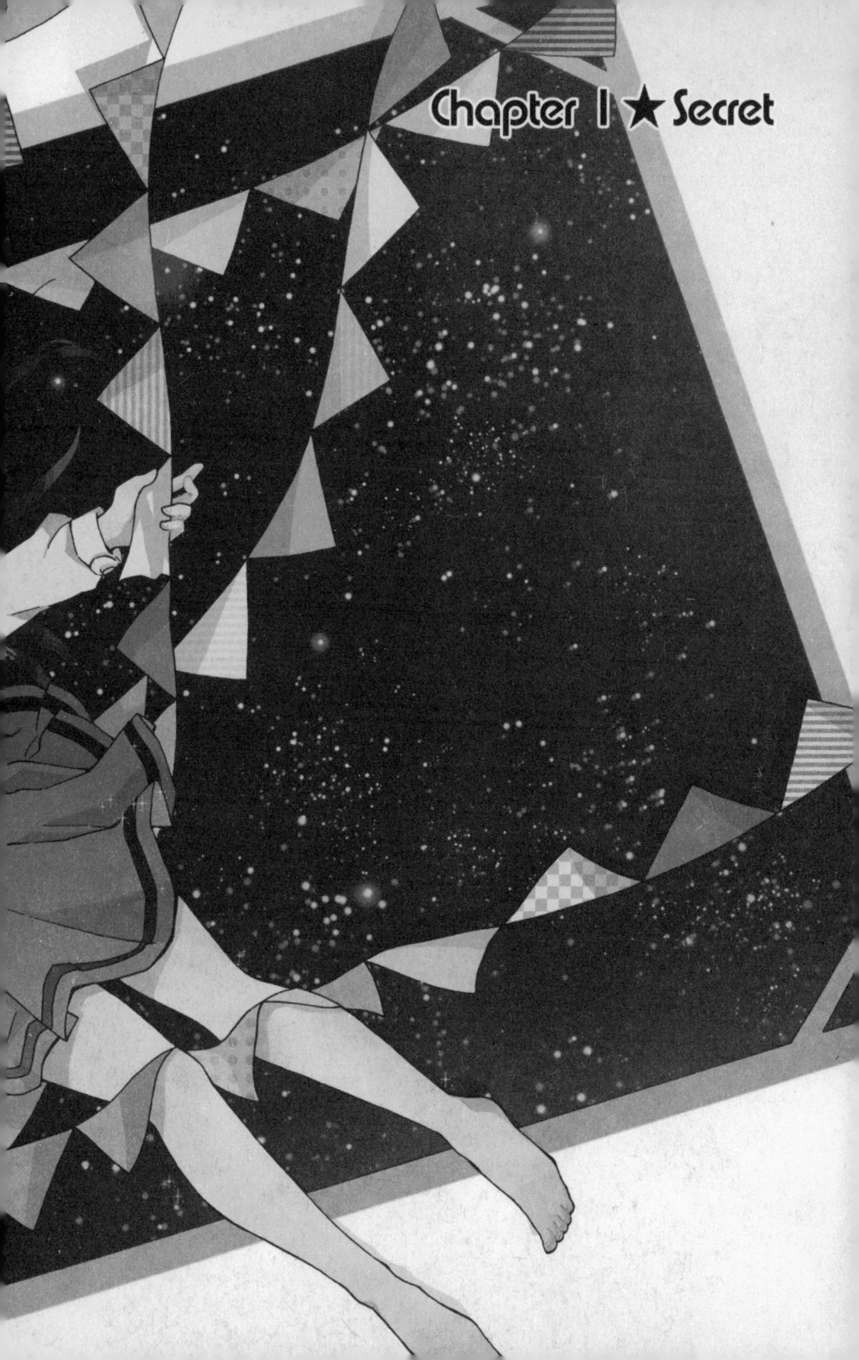
Chapter 1 ★ Secret

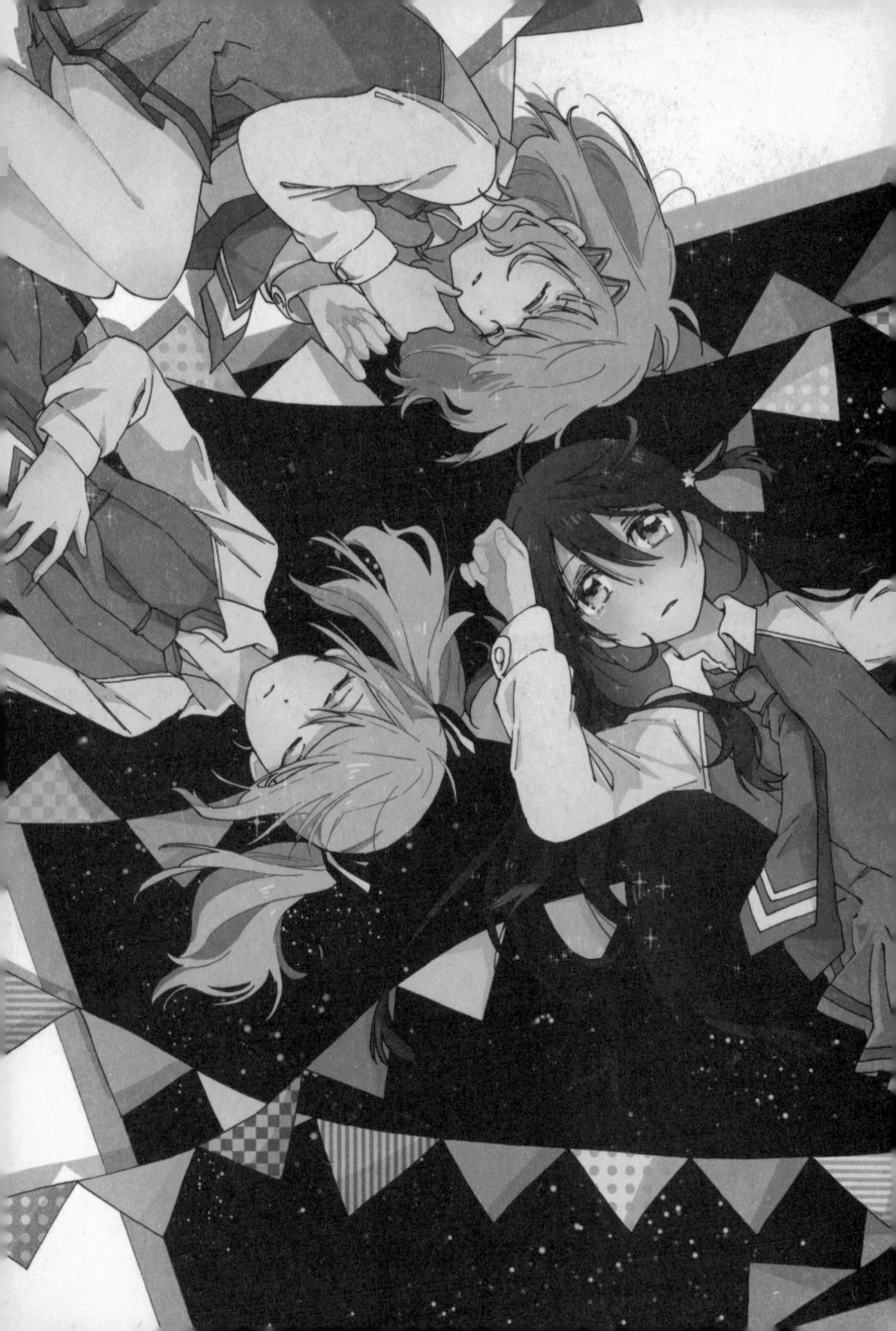

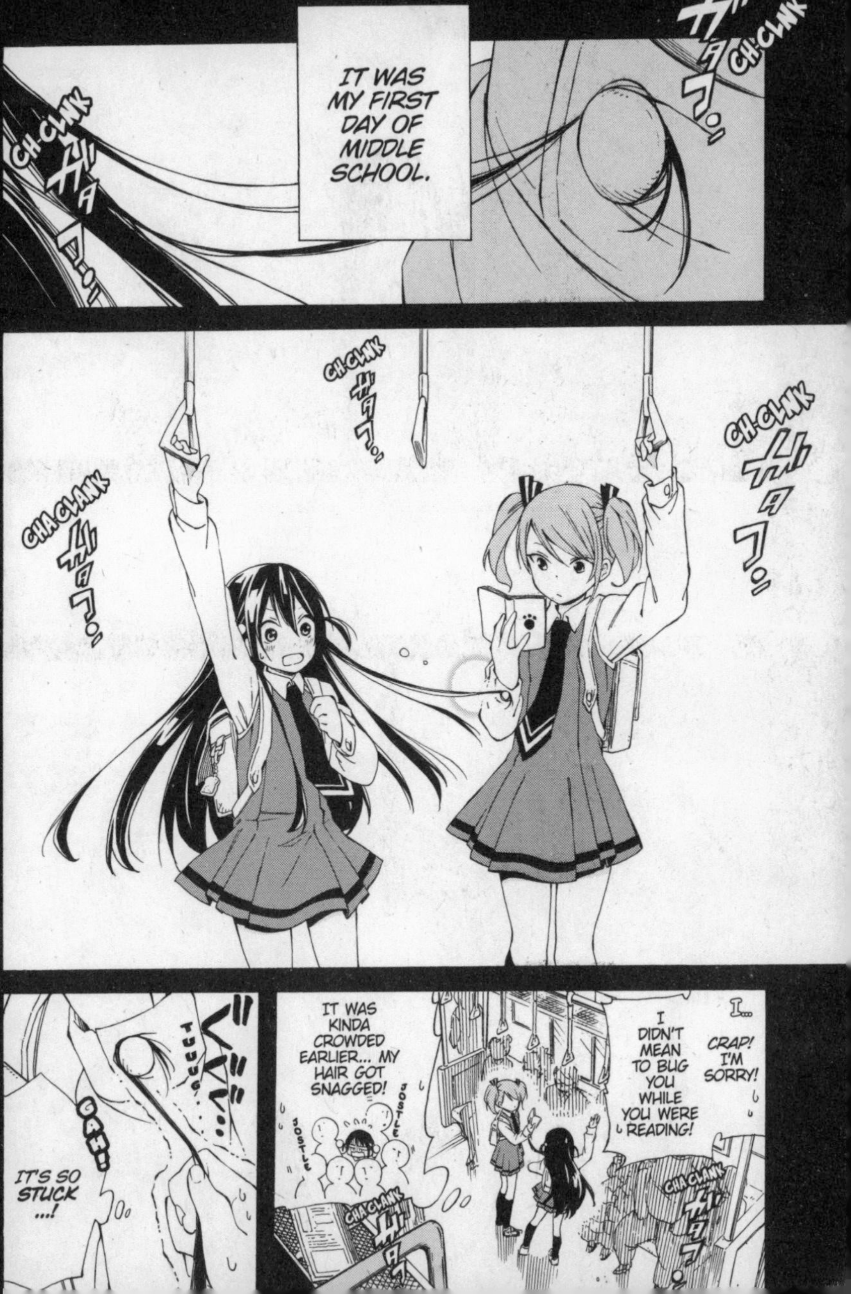
CH-CLNK
IT WAS MY FIRST DAY OF MIDDLE SCHOOL.
CH-CLNK
CH-CLNK
CH-CLNK
CHA-CLANK
I...
CRAP! I'M SORRY!
I DIDN'T MEAN TO BUG YOU WHILE YOU WERE READING!
IT WAS KINDA CROWDED EARLIER... MY HAIR GOT SNAGGED!
JOSTLE
JOSTLE
CHA-CLANK
CHA-CLANK
TUUUG...
GAH!
IT'S SO STUCK...!

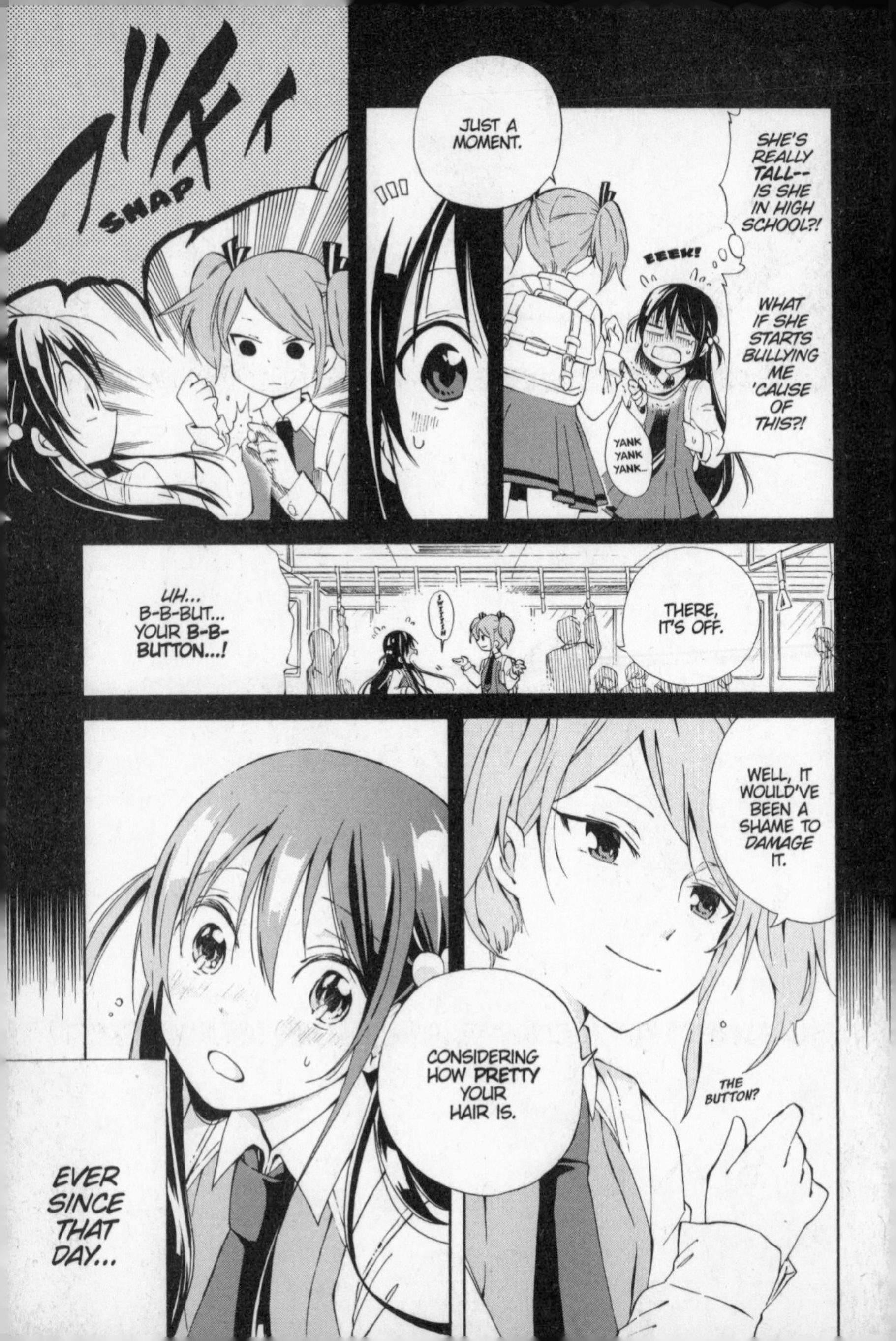
JUST A MOMENT.
SHE'S REALLY TALL-- IS SHE IN HIGH SCHOOL?!
EEEK!
WHAT IF SHE STARTS BULLYING ME 'CAUSE OF THIS?!
YANK YANK YANK...
SNAP
THERE, IT'S OFF.
UH... B-B-BUT... YOUR B-B-BUTTON...!
WELL, IT WOULD'VE BEEN A SHAME TO DAMAGE IT.
THE BUTTON?
CONSIDERING HOW PRETTY YOUR HAIR IS.
EVER SINCE THAT DAY...

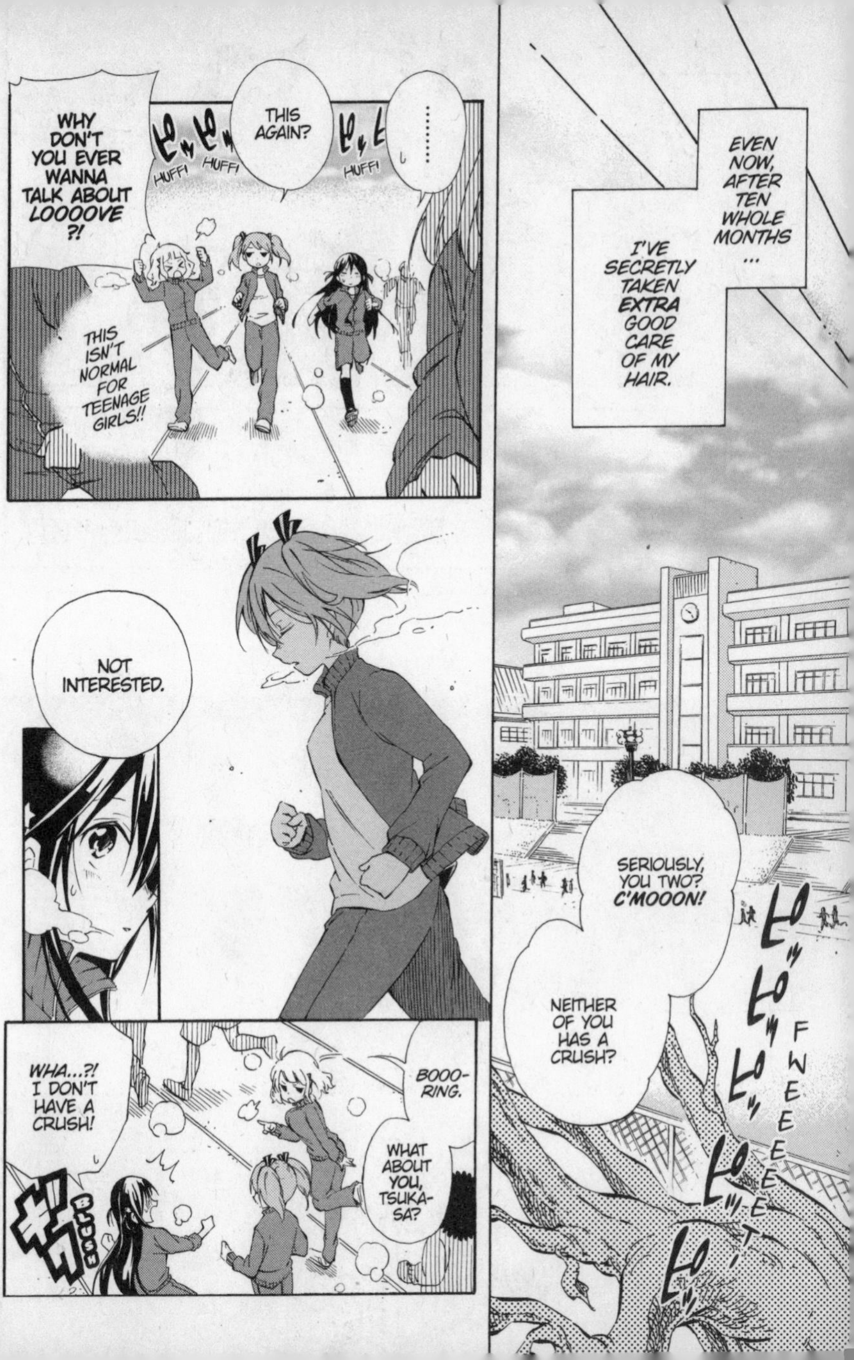

EVEN NOW, AFTER TEN WHOLE MONTHS...
I'VE SECRETLY TAKEN EXTRA GOOD CARE OF MY HAIR.
SERIOUSLY, YOU TWO? C'MOOON!
NEITHER OF YOU HAS A CRUSH?
FWEEEEE-ET!
......
THIS AGAIN?
HUFF! HUFF! HUFF!
WHY DON'T YOU EVER WANNA TALK ABOUT LOOOOVE?!
THIS ISN'T NORMAL FOR TEENAGE GIRLS!!
NOT INTERESTED.
BOOO-RING.
WHAT ABOUT YOU, TSUKA-SA?
WHA...?! I DON'T HAVE A CRUSH!
BLUSH

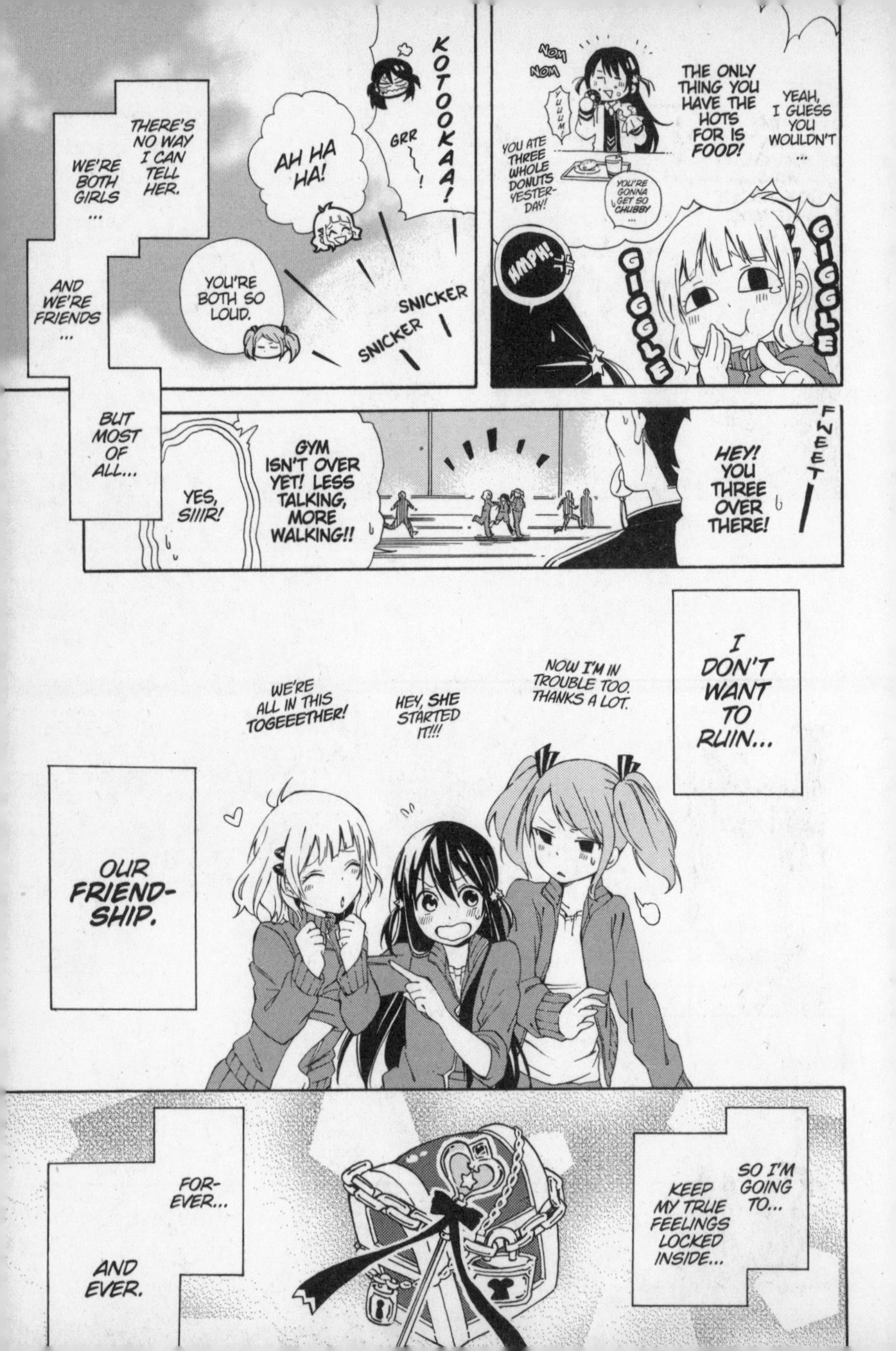
YEAH, I GUESS YOU WOULDN'T ...
THE ONLY THING YOU HAVE THE HOTS FOR IS FOOD!
NOM NOM
YUUUM!
YOU ATE THREE WHOLE DONUTS YESTER-DAY!
YOU'RE GONNA GET SO CHUBBY ...
GIGGLE GIGGLE
HMPH!
KOTOOKAA!
GRR
AH HA HA!
SNICKER SNICKER
YOU'RE BOTH SO LOUD.
THERE'S NO WAY I CAN TELL HER.
WE'RE BOTH GIRLS ...
AND WE'RE FRIENDS ...
BUT MOST OF ALL...
FWEET
HEY! YOU THREE OVER THERE!
GYM ISN'T OVER YET! LESS TALKING, MORE WALKING!!
YES, SIIIR!
I DON'T WANT TO RUIN...
NOW I'M IN TROUBLE TOO. THANKS A LOT.
HEY, SHE STARTED IT!!!
WE'RE ALL IN THIS TOGEEEETHER!
OUR FRIEND-SHIP.
SO I'M GOING TO...
KEEP MY TRUE FEELINGS LOCKED INSIDE...
FOR-EVER...
AND EVER.

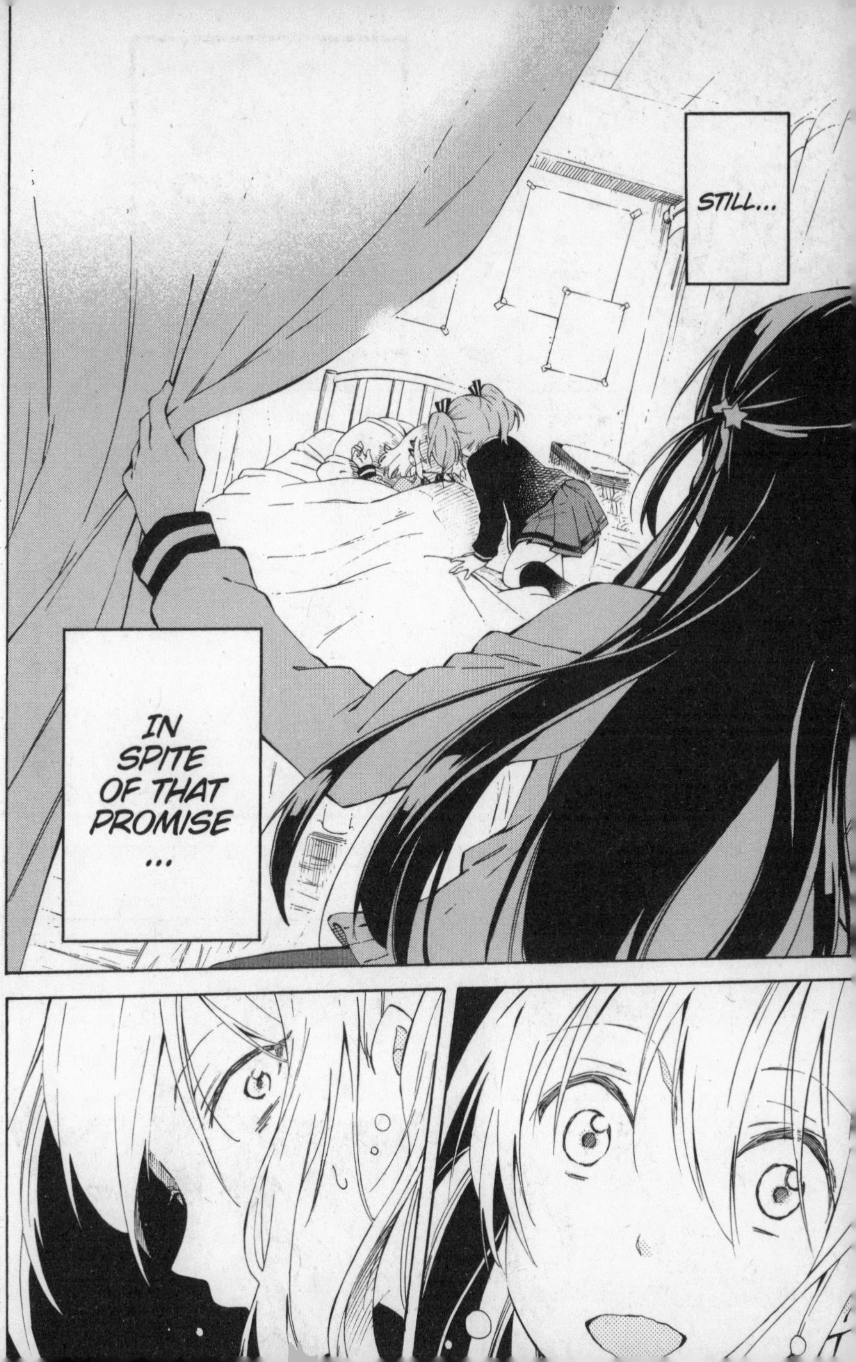
STILL...
IN SPITE OF THAT PROMISE...

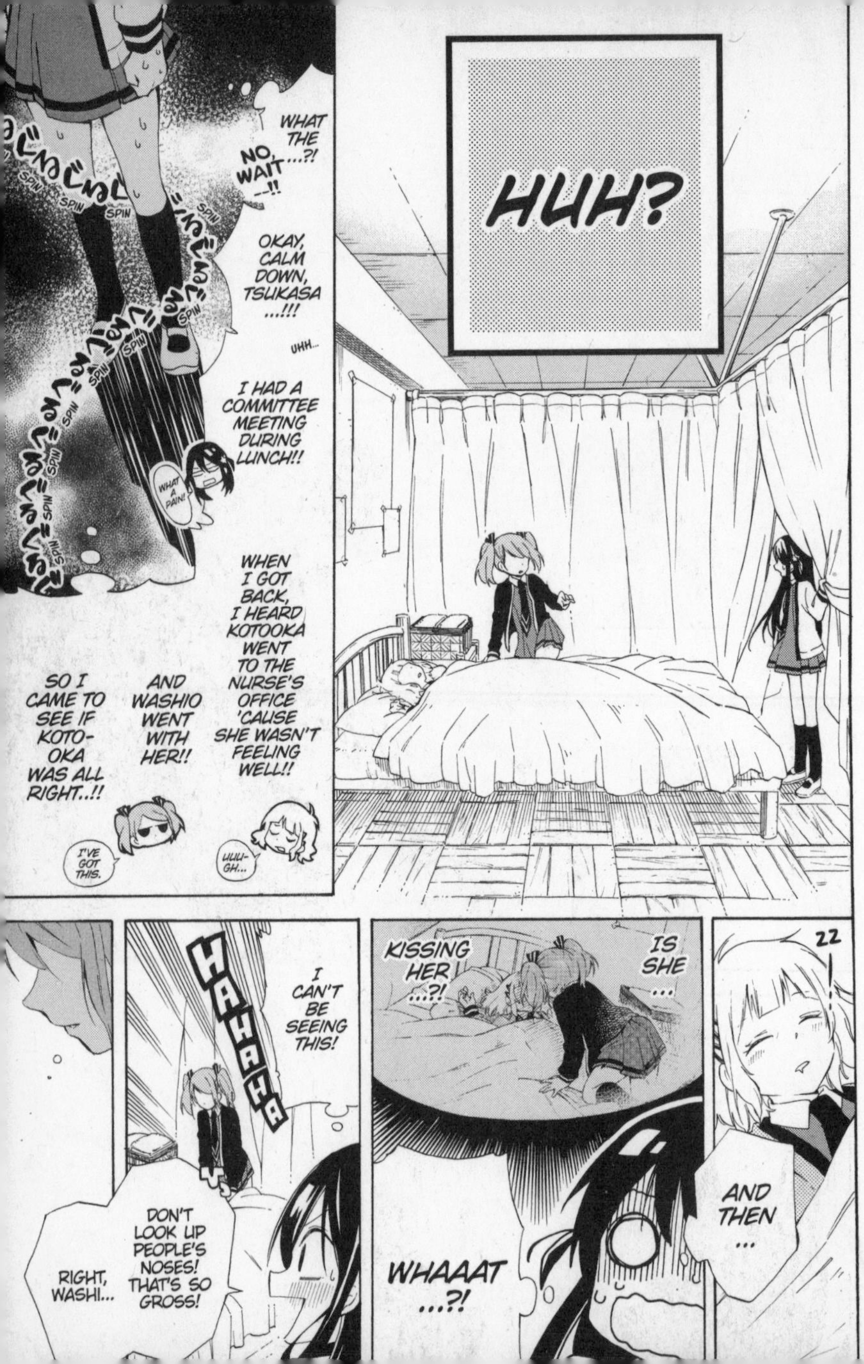
HUH?
WHAT THE...?!
NO, WAIT--!!
SPIN SPIN SPIN SPIN SPIN SPIN SPIN SPIN SPIN
OKAY, CALM DOWN, TSUKASA...!!!
UHH...
I HAD A COMMITTEE MEETING DURING LUNCH!!
WHAT A PAIN!
WHEN I GOT BACK, I HEARD KOTOOKA WENT TO THE NURSE'S OFFICE 'CAUSE SHE WASN'T FEELING WELL!!
AND WASHIO WENT WITH HER!!
SO I CAME TO SEE IF KOTO-OKA WAS ALL RIGHT..!!
UUU-GH...
I'VE GOT THIS.
22
AND THEN...
IS SHE...
KISSING HER...?!
WHAAAT...?!
HAHAHAHA
I CAN'T BE SEEING THIS!
DON'T LOOK UP PEOPLE'S NOSES! THAT'S SO GROSS!
RIGHT, WASHI...

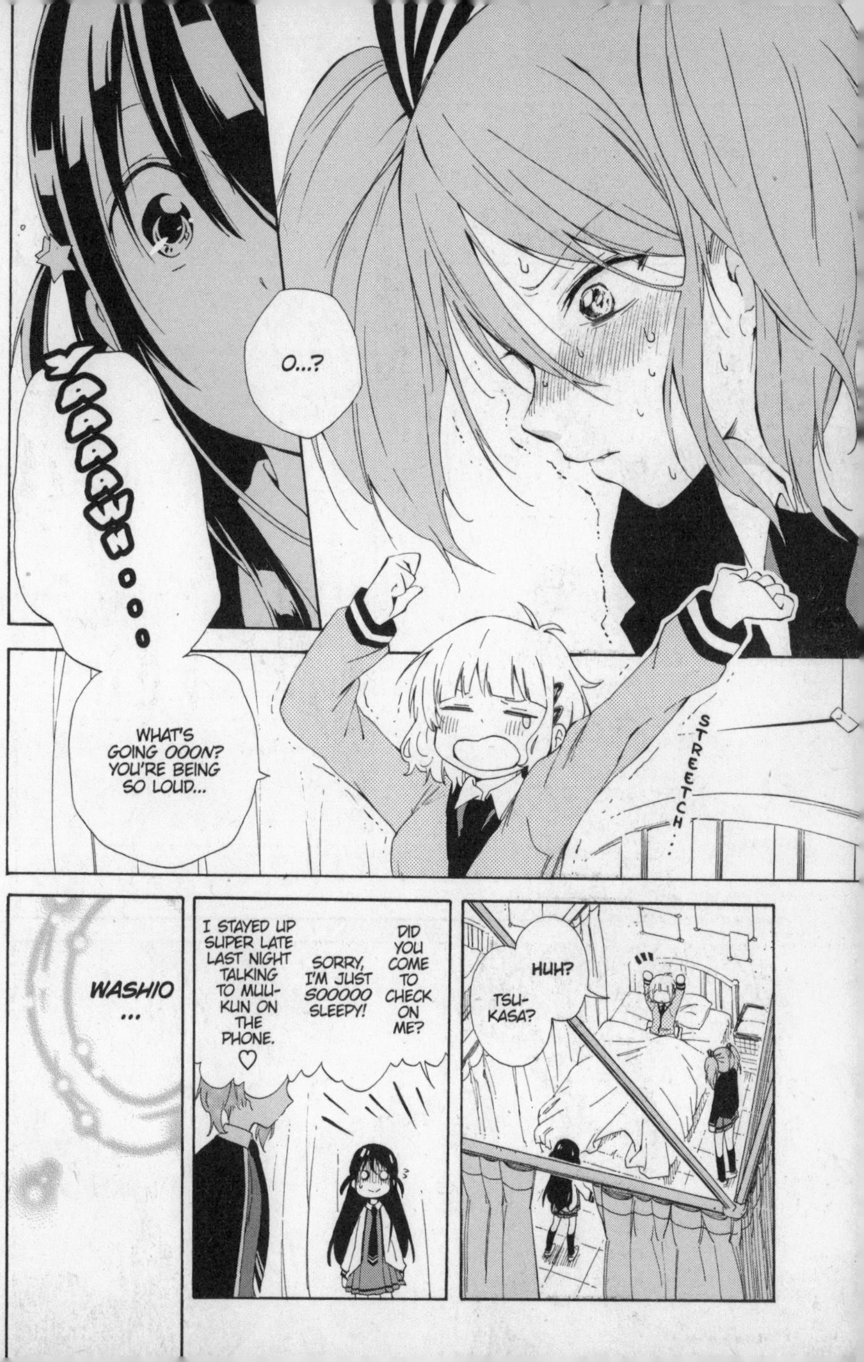
O...?
YAAAAAWN...
STREETCH...
WHAT'S GOING OOON? YOU'RE BEING SO LOUD...
HUH?
TSU-KASA?
DID YOU COME TO CHECK ON ME?
SORRY, I'M JUST SOOOOO SLEEPY!
I STAYED UP SUPER LATE LAST NIGHT TALKING TO MUU-KUN ON THE PHONE. ♡
WASHIO...

COULD YOU BE...?

OH! THAT'S RIGHT! I HAD PLANS WITH MULI-KUN!

♪

AH!

SORRY, GOTTA HANG WITH MY BOYFRIEND! ♥

LAAA-TER! ♥

....

SHIRATORI...

SPINS SPINS SPINS SP

THIS IS SO AWK-WARD...

WH-WHAT SHOULD I DO...?

I'M SORRY.

THAT MUST HAVE... GROSSED YOU OUT.

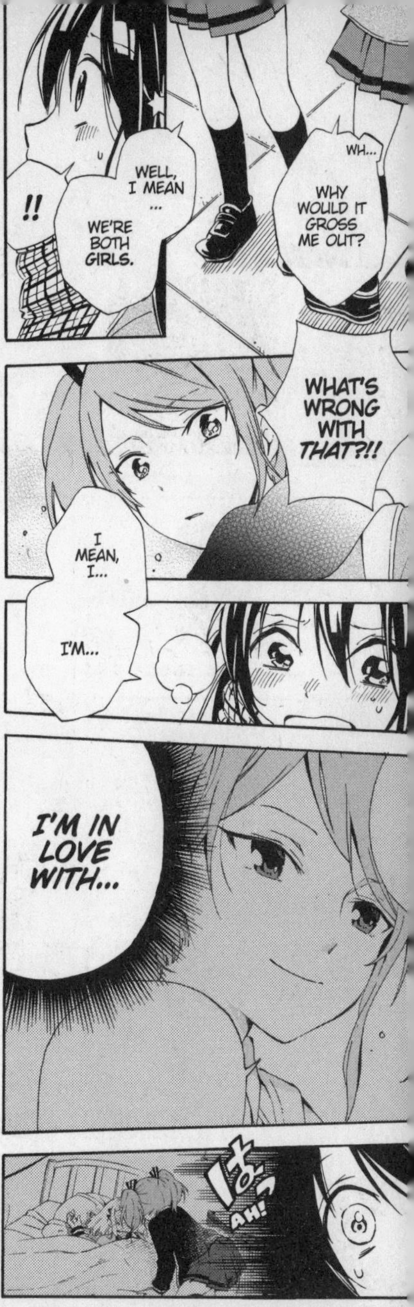
WH...
WHY WOULD IT GROSS ME OUT?
WELL, I MEAN ...
WE'RE BOTH GIRLS.
!!
WHAT'S WRONG WITH THAT?!!
I MEAN, I...
I'M...
I'M IN LOVE WITH...
はっ
AH!

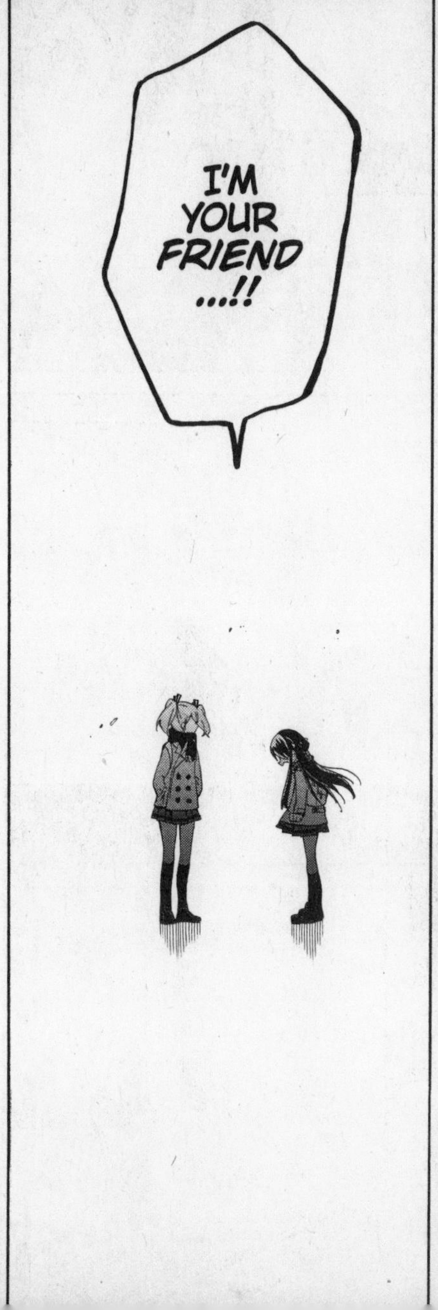
I'M YOUR FRIEND ...!!

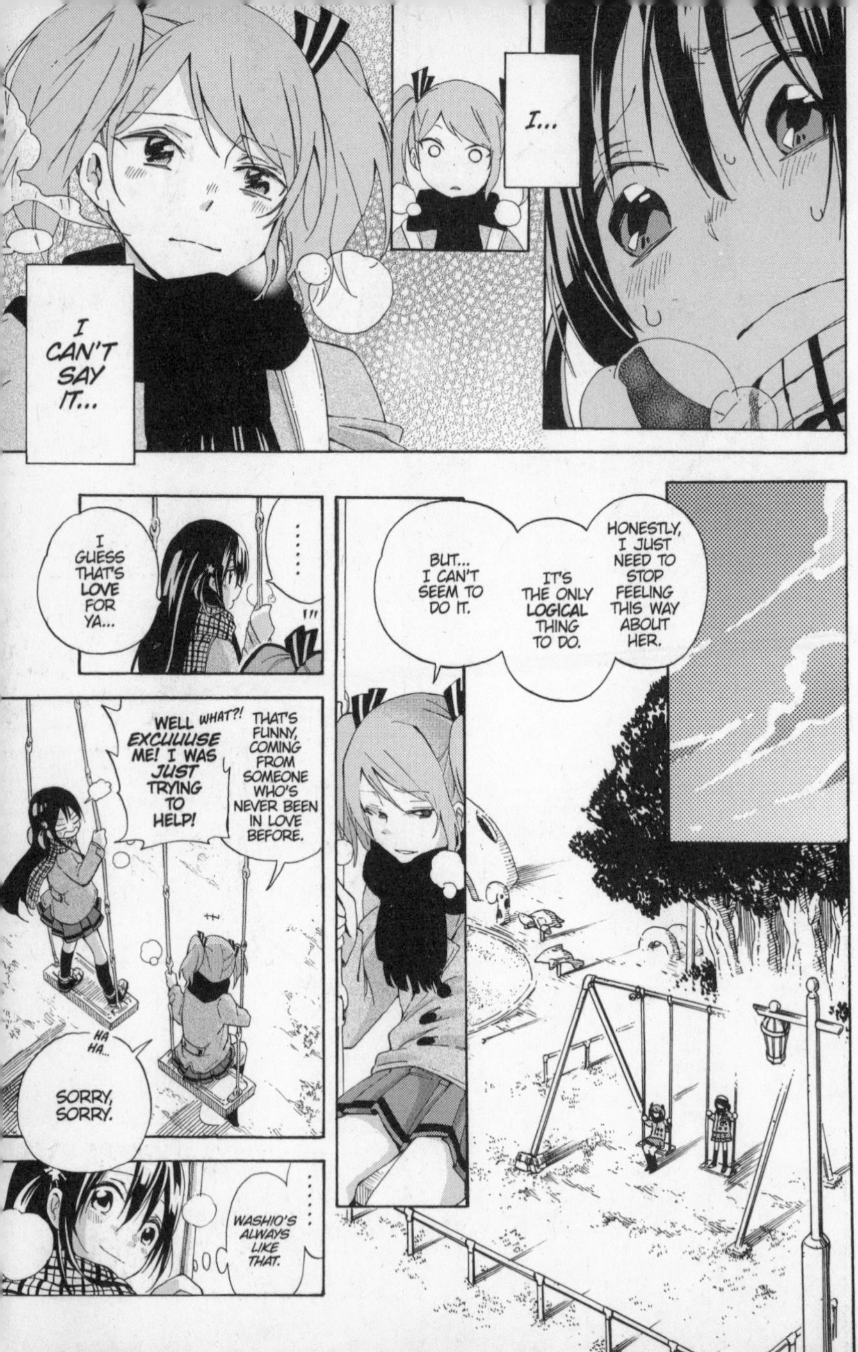
I...
I CAN'T SAY IT...
HONESTLY, I JUST NEED TO STOP FEELING THIS WAY ABOUT HER.
IT'S THE ONLY LOGICAL THING TO DO.
BUT... I CAN'T SEEM TO DO IT.
......
I GUESS THAT'S LOVE FOR YA...
THAT'S FUNNY, COMING FROM SOMEONE WHO'S NEVER BEEN IN LOVE BEFORE.
WHAT?!
WELL EXCUUUSE ME! I WAS JUST TRYING TO HELP!
HA HA...
SORRY, SORRY.
......
WASHIO'S ALWAYS LIKE THAT.

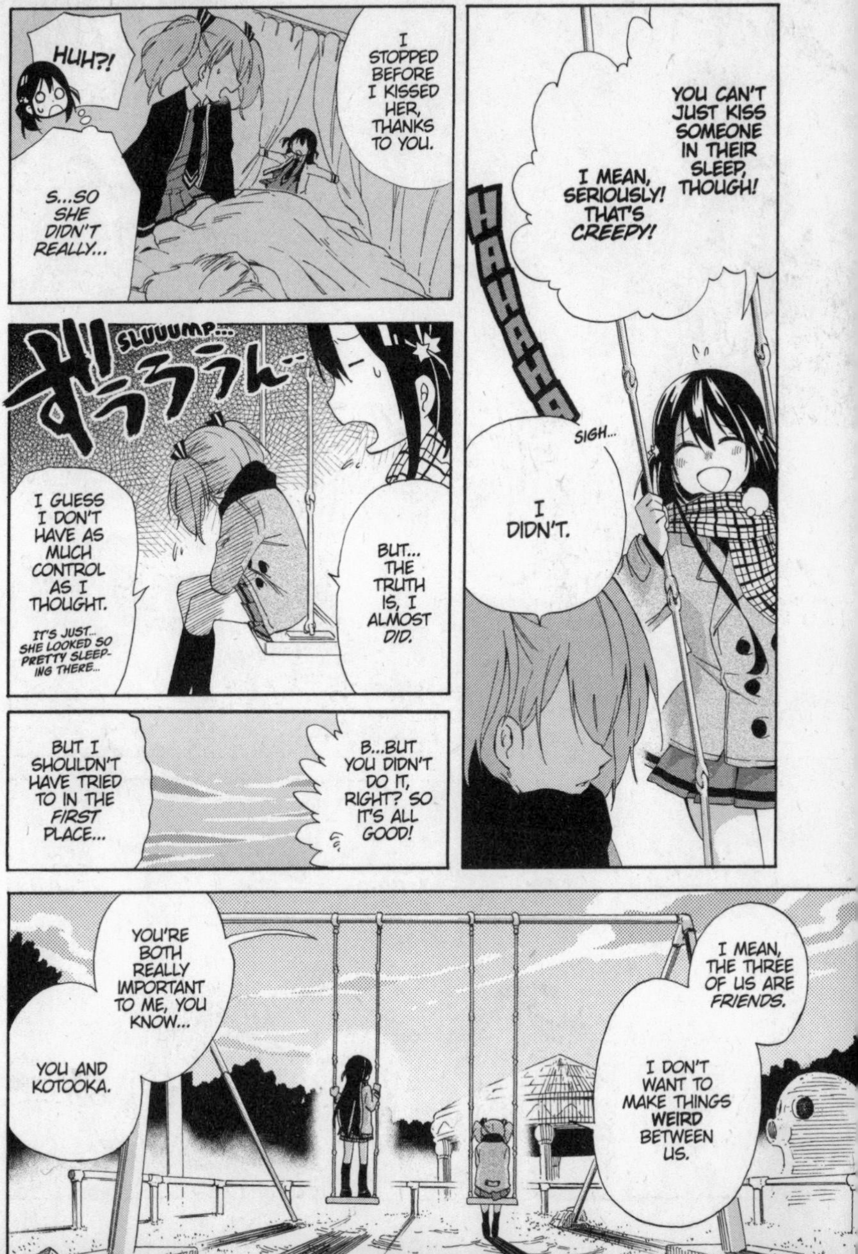
YOU CAN'T JUST KISS SOMEONE IN THEIR SLEEP, THOUGH!
I MEAN, SERIOUSLY! THAT'S CREEPY!
HAHAHAHA
SIGH...
I DIDN'T.
I STOPPED BEFORE I KISSED HER, THANKS TO YOU.
HUH?!
S...SO SHE DIDN'T REALLY...
SLUUUMP...
BUT... THE TRUTH IS, I ALMOST DID.
I GUESS I DON'T HAVE AS MUCH CONTROL AS I THOUGHT.
IT'S JUST... SHE LOOKED SO PRETTY SLEEPING THERE...
B...BUT YOU DIDN'T DO IT, RIGHT? SO IT'S ALL GOOD!
BUT I SHOULDN'T HAVE TRIED TO IN THE FIRST PLACE...
I MEAN, THE THREE OF US ARE FRIENDS.
I DON'T WANT TO MAKE THINGS WEIRD BETWEEN US.
YOU'RE BOTH REALLY IMPORTANT TO ME, YOU KNOW...
YOU AND KOTOOKA.

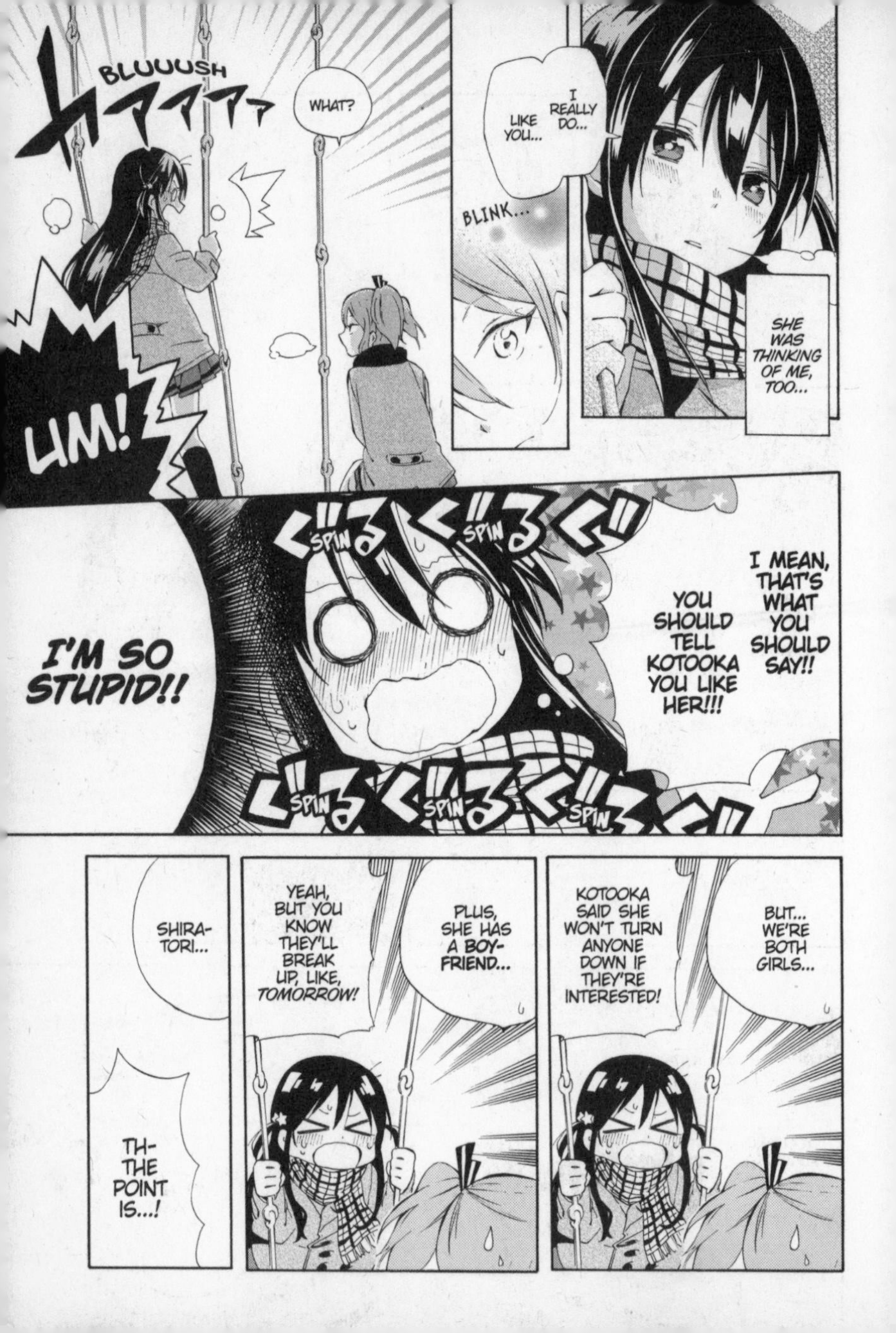
I REALLY DO... LIKE YOU...
SHE WAS THINKING OF ME, TOO...
BLINK...
WHAT?
BLUUUSH
UM!
I MEAN, THAT'S WHAT YOU SHOULD SAY!!
YOU SHOULD TELL KOTOOKA YOU LIKE HER!!!
SPIN SPIN
SPIN SPIN SPIN
I'M SO STUPID!!
BUT... WE'RE BOTH GIRLS...
KOTOOKA SAID SHE WON'T TURN ANYONE DOWN IF THEY'RE INTERESTED!
PLUS, SHE HAS A BOY-FRIEND...
YEAH, BUT YOU KNOW THEY'LL BREAK UP, LIKE, *TOMORROW!*
SHIRA-TORI...
TH-THE POINT IS...!

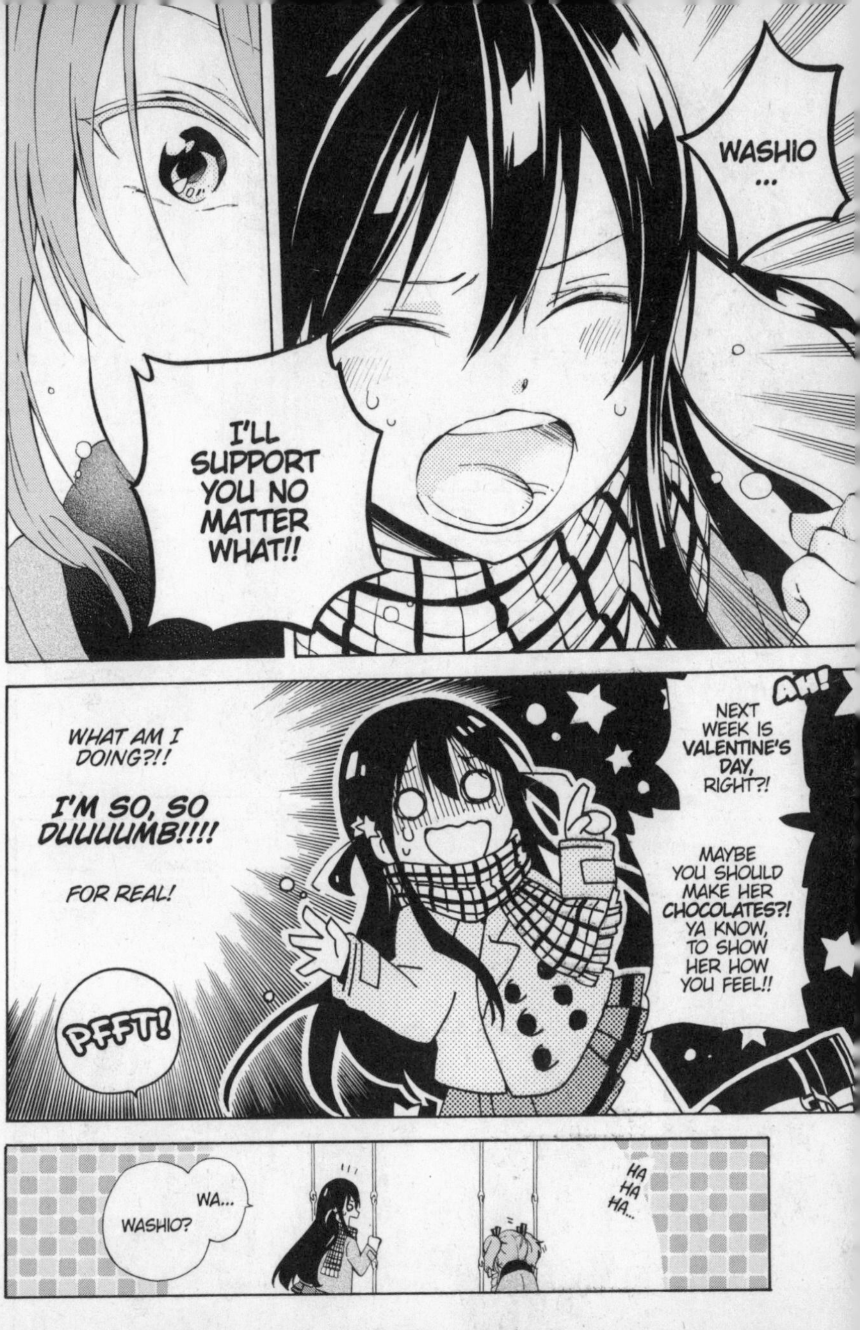

WASHIO ...
I'LL SUPPORT YOU NO MATTER WHAT!!
AH!
NEXT WEEK IS VALENTINE'S DAY, RIGHT?!
MAYBE YOU SHOULD MAKE HER CHOCOLATES?! YA KNOW, TO SHOW HER HOW YOU FEEL!!
WHAT AM I DOING?!!
I'M SO, SO DUUUUMB!!!!
FOR REAL!
PFFT!
HA HA HA...
WA... WASHIO?

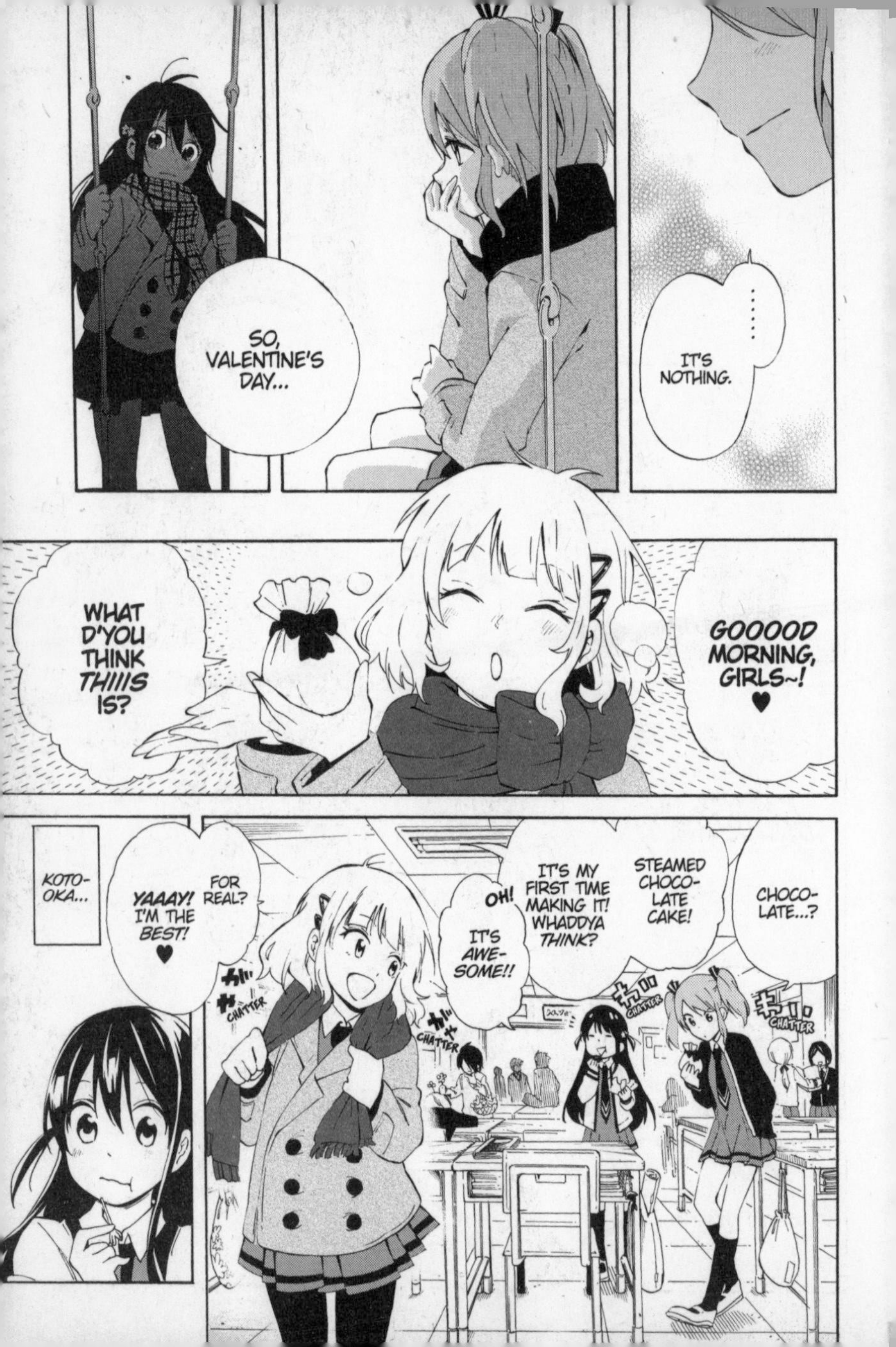
......
IT'S NOTHING.
SO, VALENTINE'S DAY...
GOOOOD MORNING, GIRLS~! ♥
WHAT D'YOU THINK THIIIS IS?
CHOCOLATE...?
STEAMED CHOCOLATE CAKE!
IT'S MY FIRST TIME MAKING IT! WHADDYA THINK?
OH! IT'S AWESOME!!
FOR REAL?
YAAAY! I'M THE BEST! ♥
CHATTER
CHATTER
CHATTER
CHATTER
KOTOOKA...

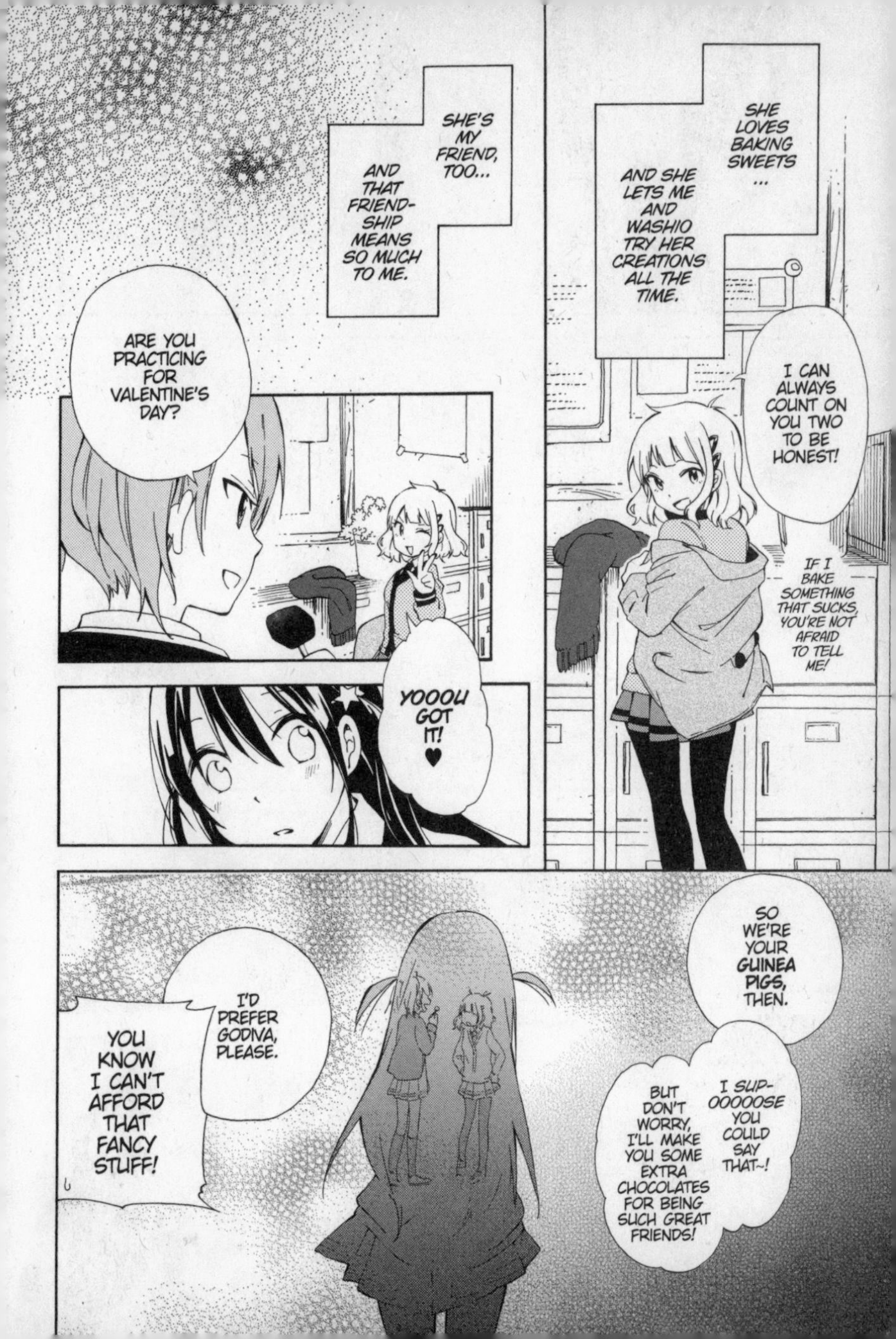
SHE LOVES BAKING SWEETS...
AND SHE LETS ME AND WASHIO TRY HER CREATIONS ALL THE TIME.
I CAN ALWAYS COUNT ON YOU TWO TO BE HONEST!
IF I BAKE SOMETHING THAT SUCKS, YOU'RE NOT AFRAID TO TELL ME!
SHE'S MY FRIEND, TOO...
AND THAT FRIENDSHIP MEANS SO MUCH TO ME.
ARE YOU PRACTICING FOR VALENTINE'S DAY?
YOOOU GOT IT! ♥
SO WE'RE YOUR GUINEA PIGS, THEN.
I SUPOOOOOSE YOU COULD SAY THAT~!
BUT DON'T WORRY, I'LL MAKE YOU SOME EXTRA CHOCOLATES FOR BEING SUCH GREAT FRIENDS!
I'D PREFER GODIVA, PLEASE.
YOU KNOW I CAN'T AFFORD THAT FANCY STUFF!

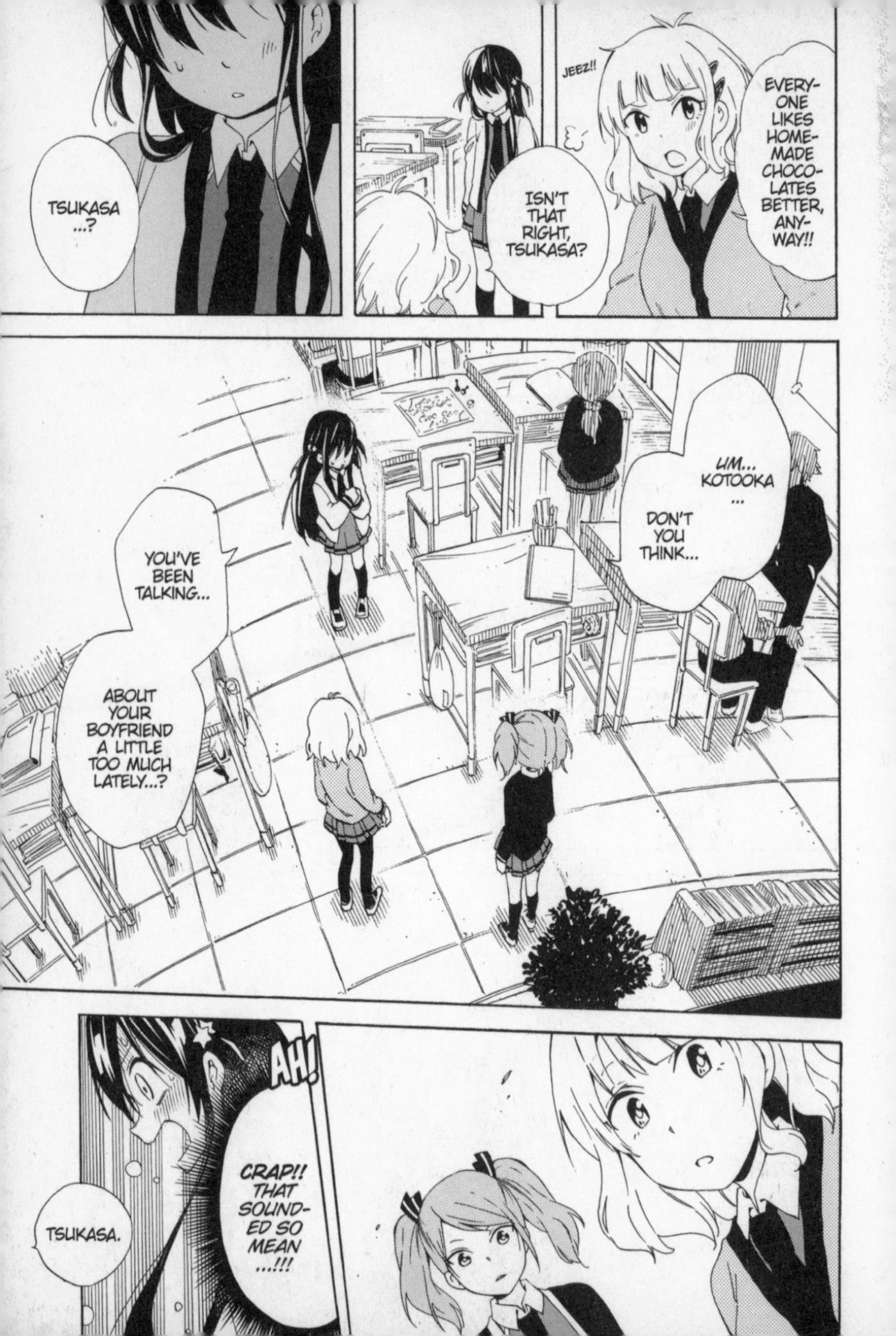
EVERY-ONE LIKES HOME-MADE CHOCO-LATES BETTER, ANY-WAY!!
JEEZ!!
ISN'T THAT RIGHT, TSUKASA?
TSUKASA ...?
UM... KOTOOKA ...
DON'T YOU THINK...
YOU'VE BEEN TALKING...
ABOUT YOUR BOYFRIEND A LITTLE TOO MUCH LATELY...?
AH!
CRAP!! THAT SOUND-ED SO MEAN ...!!!
TSUKASA.

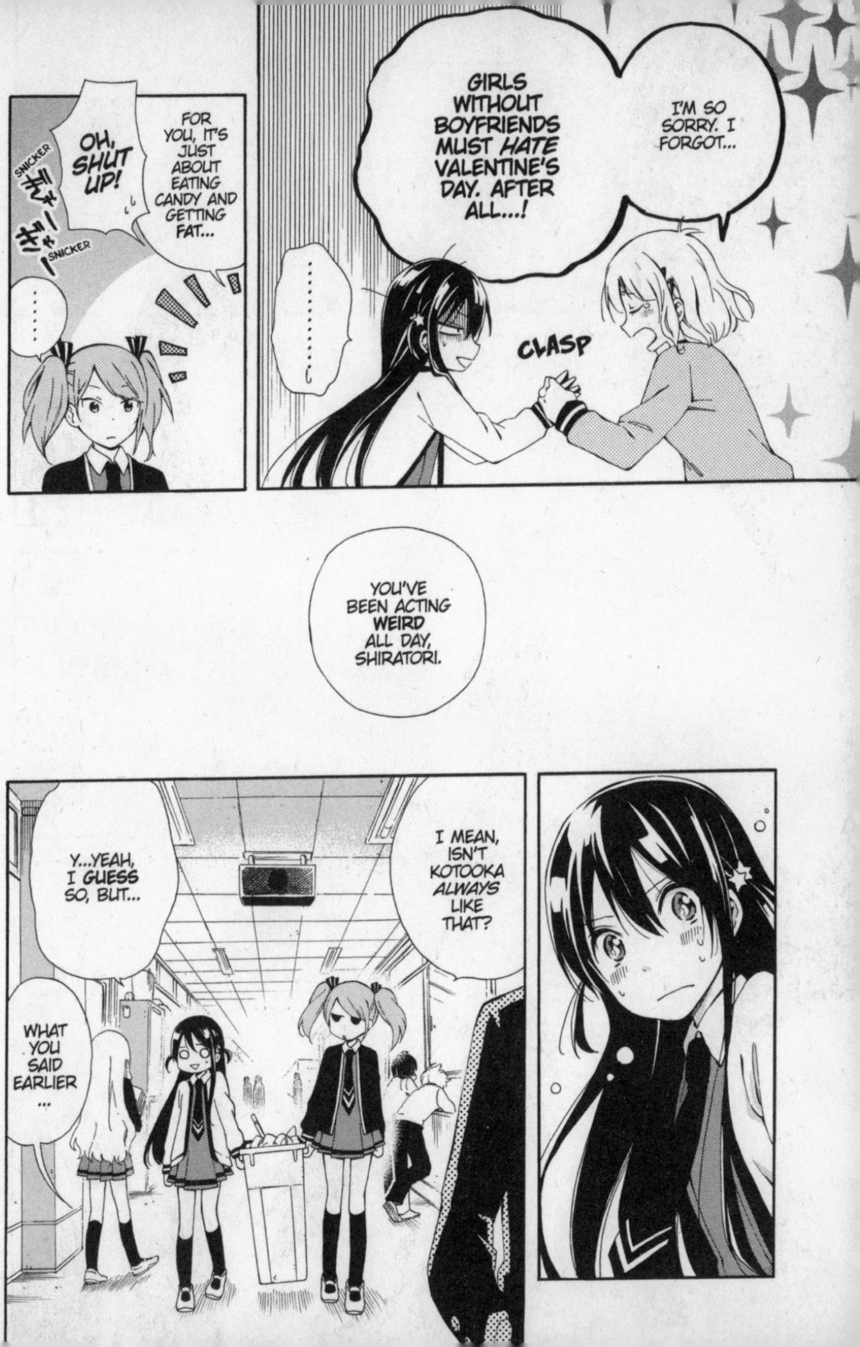
I'M SO SORRY. I FORGOT...
GIRLS WITHOUT BOYFRIENDS MUST *HATE* VALENTINE'S DAY. AFTER ALL...!
CLASP
......
FOR YOU, IT'S JUST ABOUT EATING CANDY AND GETTING FAT...
OH, SHUT UP!
SNICKER
SNICKER
......
YOU'VE BEEN ACTING **WEIRD** ALL DAY, SHIRATORI.
I MEAN, ISN'T KOTOOKA *ALWAYS* LIKE THAT?
Y...YEAH, I GUESS SO, BUT...
WHAT YOU SAID EARLIER...

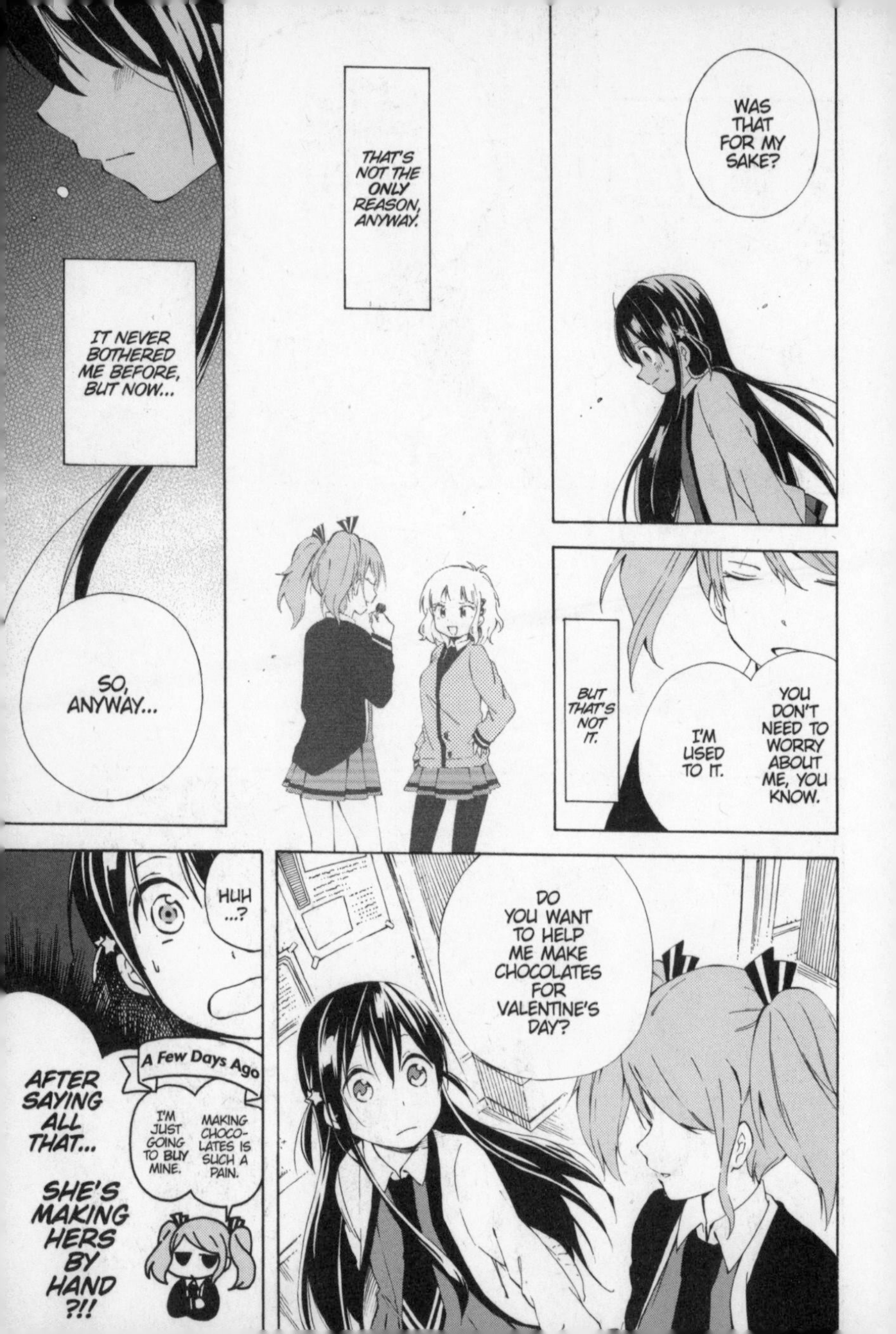
WAS THAT FOR MY SAKE?
YOU DON'T NEED TO WORRY ABOUT ME, YOU KNOW.
I'M USED TO IT.
BUT THAT'S NOT IT.
THAT'S NOT THE ONLY REASON, ANYWAY.
IT NEVER BOTHERED ME BEFORE, BUT NOW...
SO, ANYWAY...
DO YOU WANT TO HELP ME MAKE CHOCOLATES FOR VALENTINE'S DAY?
HUH ...?
A Few Days Ago
MAKING CHOCO- LATES IS SUCH A PAIN.
I'M JUST GOING TO BUY MINE.
AFTER SAYING ALL THAT...
SHE'S MAKING HERS BY HAND ?!!

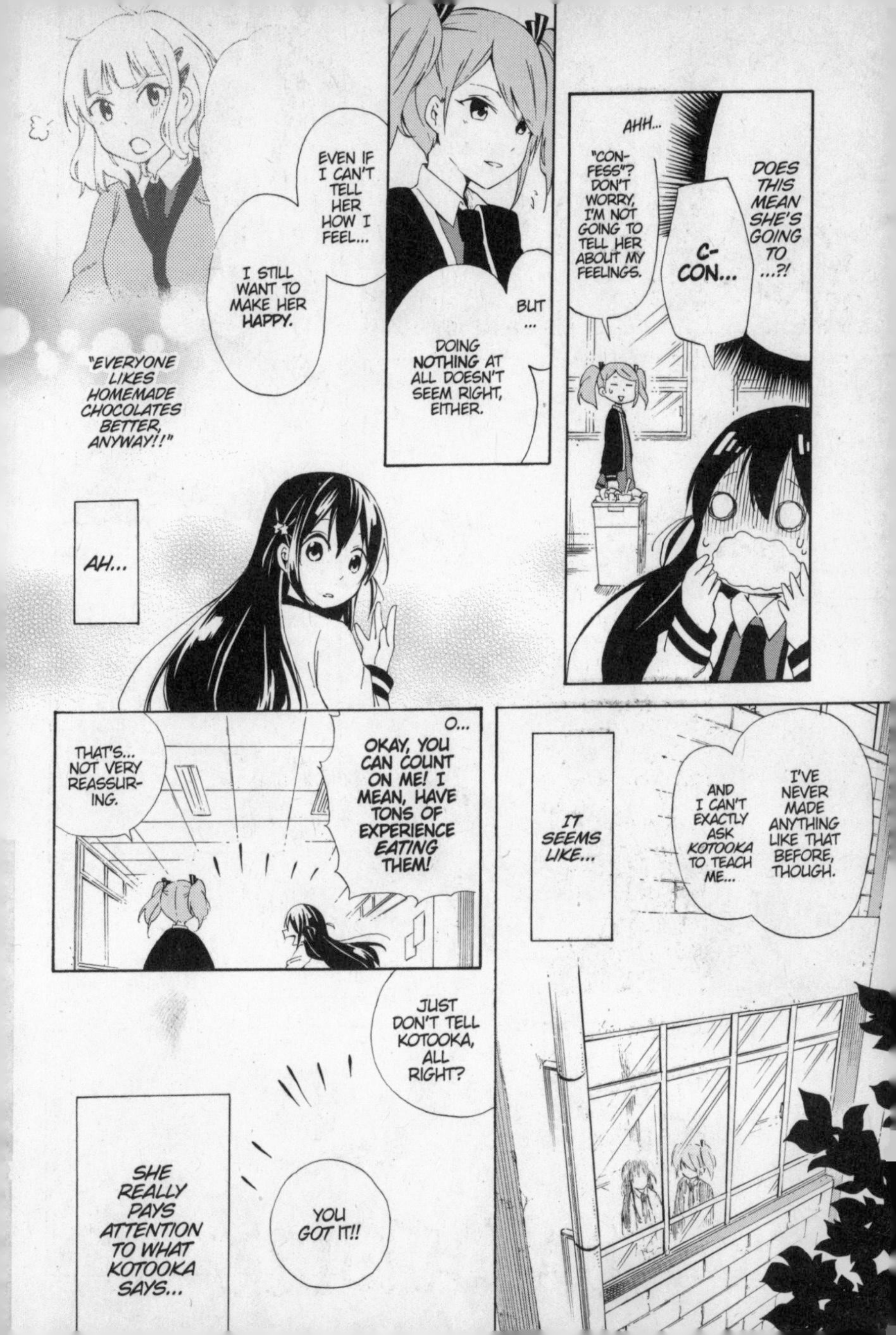
DOES THIS MEAN SHE'S GOING TO ...?!
C-CON...
AHH...
"CON-FESS"? DON'T WORRY, I'M NOT GOING TO TELL HER ABOUT MY FEELINGS.
EVEN IF I CAN'T TELL HER HOW I FEEL...
I STILL WANT TO MAKE HER HAPPY.
BUT ...
DOING NOTHING AT ALL DOESN'T SEEM RIGHT, EITHER.
"EVERYONE LIKES HOMEMADE CHOCOLATES BETTER, ANYWAY!!"
AH...
I'VE NEVER MADE ANYTHING LIKE THAT BEFORE, THOUGH.
AND I CAN'T EXACTLY ASK KOTOOKA TO TEACH ME...
IT SEEMS LIKE...
O...
OKAY, YOU CAN COUNT ON ME! I MEAN, HAVE TONS OF EXPERIENCE EATING THEM!
THAT'S... NOT VERY REASSURING.
JUST DON'T TELL KOTOOKA, ALL RIGHT?
YOU GOT IT!!
SHE REALLY PAYS ATTENTION TO WHAT KOTOOKA SAYS...

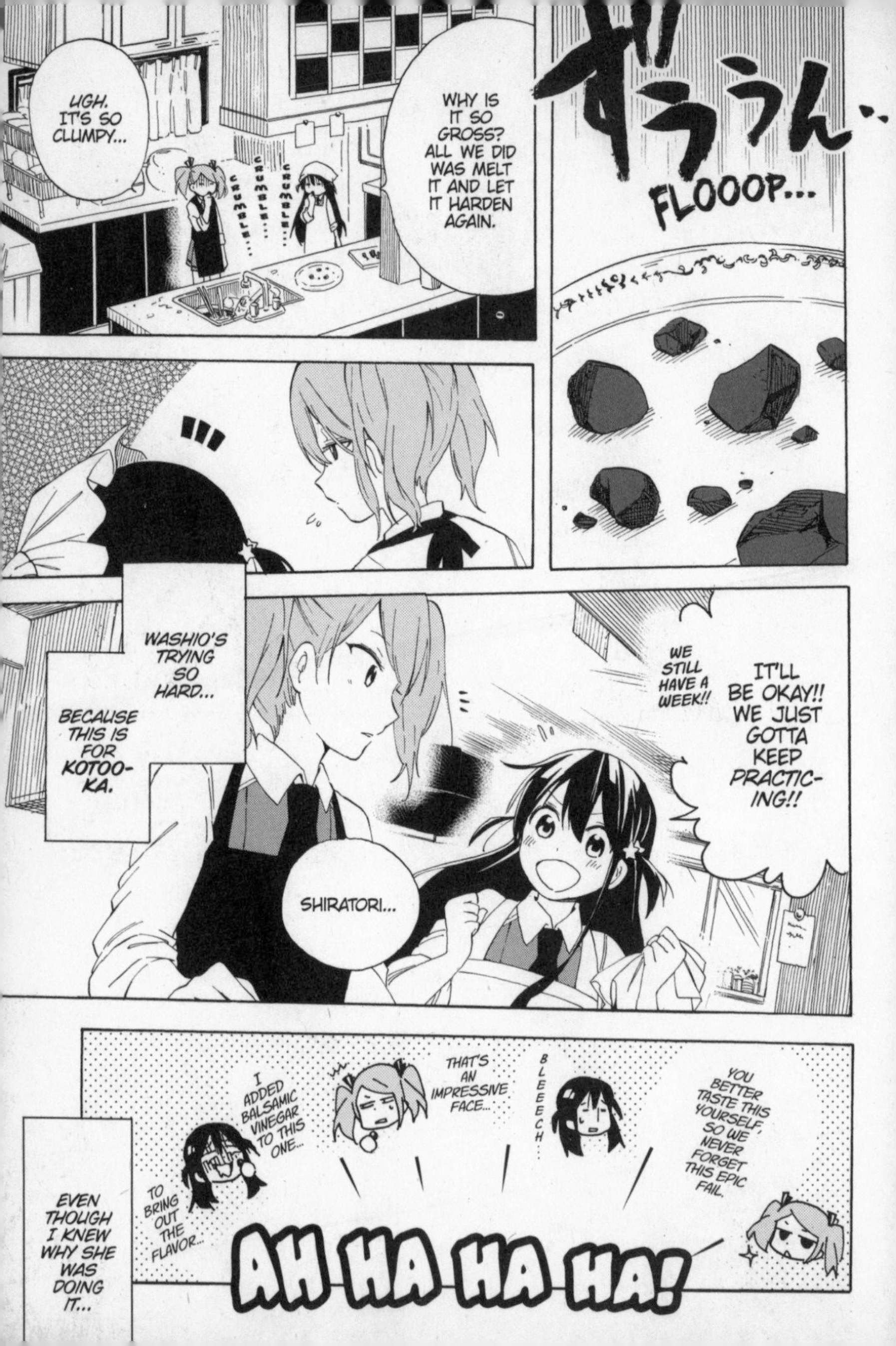
ずううん…
FLOOOP...
WHY IS IT SO GROSS? ALL WE DID WAS MELT IT AND LET IT HARDEN AGAIN.
CRUMBLE... CRUMBLE... CRUMBLE...
UGH. IT'S SO CLUMPY...
!!!
IT'LL BE OKAY!! WE JUST GOTTA KEEP PRACTIC-ING!!
WE STILL HAVE A WEEK!!
SHIRATORI...
WASHIO'S TRYING SO HARD...
BECAUSE THIS IS FOR KOTOOKA.
YOU BETTER TASTE THIS YOURSELF, SO WE NEVER FORGET THIS EPIC FAIL.
BLEEECH...
THAT'S AN IMPRESSIVE FACE...
I ADDED BALSAMIC VINEGAR TO THIS ONE...
TO BRING OUT THE FLAVOR...
AH HA HA HA HA!
EVEN THOUGH I KNEW WHY SHE WAS DOING IT...

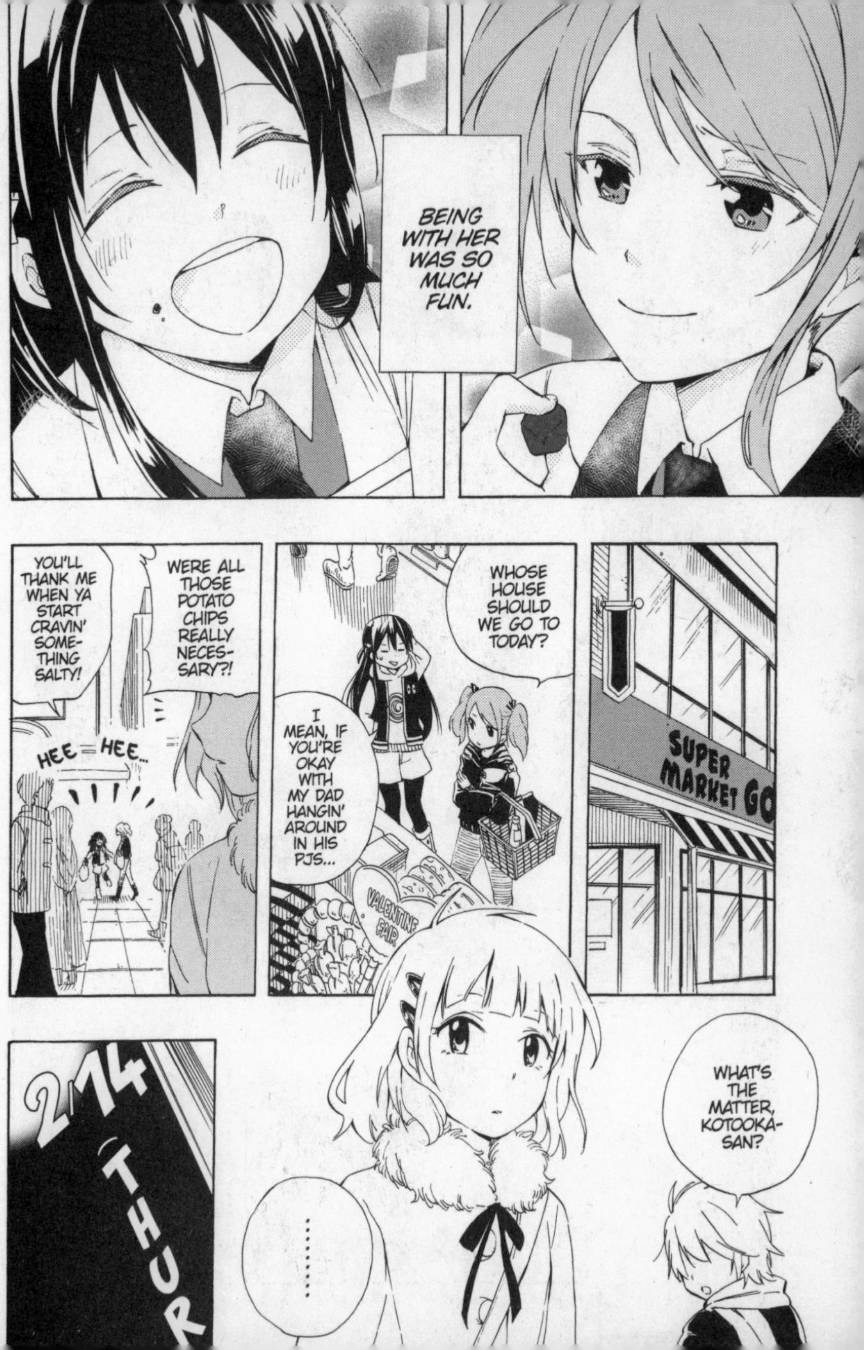
BEING WITH HER WAS SO MUCH FUN.
SUPER MARKET GO
WHOSE HOUSE SHOULD WE GO TO TODAY?
I MEAN, IF YOU'RE OKAY WITH MY DAD HANGIN' AROUND IN HIS PJS...
VALENTINE FAIR
WERE ALL THOSE POTATO CHIPS REALLY NECESSARY?!
YOU'LL THANK ME WHEN YA START CRAVIN' SOMETHING SALTY!
HEE HEE...
WHAT'S THE MATTER, KOTOOKA-SAN?
......
2/14 THUR

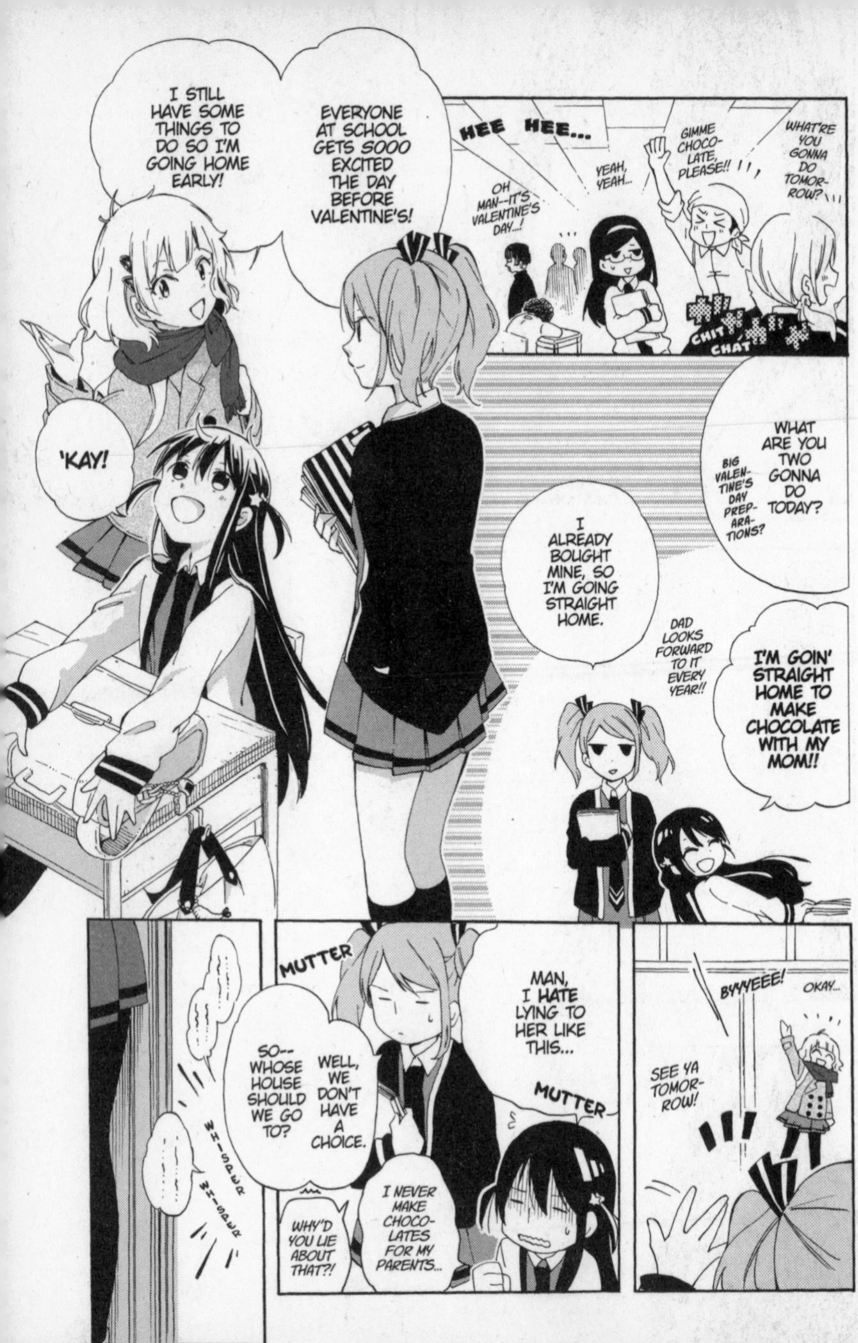
WHAT'RE YOU GONNA DO TOMOR-ROW?
GIMME CHOCO-LATE, PLEASE!!
YEAH, YEAH...
HEE HEE...
OH MAN--IT'S VALENTINE'S DAY...!
CHIT CHAT
WHAT ARE YOU TWO GONNA DO TODAY?
BIG VALEN-TINE'S DAY PREP-ARA-TIONS?
I'M GOIN' STRAIGHT HOME TO MAKE CHOCOLATE WITH MY MOM!!
DAD LOOKS FORWARD TO IT EVERY YEAR!!
I ALREADY BOUGHT MINE, SO I'M GOING STRAIGHT HOME.
EVERYONE AT SCHOOL GETS SOOO EXCITED THE DAY BEFORE VALENTINE'S!
I STILL HAVE SOME THINGS TO DO SO I'M GOING HOME EARLY!
'KAY!
BYYYEEE!
OKAY...
SEE YA TOMOR-ROW!
MAN, I HATE LYING TO HER LIKE THIS...
MUTTER
WELL, WE DON'T HAVE A CHOICE.
MUTTER
I NEVER MAKE CHOCO-LATES FOR MY PARENTS...
SO--WHOSE HOUSE SHOULD WE GO TO?
WHY'D YOU LIE ABOUT THAT?!
WHISPER WHISPER

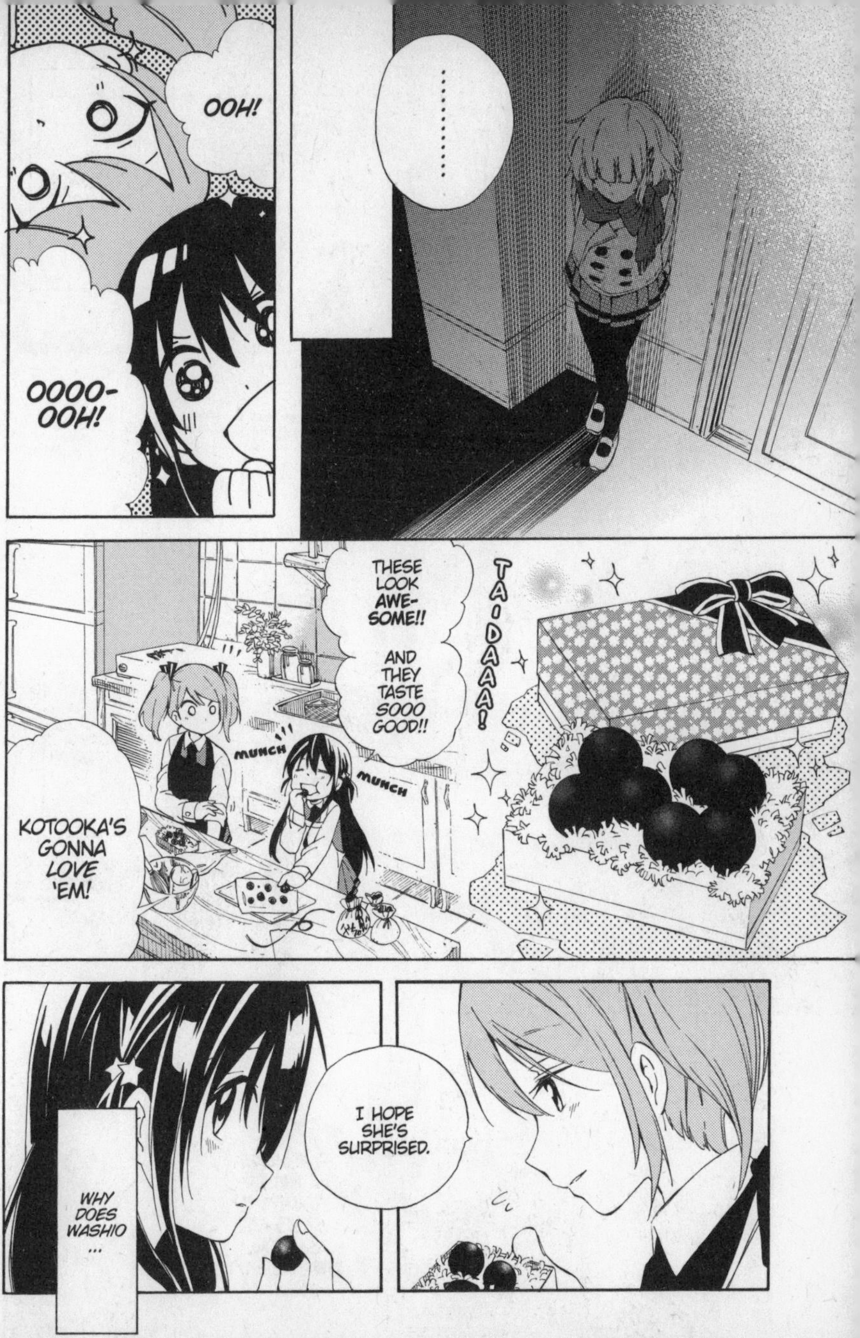
......
OOH!
OOOO-OOH!
TA-DAAAA!
THESE LOOK AWESOME!! AND THEY TASTE SOOO GOOD!!
MUNCH
MUNCH
KOTOOKA'S GONNA LOVE 'EM!
I HOPE SHE'S SURPRISED.
WHY DOES WASHIO ...

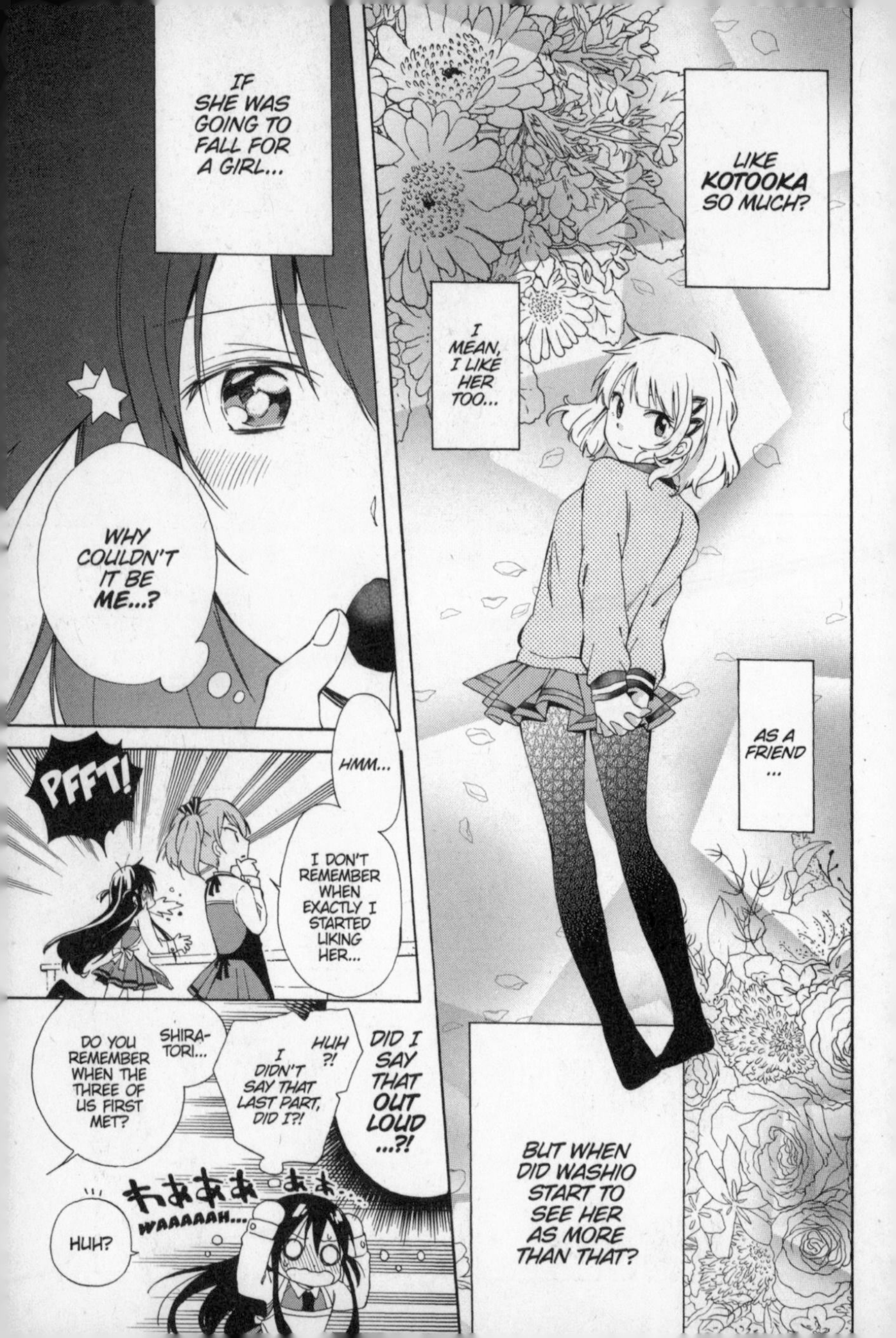
LIKE KOTOOKA SO MUCH?
I MEAN, I LIKE HER TOO...
AS A FRIEND...
BUT WHEN DID WASHIO START TO SEE HER AS MORE THAN THAT?
IF SHE WAS GOING TO FALL FOR A GIRL...
WHY COULDN'T IT BE ME...?
HMM...
PFFT!
I DON'T REMEMBER WHEN EXACTLY I STARTED LIKING HER...
DID I SAY THAT OUT LOUD...?!
HUH?!
I DIDN'T SAY THAT LAST PART, DID I?!
SHIRATORI...
DO YOU REMEMBER WHEN THE THREE OF US FIRST MET?
わあああ ああ
WAAAAAH...
HUH?

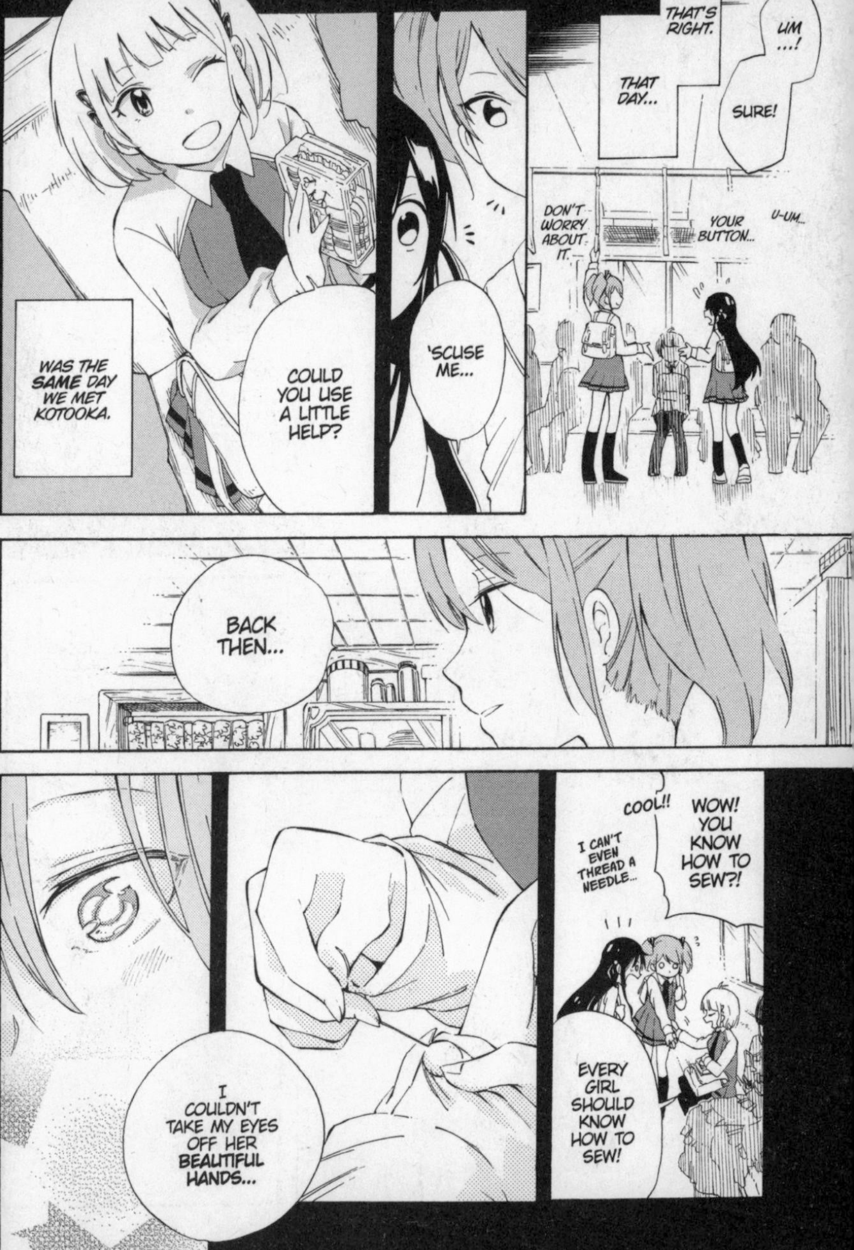
THAT'S RIGHT.
THAT DAY...
UM ...! SURE!
U-UM... YOUR BUTTON...
DON'T WORRY ABOUT IT.
'SCUSE ME...
COULD YOU USE A LITTLE HELP?
WAS THE SAME DAY WE MET KOTOOKA.
BACK THEN...
WOW! YOU KNOW HOW TO SEW?!
COOL!!
I CAN'T EVEN THREAD A NEEDLE...
EVERY GIRL SHOULD KNOW HOW TO SEW!
I COULDN'T TAKE MY EYES OFF HER BEAUTIFUL HANDS...

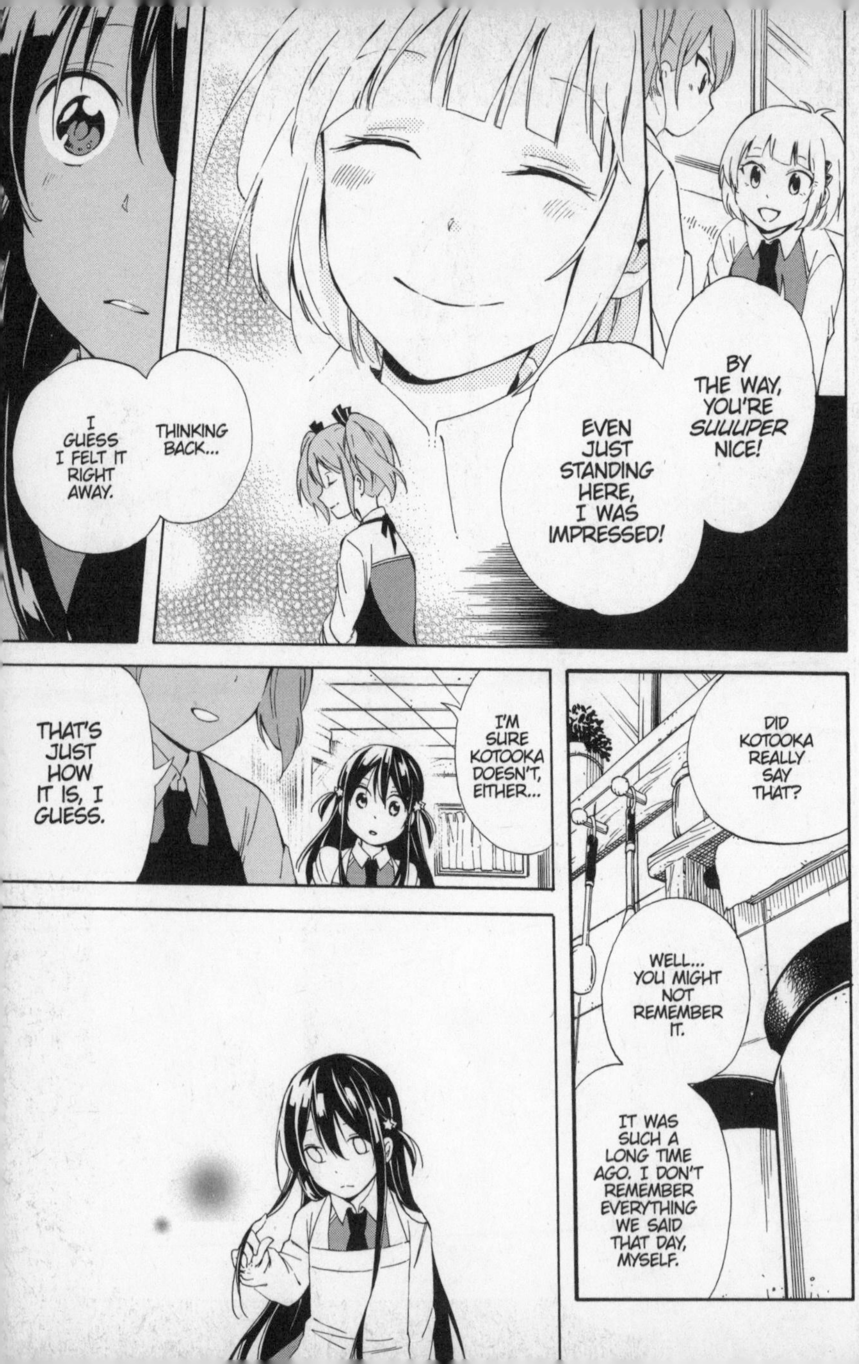
BY THE WAY, YOU'RE SUUUPER NICE!
EVEN JUST STANDING HERE, I WAS IMPRESSED!
THINKING BACK...
I GUESS I FELT IT RIGHT AWAY.
DID KOTOOKA REALLY SAY THAT?
WELL... YOU MIGHT NOT REMEMBER IT.
IT WAS SUCH A LONG TIME AGO. I DON'T REMEMBER EVERYTHING WE SAID THAT DAY, MYSELF.
I'M SURE KOTOOKA DOESN'T, EITHER...
THAT'S JUST HOW IT IS, I GUESS.

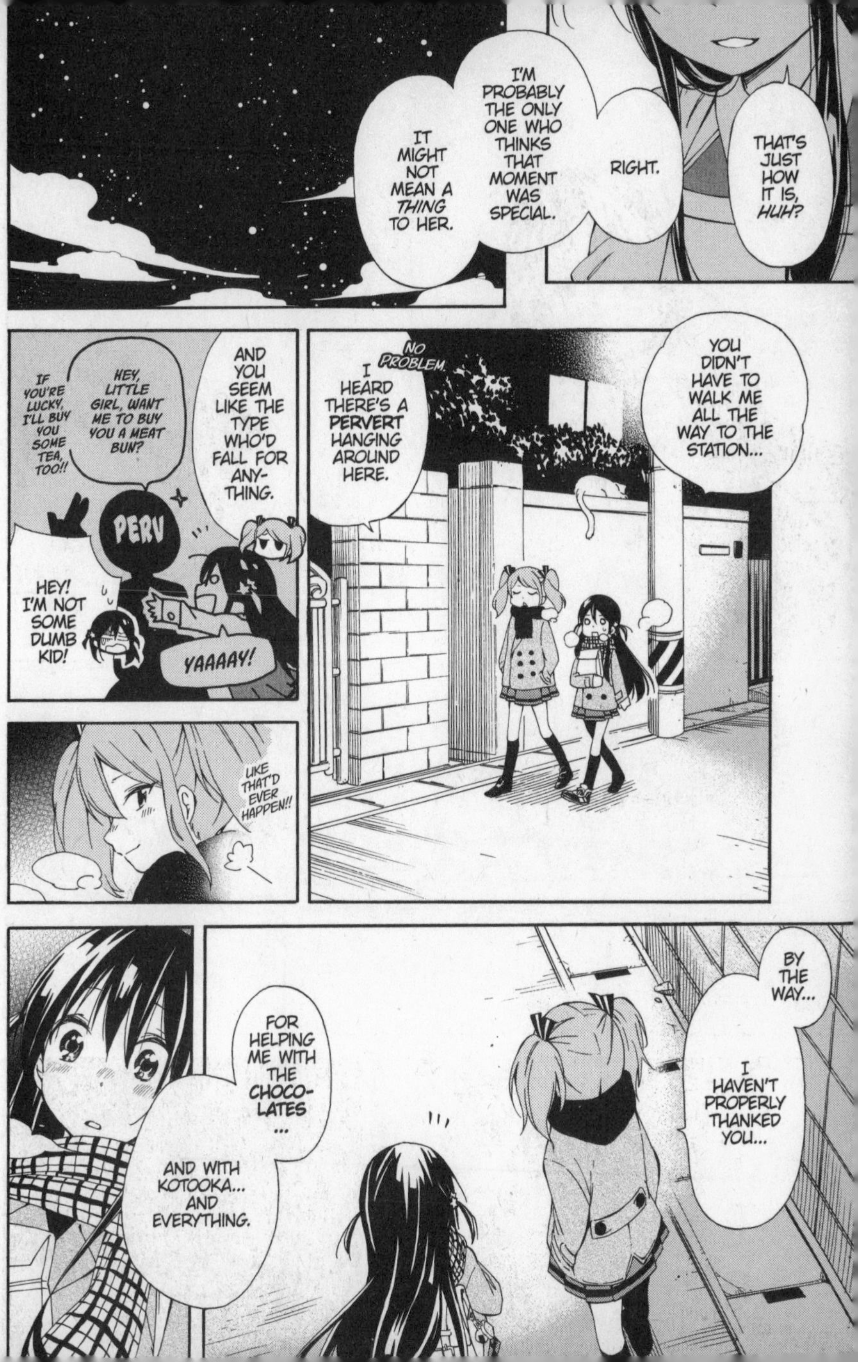
THAT'S JUST HOW IT IS, *HUH?*
RIGHT.
I'M PROBABLY THE ONLY ONE WHO THINKS THAT MOMENT WAS SPECIAL.
IT MIGHT NOT MEAN A *THING* TO HER.
YOU DIDN'T HAVE TO WALK ME ALL THE WAY TO THE STATION...
NO PROBLEM.
I HEARD THERE'S A **PERVERT** HANGING AROUND HERE.
AND YOU SEEM LIKE THE TYPE WHO'D FALL FOR ANY-THING.
HEY, LITTLE GIRL, WANT ME TO BUY YOU A MEAT BUN?
IF YOU'RE LUCKY, I'LL BUY YOU SOME TEA, TOO!!
PERV
YAAAAY!
HEY! I'M NOT SOME DUMB KID!
LIKE THAT'D EVER HAPPEN!!
BY THE WAY...
I HAVEN'T PROPERLY THANKED YOU...
FOR HELPING ME WITH THE CHOCO-LATES...
AND WITH KOTOOKA... AND EVERYTHING.

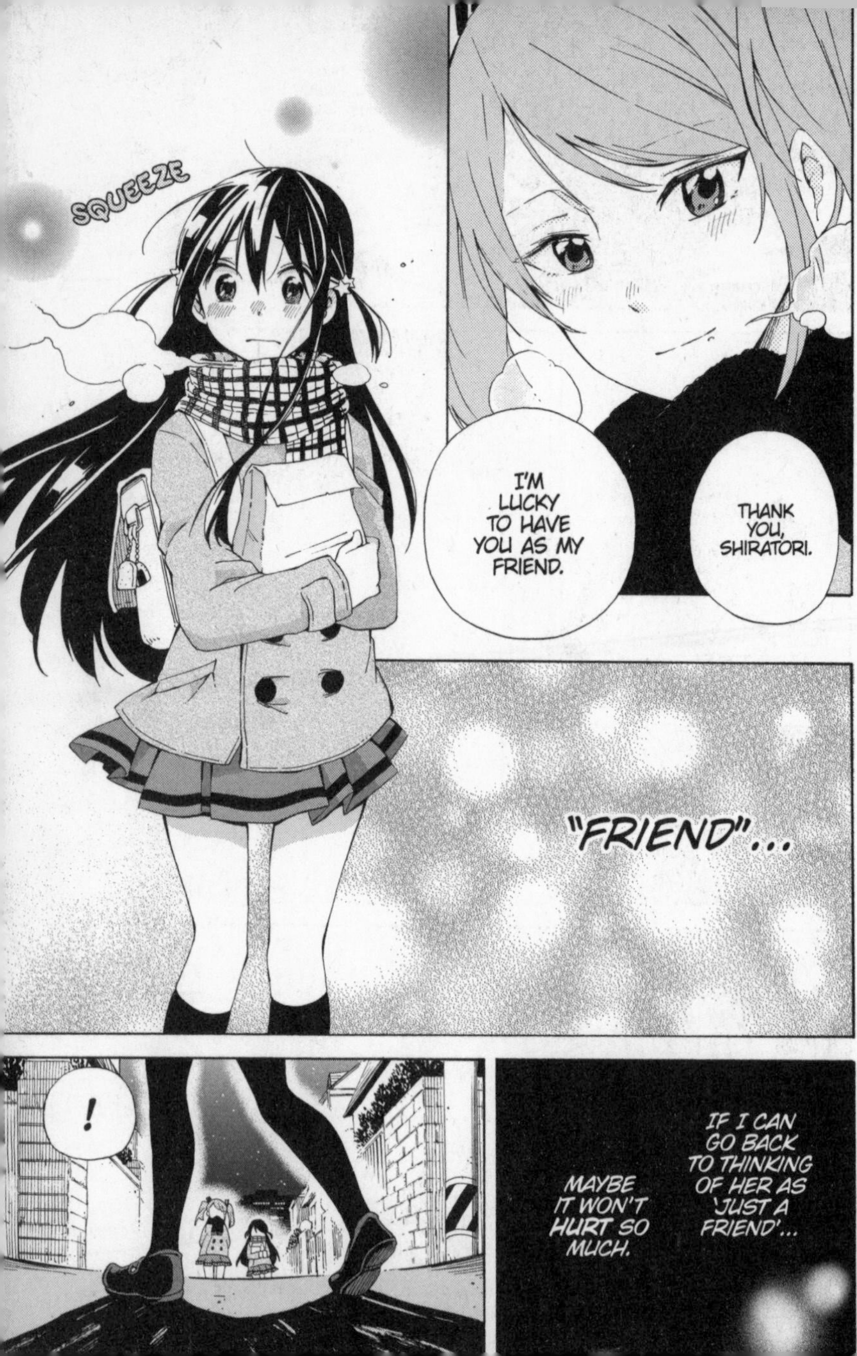
THANK YOU, SHIRATORI.
I'M LUCKY TO HAVE YOU AS MY FRIEND.
"FRIEND"...
SQUEEZE
IF I CAN GO BACK TO THINKING OF HER AS 'JUST A FRIEND'...
MAYBE IT WON'T HURT SO MUCH.
!

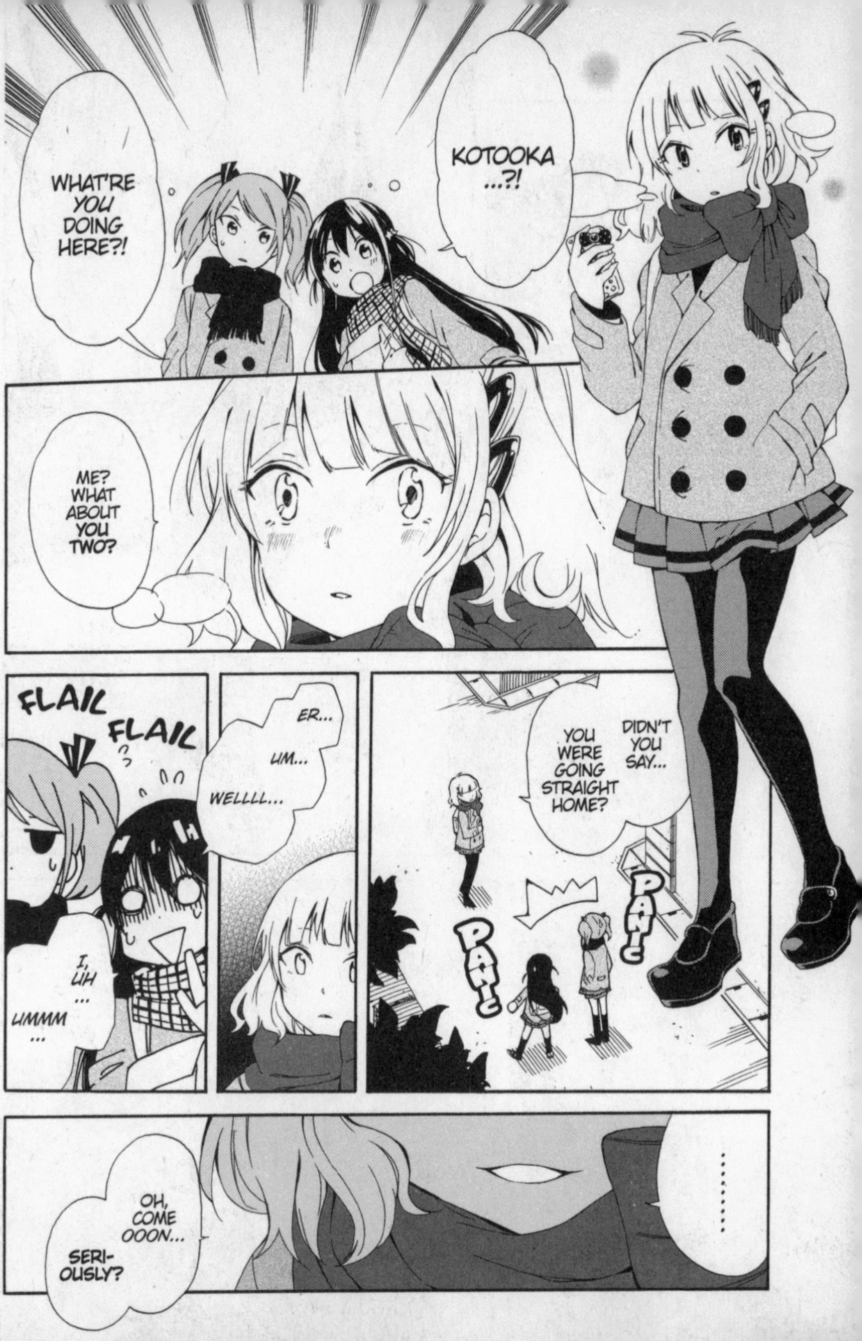
KOTOOKA ...?!
WHAT'RE YOU DOING HERE?!
ME? WHAT ABOUT YOU TWO?
DIDN'T YOU SAY...
YOU WERE GOING STRAIGHT HOME?
PANIC
PANIC
ER...
UM...
WELLLL...
FLAIL
FLAIL
I, UH ...
UMMM ...
......
OH, COME OOON...
SERI-OUSLY?

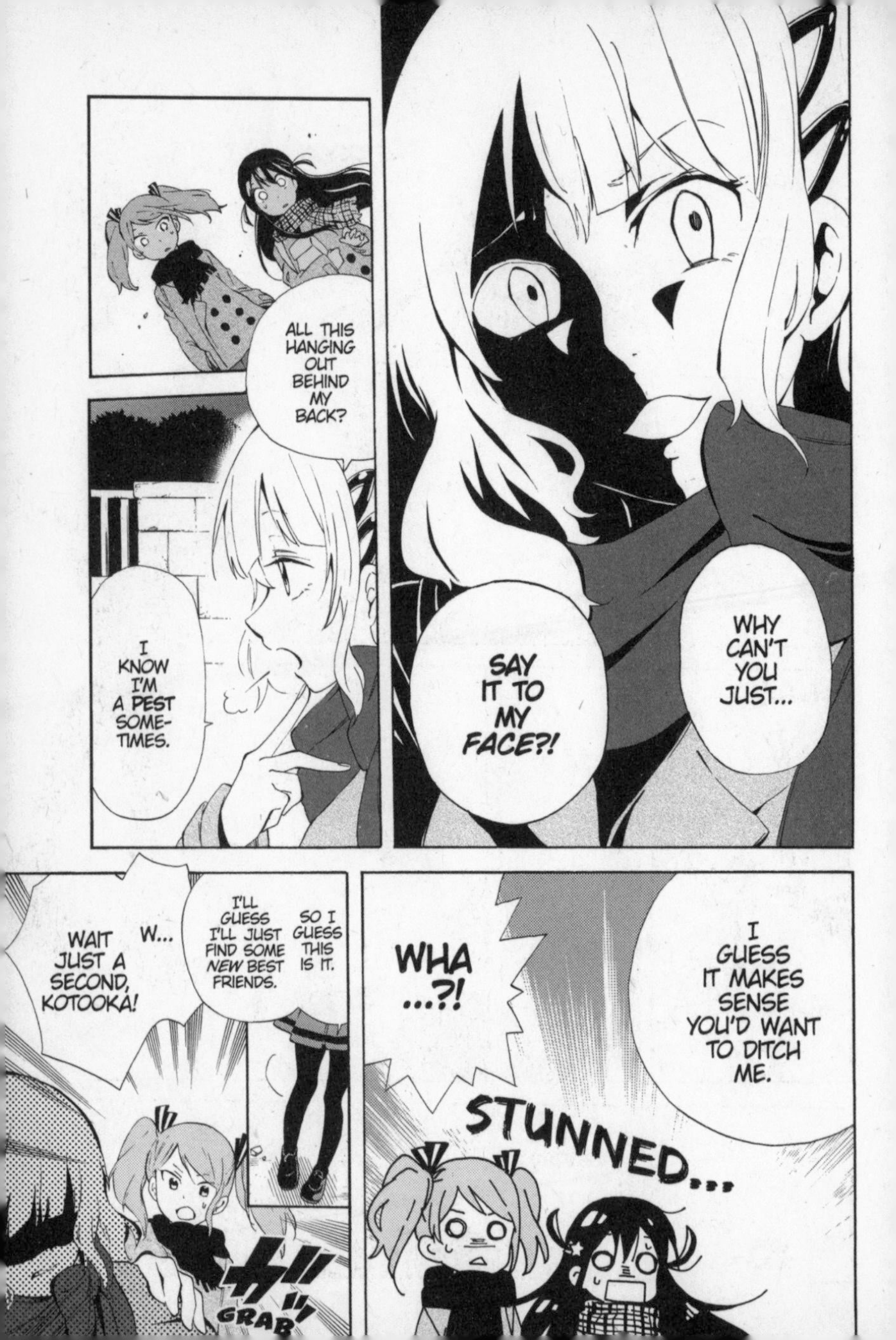
WHY CAN'T YOU JUST...
SAY IT TO MY FACE?!
ALL THIS HANGING OUT BEHIND MY BACK?
I KNOW I'M A PEST SOME-TIMES.
I GUESS IT MAKES SENSE YOU'D WANT TO DITCH ME.
WHA ...?!
STUNNED...
SO I GUESS THIS IS IT.
I'LL GUESS I'LL JUST FIND SOME NEW BEST FRIENDS.
W...
WAIT JUST A SECOND, KOTOOKA!
GRAB

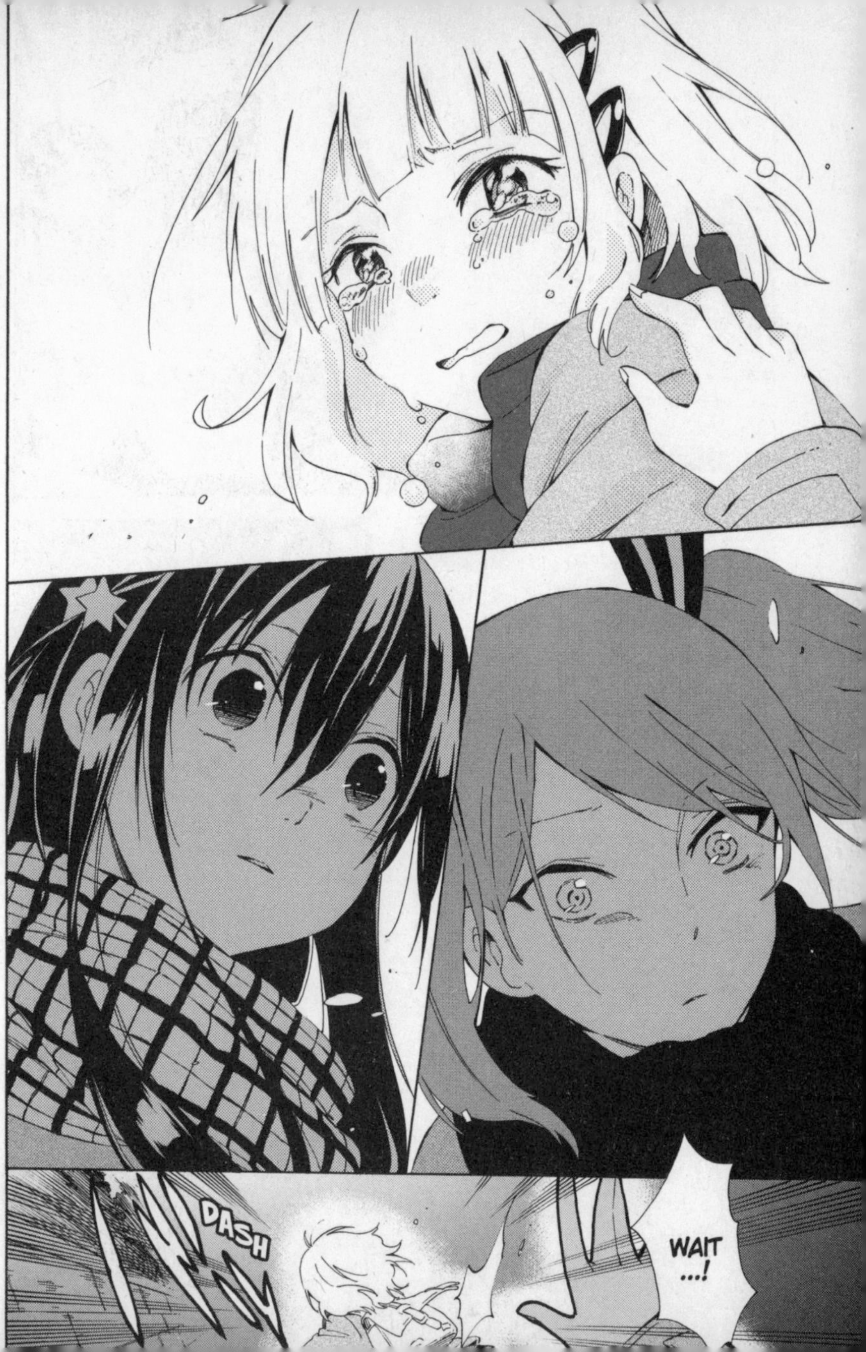
WAIT ...!
DASH

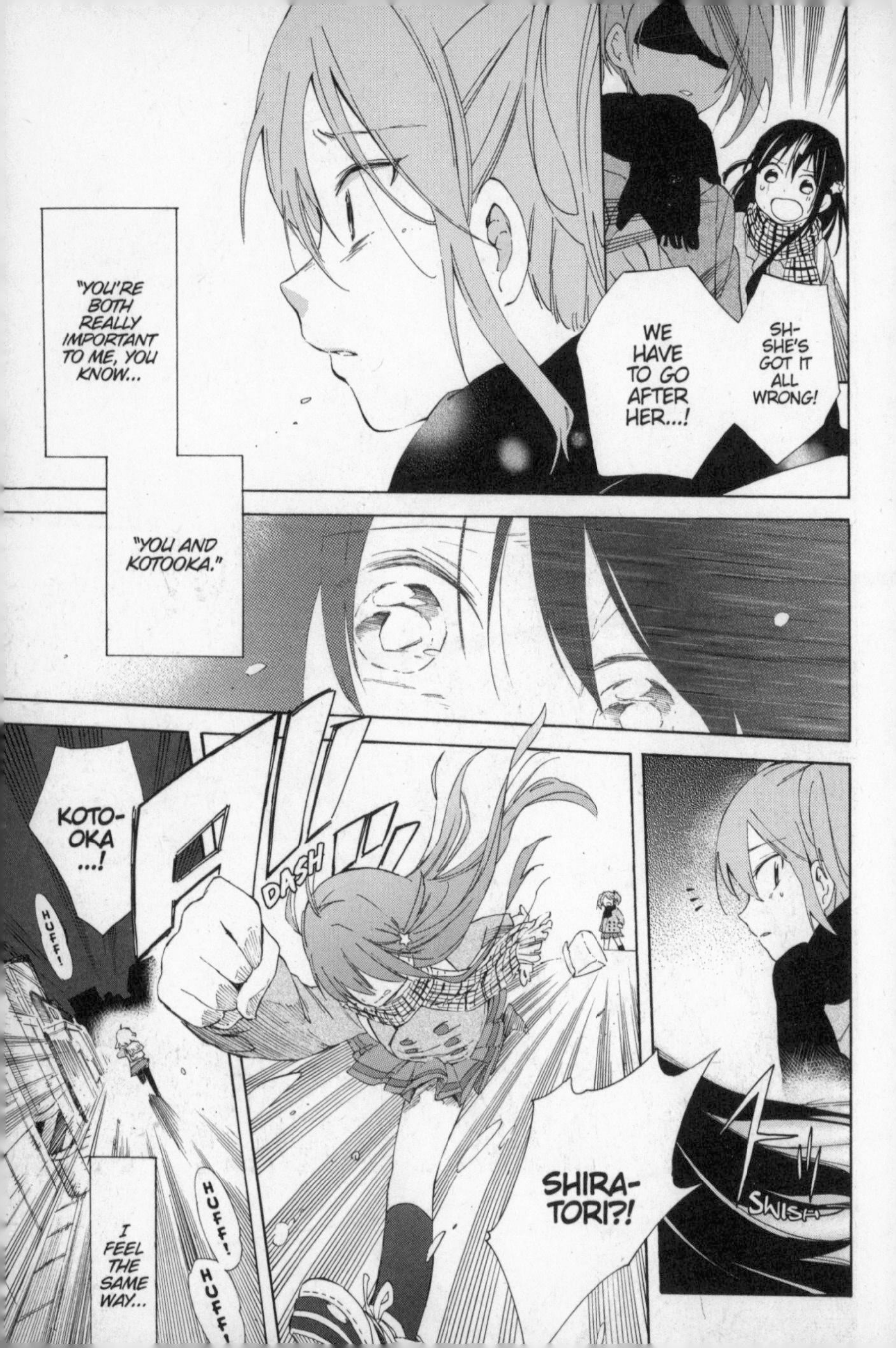
SH-SHE'S GOT IT ALL WRONG!
WE HAVE TO GO AFTER HER...!
"YOU'RE BOTH REALLY IMPORTANT TO ME, YOU KNOW...
"YOU AND KOTOOKA."
SHIRA-TORI?!
SWISH
KOTO-OKA ...!
DASH
HUFF!
HUFF!
HUFF!
I FEEL THE SAME WAY...

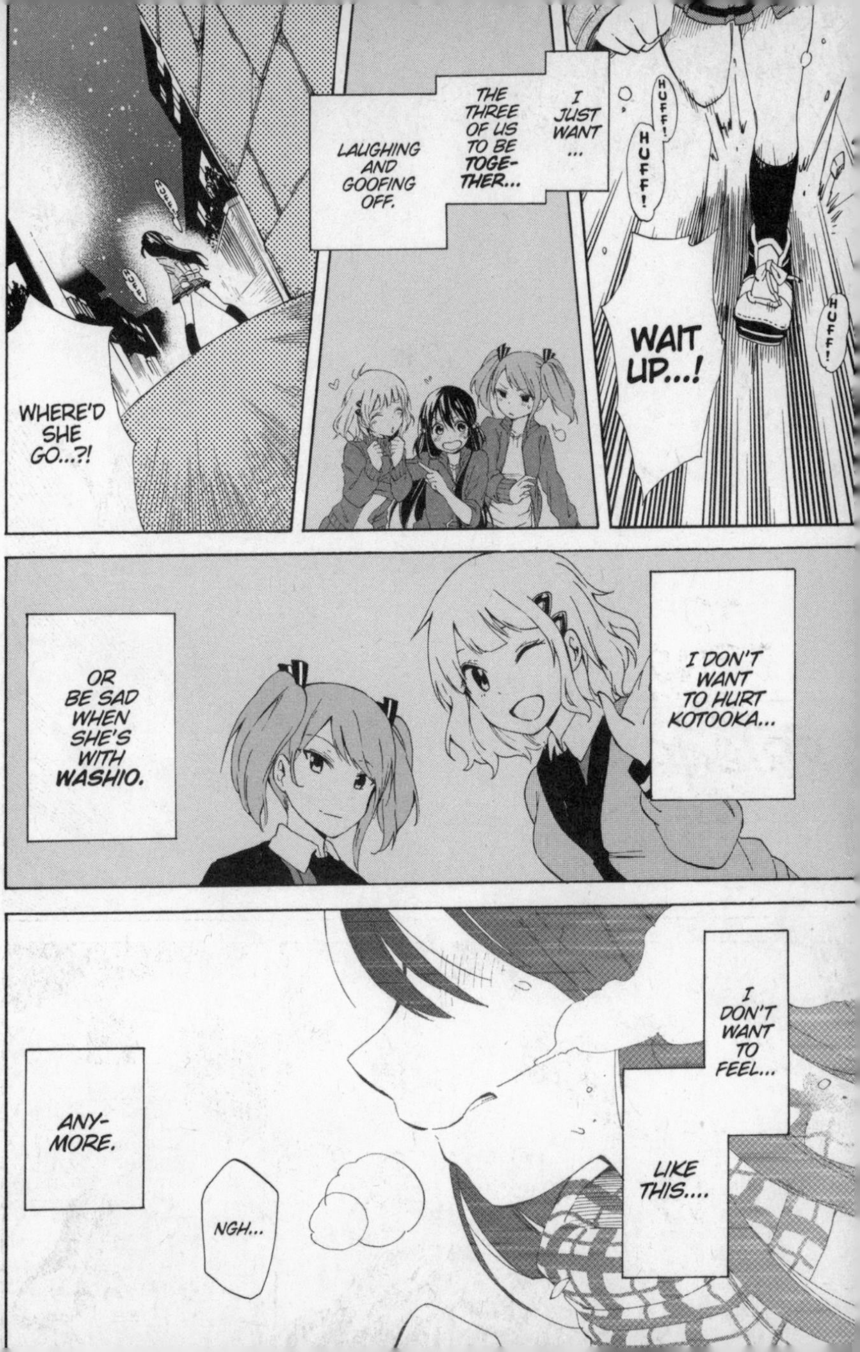
HUFF! HUFF! HUFF!
WAIT UP...!
HUFF!
I JUST WANT...
THE THREE OF US TO BE TOGE-THER...
LAUGHING AND GOOFING OFF.
WHERE'D SHE GO...?!
I DON'T WANT TO HURT KOTOOKA...
OR BE SAD WHEN SHE'S WITH WASHIO.
I DON'T WANT TO FEEL...
LIKE THIS....
ANY-MORE.
NGH...

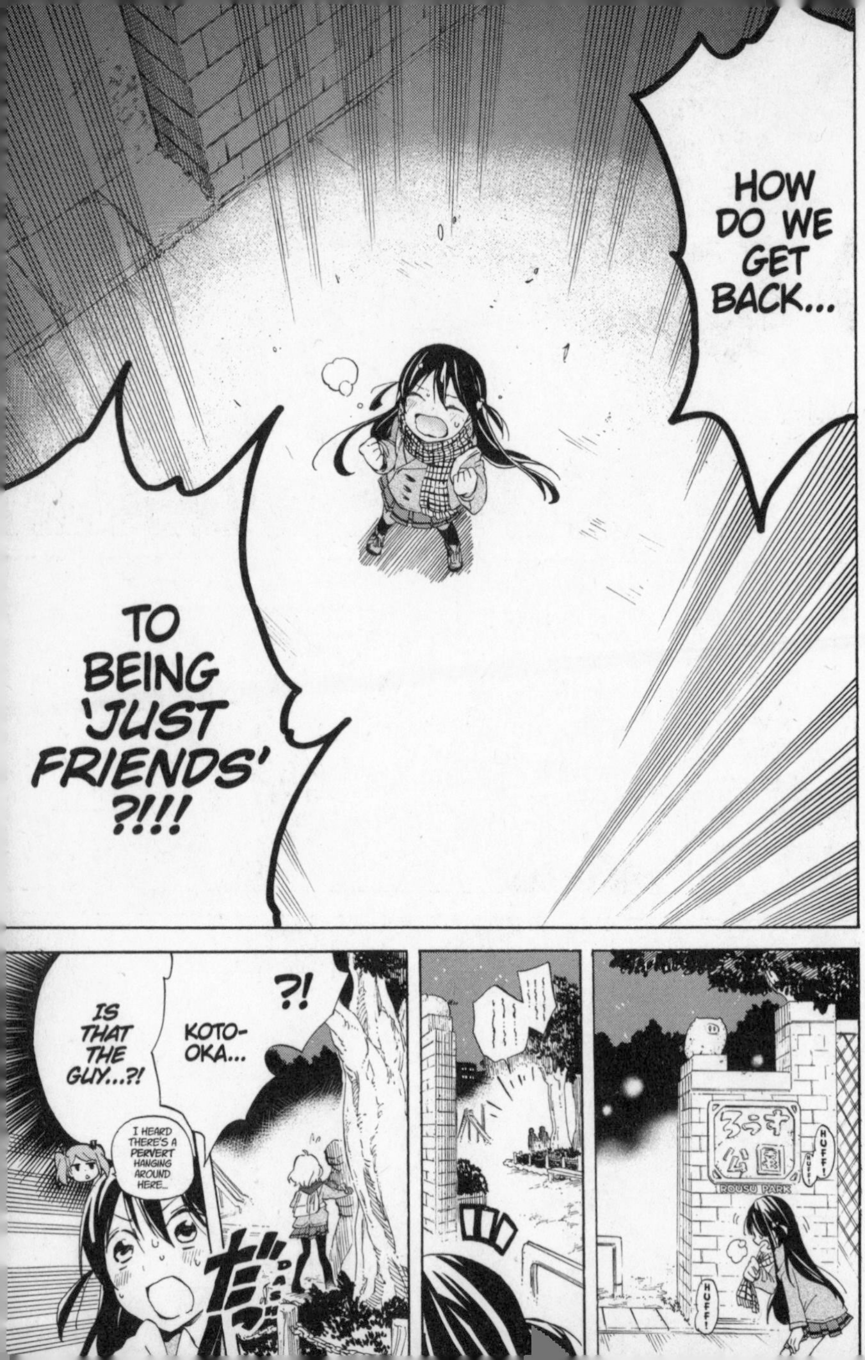
HOW DO WE GET BACK...
TO BEING 'JUST FRIENDS' ?!!!
ろうす公園
ROUSU PARK
HUFF! HUFF!
HUFF!
?!
KOTO-OKA...
IS THAT THE GUY...?!
I HEARD THERE'S A PERVERT HANGING AROUND HERE...
DASH

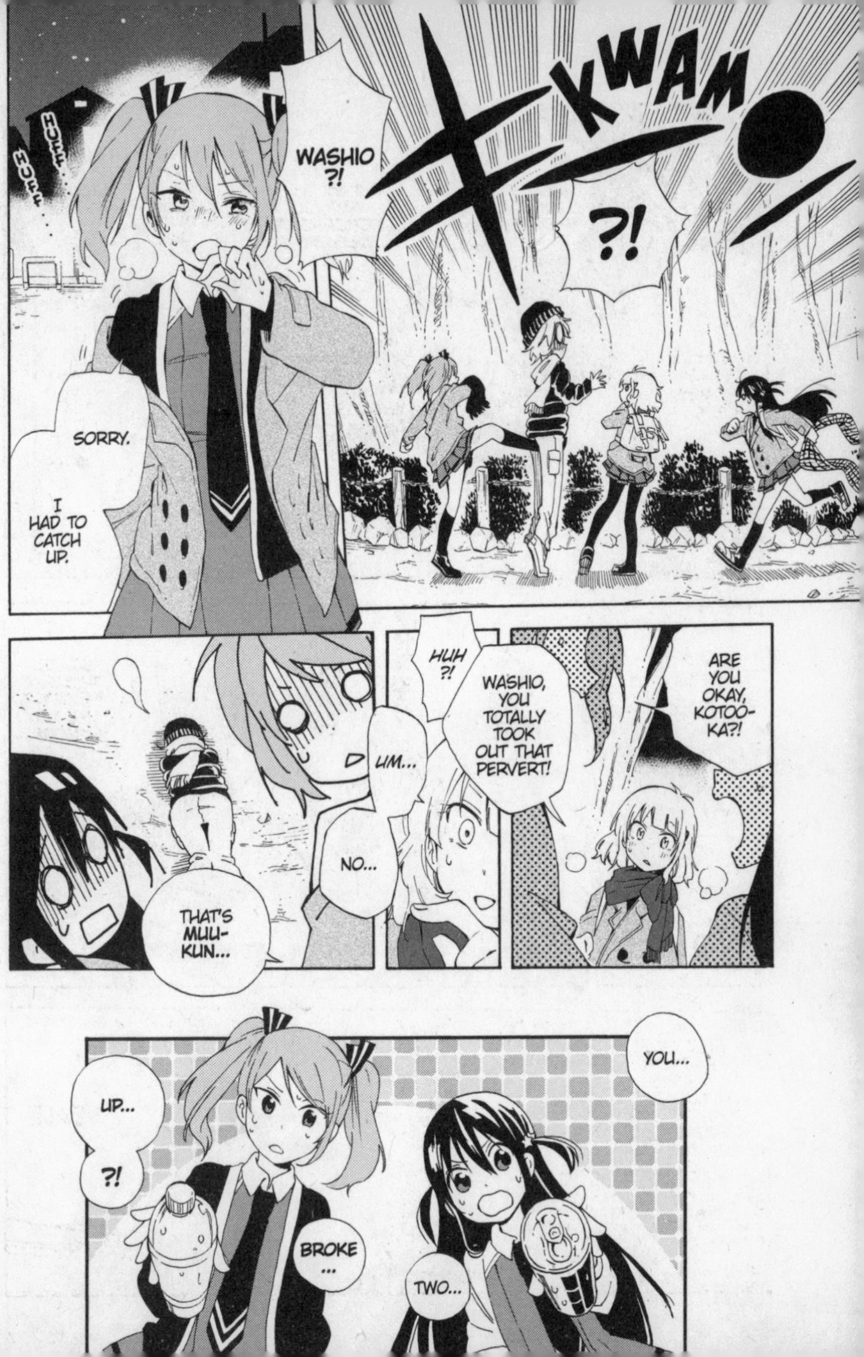
KWAM
?!
WASHIO ?!
HUFF HUFF...
SORRY.
I HAD TO CATCH UP.
ARE YOU OKAY, KOTOO-KA?!
HUH ?!
WASHIO, YOU TOTALLY TOOK OUT THAT PERVERT!
UM...
NO...
THAT'S MUU-KUN...
YOU...
TWO...
BROKE ...
UP...
?!

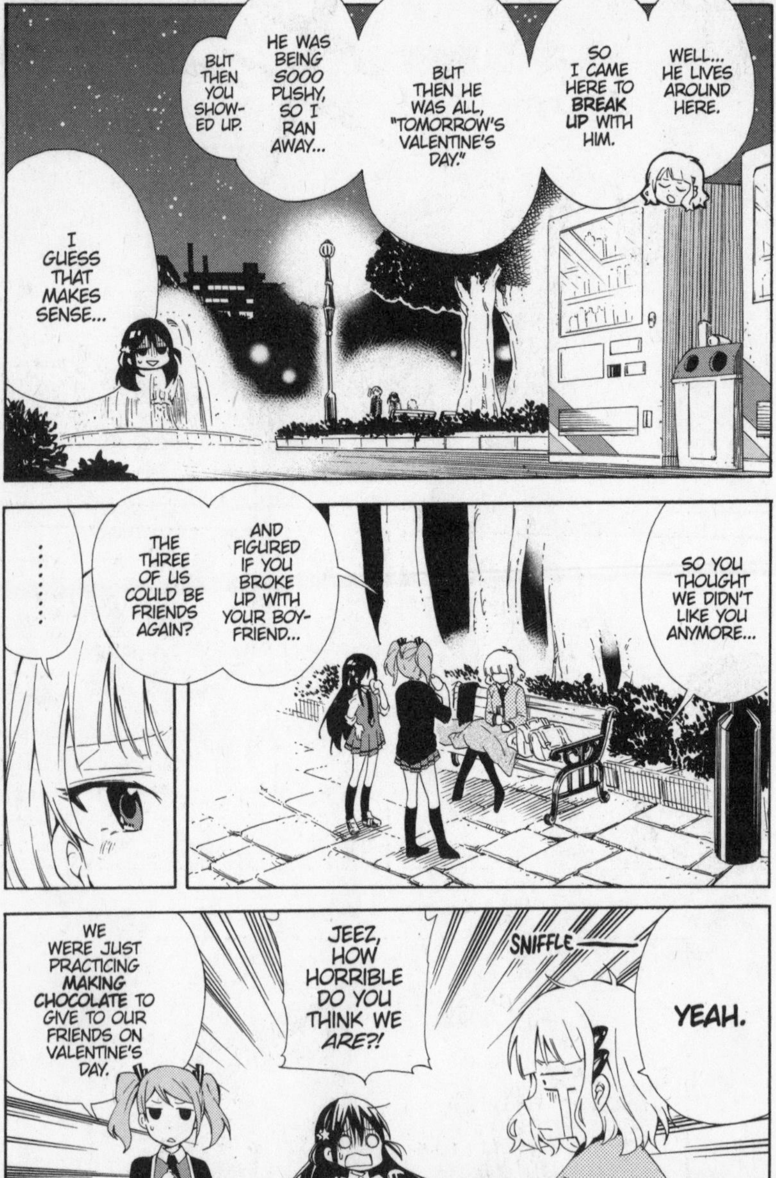
WELL... HE LIVES AROUND HERE.
SO I CAME HERE TO **BREAK UP** WITH HIM.
BUT THEN HE WAS ALL, "TOMORROW'S VALENTINE'S DAY."
HE WAS BEING *SOOO* PUSHY, SO I RAN AWAY...
BUT THEN YOU SHOWED UP.
I GUESS THAT MAKES SENSE...
SO YOU THOUGHT WE DIDN'T LIKE YOU ANYMORE...
AND FIGURED IF YOU BROKE UP WITH YOUR BOYFRIEND...
THE THREE OF US COULD BE FRIENDS AGAIN?
......
SNIFFLE——
YEAH.
JEEZ, HOW HORRIBLE DO YOU THINK WE *ARE*?!
WE WERE JUST PRACTICING MAKING **CHOCOLATE** TO GIVE TO OUR FRIENDS ON VALENTINE'S DAY.

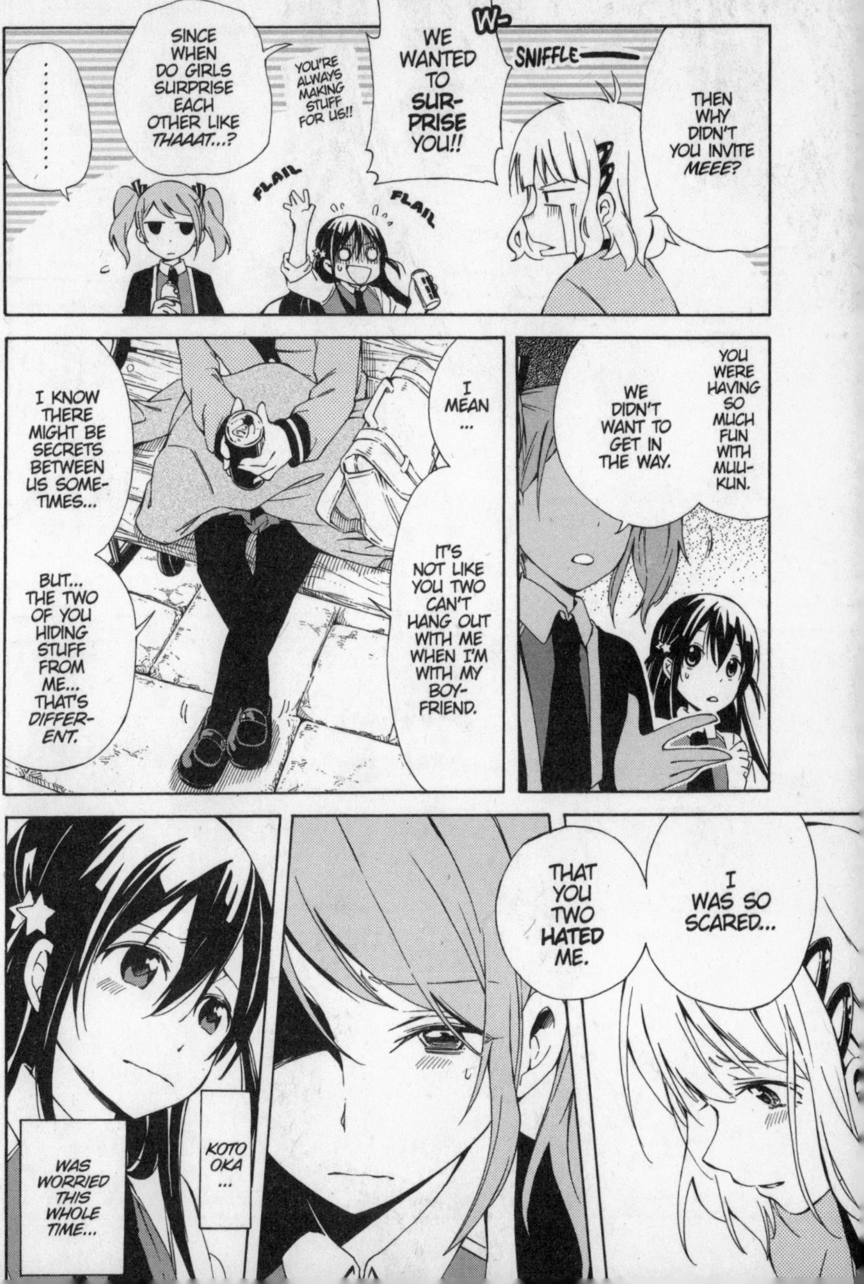
THEN WHY DIDN'T YOU INVITE MEEE?
W- SNIFFLE——
WE WANTED TO SURPRISE YOU!!
YOU'RE ALWAYS MAKING STUFF FOR US!!
FLAIL
FLAIL
SINCE WHEN DO GIRLS SURPRISE EACH OTHER LIKE THAAAT...?
......
YOU WERE HAVING SO MUCH FUN WITH MUU-KUN.
WE DIDN'T WANT TO GET IN THE WAY.
I MEAN...
IT'S NOT LIKE YOU TWO CAN'T HANG OUT WITH ME WHEN I'M WITH MY BOYFRIEND.
I KNOW THERE MIGHT BE SECRETS BETWEEN US SOMETIMES...
BUT... THE TWO OF YOU HIDING STUFF FROM ME... THAT'S DIFFERENT.
I WAS SO SCARED...
THAT YOU TWO HATED ME.
KOTOOKA...
WAS WORRIED THIS WHOLE TIME...

IF I WAS IN HER SHOES, I'D HAVE BEEN WORRIED TOO.

BUT...

I'M SORRY...

WILL ALWAYS BE FRIENDS, RIGHT?

SQUEEZE

THE THREE OF US...

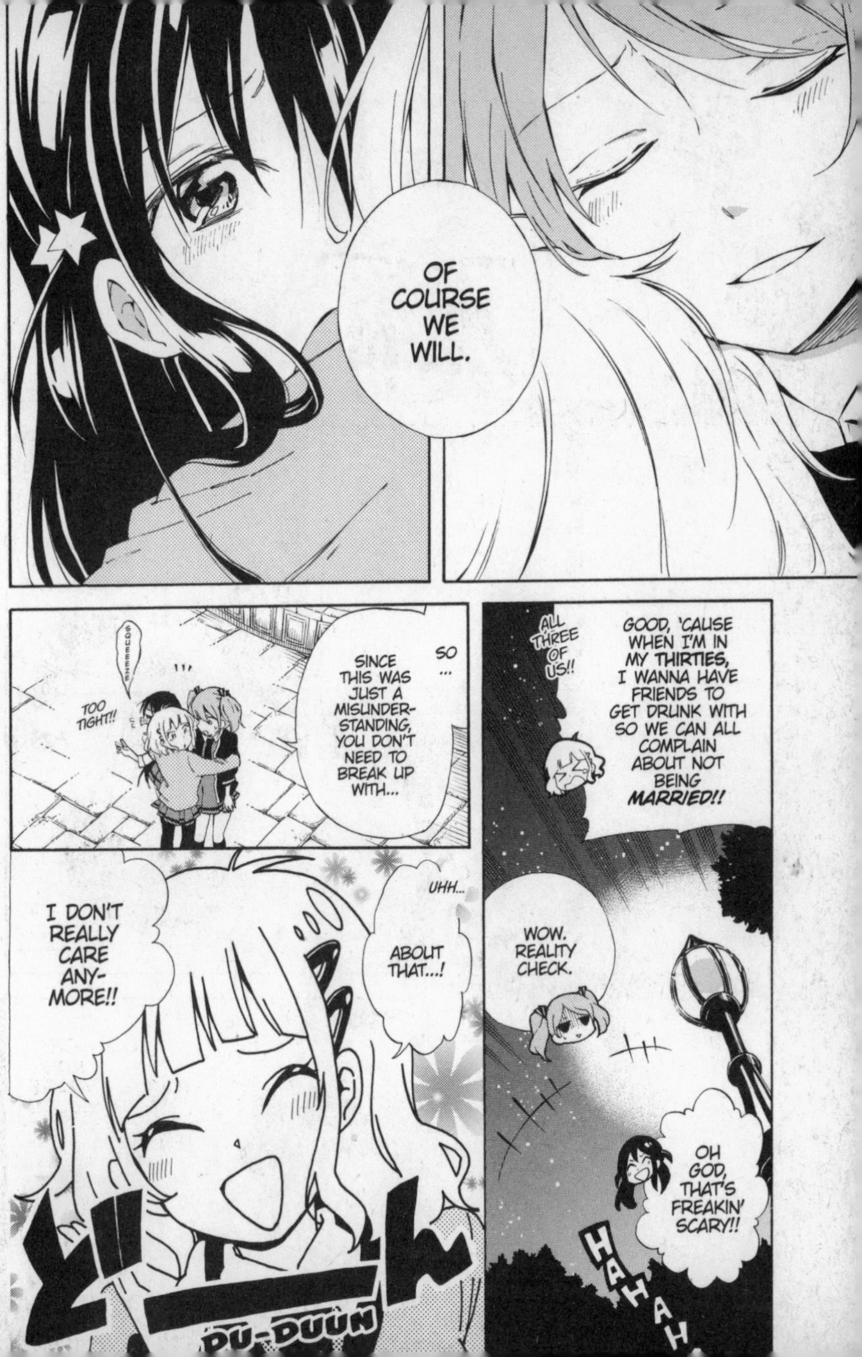
OF COURSE WE WILL.
GOOD, 'CAUSE WHEN I'M IN MY THIRTIES, I WANNA HAVE FRIENDS TO GET DRUNK WITH SO WE CAN ALL COMPLAIN ABOUT NOT BEING MARRIED!!
ALL THREE OF US!!
WOW. REALITY CHECK.
OH GOD, THAT'S FREAKIN' SCARY!!
HAHAHAH
SO...
SINCE THIS WAS JUST A MISUNDER-STANDING, YOU DON'T NEED TO BREAK UP WITH...
SQUEEEEZE
TOO TIGHT!!
UHH...
ABOUT THAT...!
I DON'T REALLY CARE ANY-MORE!!
DU-DUUN

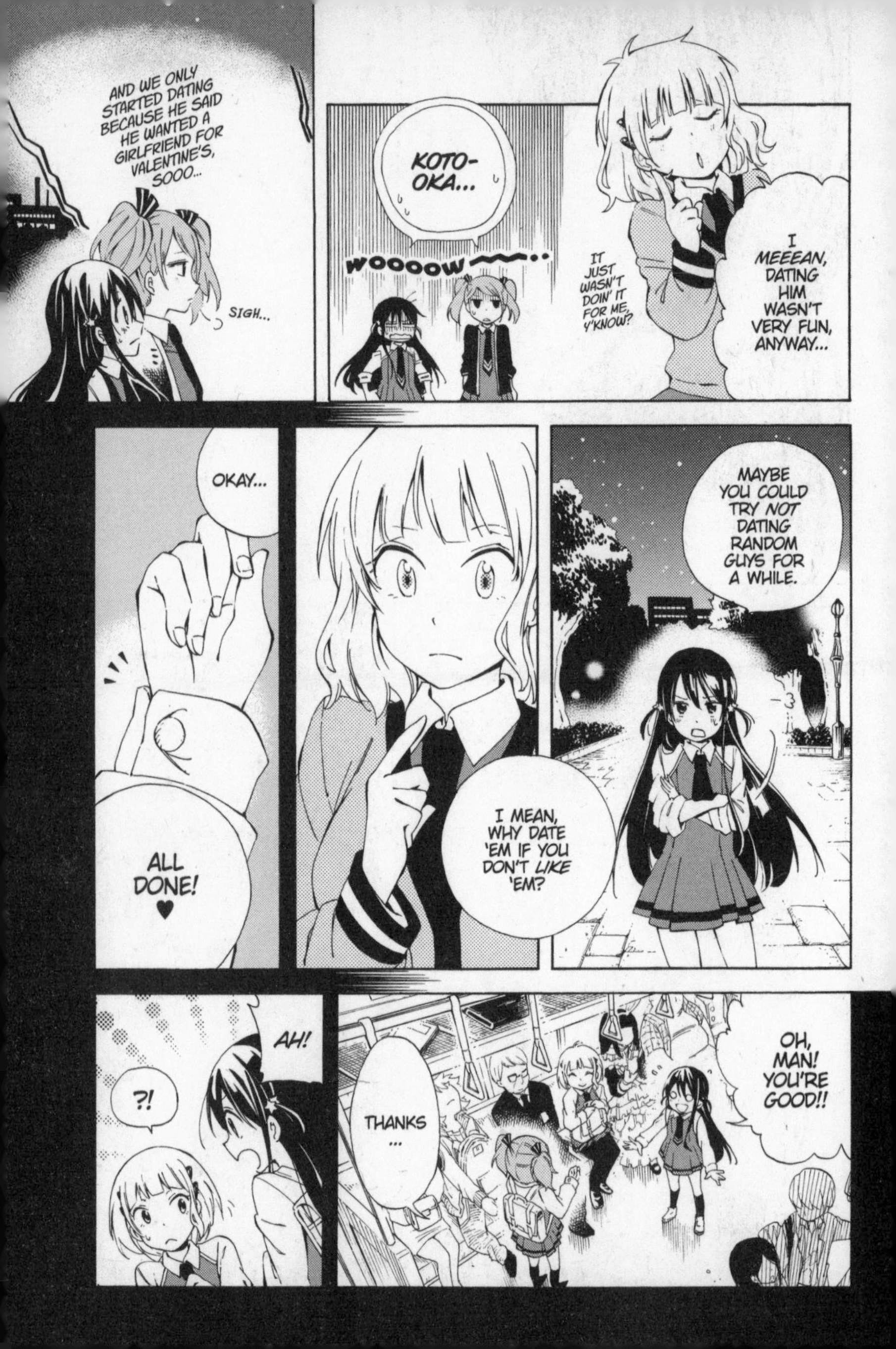
I MEEEAN, DATING HIM WASN'T VERY FUN, ANYWAY...
IT JUST WASN'T DOIN' IT FOR ME, Y'KNOW?
KOTO-OKA...
WOOOOW~~..
AND WE ONLY STARTED DATING BECAUSE HE SAID HE WANTED A GIRLFRIEND FOR VALENTINE'S, SOOO...
SIGH...
MAYBE YOU COULD TRY *NOT* DATING RANDOM GUYS FOR A WHILE.
I MEAN, WHY DATE 'EM IF YOU DON'T *LIKE* 'EM?
OKAY...
ALL DONE! ♥
OH, MAN! YOU'RE GOOD!!
THANKS ...
AH!
?!

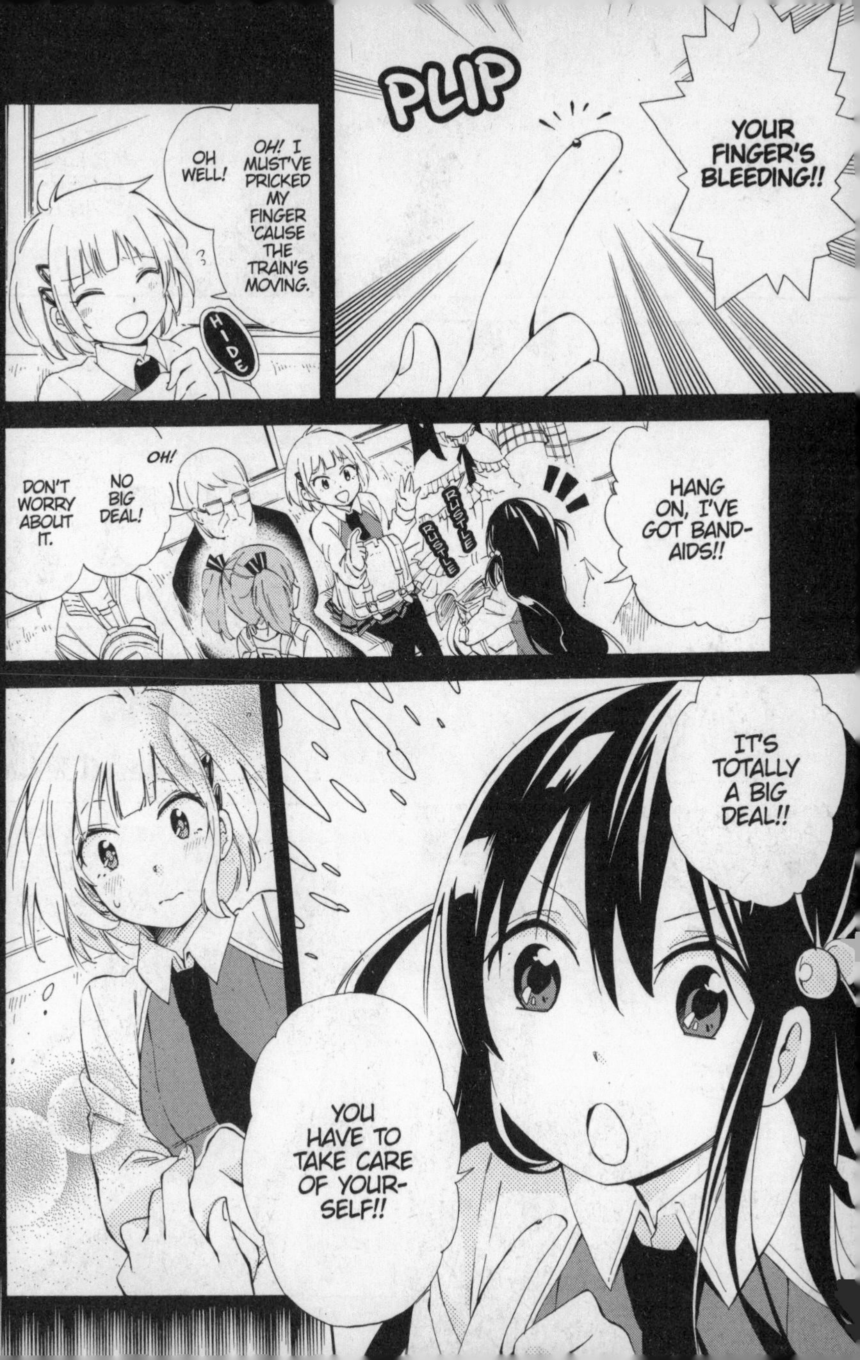
PLIP
YOUR FINGER'S BLEEDING!!
OH! I MUST'VE PRICKED MY FINGER 'CAUSE THE TRAIN'S MOVING.
OH WELL!
HIDE
HANG ON, I'VE GOT BAND-AIDS!!
RUSTLE
RUSTLE
OH!
NO BIG DEAL!
DON'T WORRY ABOUT IT.
IT'S TOTALLY A BIG DEAL!!
YOU HAVE TO TAKE CARE OF YOUR-SELF!!

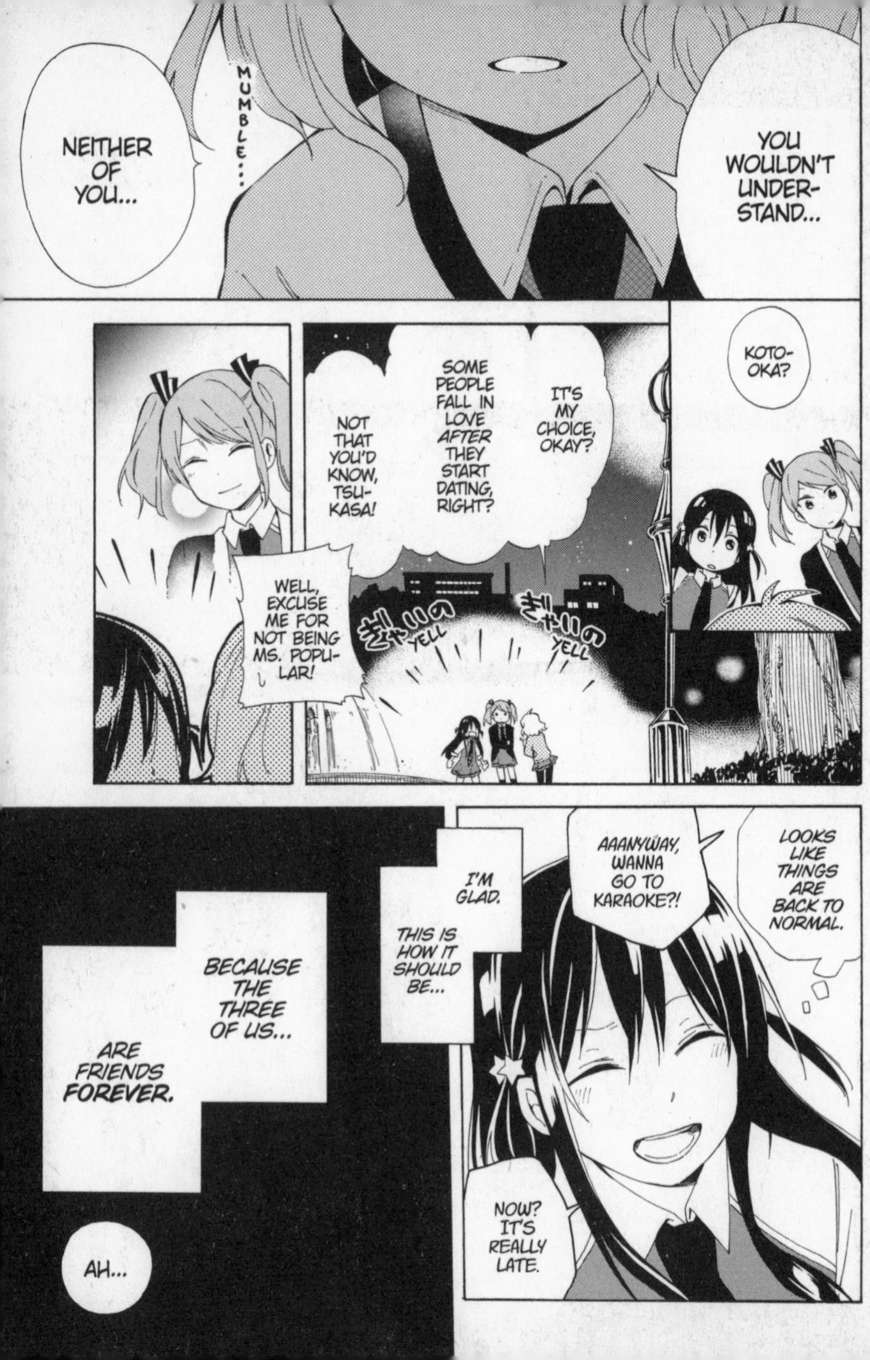
YOU WOULDN'T UNDER-STAND...
MUMBLE...
NEITHER OF YOU...
KOTO-OKA?
IT'S MY CHOICE, OKAY?
SOME PEOPLE FALL IN LOVE AFTER THEY START DATING, RIGHT?
NOT THAT YOU'D KNOW, TSU-KASA!
きゃいの YELL
きゃいの YELL
WELL, EXCUSE ME FOR NOT BEING MS. POPU-LAR!
LOOKS LIKE THINGS ARE BACK TO NORMAL.
AAANYWAY, WANNA GO TO KARAOKE?!
I'M GLAD.
THIS IS HOW IT SHOULD BE...
NOW? IT'S REALLY LATE.
BECAUSE THE THREE OF US...
ARE FRIENDS FOREVER.
AH...

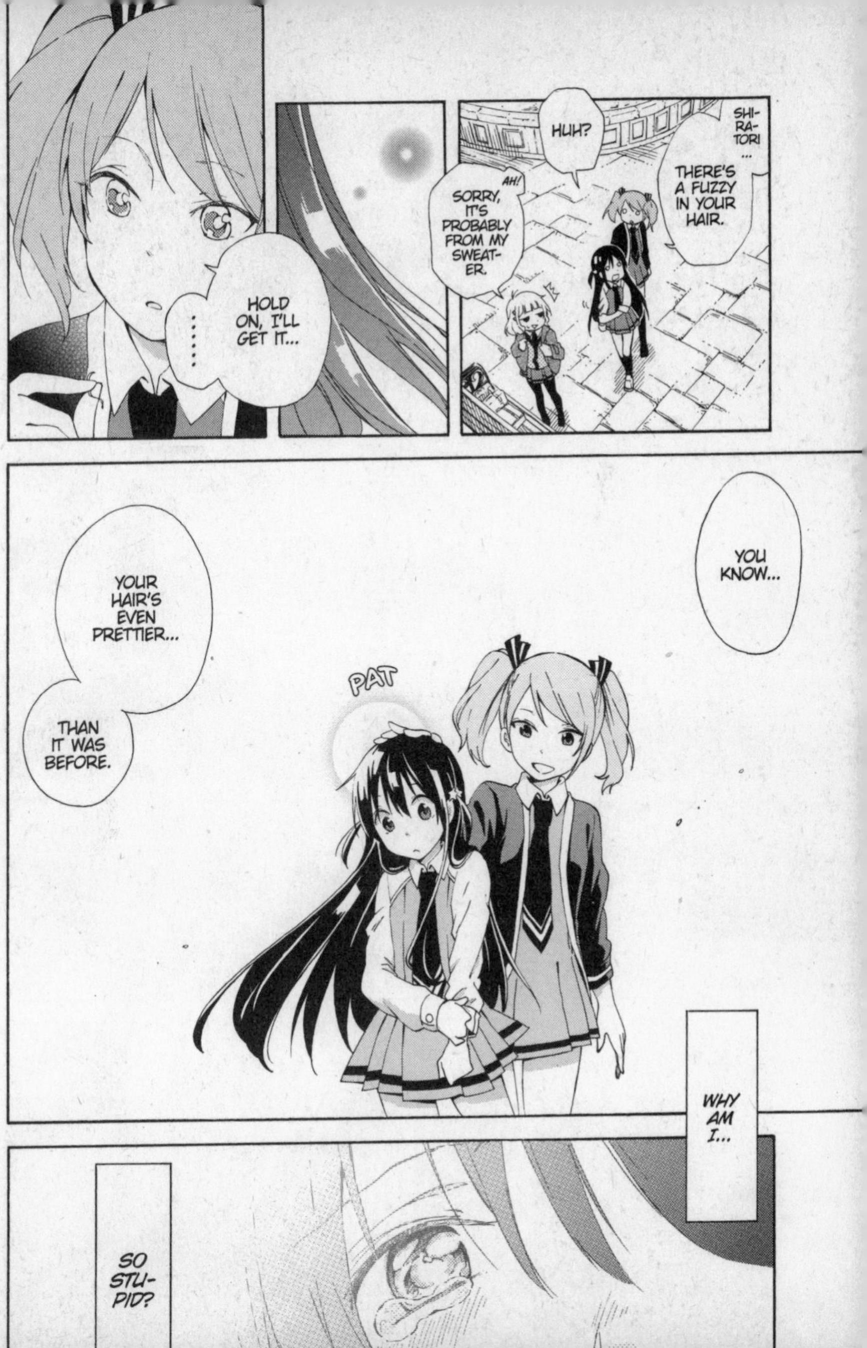
SHI-RA-TORI...
THERE'S A FUZZY IN YOUR HAIR.
HUH?
AH! SORRY, IT'S PROBABLY FROM MY SWEAT-ER.
HOLD ON, I'LL GET IT...
......
YOU KNOW...
PAT
YOUR HAIR'S EVEN PRETTIER...
THAN IT WAS BEFORE.
WHY AM I...
SO STU-PID?

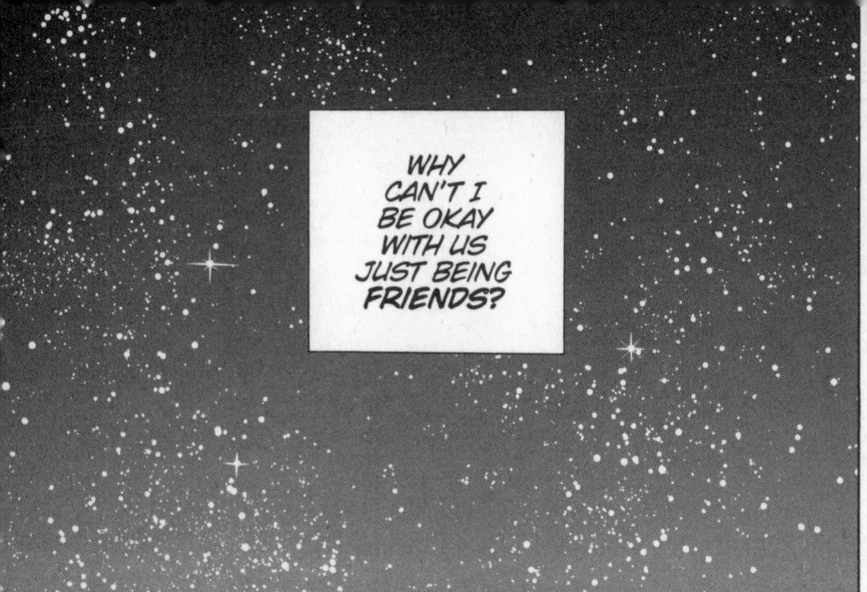
WHY CAN'T I BE OKAY WITH US JUST BEING FRIENDS?
HEY... WHAT'S WRONG?!
ARE YOU UPSET ABOUT WHAT HAPPENED EARLIER?

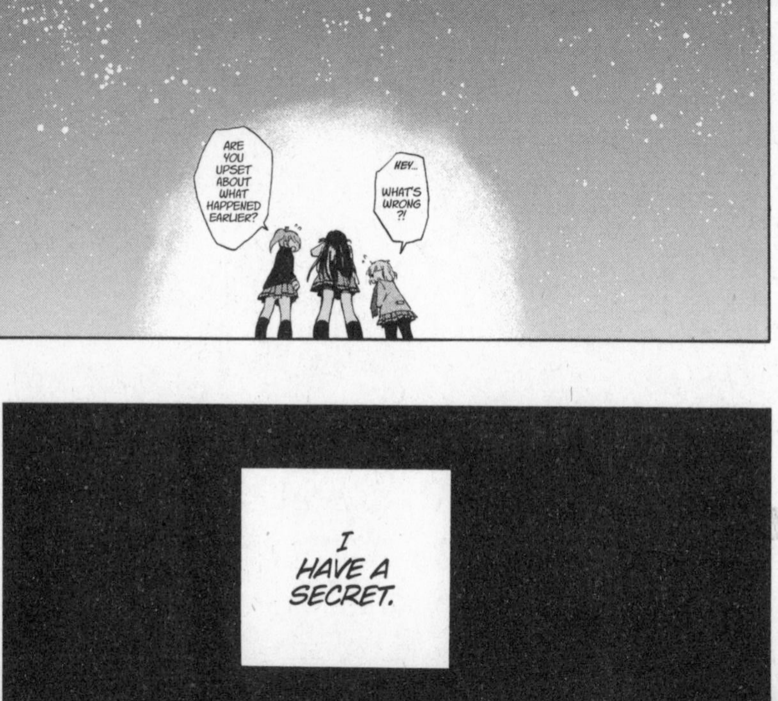
I HAVE A SECRET.

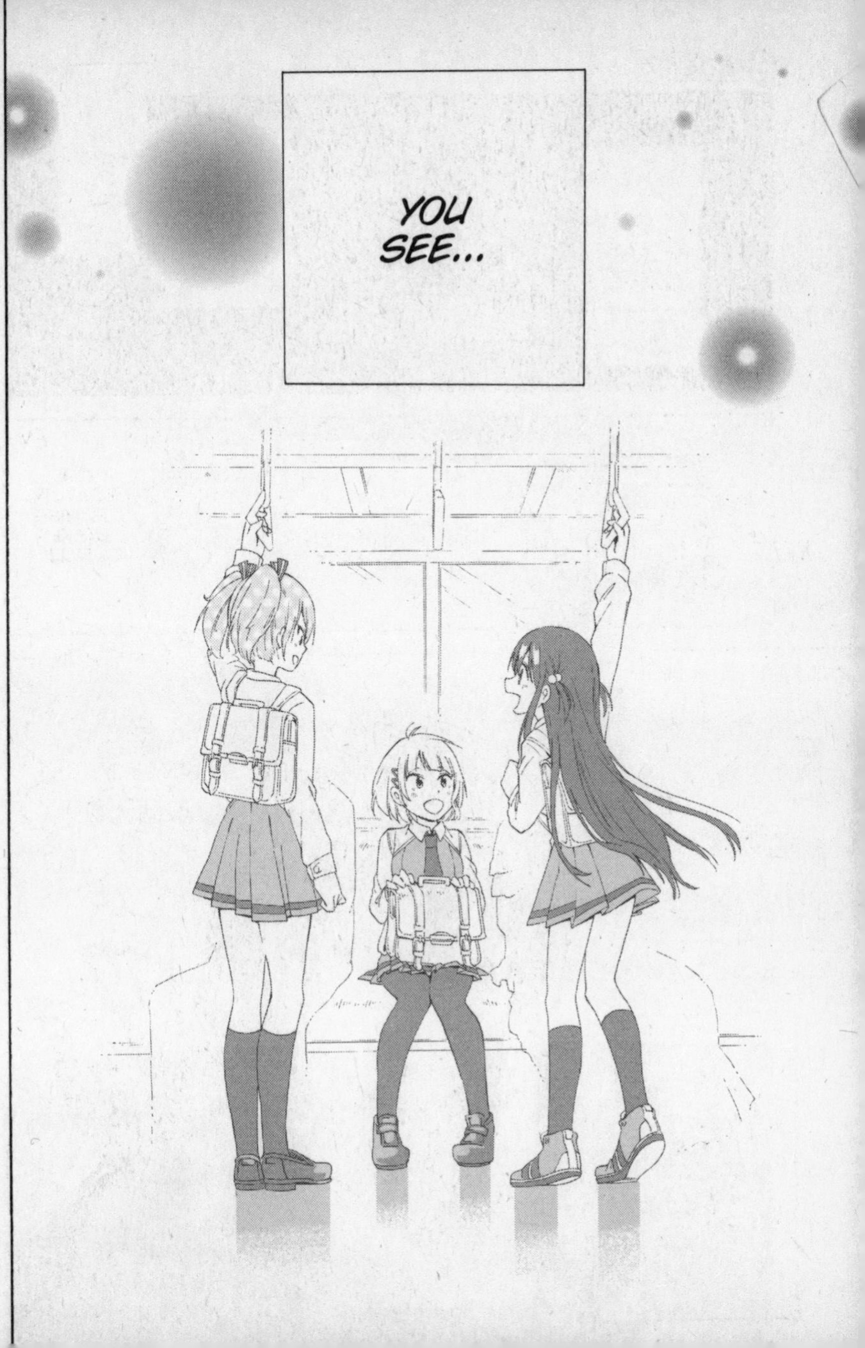
YOU SEE...

Chapter 2

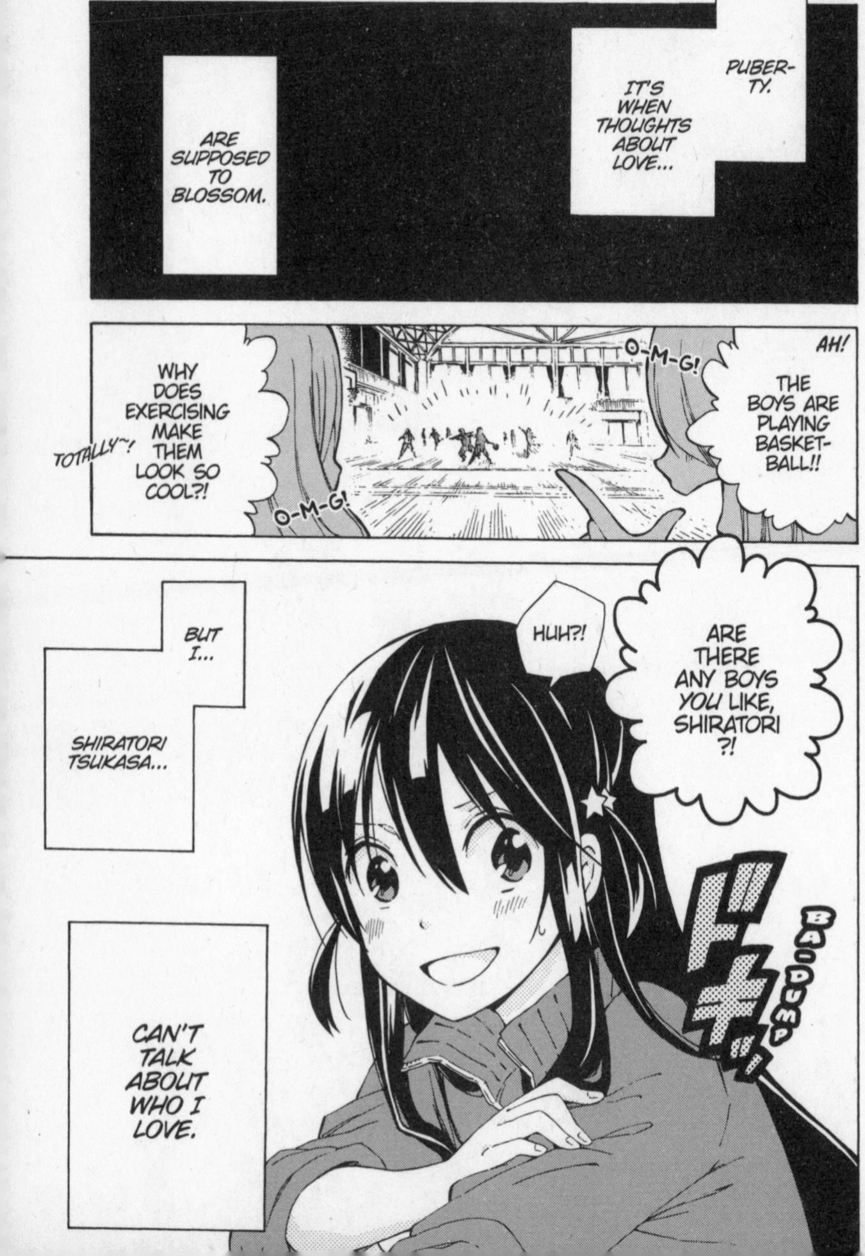
PUBER-TY.
IT'S WHEN THOUGHTS ABOUT LOVE...
ARE SUPPOSED TO BLOSSOM.
AH!
THE BOYS ARE PLAYING BASKET-BALL!!
O-M-G!
WHY DOES EXERCISING MAKE THEM LOOK SO COOL?!
TOTALLY~!
O-M-G!
ARE THERE ANY BOYS YOU LIKE, SHIRATORI ?!
HUH?!
BA-DUMP
BUT I...
SHIRATORI TSUKASA...
CAN'T TALK ABOUT WHO I LOVE.

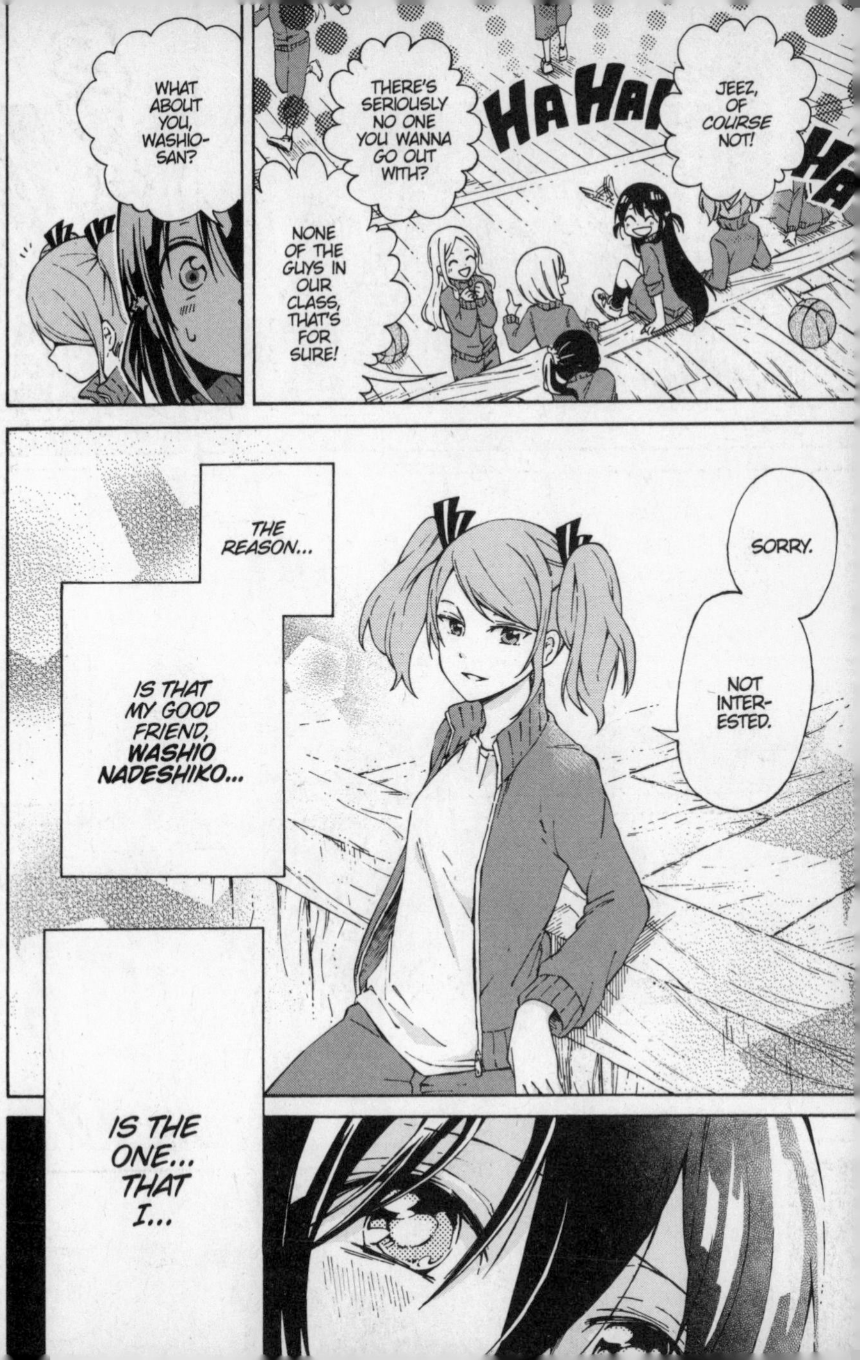
THERE'S SERIOUSLY NO ONE YOU WANNA GO OUT WITH?
JEEZ, OF COURSE NOT!
HAHA HA
NONE OF THE GUYS IN OUR CLASS, THAT'S FOR SURE!
WHAT ABOUT YOU, WASHIO-SAN?
SORRY.
NOT INTER-ESTED.
THE REASON...
IS THAT MY GOOD FRIEND, WASHIO NADESHIKO...
IS THE ONE... THAT I...

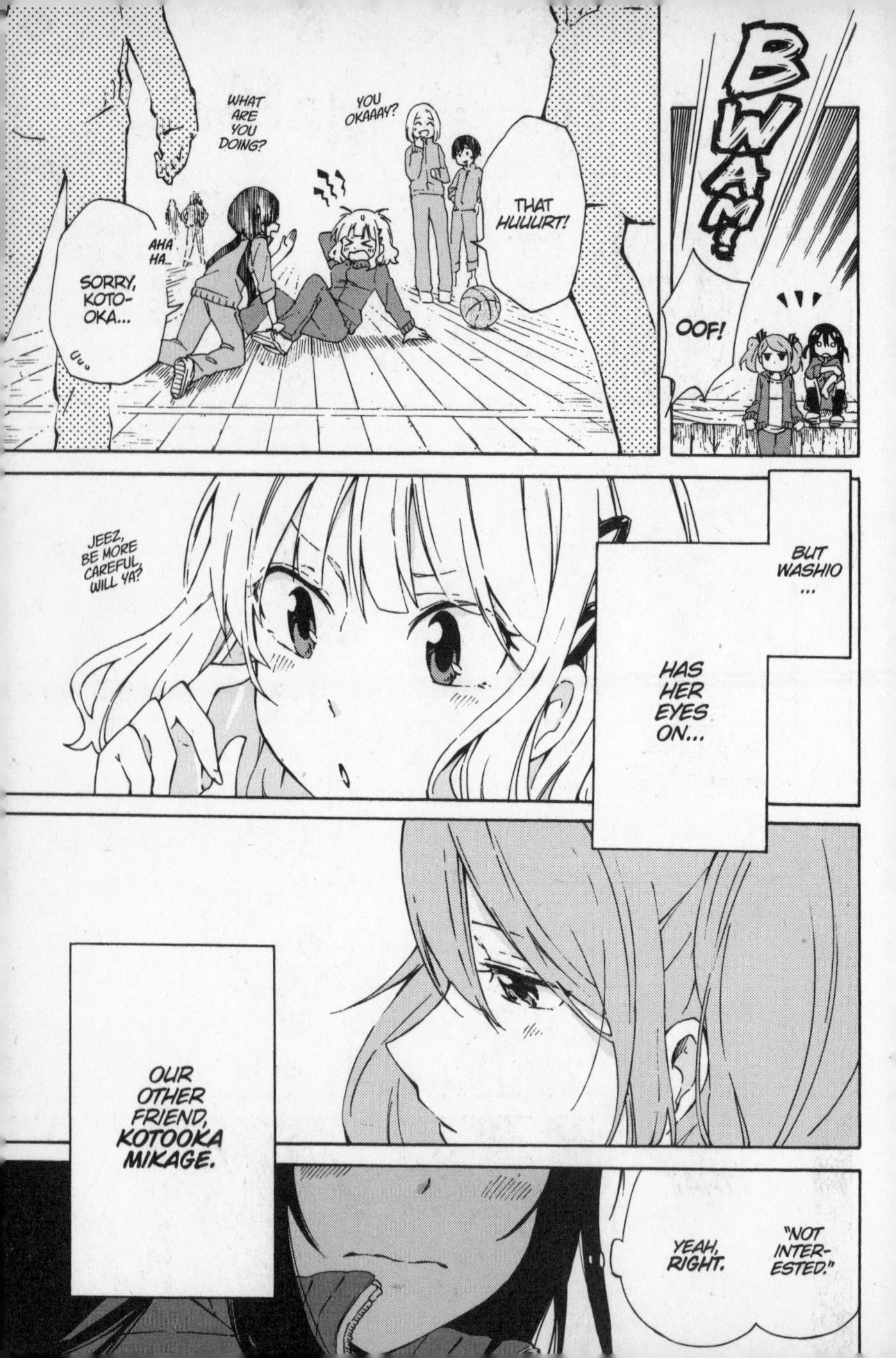
BWAM!
OOF!
THAT HUUURT!
YOU OKAAAY?
WHAT ARE YOU DOING?
AHA HA...
SORRY, KOTO-OKA...
BUT WASHIO...
HAS HER EYES ON...
JEEZ, BE MORE CAREFUL, WILL YA?
OUR OTHER FRIEND, KOTOOKA MIKAGE.
"NOT INTER-ESTED."
YEAH, RIGHT.

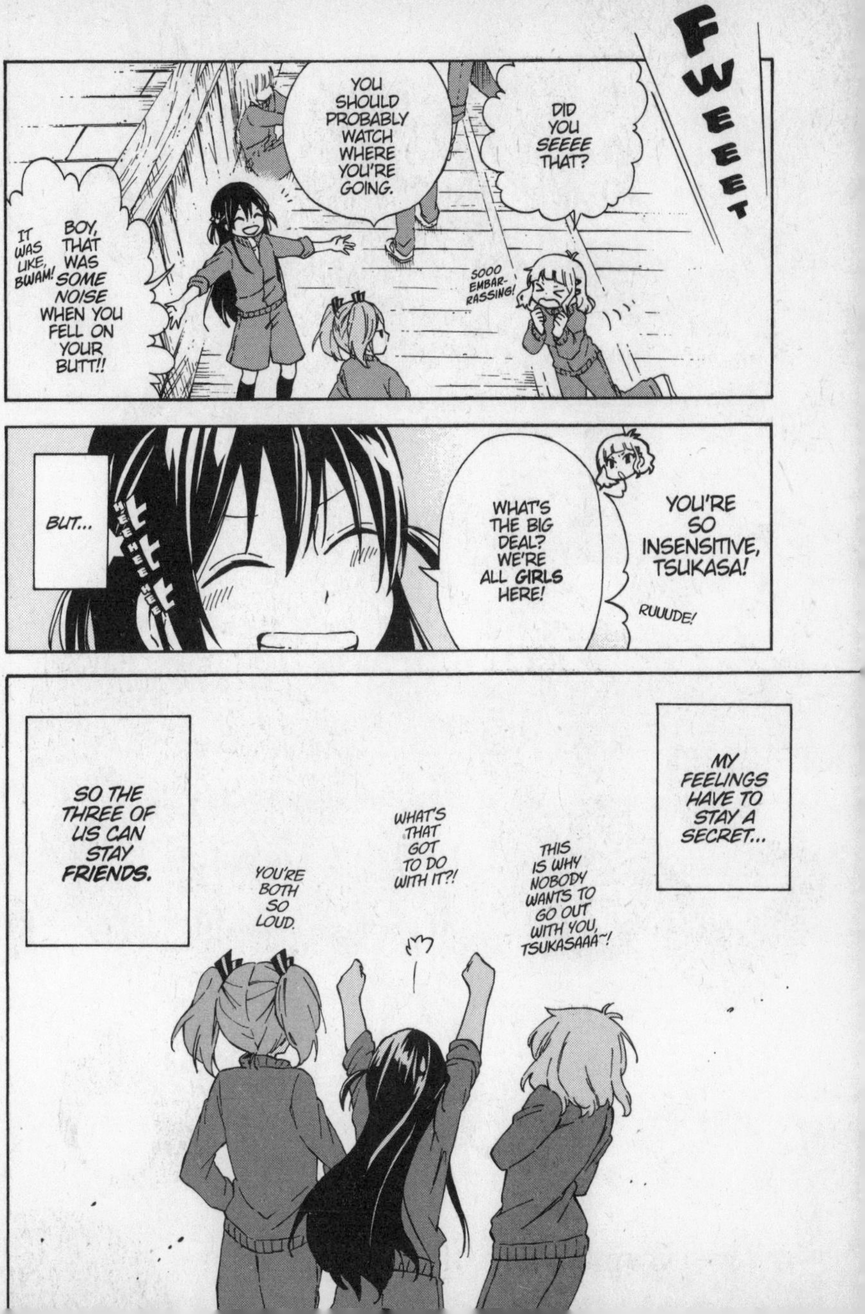
FWEEET
DID YOU SEEEE THAT?
YOU SHOULD PROBABLY WATCH WHERE YOU'RE GOING.
SOOO EMBARRASSING!
BOY, THAT WAS SOME NOISE WHEN YOU FELL ON YOUR BUTT!!
IT WAS LIKE, BWAM!
YOU'RE SO INSENSITIVE, TSUKASA!
RUUUDE!
WHAT'S THE BIG DEAL? WE'RE ALL GIRLS HERE!
HEE HEE HEE
BUT...
MY FEELINGS HAVE TO STAY A SECRET...
THIS IS WHY NOBODY WANTS TO GO OUT WITH YOU, TSUKASAAA~!
WHAT'S THAT GOT TO DO WITH IT?!
YOU'RE BOTH SO LOUD.
SO THE THREE OF US CAN STAY FRIENDS.

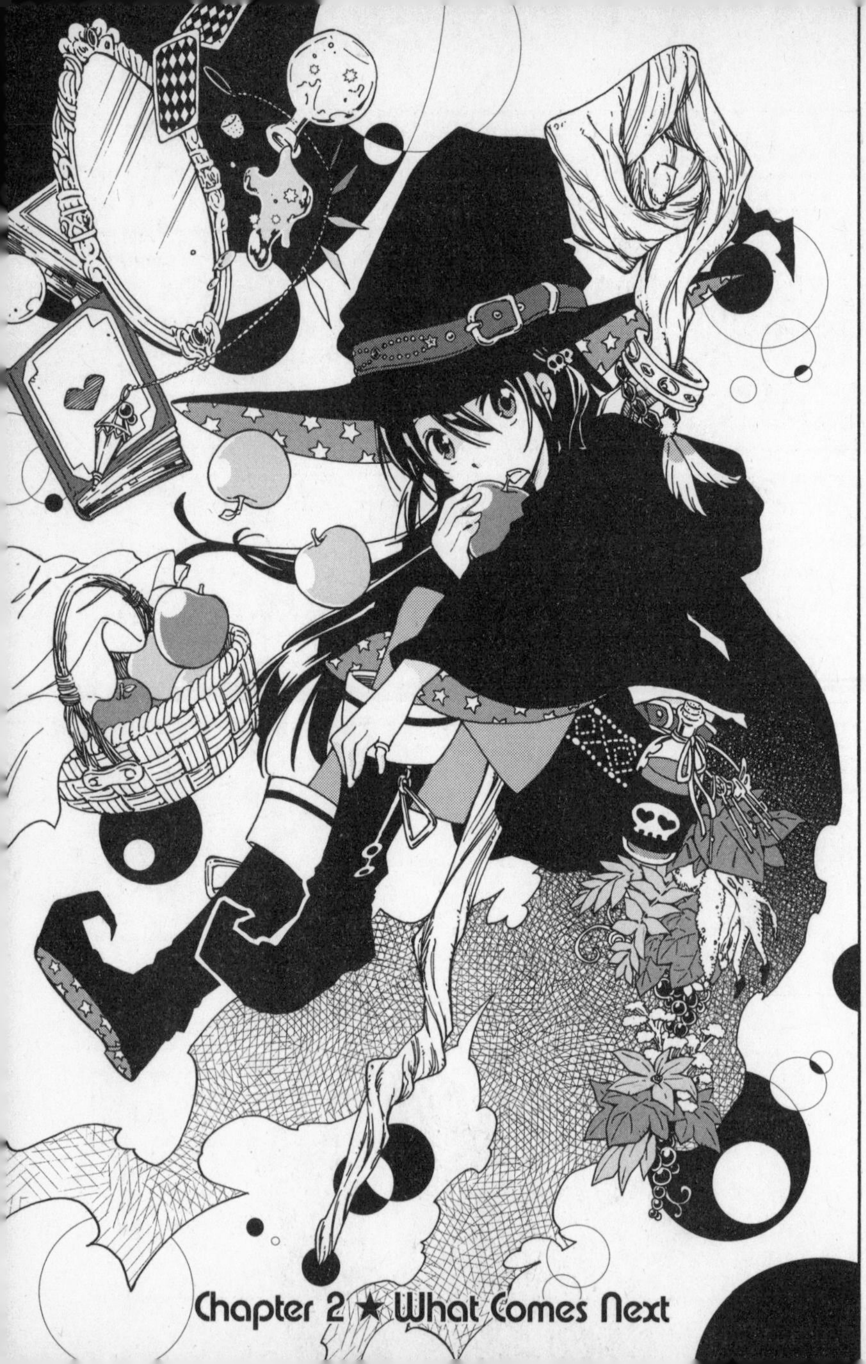

Chapter 2 ★ What Comes Next

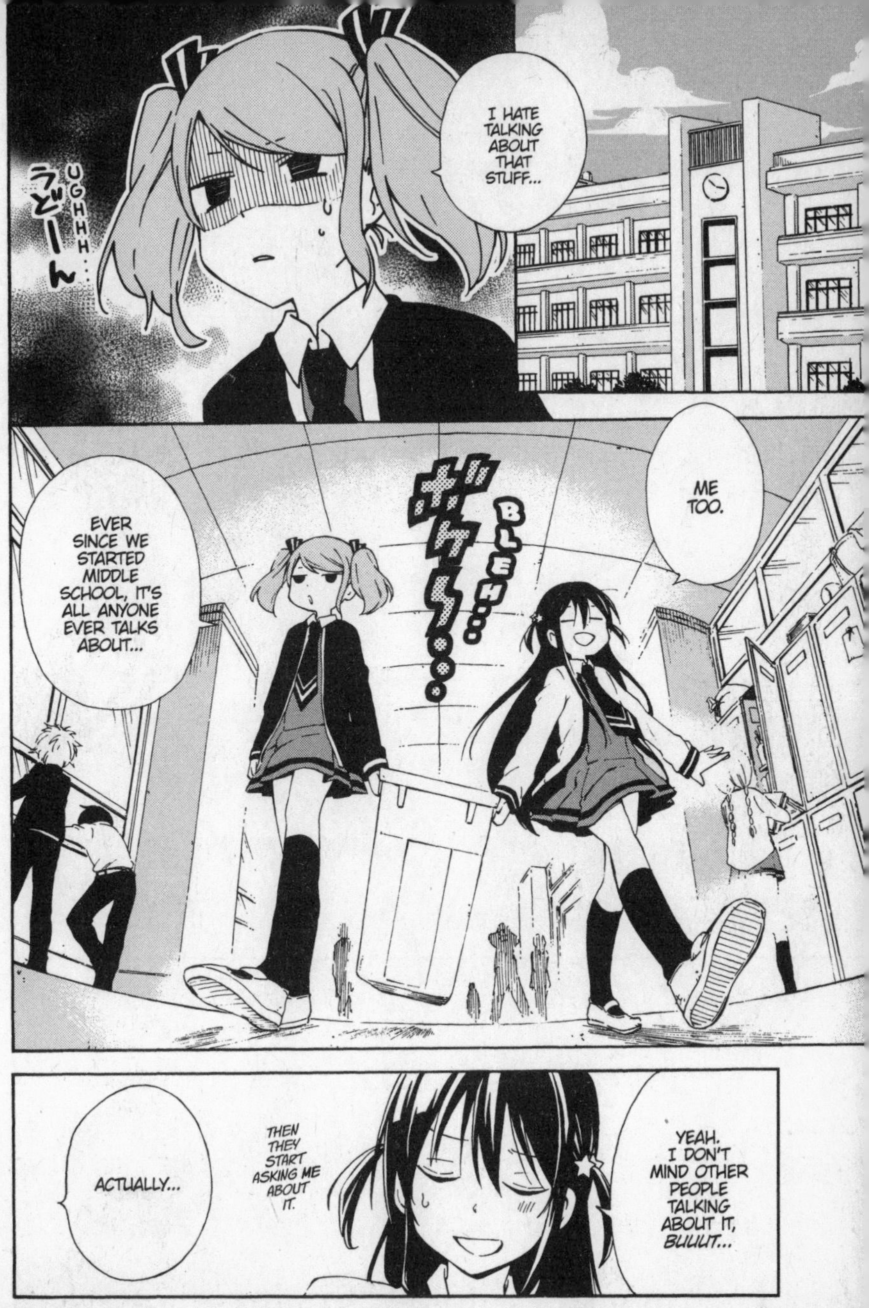
I HATE TALKING ABOUT THAT STUFF...
うどーん
UGHHH...
ME TOO.
BLEH...
EVER SINCE WE STARTED MIDDLE SCHOOL, IT'S ALL ANYONE EVER TALKS ABOUT...
YEAH. I DON'T MIND OTHER PEOPLE TALKING ABOUT IT, BUUUT...
THEN THEY START ASKING ME ABOUT IT.
ACTUALLY...

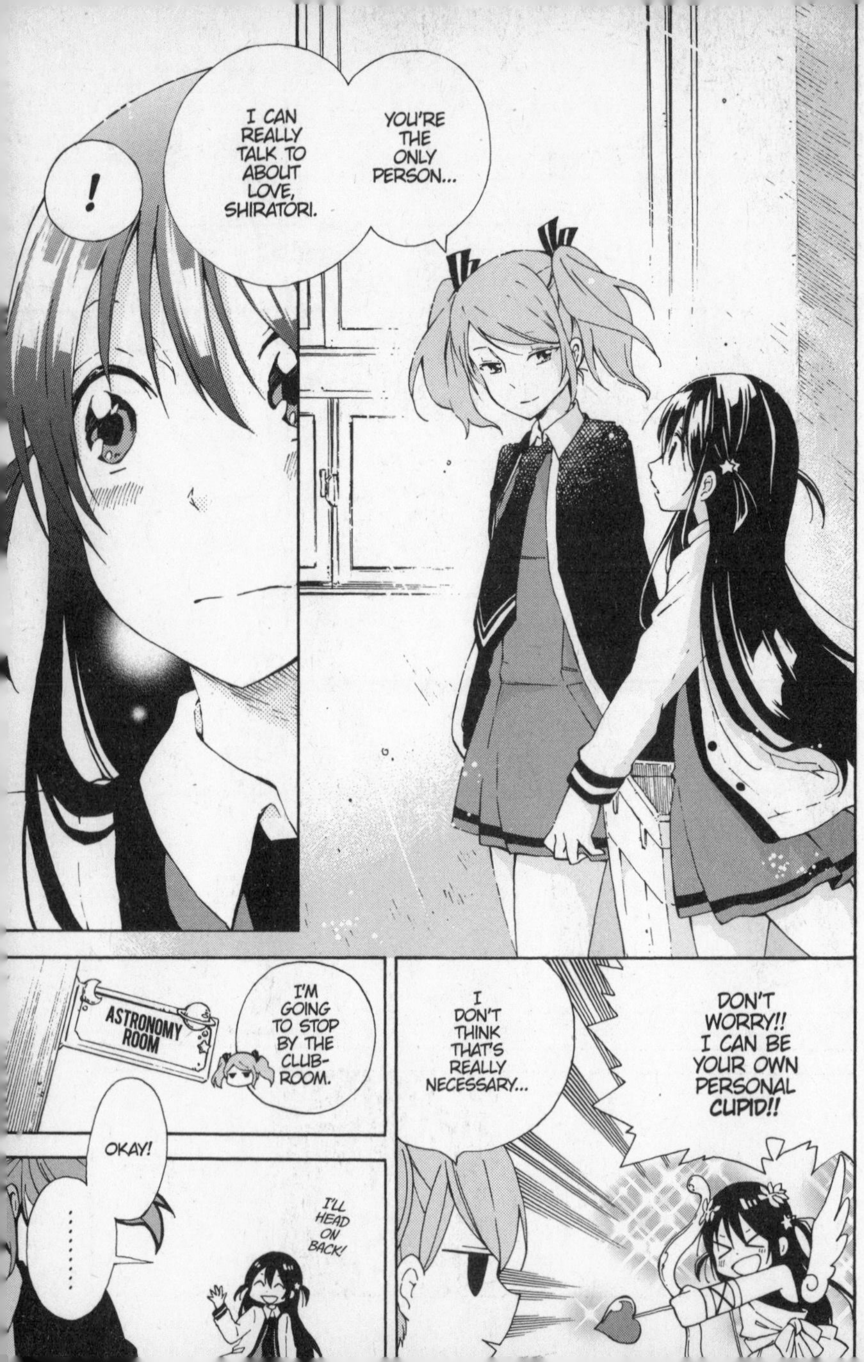
YOU'RE THE ONLY PERSON...
I CAN REALLY TALK TO ABOUT LOVE, SHIRATORI.
!
DON'T WORRY!! I CAN BE YOUR OWN PERSONAL CUPID!!
I DON'T THINK THAT'S REALLY NECESSARY...
ASTRONOMY ROOM
I'M GOING TO STOP BY THE CLUB-ROOM.
OKAY!
I'LL HEAD ON BACK!
......

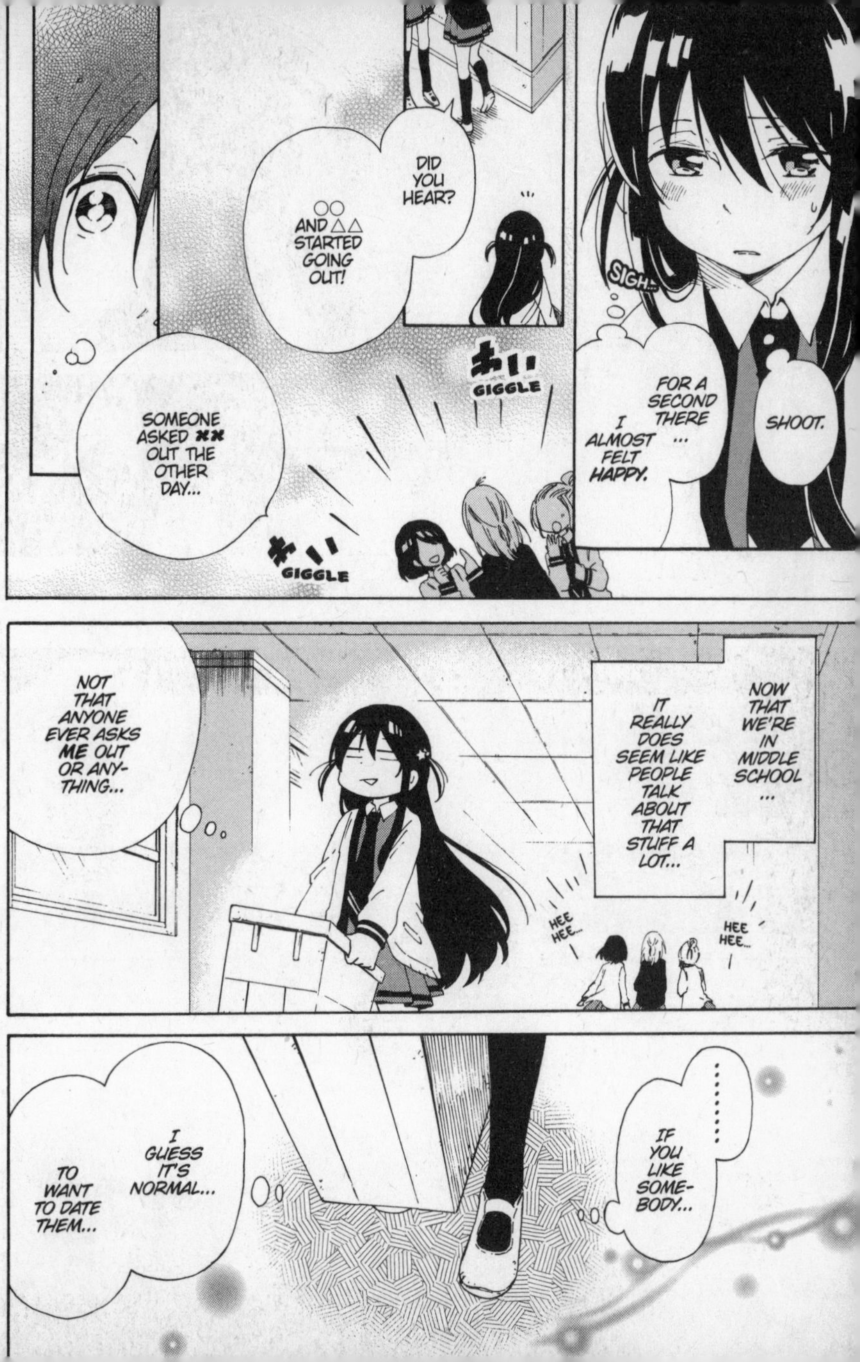
SIGH...
FOR A SECOND THERE... I ALMOST FELT HAPPY.
SHOOT.
DID YOU HEAR?
○○ AND △△ STARTED GOING OUT!
GIGGLE
SOMEONE ASKED ※※ OUT THE OTHER DAY...
GIGGLE
NOW THAT WE'RE IN MIDDLE SCHOOL...
IT REALLY DOES SEEM LIKE PEOPLE TALK ABOUT THAT STUFF A LOT...
HEE HEE...
HEE HEE...
NOT THAT ANYONE EVER ASKS ME OUT OR ANYTHING...
......
IF YOU LIKE SOMEBODY...
I GUESS IT'S NORMAL...
TO WANT TO DATE THEM...

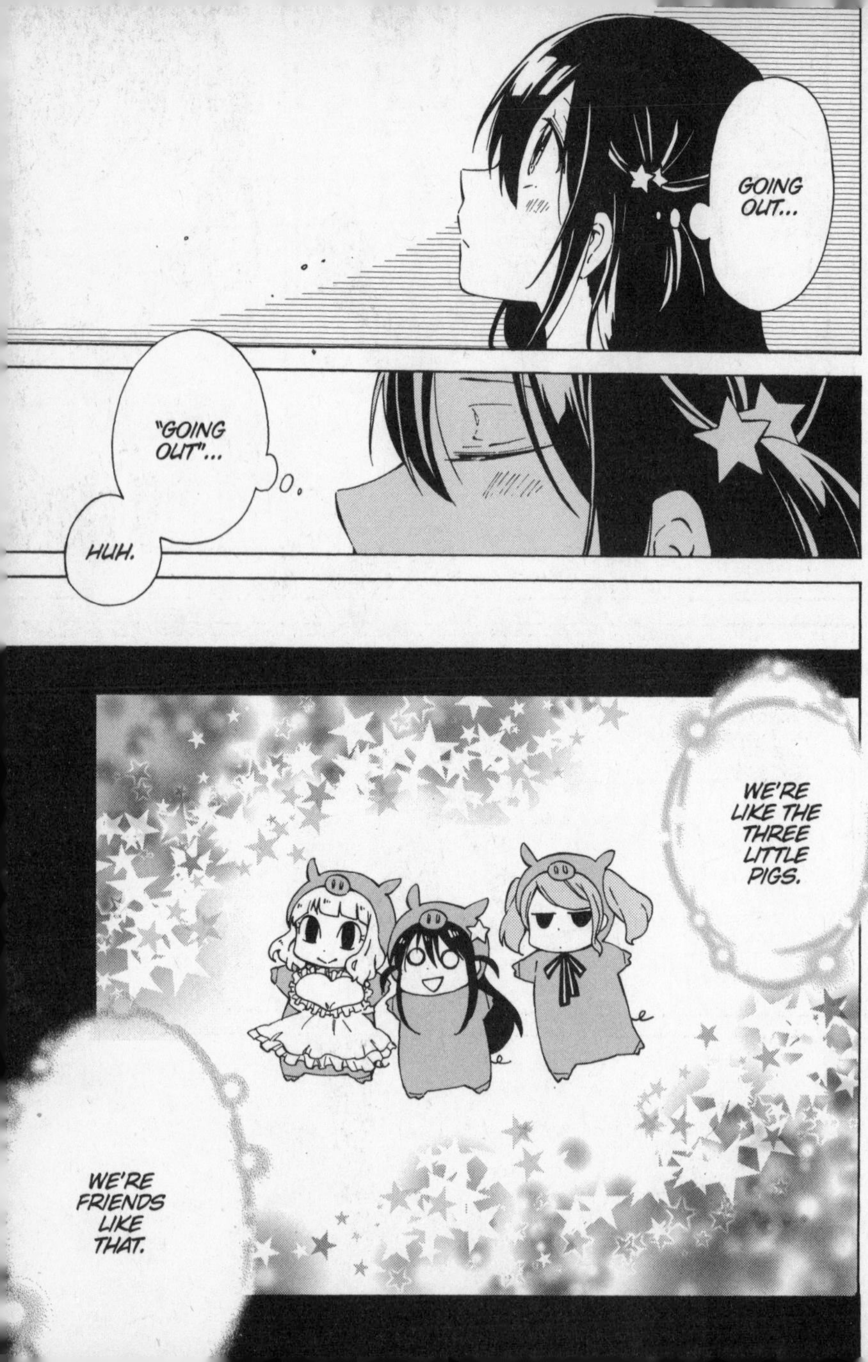
GOING OUT...
"GOING OUT"...
HUH.
WE'RE LIKE THE THREE LITTLE PIGS.
WE'RE FRIENDS LIKE THAT.

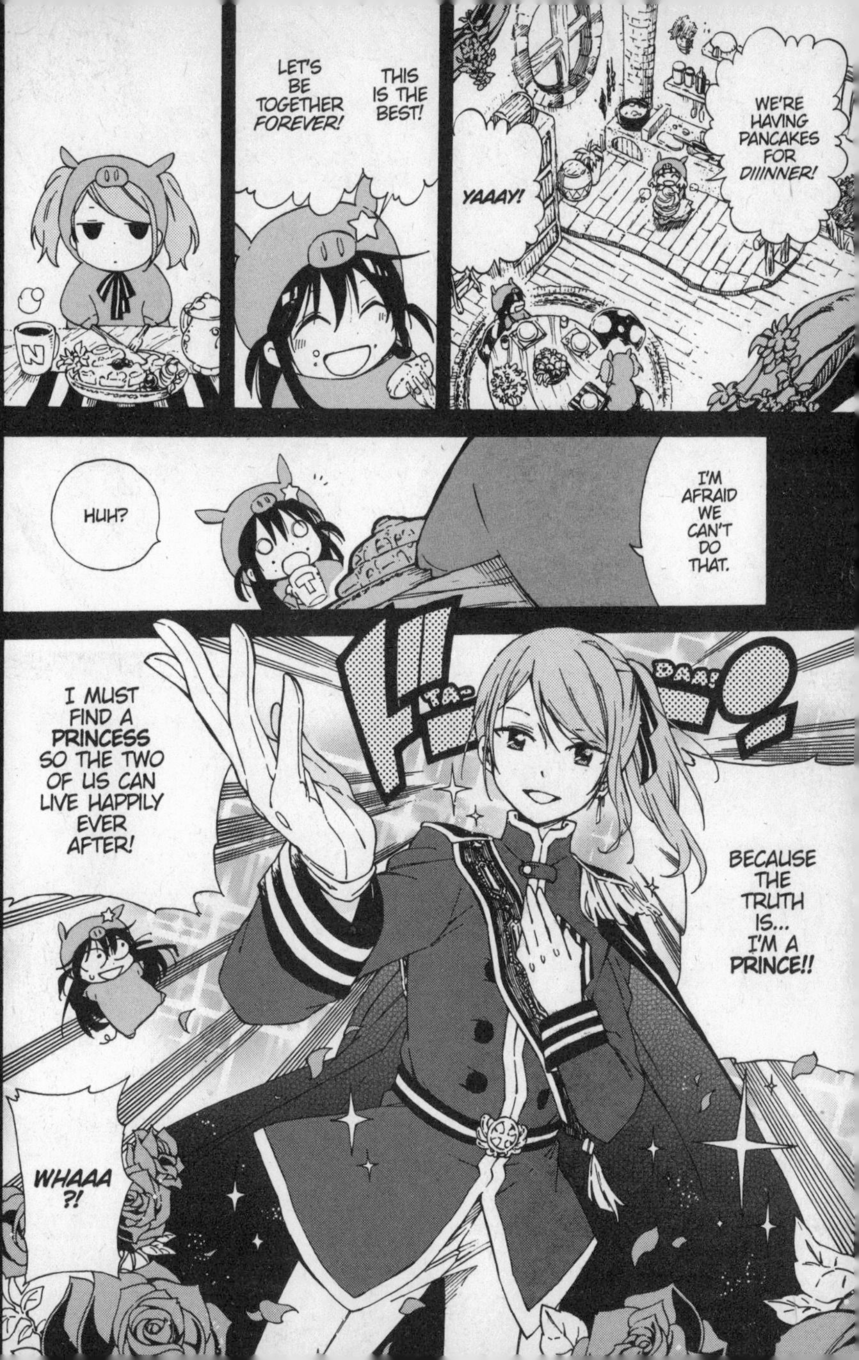
WE'RE HAVING PANCAKES FOR DIIINNER!
YAAAY!
THIS IS THE BEST!
LET'S BE TOGETHER FOREVER!
I'M AFRAID WE CAN'T DO THAT.
HUH?
BECAUSE THE TRUTH IS... I'M A PRINCE!!
TA-DAA!
I MUST FIND A PRINCESS SO THE TWO OF US CAN LIVE HAPPILY EVER AFTER!
WHAAA?!

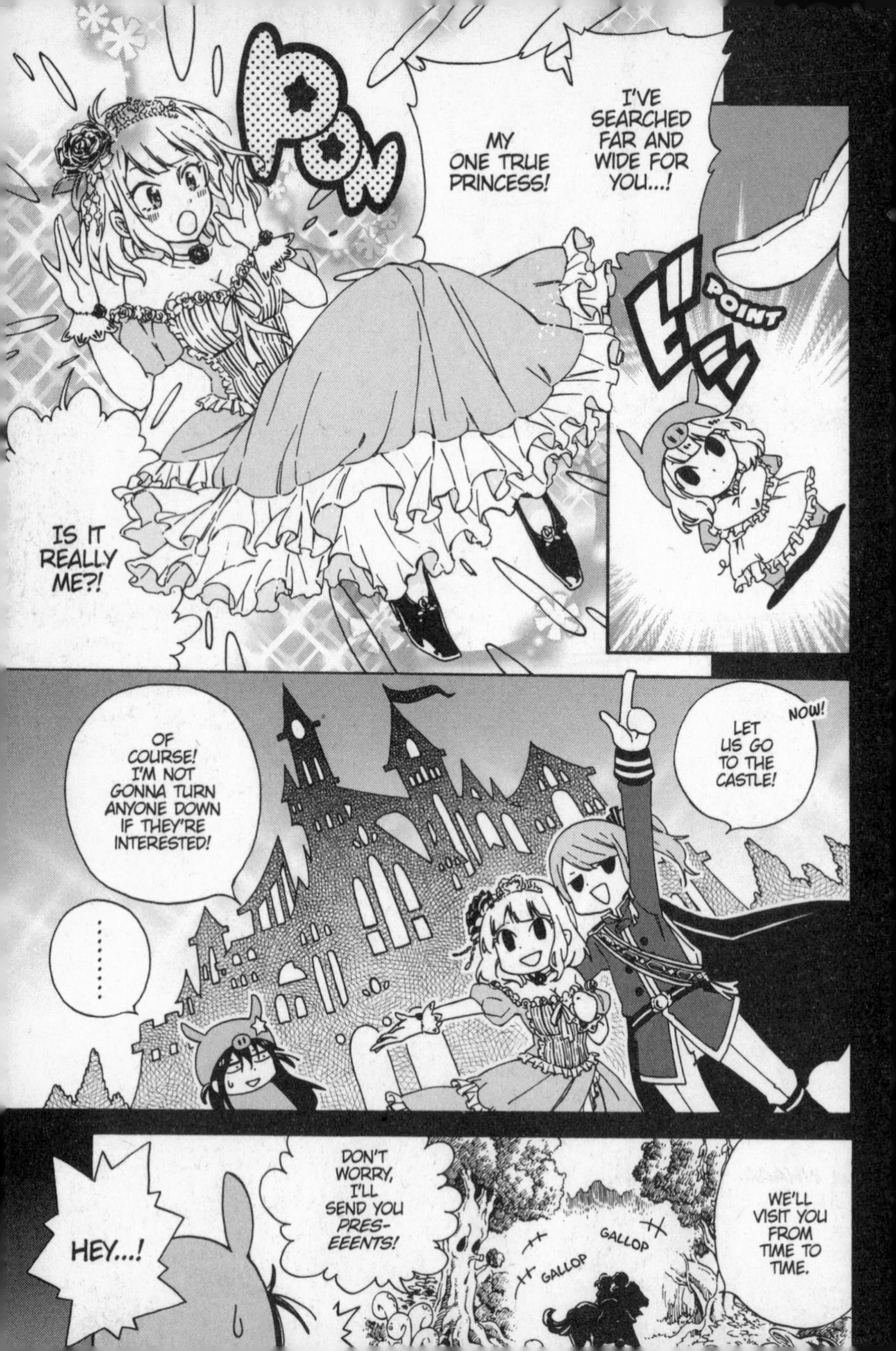
I'VE SEARCHED FAR AND WIDE FOR YOU...!
MY ONE TRUE PRINCESS!
POINT
POW
IS IT REALLY ME?!
NOW! LET US GO TO THE CASTLE!
OF COURSE! I'M NOT GONNA TURN ANYONE DOWN IF THEY'RE INTERESTED!
......
WE'LL VISIT YOU FROM TIME TO TIME.
GALLOP
GALLOP
DON'T WORRY, I'LL SEND YOU PRES-EEENTS!
HEY...!

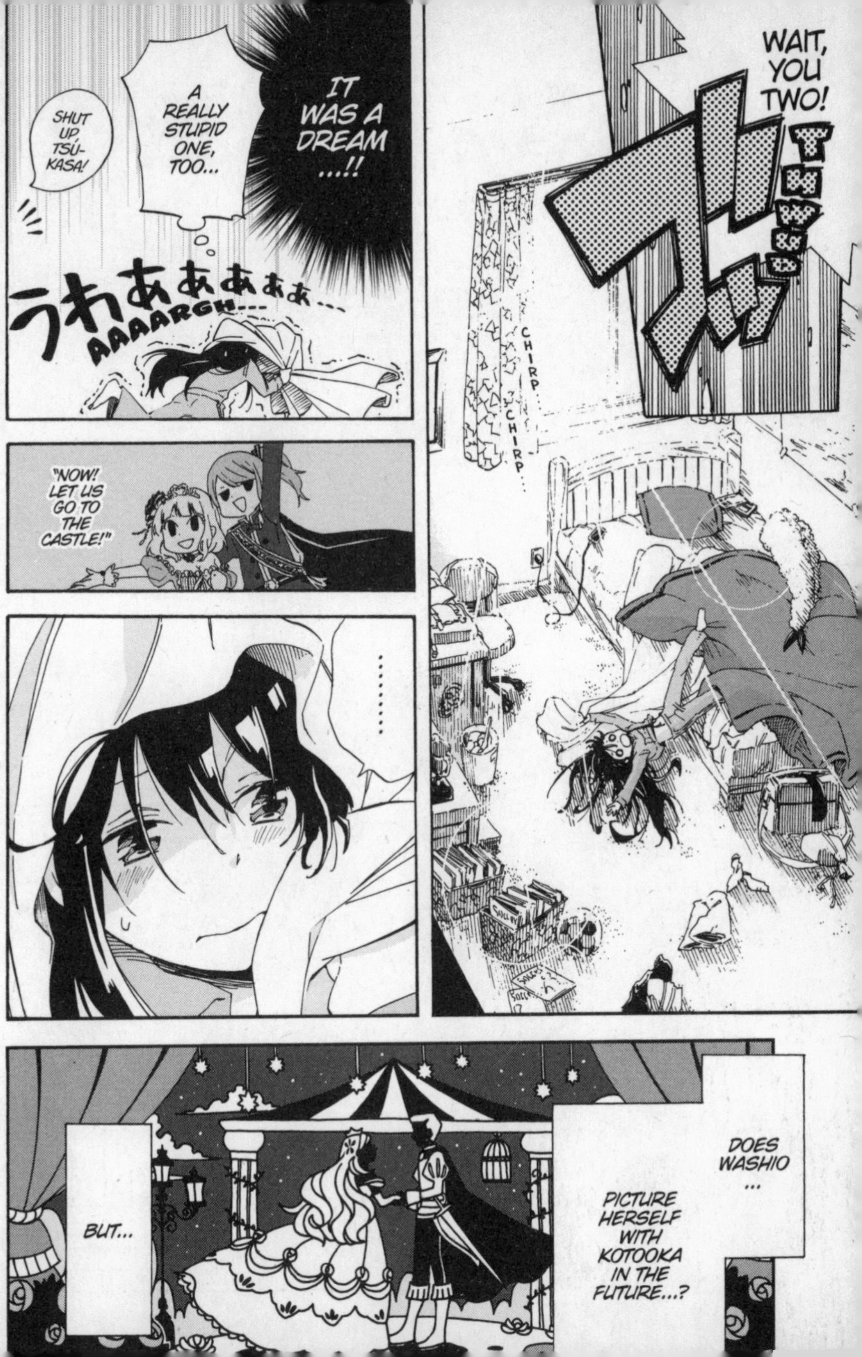
WAIT, YOU TWO!
CHIRP... CHIRP...
IT WAS A DREAM...!!
A REALLY STUPID ONE, TOO...
SHUT UP, TSÚ-KASA!
うわあああぁぁぁ...
AAAARGH...
"NOW! LET US GO TO THE CASTLE!"
......
DOES WASHIO ...
PICTURE HERSELF WITH KOTOOKA IN THE FUTURE...?
BUT...

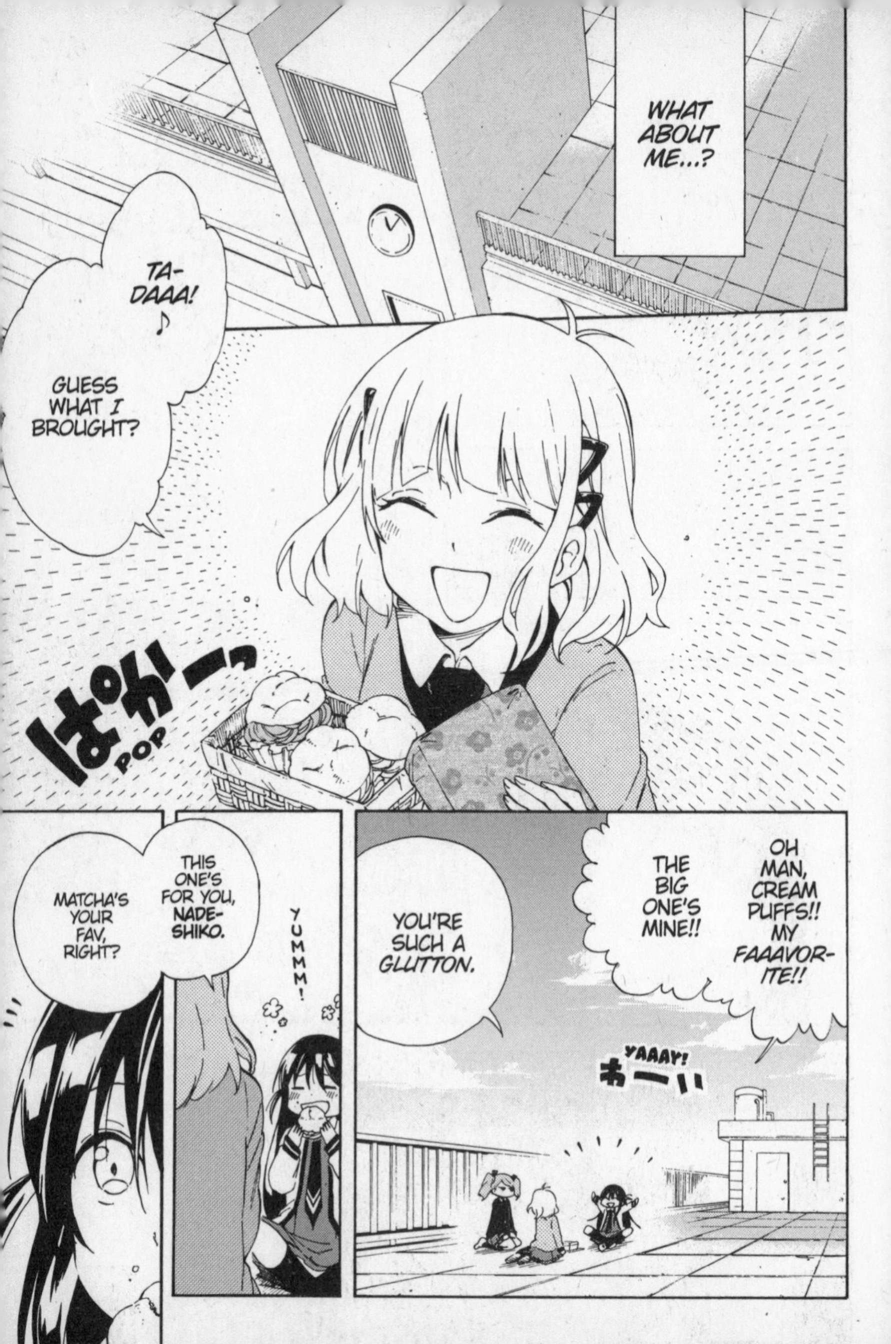
WHAT ABOUT ME...?
TA-DAAA! ♪
GUESS WHAT I BROUGHT?
ぱかーっ
POP
OH MAN, CREAM PUFFS!! MY FAAAVORITE!!
THE BIG ONE'S MINE!!
YOU'RE SUCH A GLUTTON.
YAAAY!
わーい
THIS ONE'S FOR YOU, NADE-SHIKO.
YUMMM!
MATCHA'S YOUR FAV, RIGHT?

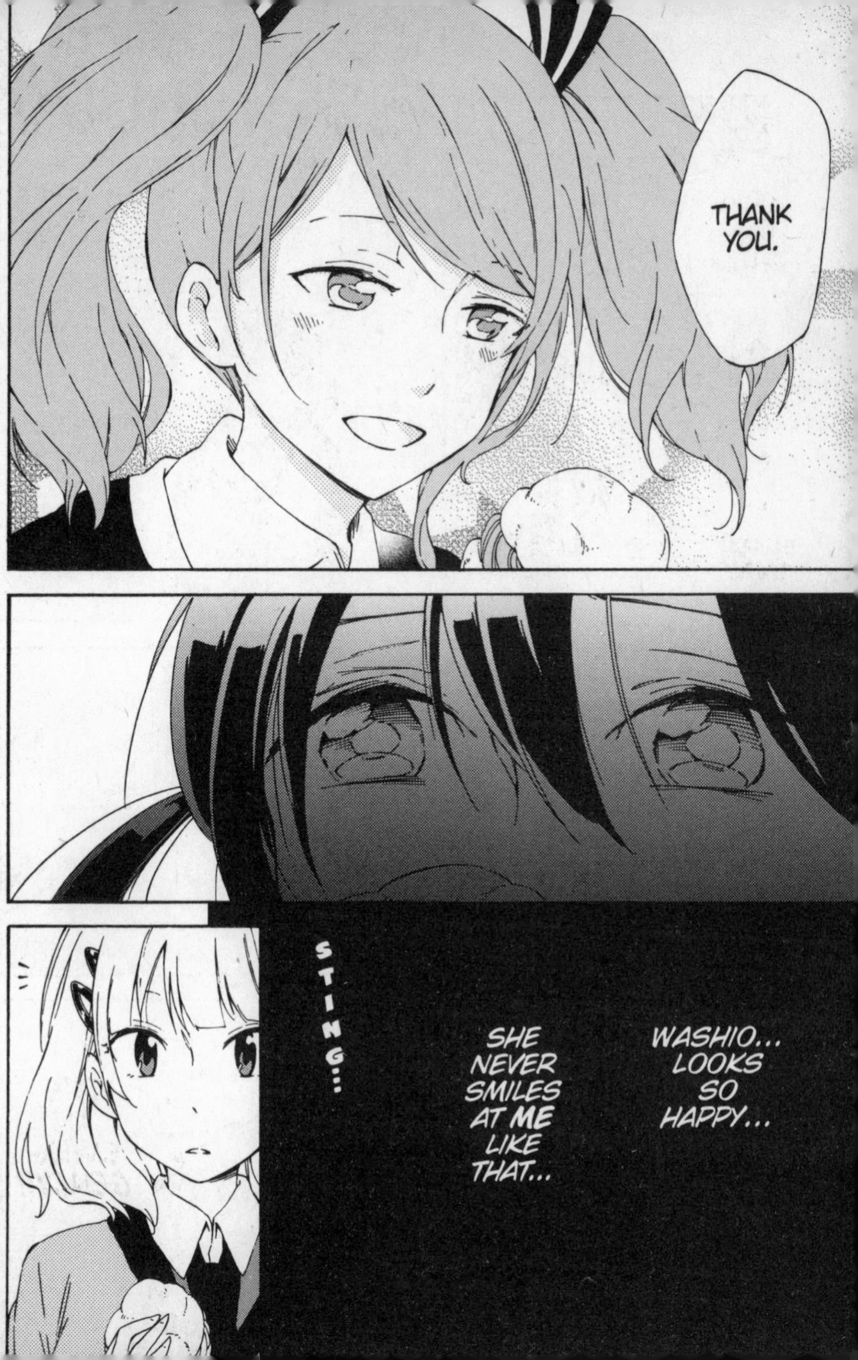
THANK YOU.
WASHIO... LOOKS SO HAPPY...
SHE NEVER SMILES AT ME LIKE THAT...
STING...

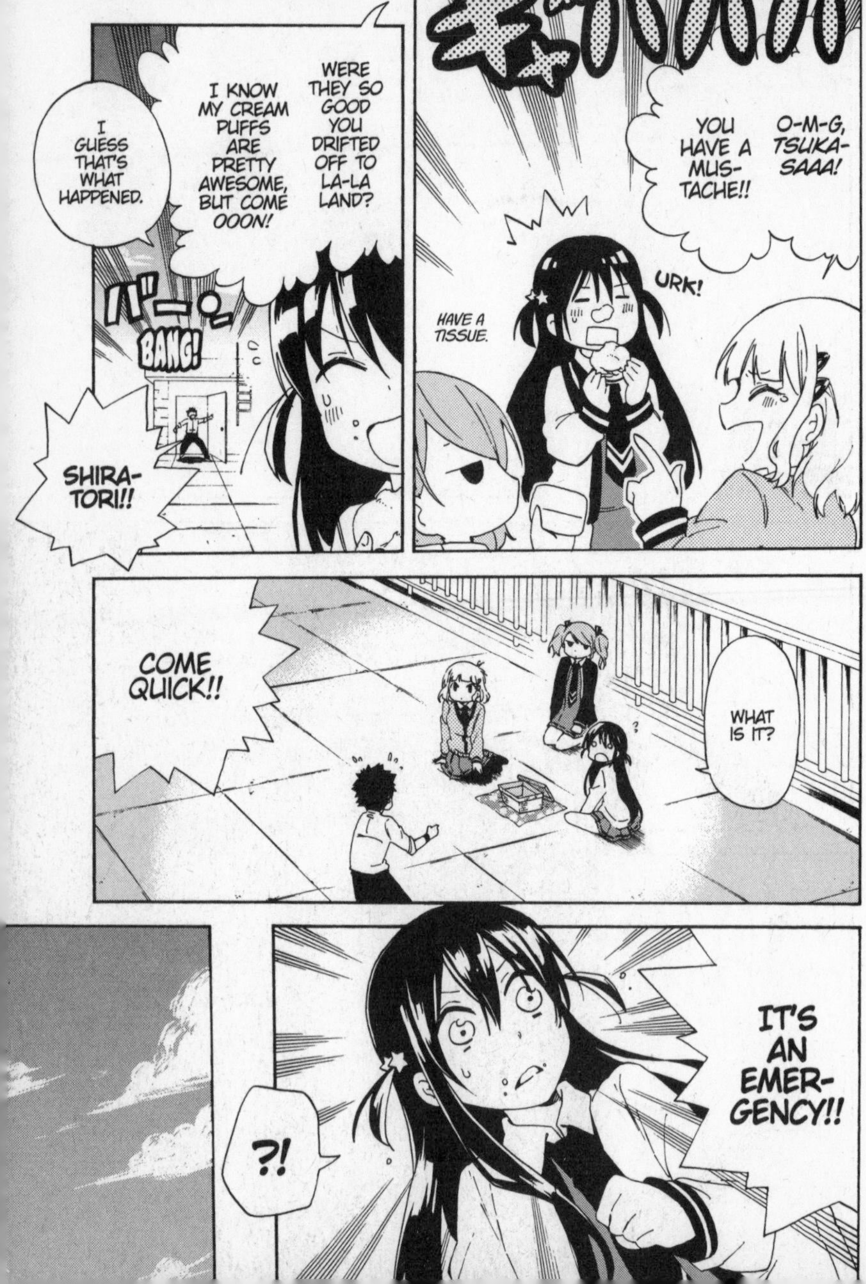
AHA HA HA!
O-M-G, TSUKASAAA!
YOU HAVE A MUSTACHE!!
URK!
HAVE A TISSUE.
WERE THEY SO GOOD YOU DRIFTED OFF TO LA-LA LAND?
I KNOW MY CREAM PUFFS ARE PRETTY AWESOME, BUT COME OOON!
I GUESS THAT'S WHAT HAPPENED.
BANG!
SHIRA-TORI!!
WHAT IS IT?
COME QUICK!!
IT'S AN EMERGENCY!!
?!

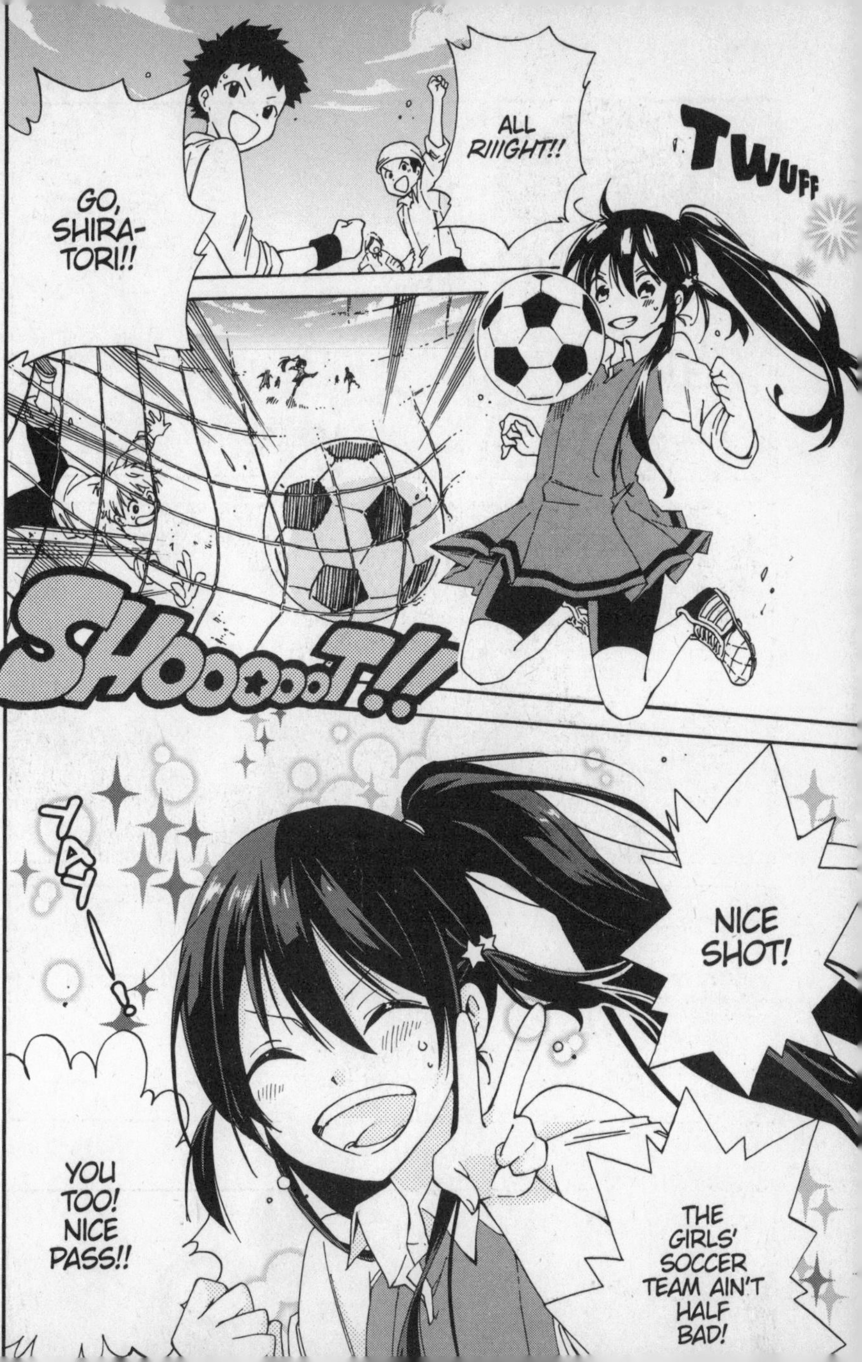
TWUFF
ALL RIIIGHT!!
GO, SHIRA-TORI!!
SHOOooOT!!
NICE SHOT!
YAY!!
THE GIRLS' SOCCER TEAM AIN'T HALF BAD!
YOU TOO! NICE PASS!!

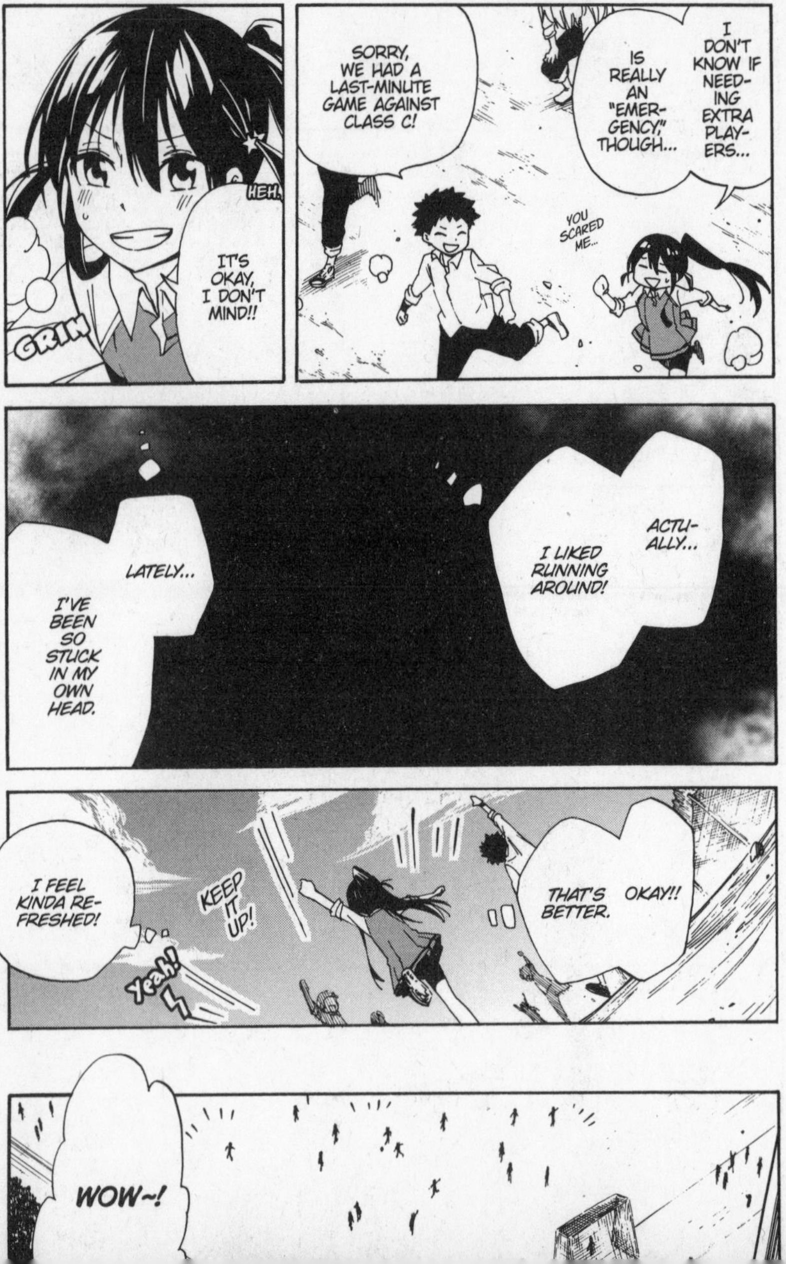
SORRY, WE HAD A LAST-MINUTE GAME AGAINST CLASS C!
I DON'T KNOW IF NEEDING EXTRA PLAYERS...
IS REALLY AN "EMERGENCY," THOUGH...
YOU SCARED ME...
HEH.
IT'S OKAY, I DON'T MIND!!
GRIN
ACTUALLY...
I LIKED RUNNING AROUND!
LATELY...
I'VE BEEN SO STUCK IN MY OWN HEAD.
OKAY!!
THAT'S BETTER.
KEEP IT UP!
I FEEL KINDA REFRESHED!
Yeah!
WOW~!

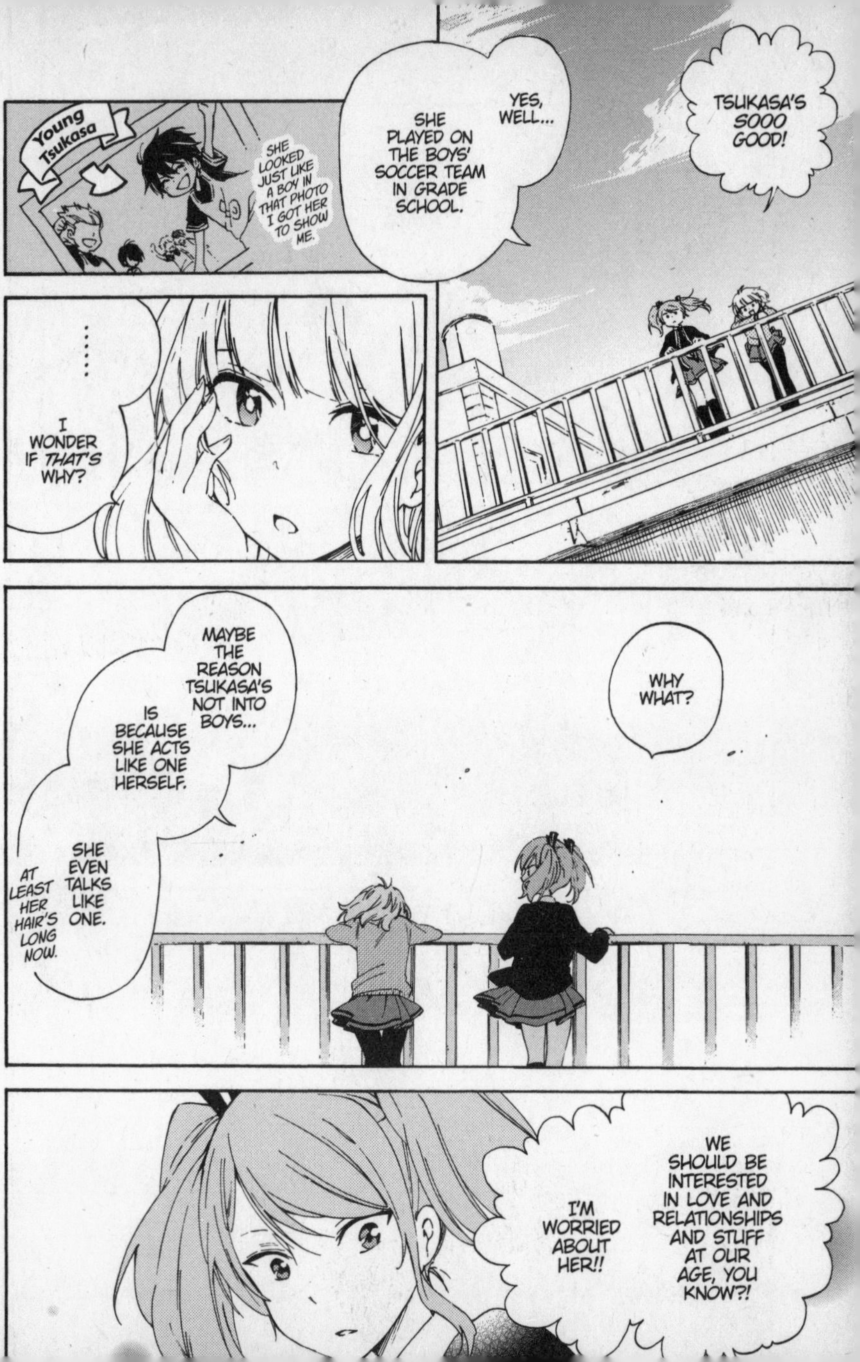
TSUKASA'S SOOO GOOD!
YES, WELL...
SHE PLAYED ON THE BOYS' SOCCER TEAM IN GRADE SCHOOL.
Young Tsukasa
SHE LOOKED JUST LIKE A BOY IN THAT PHOTO I GOT HER TO SHOW ME.
......
I WONDER IF *THAT'S* WHY?
WHY WHAT?
MAYBE THE REASON TSUKASA'S NOT INTO BOYS...
IS BECAUSE SHE ACTS LIKE ONE HERSELF.
SHE EVEN TALKS LIKE ONE.
AT LEAST HER HAIR'S LONG NOW.
WE SHOULD BE INTERESTED IN LOVE AND RELATIONSHIPS AND STUFF AT OUR AGE, YOU KNOW?!
I'M WORRIED ABOUT HER!!

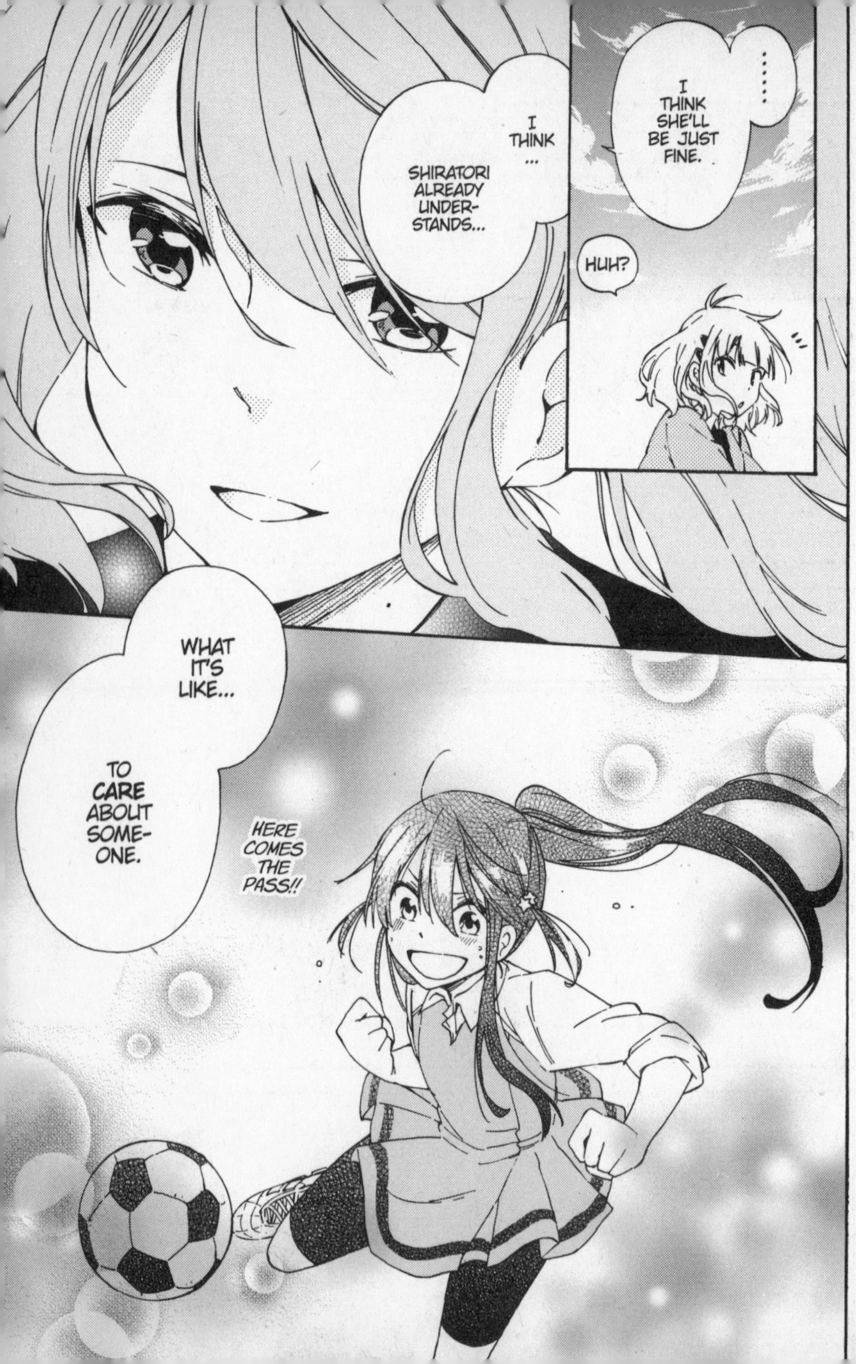
......
I THINK SHE'LL BE JUST FINE.
HUH?
I THINK ...
SHIRATORI ALREADY UNDER-STANDS...
WHAT IT'S LIKE...
TO **CARE** ABOUT SOME-ONE.
HERE COMES THE PASS!!

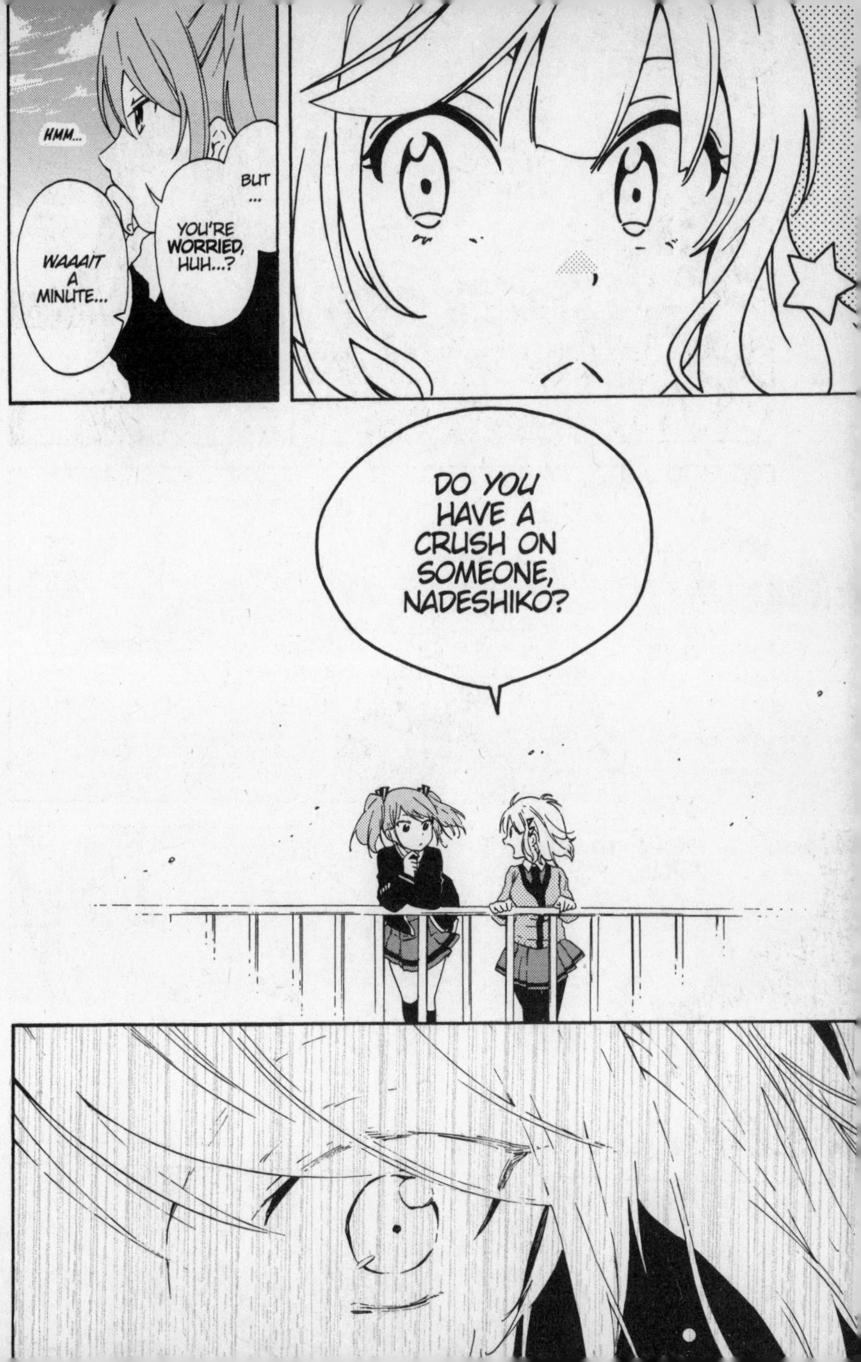
BUT ... YOU'RE WORRIED, HUH...?
HMM...
WAAAIT A MINUTE...
DO YOU HAVE A CRUSH ON SOMEONE, NADESHIKO?

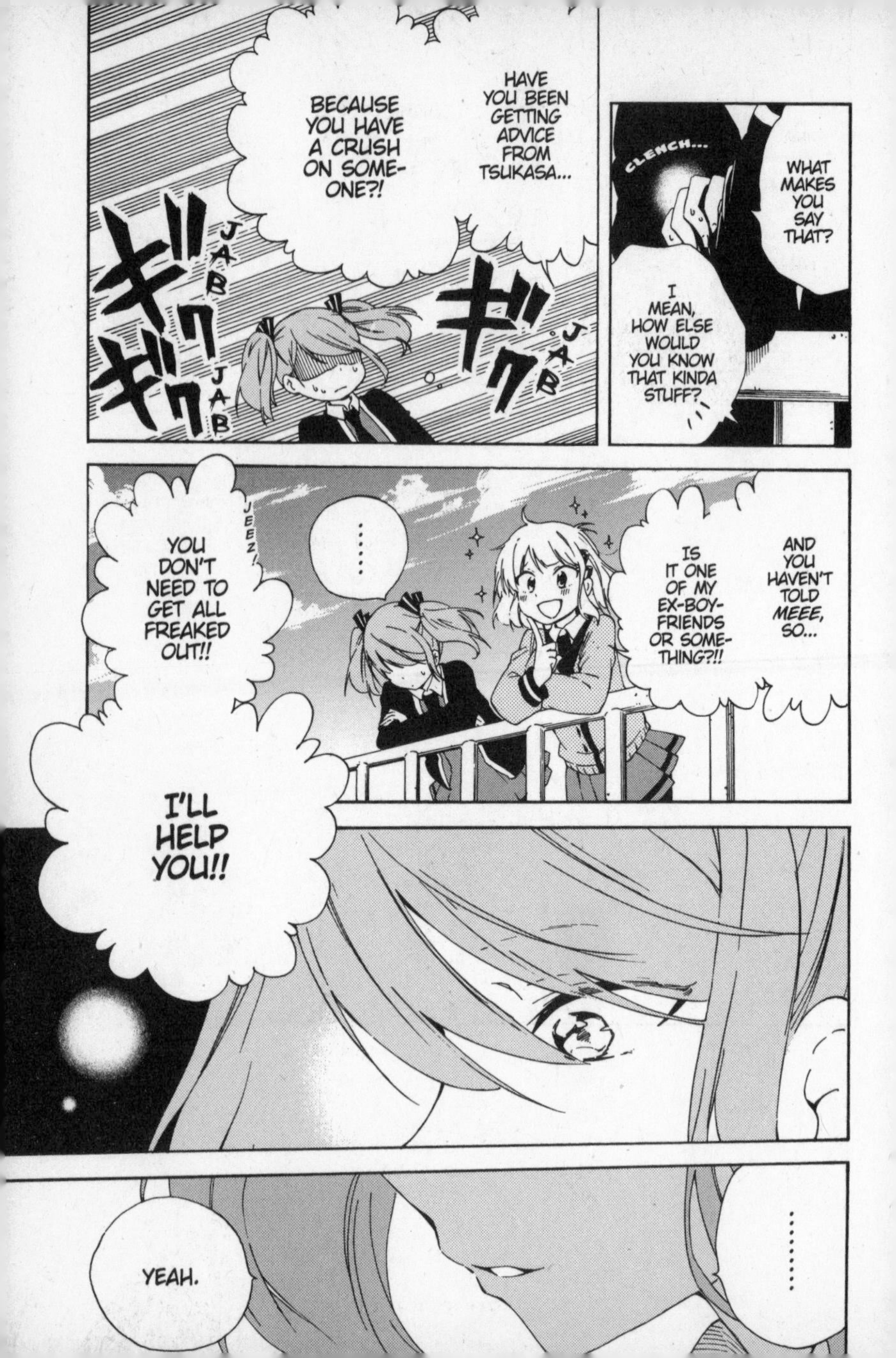
CLENCH...
WHAT MAKES YOU SAY THAT?
I MEAN, HOW ELSE WOULD YOU KNOW THAT KINDA STUFF?
HAVE YOU BEEN GETTING ADVICE FROM TSUKASA...
BECAUSE YOU HAVE A CRUSH ON SOME-ONE?!
JAB
JAB JAB
AND YOU HAVEN'T TOLD MEEE, SO...
IS IT ONE OF MY EX-BOY-FRIENDS OR SOME-THING?!!
......
JEEZ!
YOU DON'T NEED TO GET ALL FREAKED OUT!!
I'LL HELP YOU!!
......
YEAH.

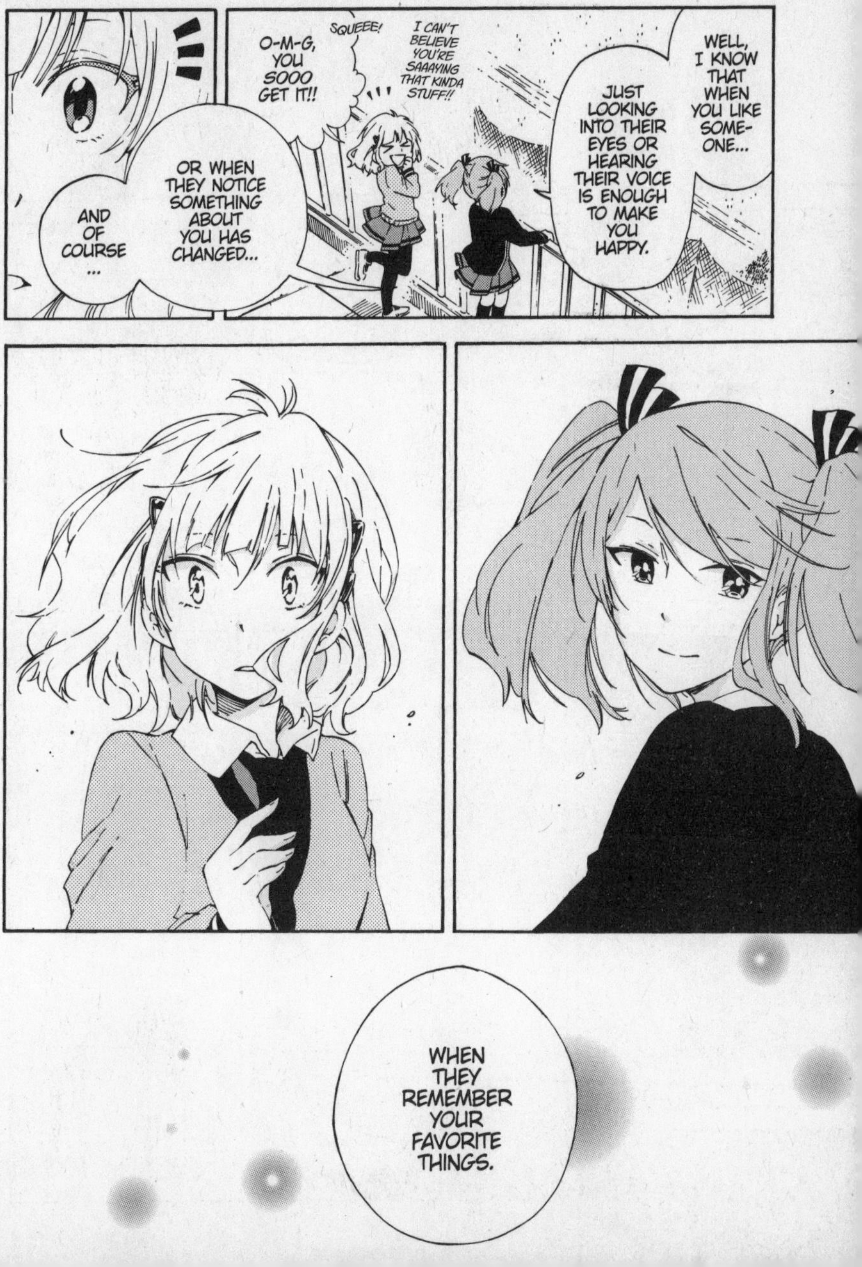
WELL, I KNOW THAT WHEN YOU LIKE SOME-ONE...
JUST LOOKING INTO THEIR EYES OR HEARING THEIR VOICE IS ENOUGH TO MAKE YOU HAPPY.
I CAN'T BELIEVE YOU'RE SAAAYING THAT KINDA STUFF!!
SQUEEE!
O-M-G, YOU SOOO GET IT!!
OR WHEN THEY NOTICE SOMETHING ABOUT YOU HAS CHANGED...
AND OF COURSE ...
WHEN THEY REMEMBER YOUR FAVORITE THINGS.

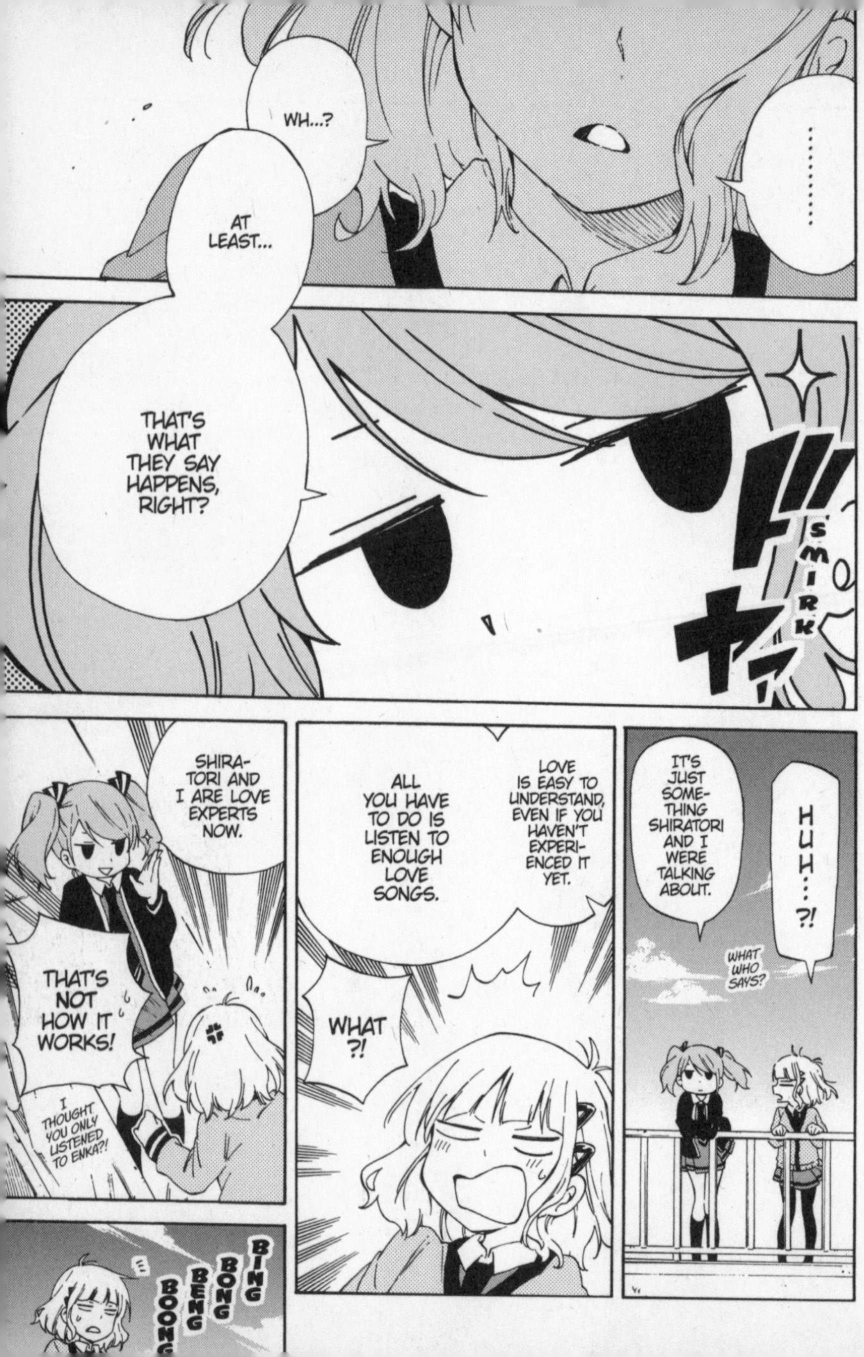
......
WH...?
AT LEAST...
THAT'S WHAT THEY SAY HAPPENS, RIGHT?
SMIRK
HUH...?!
IT'S JUST SOME-THING SHIRATORI AND I WERE TALKING ABOUT.
WHAT WHO SAYS?
LOVE IS EASY TO UNDERSTAND, EVEN IF YOU HAVEN'T EXPERI-ENCED IT YET.
ALL YOU HAVE TO DO IS LISTEN TO ENOUGH LOVE SONGS.
WHAT ?!
SHIRA-TORI AND I ARE LOVE EXPERTS NOW.
THAT'S NOT HOW IT WORKS!
I THOUGHT YOU ONLY LISTENED TO ENKA?!
BING BONG BENG BOONG

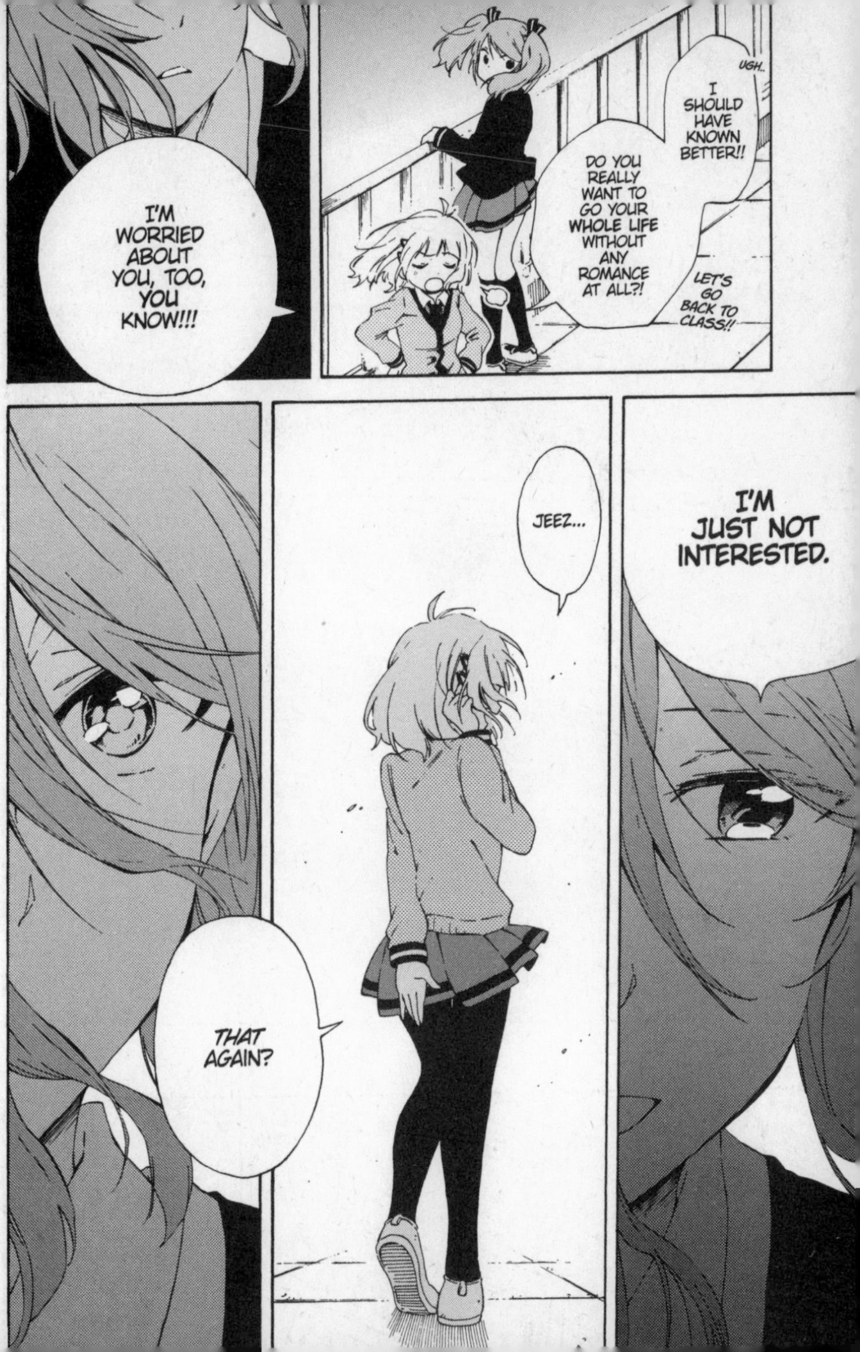
UGH..
I SHOULD HAVE KNOWN BETTER!!
DO YOU REALLY WANT TO GO YOUR WHOLE LIFE WITHOUT ANY ROMANCE AT ALL?!
LET'S GO BACK TO CLASS!!
I'M WORRIED ABOUT YOU, TOO, YOU KNOW!!!
I'M JUST NOT INTERESTED.
JEEZ...
THAT AGAIN?

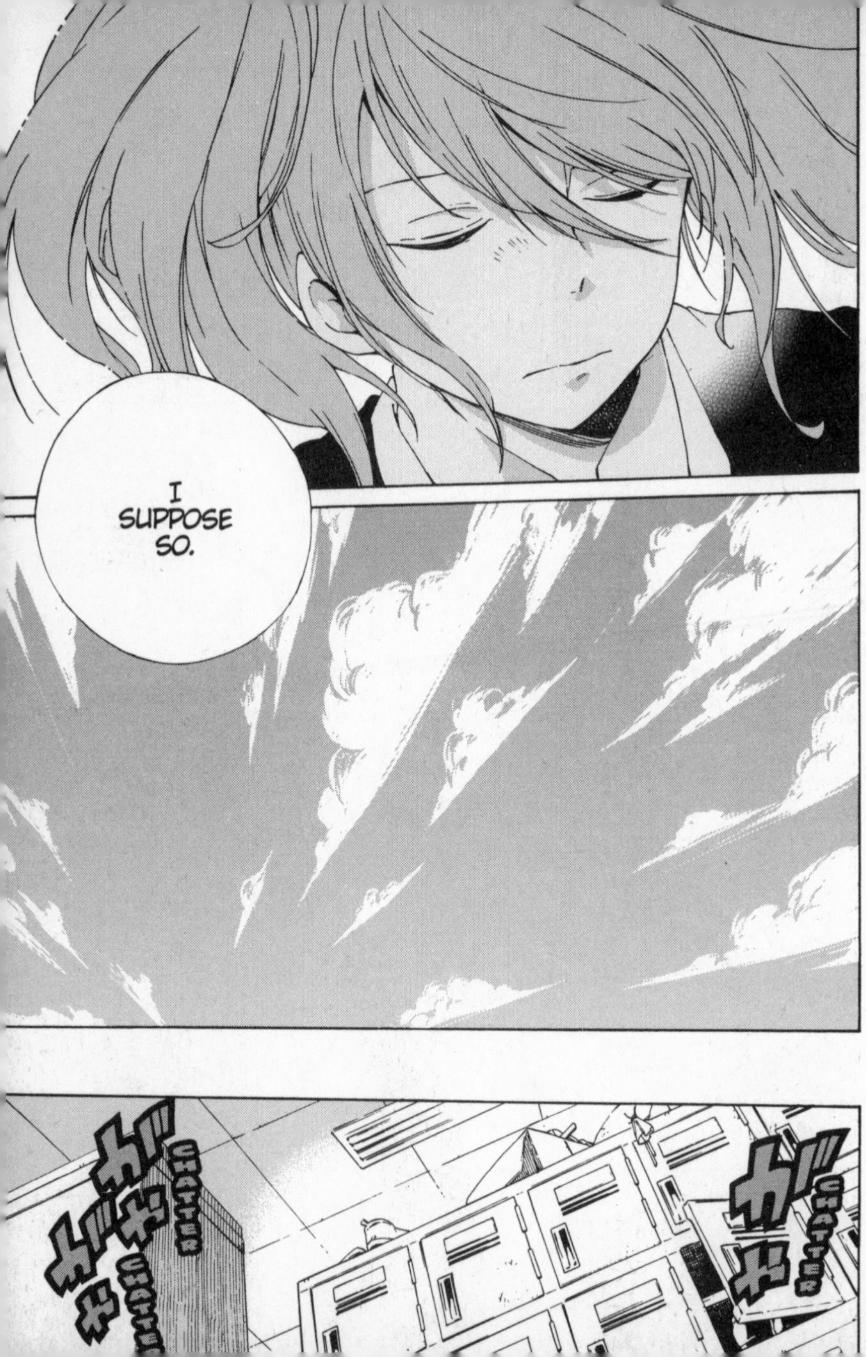

I SUPPOSE SO.
ガヤ
CHATTER
ガヤ
CHATTER
ガヤ
CHATTER

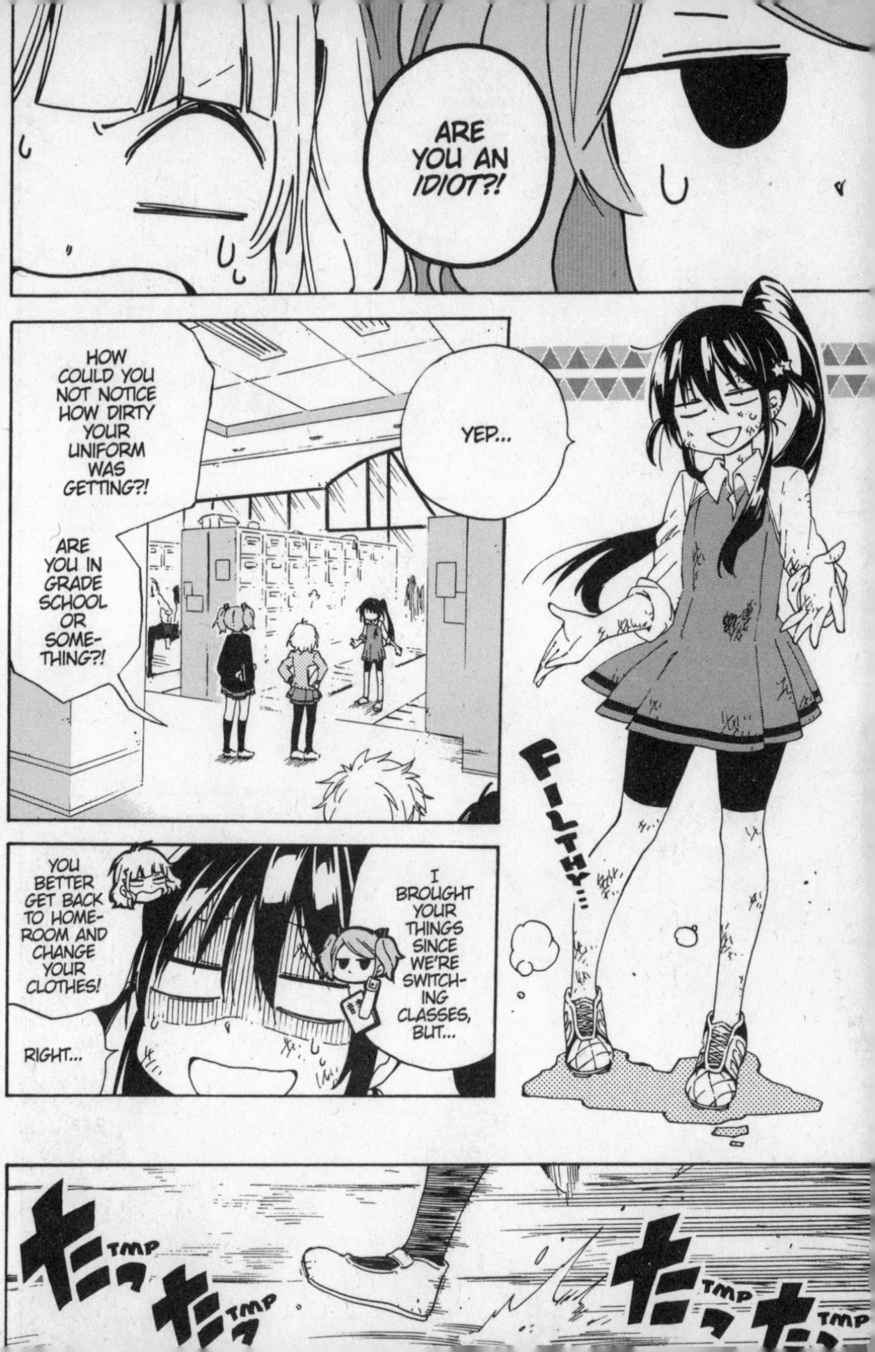
ARE YOU AN IDIOT?!
FILTHY...
YEP...
HOW COULD YOU NOT NOTICE HOW DIRTY YOUR UNIFORM WAS GETTING?!
ARE YOU IN GRADE SCHOOL OR SOME-THING?!
I BROUGHT YOUR THINGS SINCE WE'RE SWITCH-ING CLASSES, BUT...
YOU BETTER GET BACK TO HOME-ROOM AND CHANGE YOUR CLOTHES!
RIGHT...
TMP
TMP
TMP
TMP

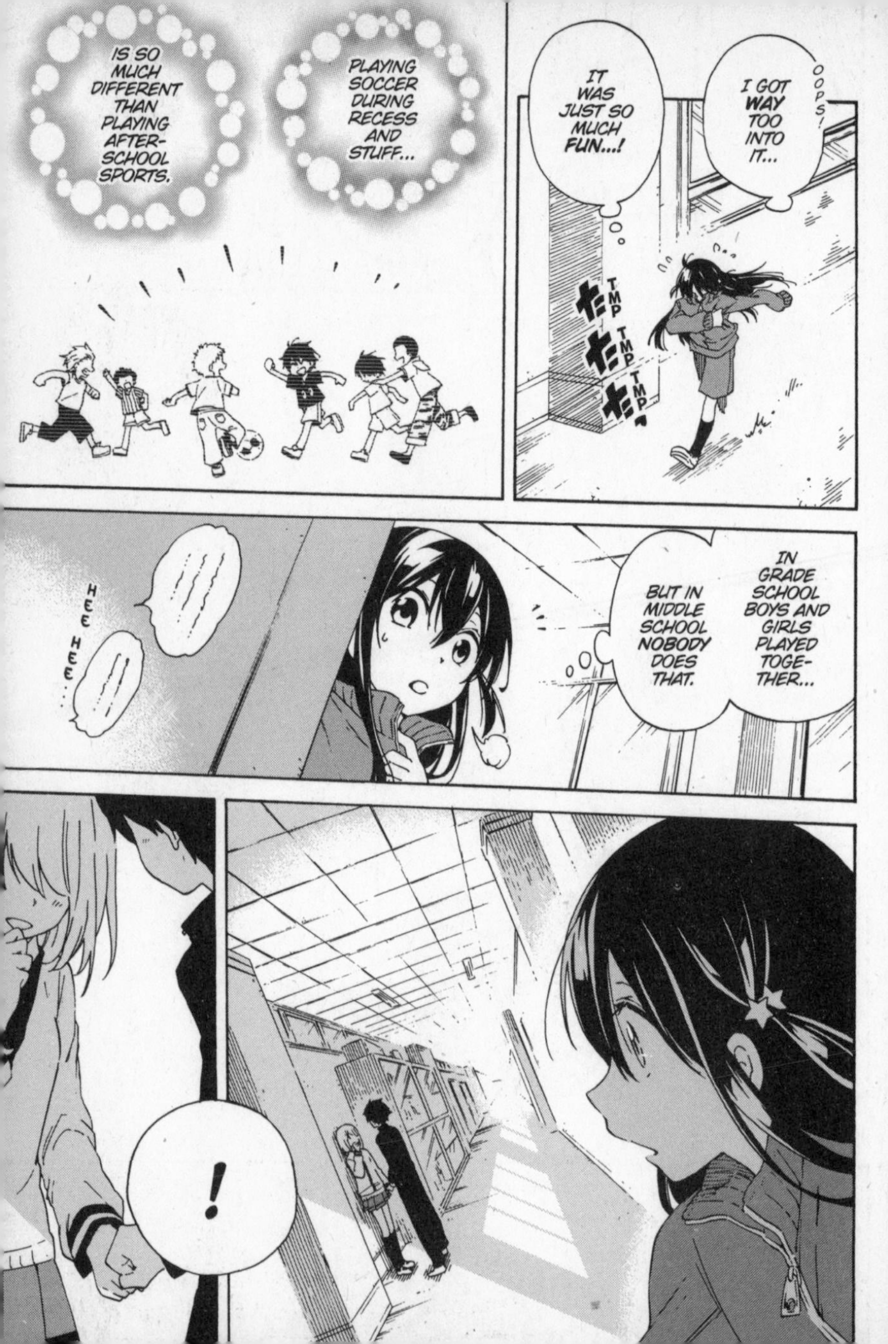
OOPS!
I GOT WAY TOO INTO IT...
IT WAS JUST SO MUCH FUN...!
TMP TMP TMP TMP
PLAYING SOCCER DURING RECESS AND STUFF...
IS SO MUCH DIFFERENT THAN PLAYING AFTER-SCHOOL SPORTS.
IN GRADE SCHOOL BOYS AND GIRLS PLAYED TOGE-THER...
BUT IN MIDDLE SCHOOL NOBODY DOES THAT.
HEE HEE...
!

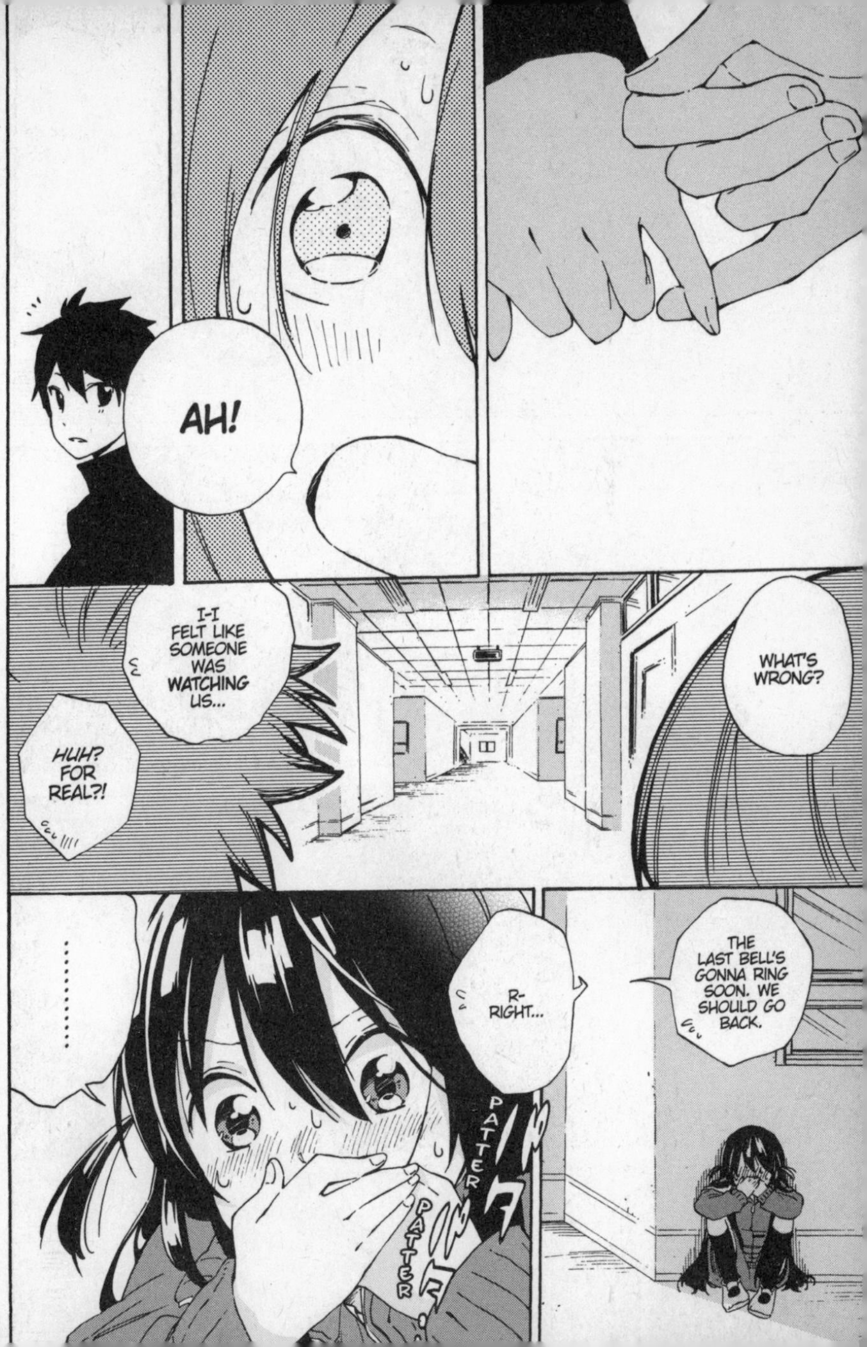
AH!
WHAT'S WRONG?
I-I FELT LIKE SOMEONE WAS WATCHING US...
HUH? FOR REAL?!
THE LAST BELL'S GONNA RING SOON. WE SHOULD GO BACK.
R-RIGHT...
PATTER
PATTER
......

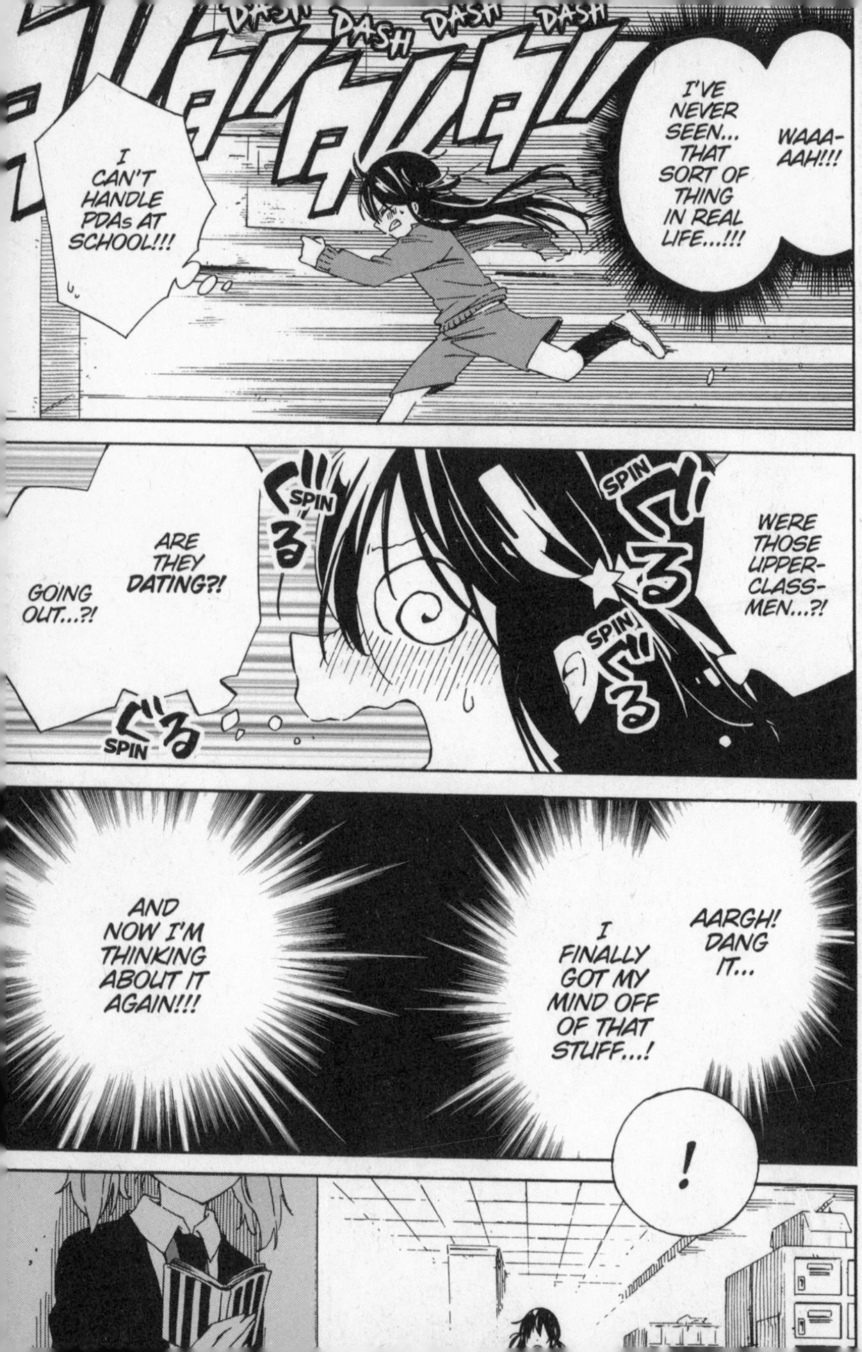
DASH DASH DASH DASH
WAAA-AAH!!!
I'VE NEVER SEEN... THAT SORT OF THING IN REAL LIFE...!!!
I CAN'T HANDLE PDAs AT SCHOOL!!!
ぐる SPIN
ぐる SPIN
WERE THOSE UPPER-CLASS-MEN...?!
ぐる SPIN
ARE THEY DATING?!
GOING OUT...?!
ぐる SPIN
AARGH! DANG IT...
I FINALLY GOT MY MIND OFF OF THAT STUFF...!
AND NOW I'M THINKING ABOUT IT AGAIN!!!
!

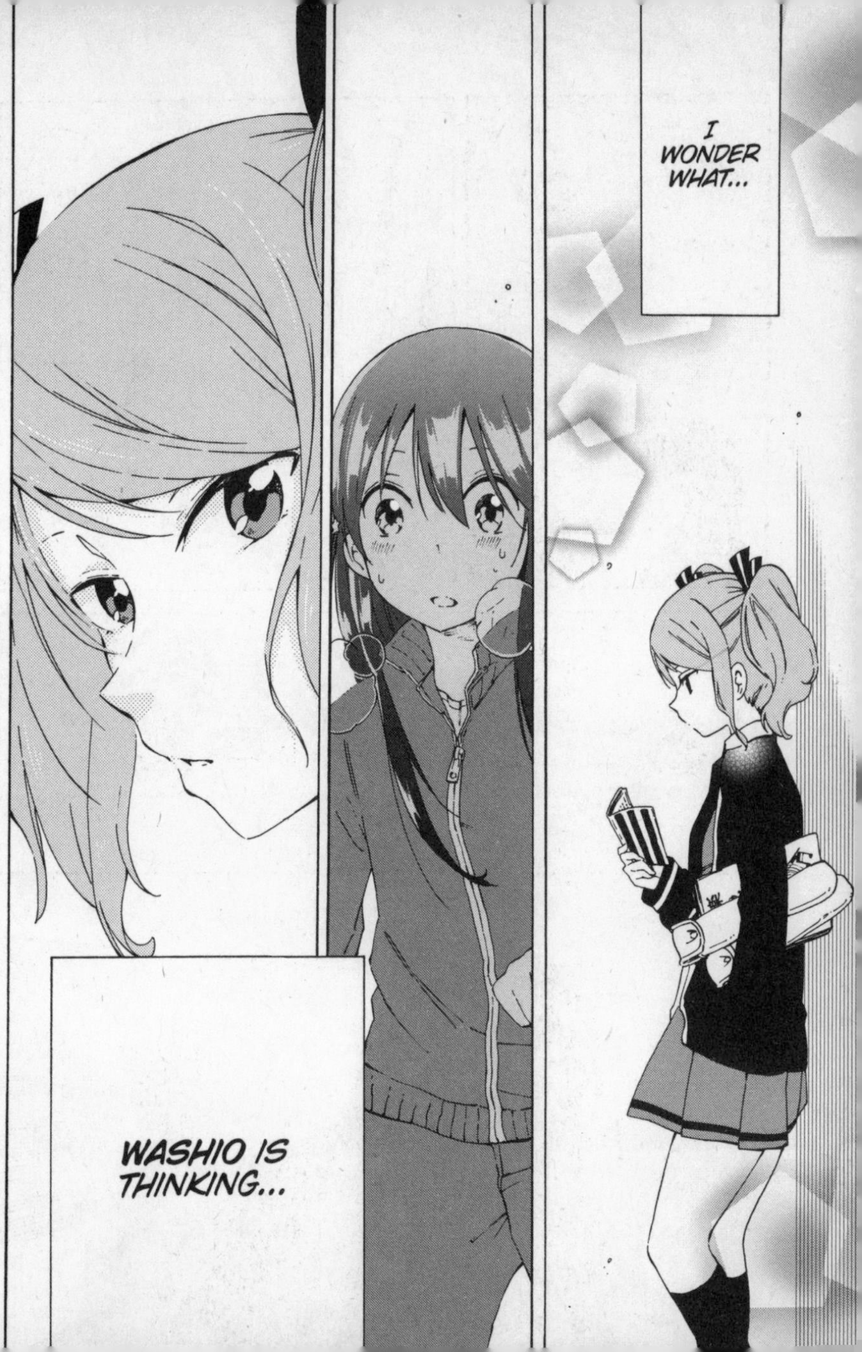
I WONDER WHAT...
WASHIO IS THINKING...

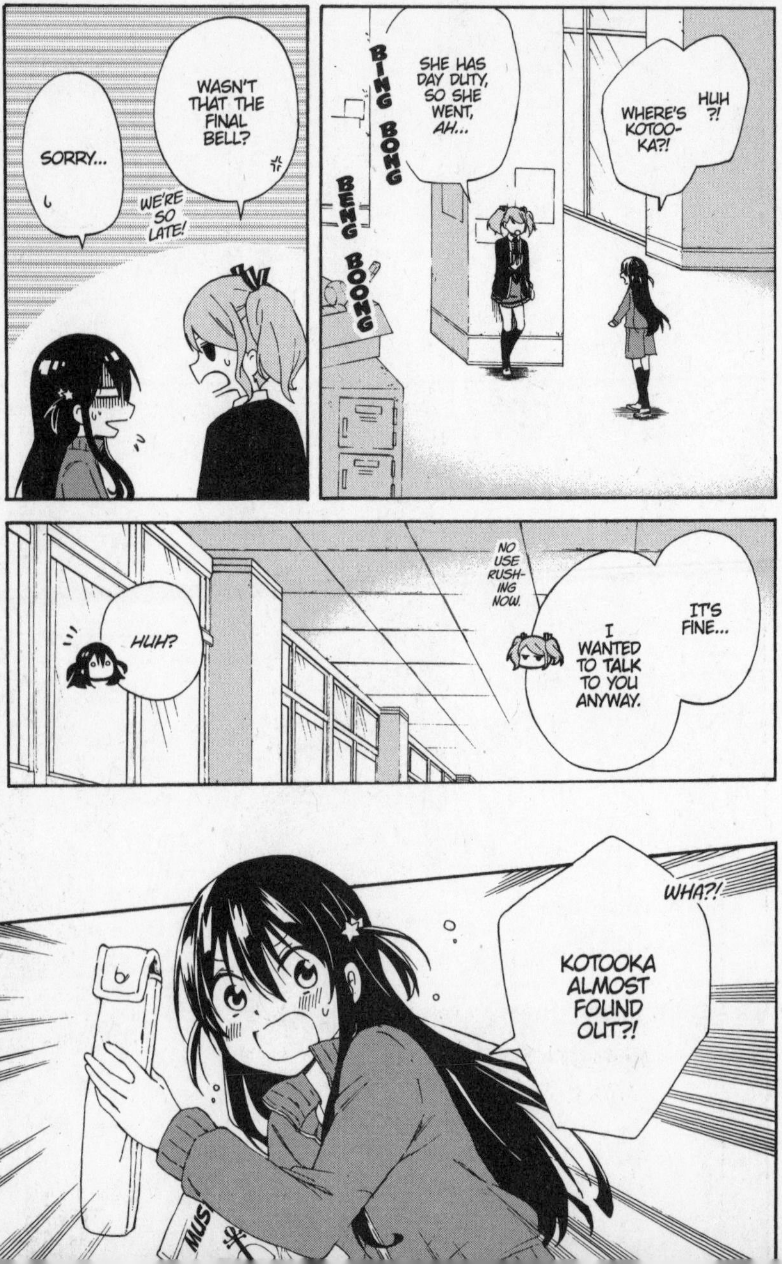
HUH ?!
WHERE'S KOTOO-KA?!
SHE HAS DAY DUTY, SO SHE WENT, AH...
BING BONG
BENG BOONG
WASN'T THAT THE FINAL BELL?
WE'RE SO LATE!
SORRY...
IT'S FINE... I WANTED TO TALK TO YOU ANYWAY.
NO USE RUSH-ING NOW.
HUH?
WHA?!
KOTOOKA ALMOST FOUND OUT?!

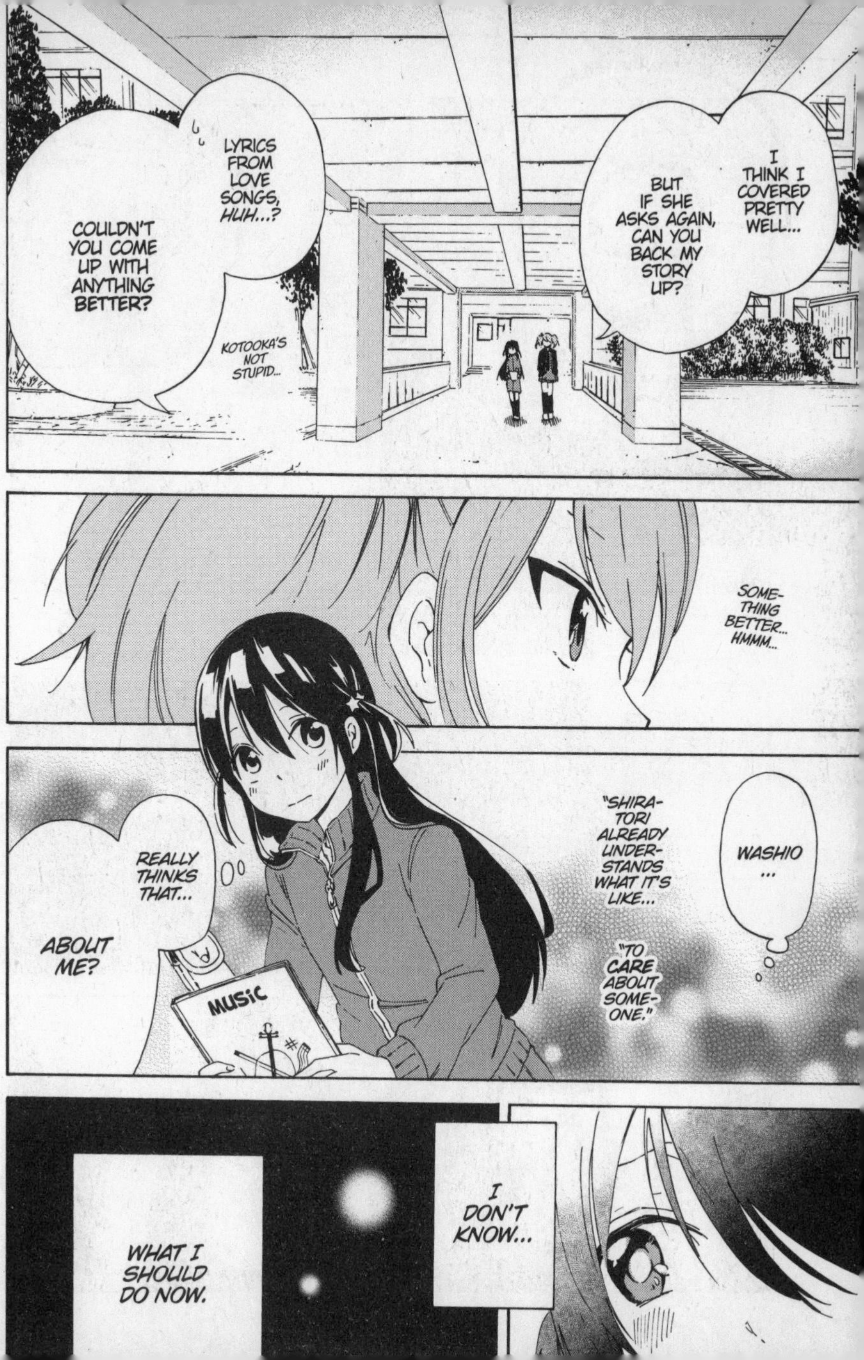
I THINK I COVERED PRETTY WELL...
BUT IF SHE ASKS AGAIN, CAN YOU BACK MY STORY UP?
LYRICS FROM LOVE SONGS, HUH...?
COULDN'T YOU COME UP WITH ANYTHING BETTER?
KOTOOKA'S NOT STUPID...
SOME-THING BETTER... HMMM...
WASHIO ...
"SHIRATORI ALREADY UNDER-STANDS WHAT IT'S LIKE...
"TO CARE ABOUT SOME-ONE."
REALLY THINKS THAT...
ABOUT ME?
MUSIC
I DON'T KNOW...
WHAT I SHOULD DO NOW.

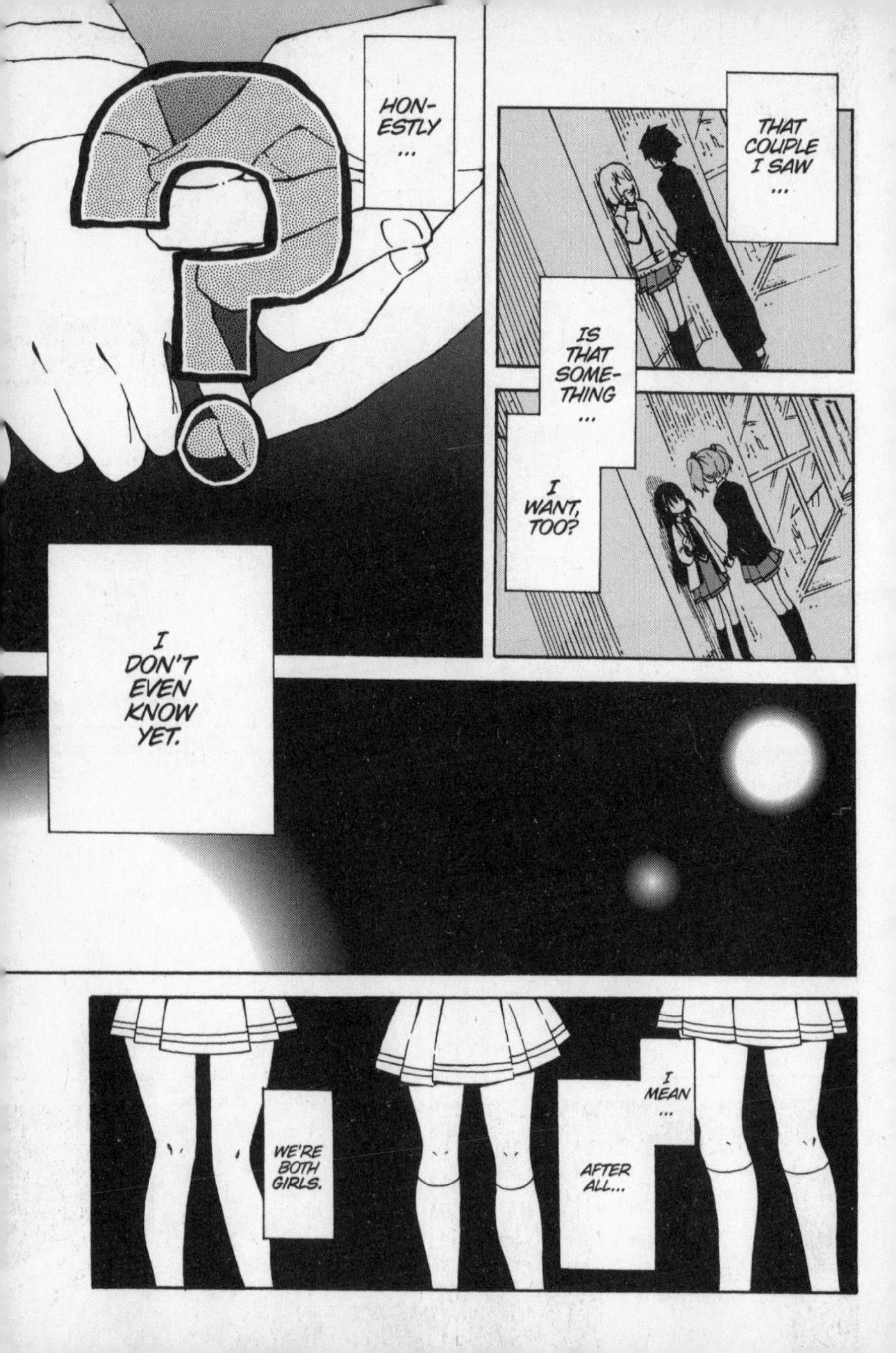
THAT COUPLE I SAW ...
IS THAT SOMETHING ... I WANT, TOO?
HON-ESTLY ...
I DON'T EVEN KNOW YET.
I MEAN ... AFTER ALL...
WE'RE BOTH GIRLS.

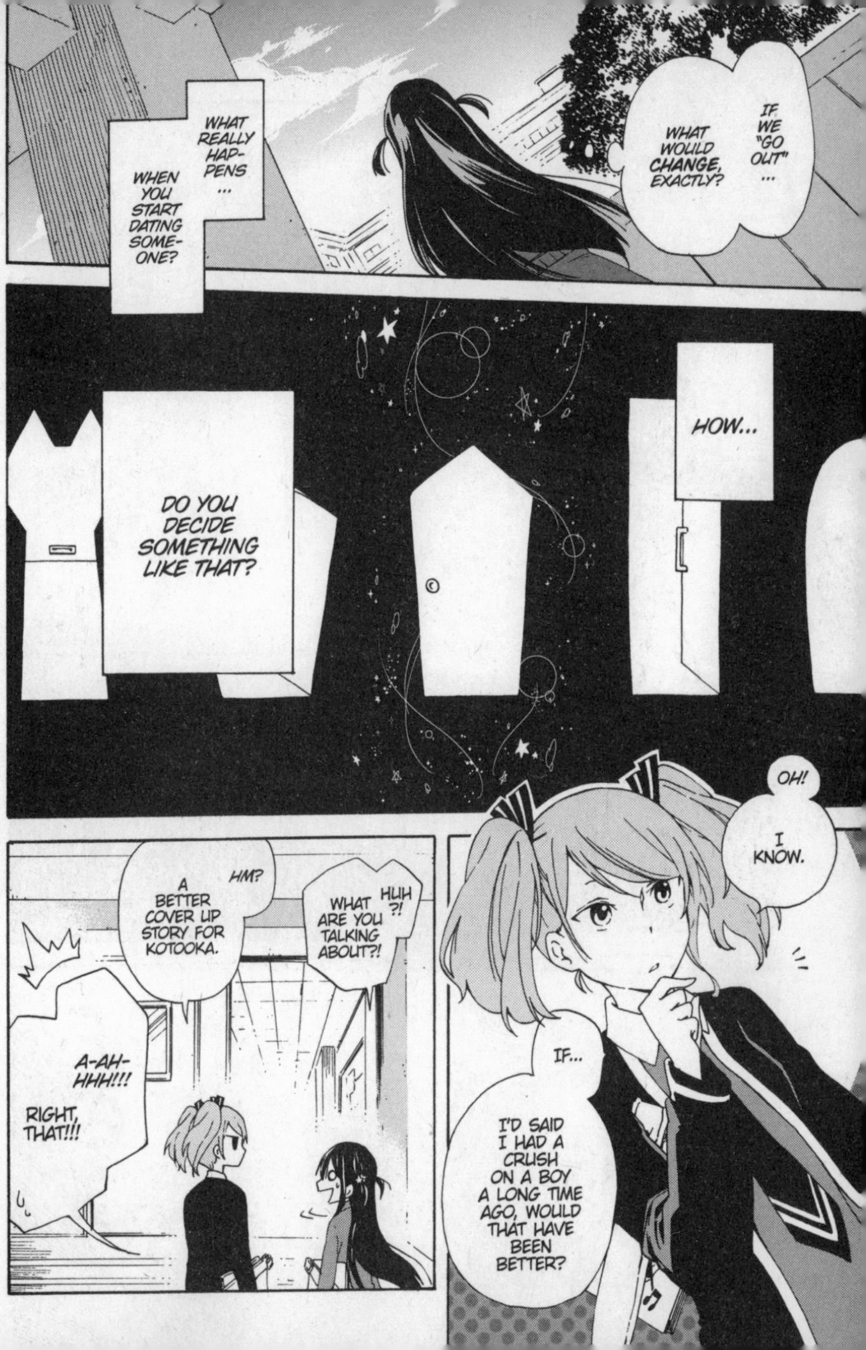
IF WE "GO OUT"...
WHAT WOULD CHANGE, EXACTLY?
WHAT REALLY HAPPENS... WHEN YOU START DATING SOMEONE?
HOW...
DO YOU DECIDE SOMETHING LIKE THAT?
OH!
I KNOW.
IF...
I'D SAID I HAD A CRUSH ON A BOY A LONG TIME AGO, WOULD THAT HAVE BEEN BETTER?
HUH?!
WHAT ARE YOU TALKING ABOUT?!
HM?
A BETTER COVER UP STORY FOR KOTOOKA.
A-AHHHH!!!
RIGHT, THAT!!!

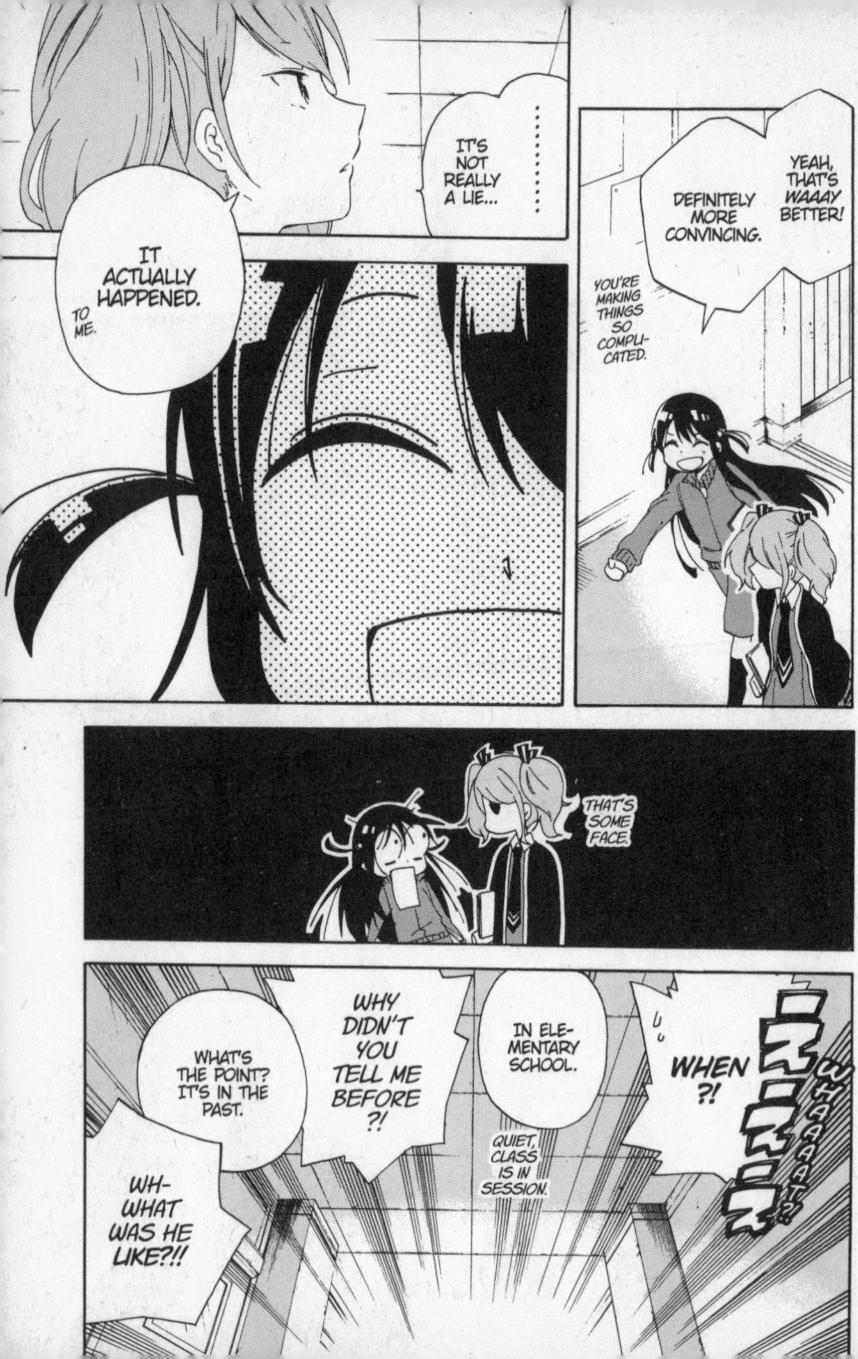
IT'S NOT REALLY A LIE...
IT ACTUALLY HAPPENED.
TO ME.
YEAH, THAT'S WAAAY BETTER!
DEFINITELY MORE CONVINCING.
YOU'RE MAKING THINGS SO COMPLICATED.
THAT'S SOME FACE.
WHAAAAAT?!
WHEN?!
IN ELEMENTARY SCHOOL.
QUIET, CLASS IS IN SESSION.
WHY DIDN'T YOU TELL ME BEFORE?!
WHAT'S THE POINT? IT'S IN THE PAST.
WH-WHAT WAS HE LIKE?!!

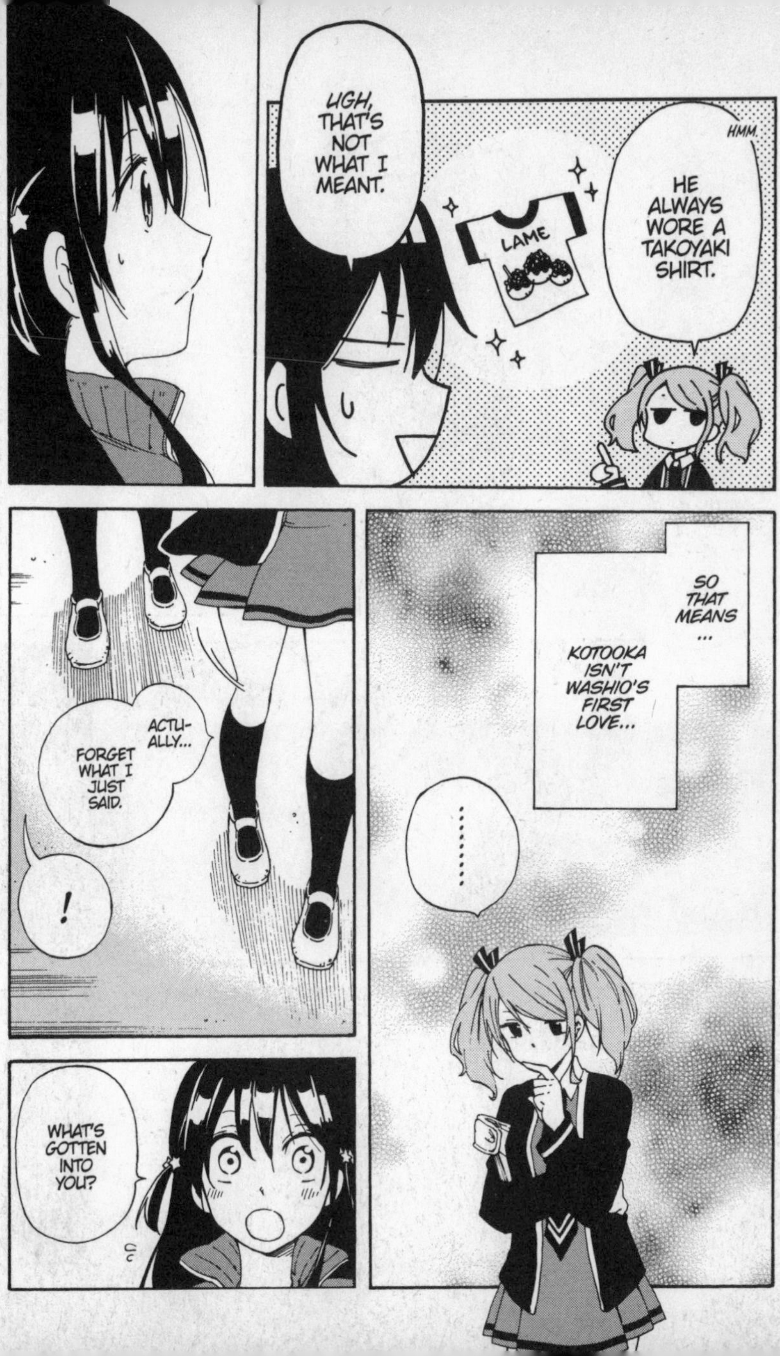
HMM.
HE ALWAYS WORE A TAKOYAKI SHIRT.
LAME
UGH, THAT'S NOT WHAT I MEANT.
SO THAT MEANS ...
KOTOOKA ISN'T WASHIO'S FIRST LOVE...
....
ACTUALLY...
FORGET WHAT I JUST SAID.
!
WHAT'S GOTTEN INTO YOU?

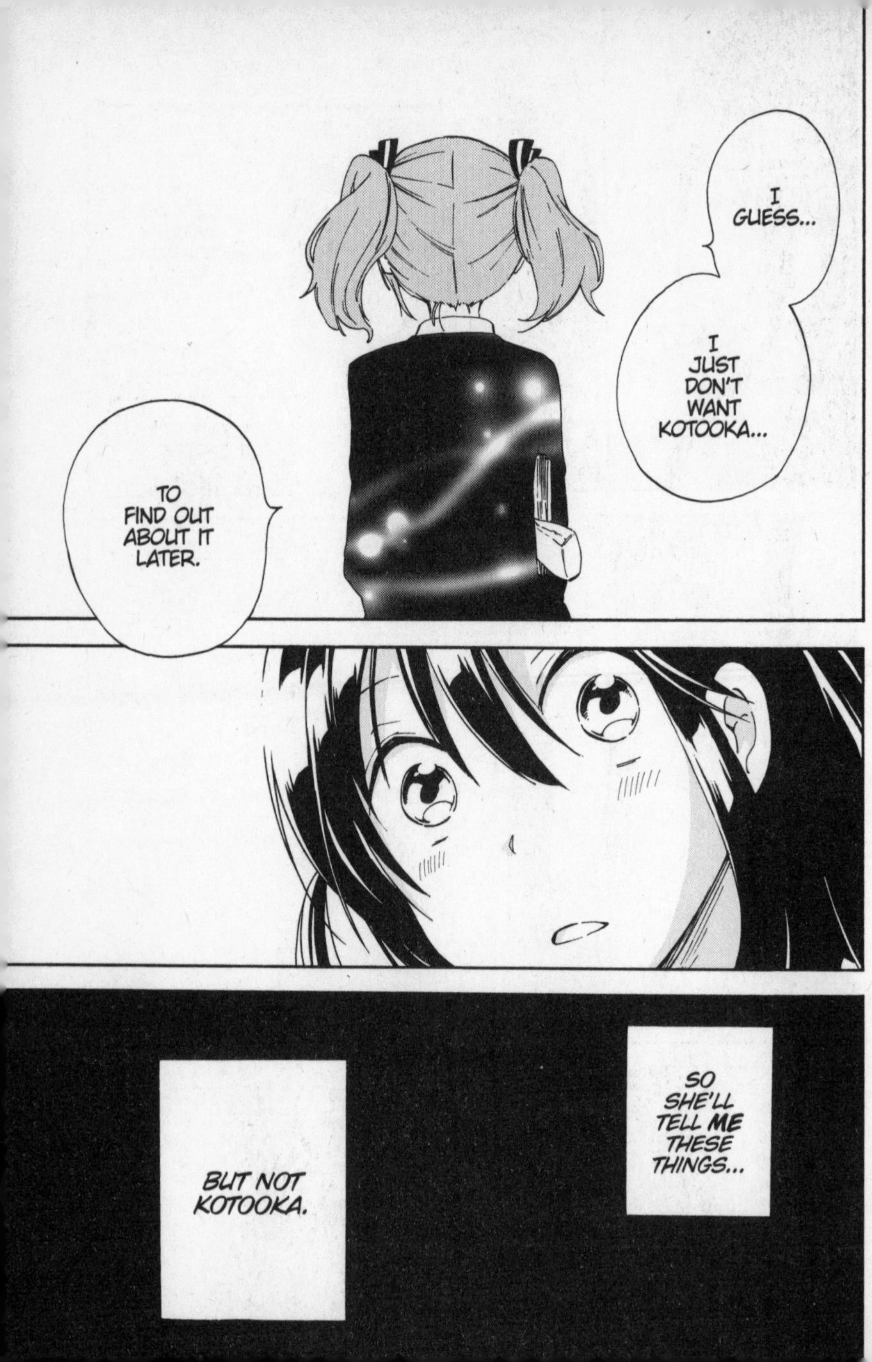
I GUESS...
I JUST DON'T WANT KOTOOKA...
TO FIND OUT ABOUT IT LATER.
SO SHE'LL TELL ME THESE THINGS...
BUT NOT KOTOOKA.

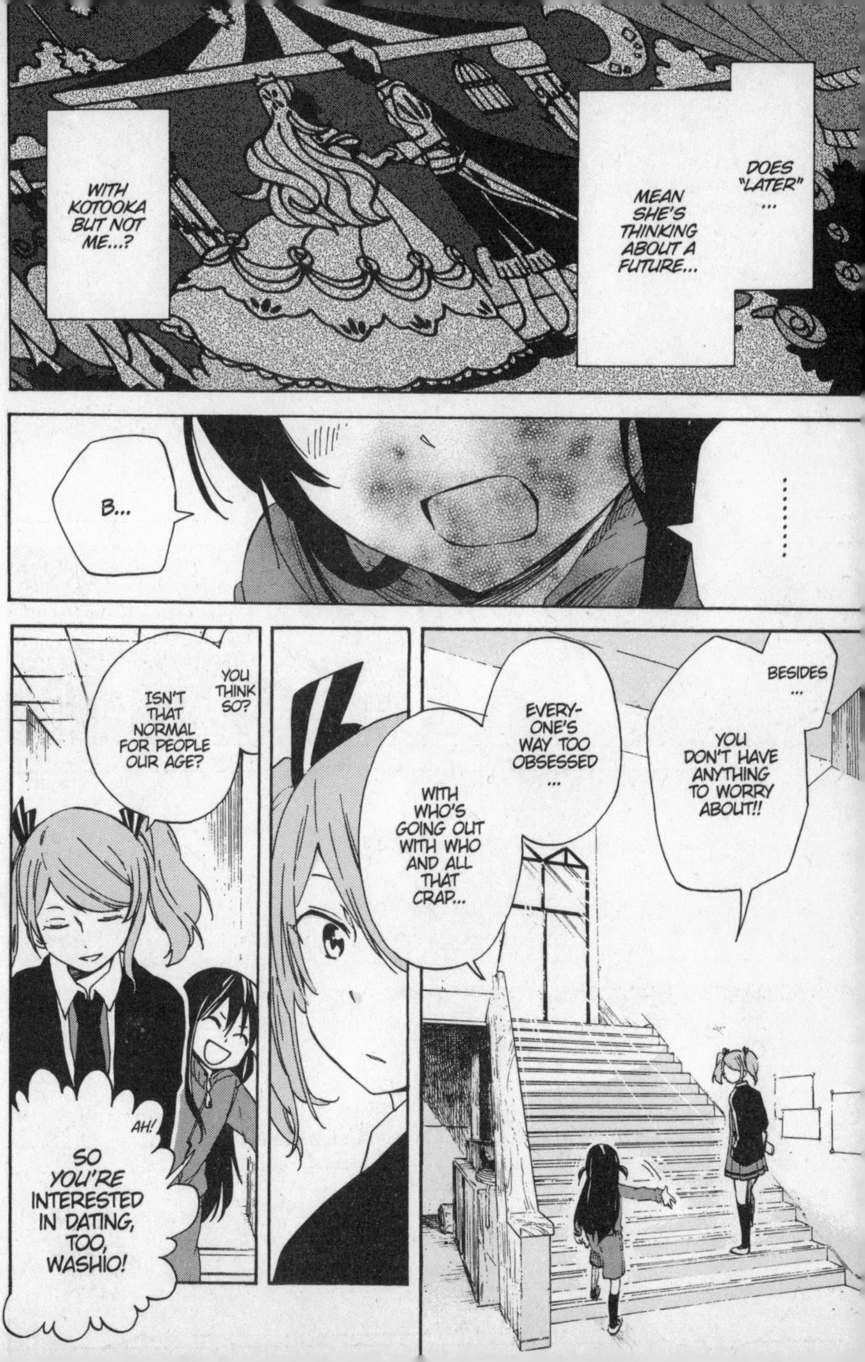
DOES "LATER"... MEAN SHE'S THINKING ABOUT A FUTURE...
WITH KOTOOKA BUT NOT ME...?
......
B...
BESIDES...
YOU DON'T HAVE ANYTHING TO WORRY ABOUT!!
EVERYONE'S WAY TOO OBSESSED...
WITH WHO'S GOING OUT WITH WHO AND ALL THAT CRAP...
YOU THINK SO?
ISN'T THAT NORMAL FOR PEOPLE OUR AGE?
AH!
SO YOU'RE INTERESTED IN DATING, TOO, WASHIO!

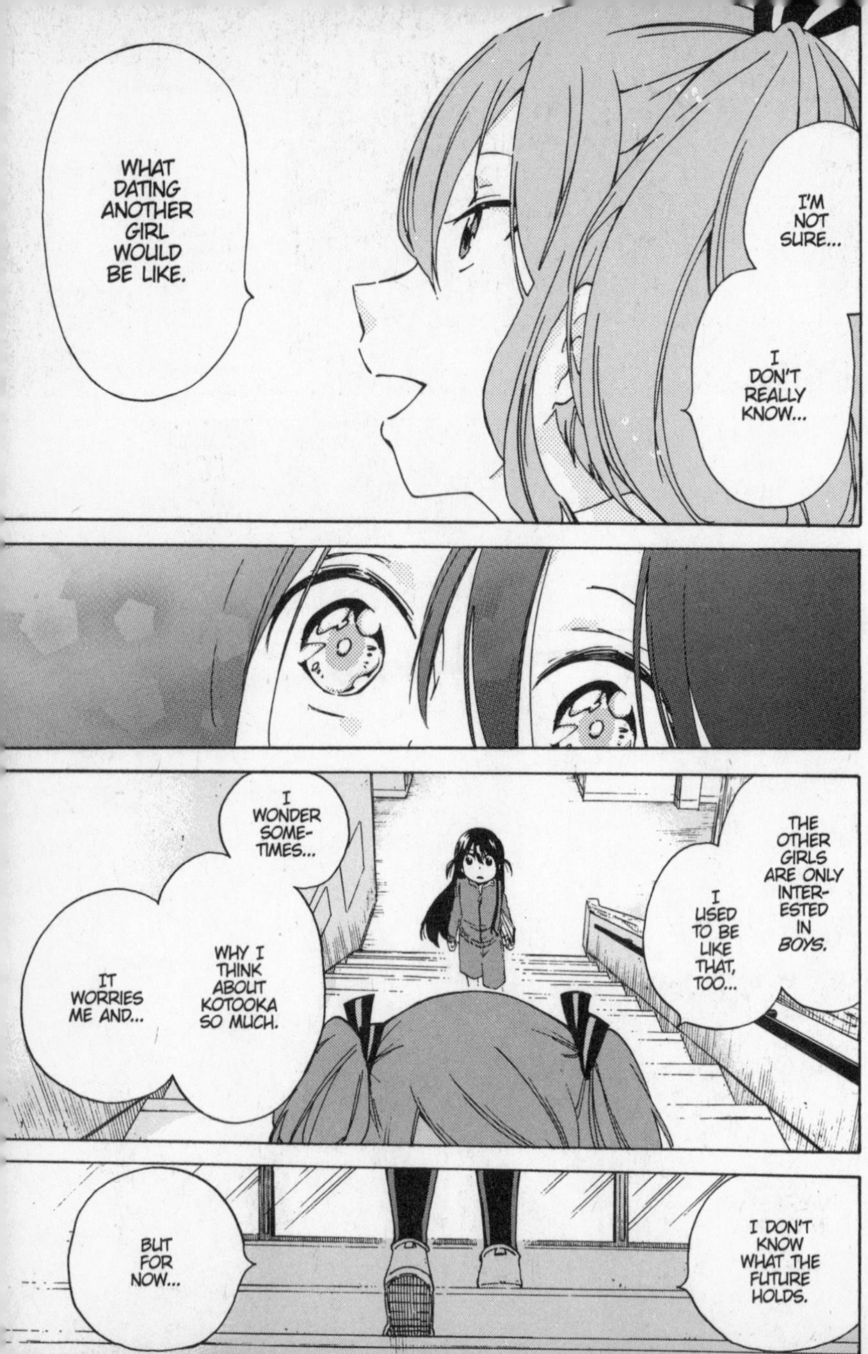
I'M NOT SURE...
I DON'T REALLY KNOW...
WHAT DATING ANOTHER GIRL WOULD BE LIKE.
THE OTHER GIRLS ARE ONLY INTERESTED IN *BOYS.*
I USED TO BE LIKE THAT, TOO...
I WONDER SOMETIMES...
WHY I THINK ABOUT KOTOOKA SO MUCH.
IT WORRIES ME AND...
I DON'T KNOW WHAT THE FUTURE HOLDS.
BUT FOR NOW...

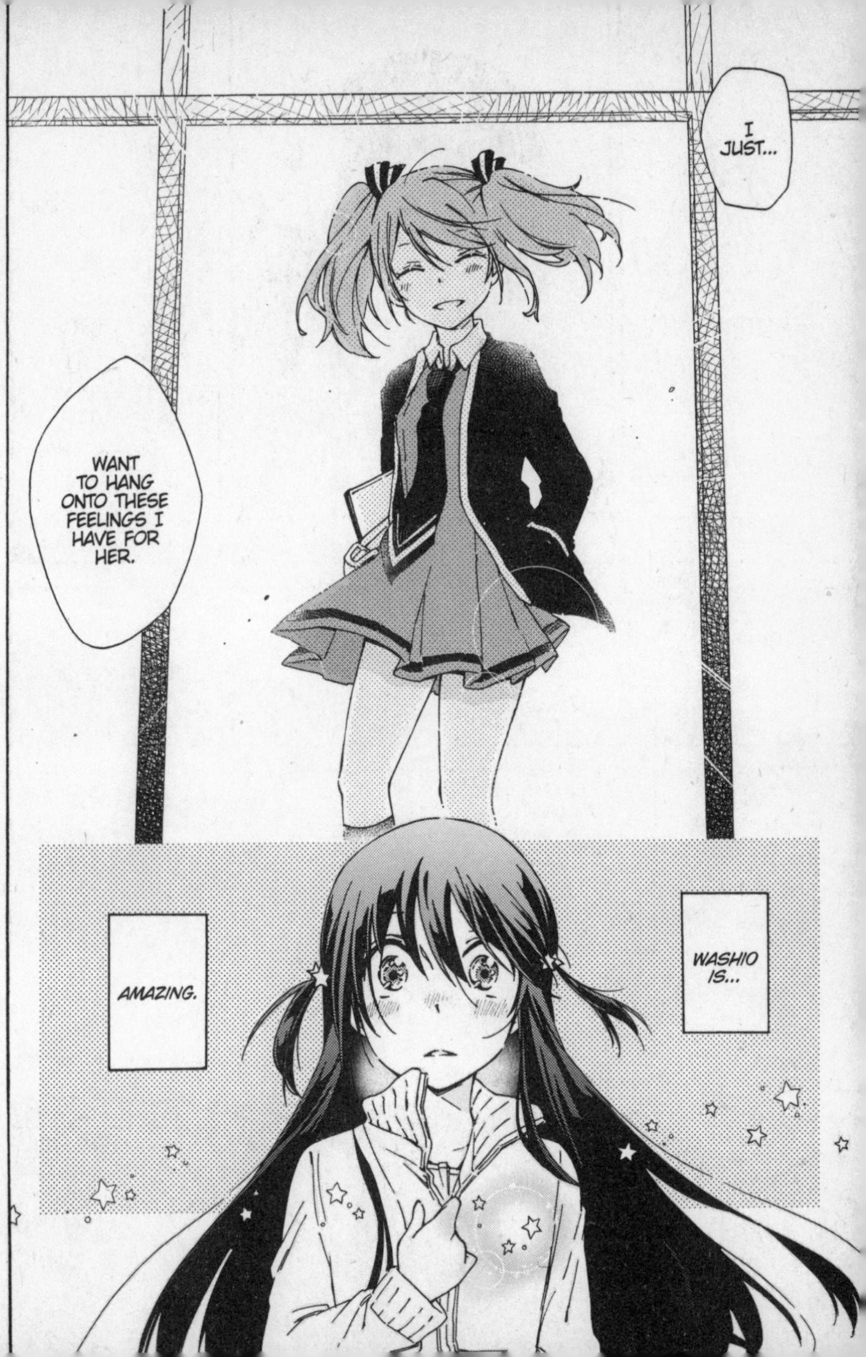
I JUST...
WANT TO HANG ONTO THESE FEELINGS I HAVE FOR HER.
WASHIO IS...
AMAZING.

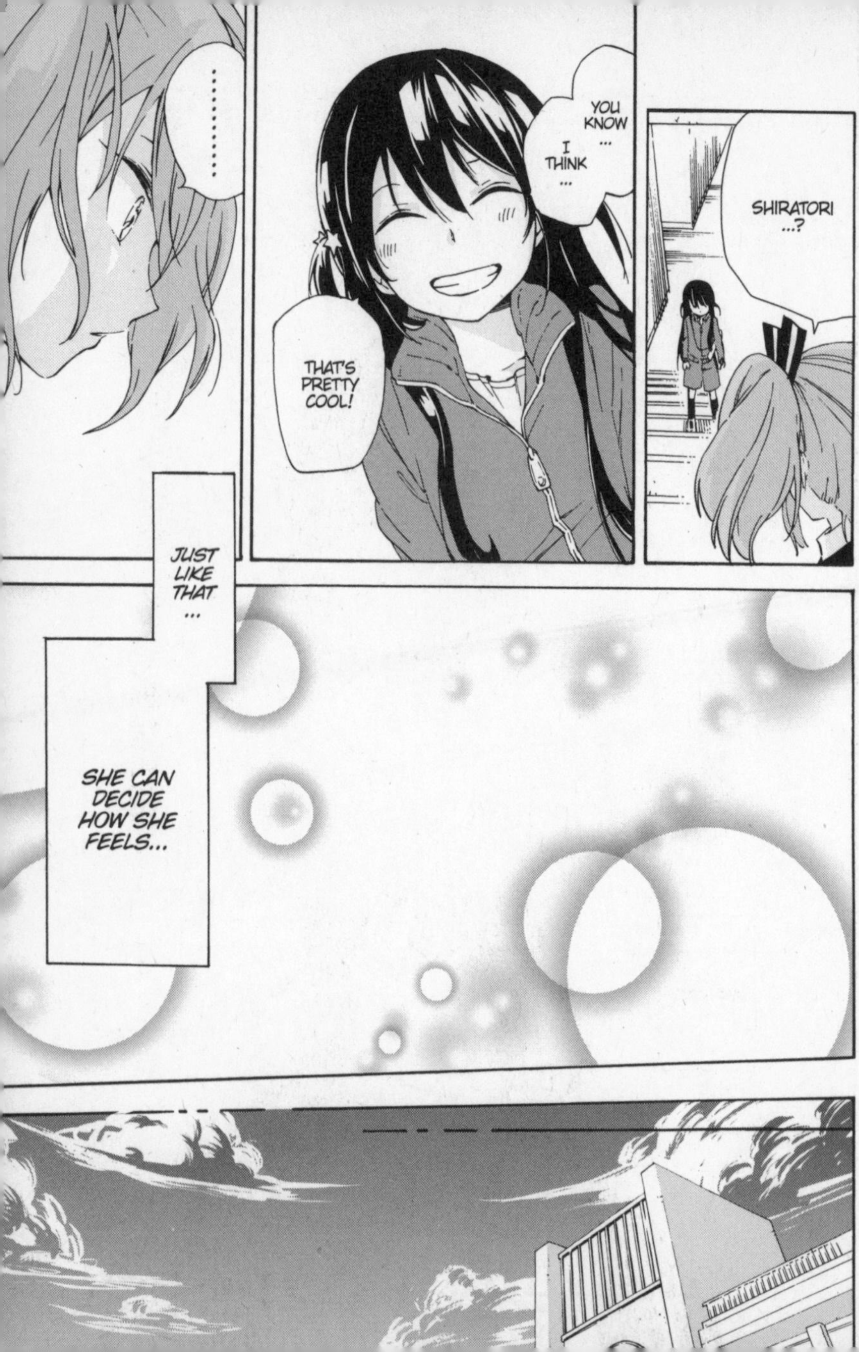
SHIRATORI ...?
YOU KNOW ... I THINK ...
THAT'S PRETTY COOL!
......
JUST LIKE THAT ...
SHE CAN DECIDE HOW SHE FEELS...

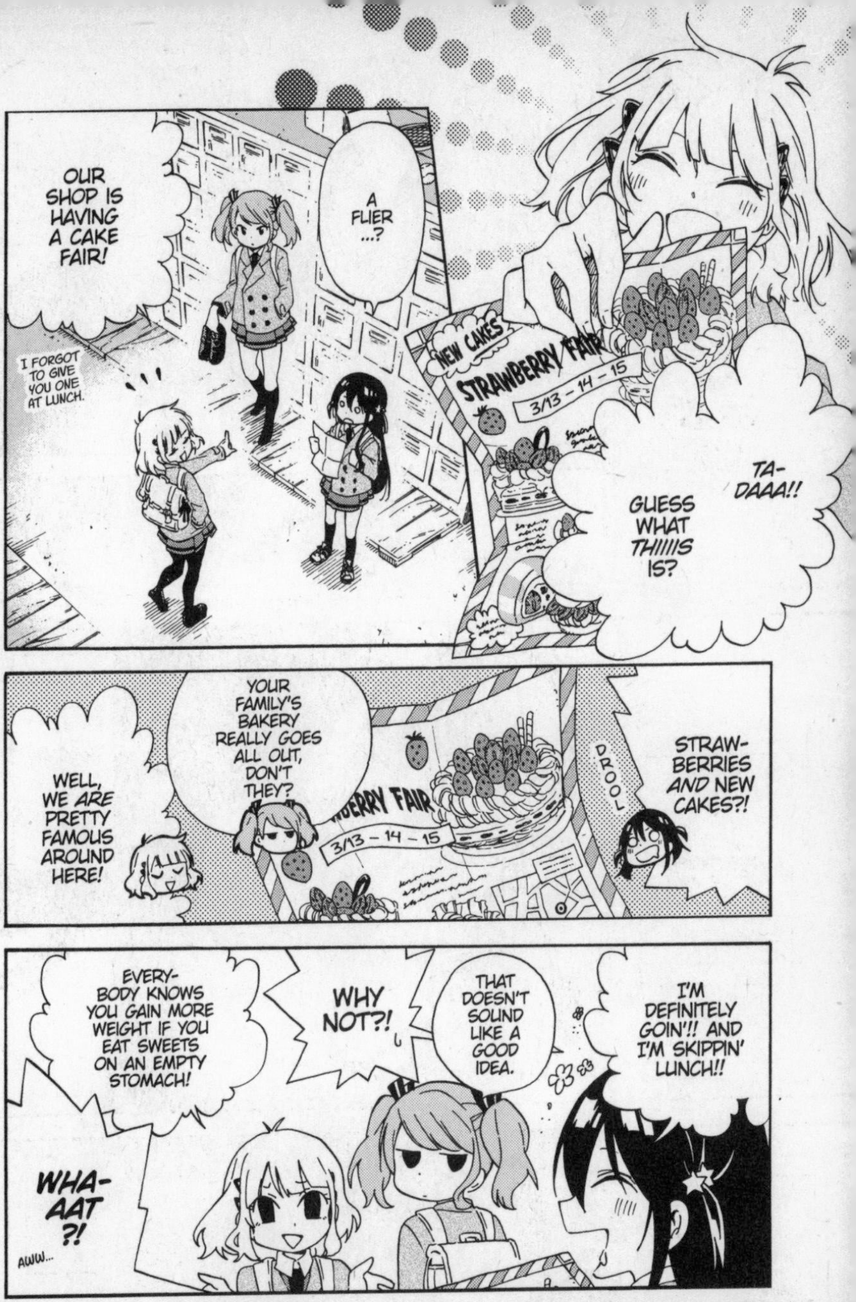
TA-DAAA!!
GUESS WHAT THIIIIS IS?
NEW CAKES
STRAWBERRY FAIR
3/13 – 14 – 15
A FLIER ...?
OUR SHOP IS HAVING A CAKE FAIR!
I FORGOT TO GIVE YOU ONE AT LUNCH.
STRAW-BERRIES AND NEW CAKES?!
DROOL
YOUR FAMILY'S BAKERY REALLY GOES ALL OUT, DON'T THEY?
RRY FAIR
3/13 – 14 – 15
WELL, WE ARE PRETTY FAMOUS AROUND HERE!
I'M DEFINITELY GOIN'!! AND I'M SKIPPIN' LUNCH!!
THAT DOESN'T SOUND LIKE A GOOD IDEA.
WHY NOT?!
EVERY-BODY KNOWS YOU GAIN MORE WEIGHT IF YOU EAT SWEETS ON AN EMPTY STOMACH!
WHA-AAT?!
AWW...

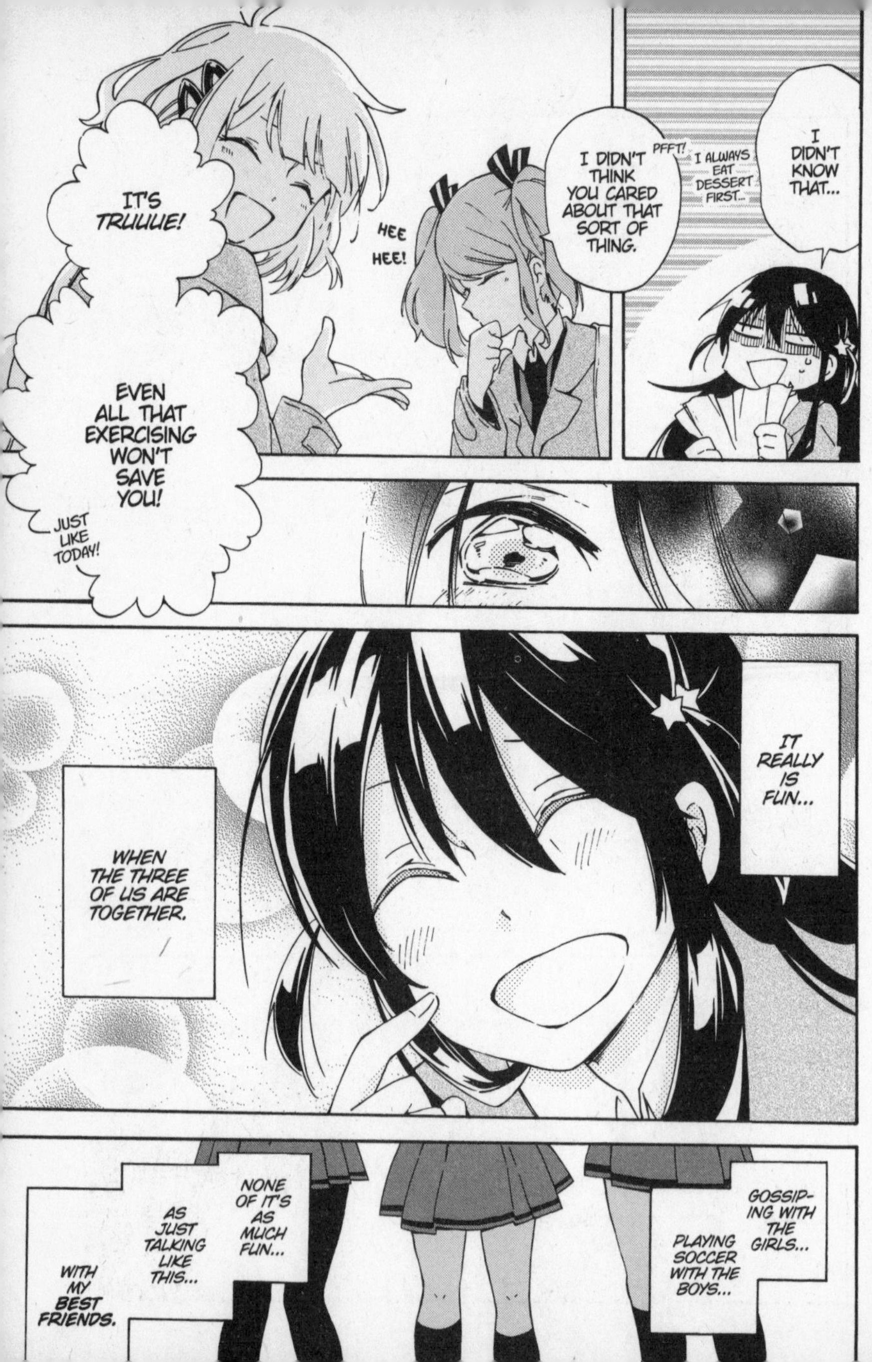
I DIDN'T KNOW THAT...
I ALWAYS EAT DESSERT FIRST...
PFFT!
I DIDN'T THINK YOU CARED ABOUT THAT SORT OF THING.
HEE HEE!
IT'S TRUUUE!
EVEN ALL THAT EXERCISING WON'T SAVE YOU!
JUST LIKE TODAY!
IT REALLY IS FUN...
WHEN THE THREE OF US ARE TOGETHER.
GOSSIPING WITH THE GIRLS...
PLAYING SOCCER WITH THE BOYS...
NONE OF IT'S AS MUCH FUN...
AS JUST TALKING LIKE THIS...
WITH MY BEST FRIENDS.

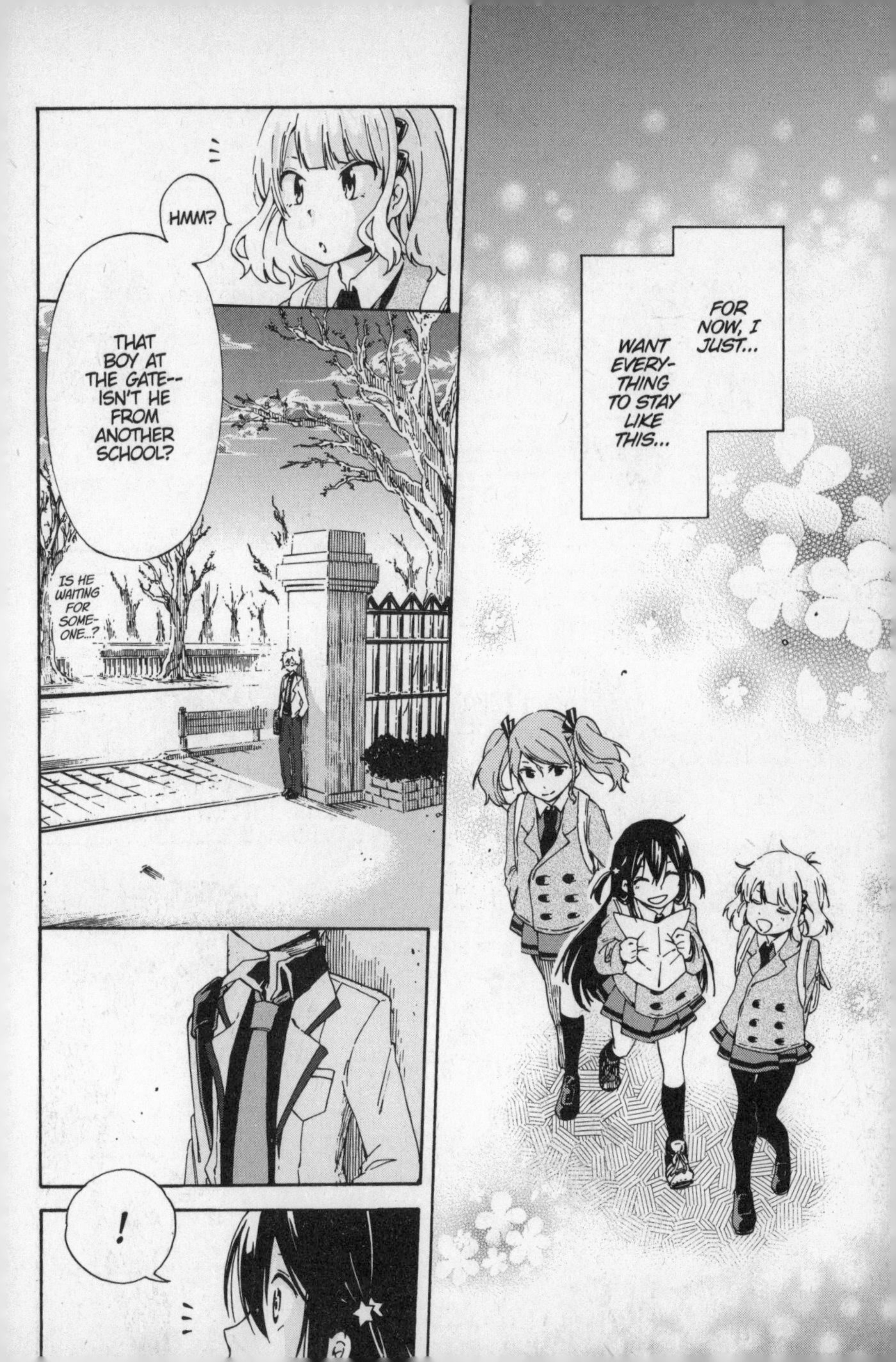

FOR NOW, I JUST...
WANT EVERY-THING TO STAY LIKE THIS...
HMM?
THAT BOY AT THE GATE--ISN'T HE FROM ANOTHER SCHOOL?
IS HE WAITING FOR SOME-ONE...?
!

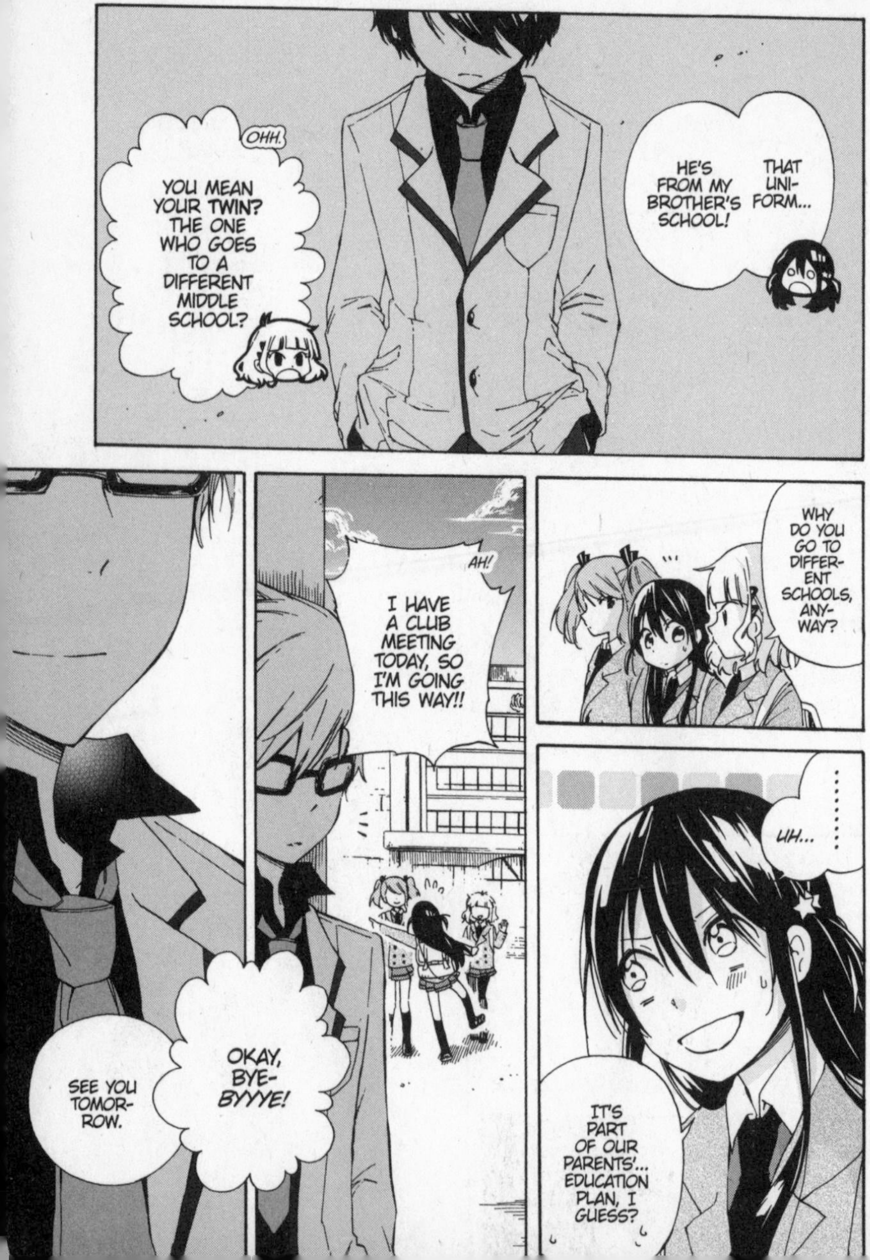
THAT UNI-FORM...
HE'S FROM MY BROTHER'S SCHOOL!
OHH.
YOU MEAN YOUR TWIN? THE ONE WHO GOES TO A DIFFERENT MIDDLE SCHOOL?
WHY DO YOU GO TO DIFFER-ENT SCHOOLS, ANY-WAY?
...
......
UH...
IT'S PART OF OUR PARENTS'... EDUCATION PLAN, I GUESS?
AH!
I HAVE A CLUB MEETING TODAY, SO I'M GOING THIS WAY!!
OKAY, BYE-BYYYE!
SEE YOU TOMOR-ROW.

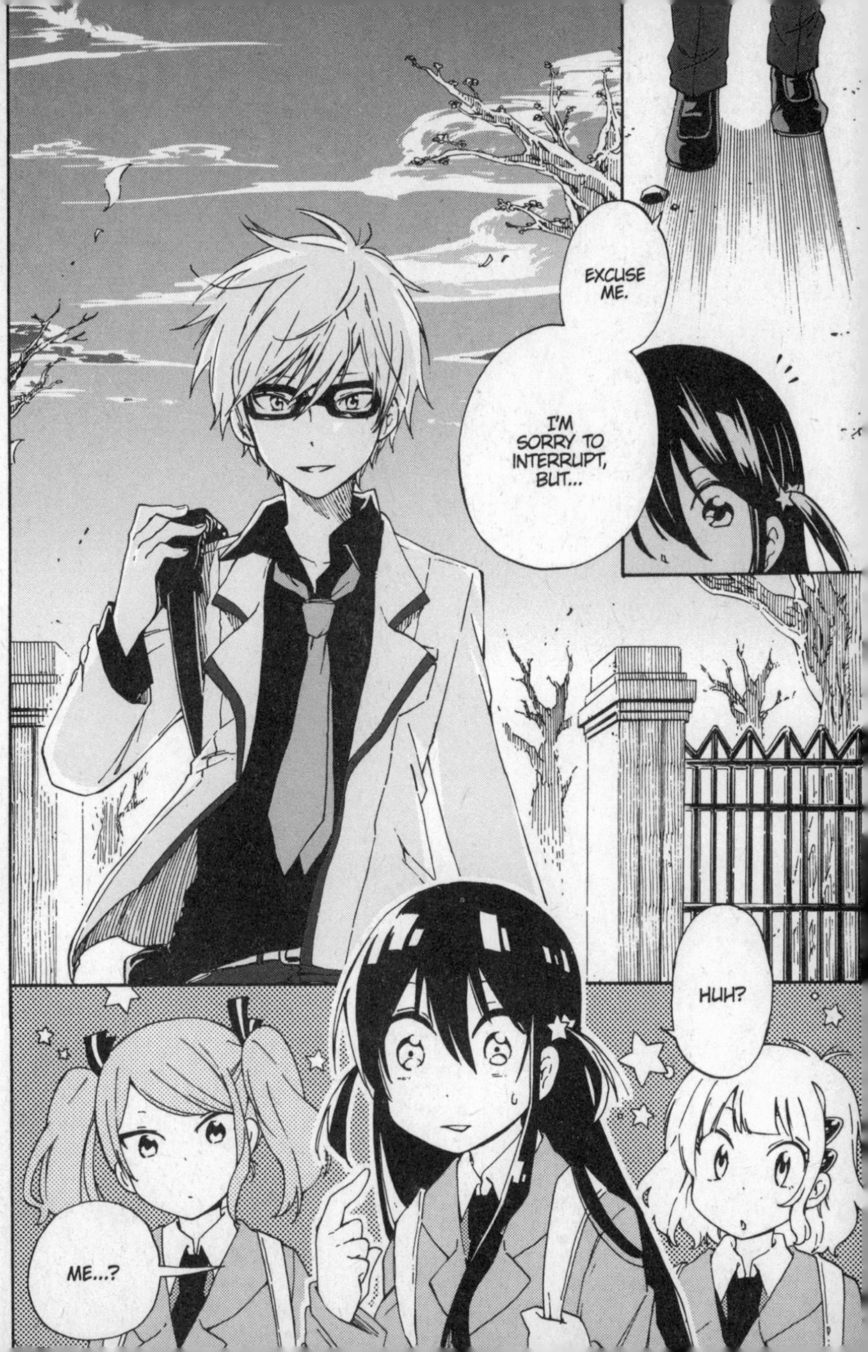
EXCUSE ME.
I'M SORRY TO INTERRUPT, BUT...
HUH?
ME...?

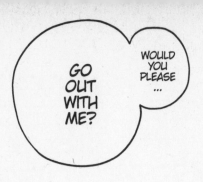

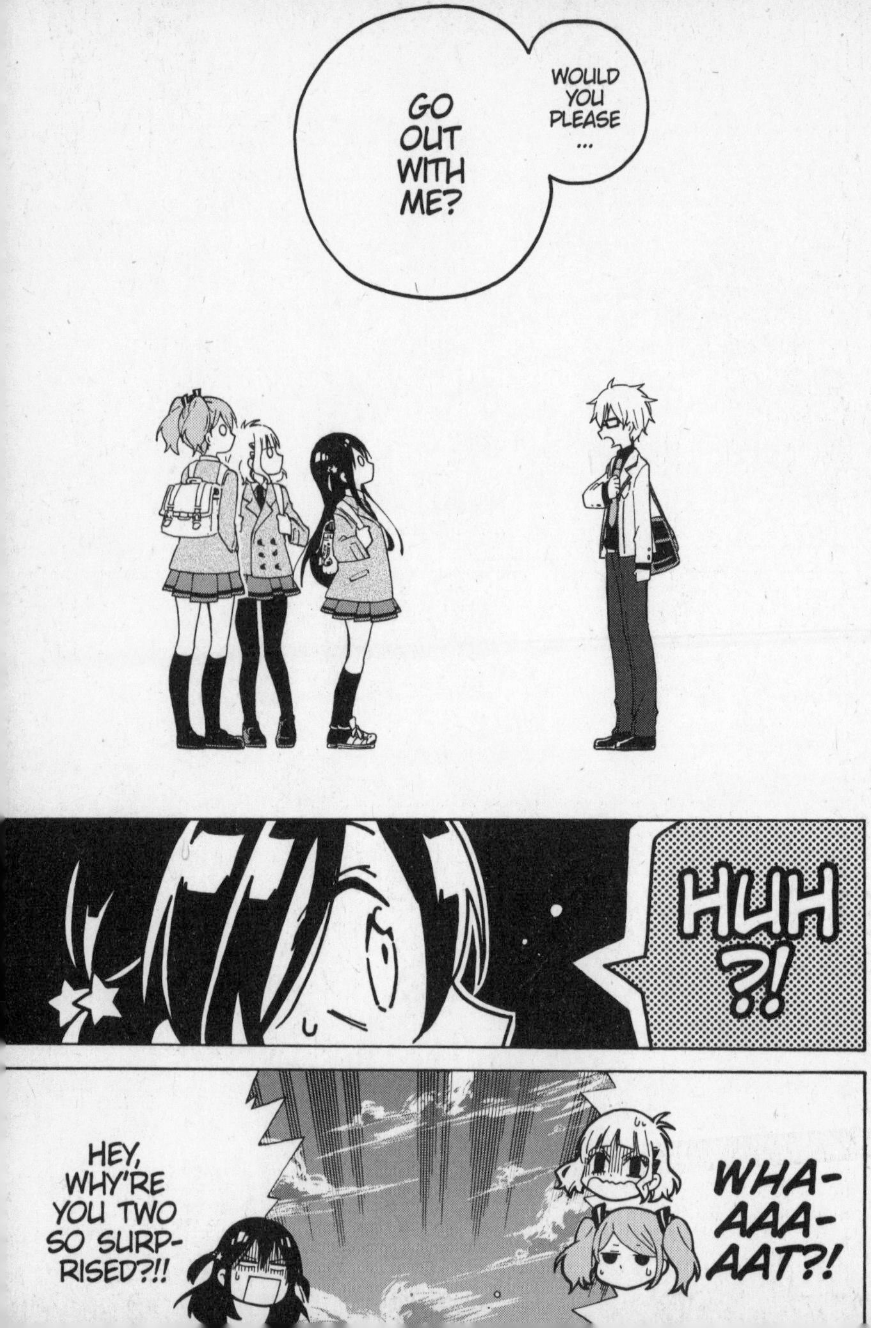
WOULD YOU PLEASE ... GO OUT WITH ME?
HUH ?!
WHA-AAA-AAT?!
HEY, WHY'RE YOU TWO SO SURP-RISED?!!

Nameless Asterism

Chapter 3

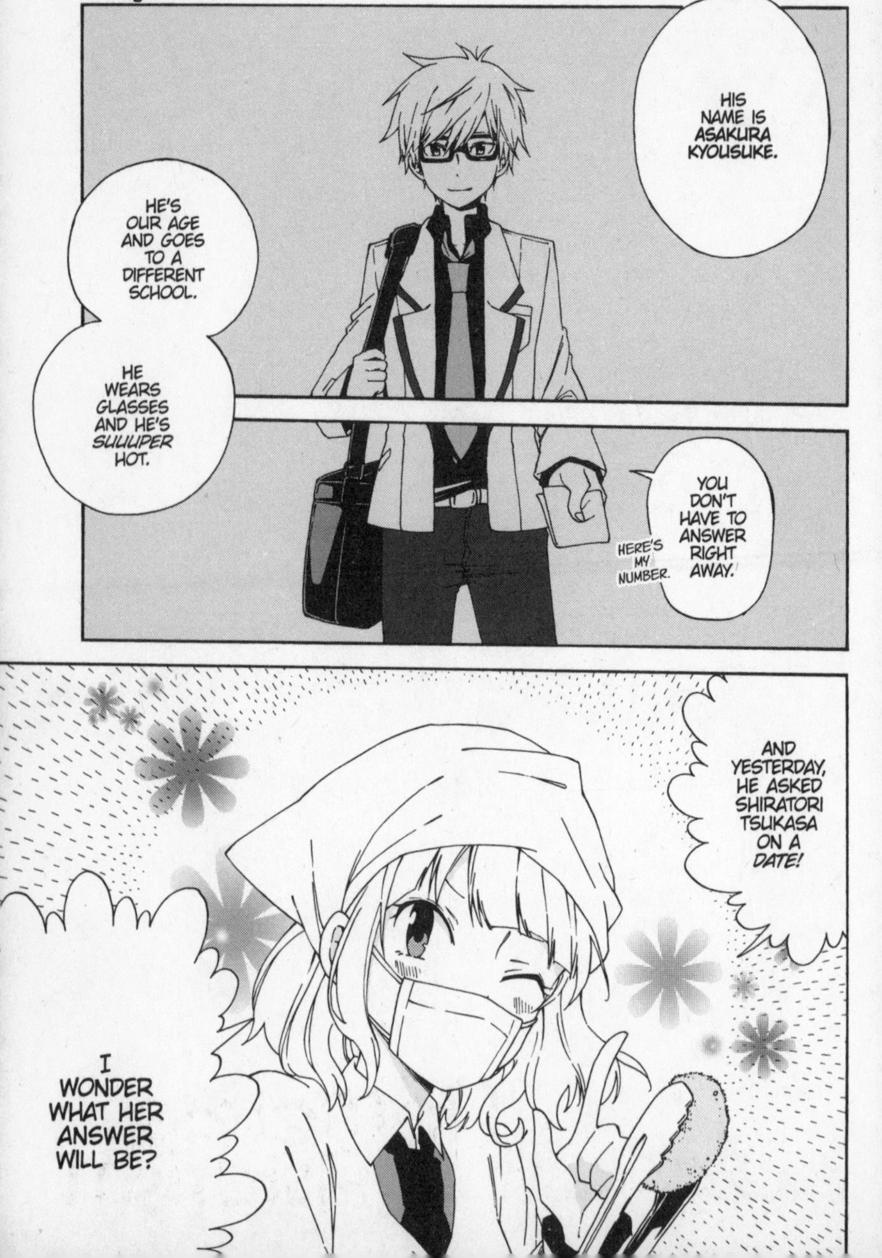
HIS NAME IS ASAKURA KYOUSUKE.
HE'S OUR AGE AND GOES TO A DIFFERENT SCHOOL.
HE WEARS GLASSES AND HE'S *SUUUPER* HOT.
YOU DON'T HAVE TO ANSWER RIGHT AWAY.
HERE'S MY NUMBER.
AND YESTERDAY, HE ASKED SHIRATORI TSUKASA ON A *DATE!*
I WONDER WHAT HER ANSWER WILL BE?

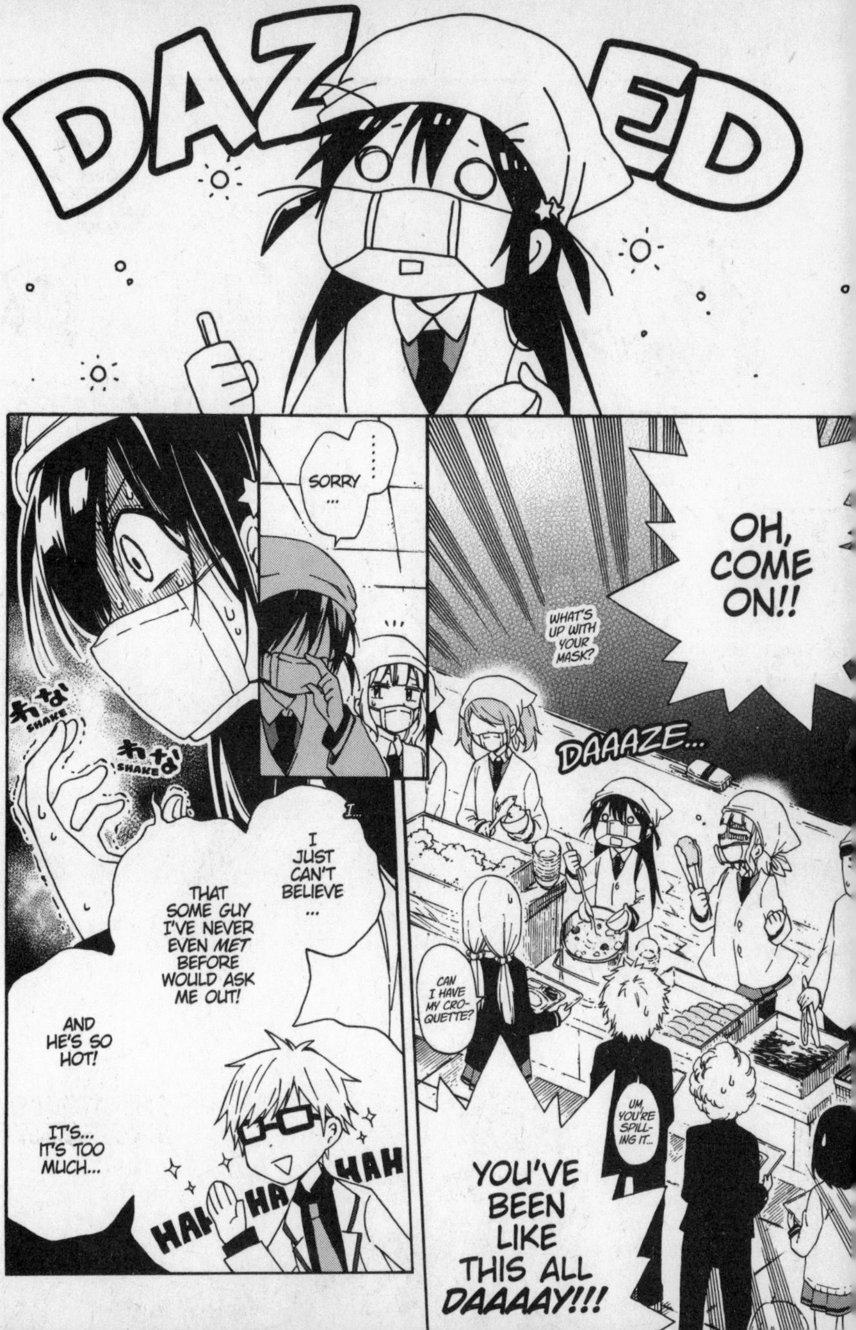
DAZED
OH, COME ON!!
WHAT'S UP WITH YOUR MASK?
DAAAZE...
CAN I HAVE MY CROQUETTE?
UM, YOU'RE SPILLING IT...
YOU'VE BEEN LIKE THIS ALL DAAAAY!!!
......
SORRY...
SHAKE
SHAKE
I...
I JUST CAN'T BELIEVE...
THAT SOME GUY I'VE NEVER EVEN MET BEFORE WOULD ASK ME OUT!
AND HE'S SO HOT!
IT'S... IT'S TOO MUCH...
HAH
HA
HAH

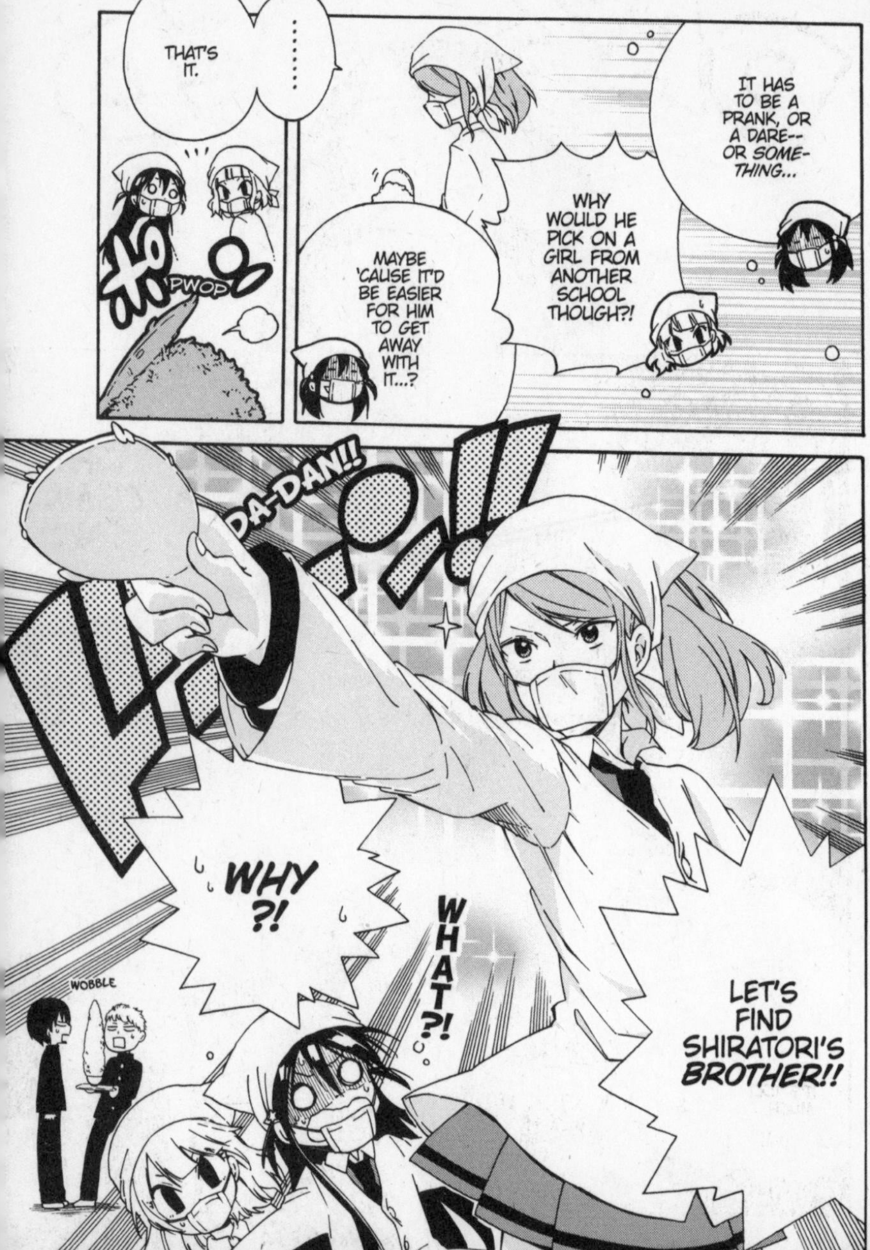
IT HAS TO BE A PRANK, OR A DARE-- OR SOMETHING...
WHY WOULD HE PICK ON A GIRL FROM ANOTHER SCHOOL THOUGH?!
MAYBE 'CAUSE IT'D BE EASIER FOR HIM TO GET AWAY WITH IT...?
......
THAT'S IT.
PWOP
DA-DAN!!
LET'S FIND SHIRATORI'S BROTHER!!
WHAT?!
WHY?!
WOBBLE

Chapter 3 ★ Little Brother

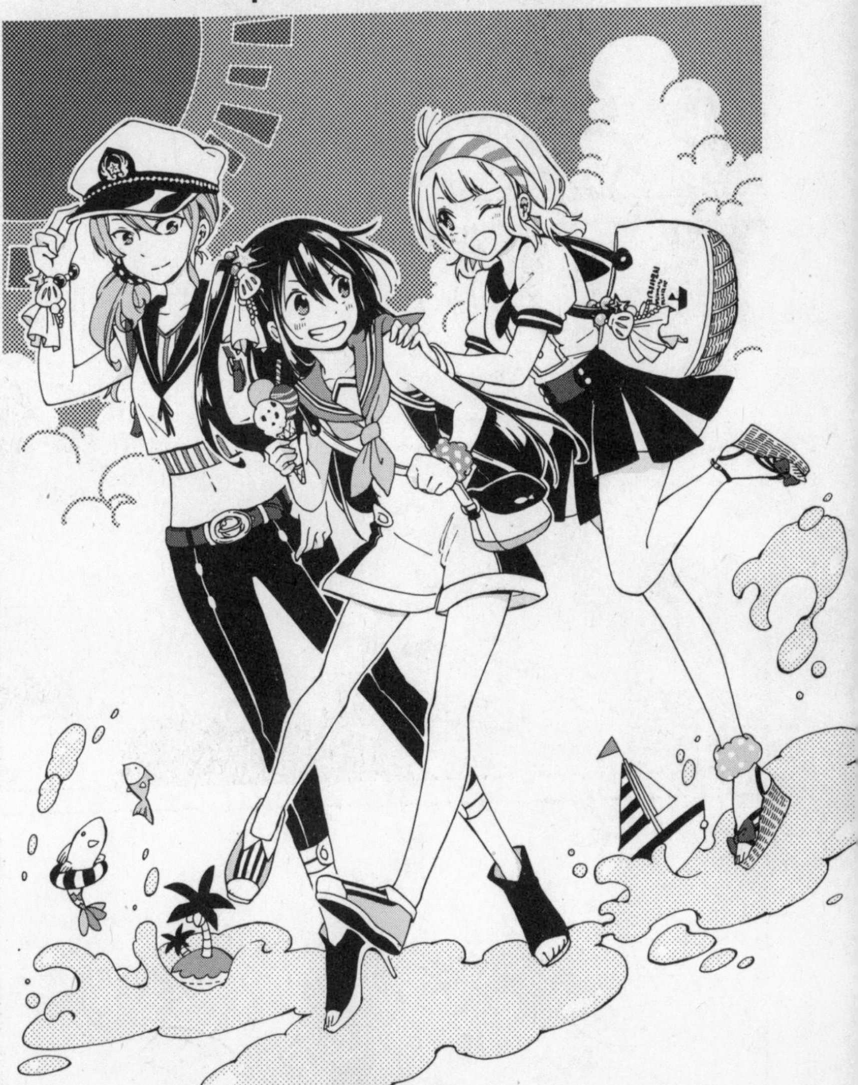

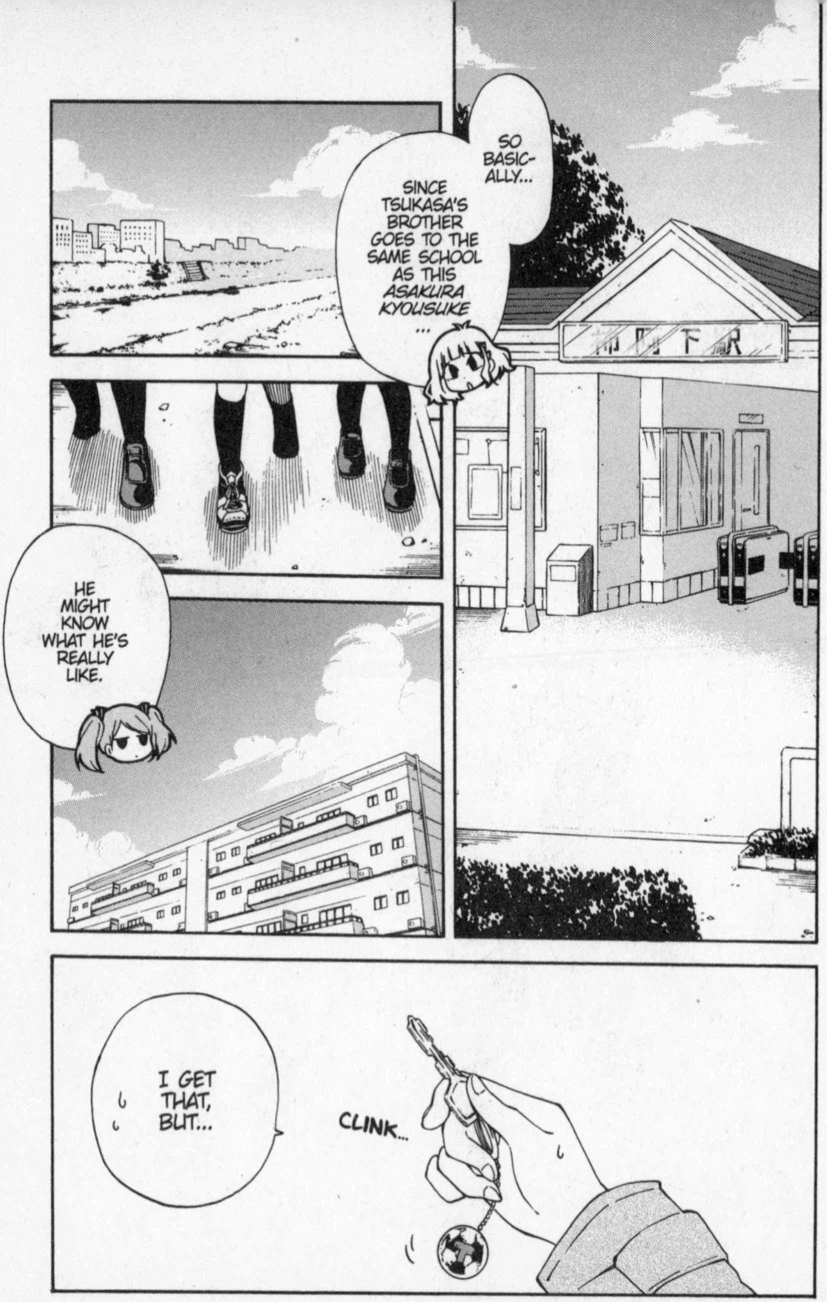
SO BASIC-ALLY...
SINCE TSUKASA'S BROTHER GOES TO THE SAME SCHOOL AS THIS ASAKURA KYOUSUKE ...
HE MIGHT KNOW WHAT HE'S REALLY LIKE.
I GET THAT, BUT...
CLINK...

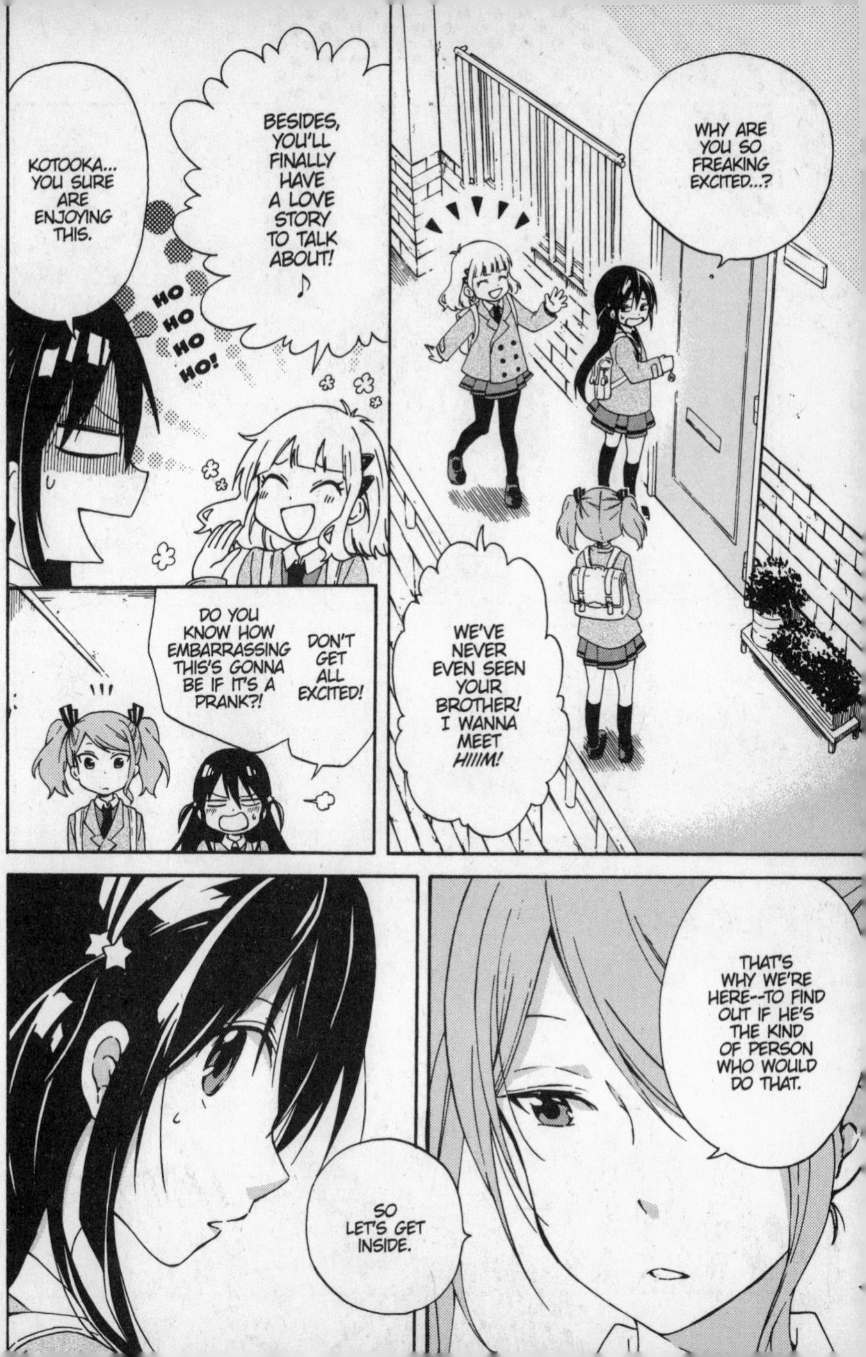
WHY ARE YOU SO FREAKING EXCITED...?
WE'VE NEVER EVEN SEEN YOUR BROTHER! I WANNA MEET *HIIIM!*
BESIDES, YOU'LL FINALLY HAVE A LOVE STORY TO TALK ABOUT! ♪
HO HO HO HO!
KOTOOKA... YOU SURE ARE ENJOYING THIS.
DON'T GET ALL EXCITED!
DO YOU KNOW HOW EMBARRASSING THIS'S GONNA BE IF IT'S A PRANK?!
THAT'S WHY WE'RE HERE--TO FIND OUT IF HE'S THE KIND OF PERSON WHO WOULD DO THAT.
SO LET'S GET INSIDE.

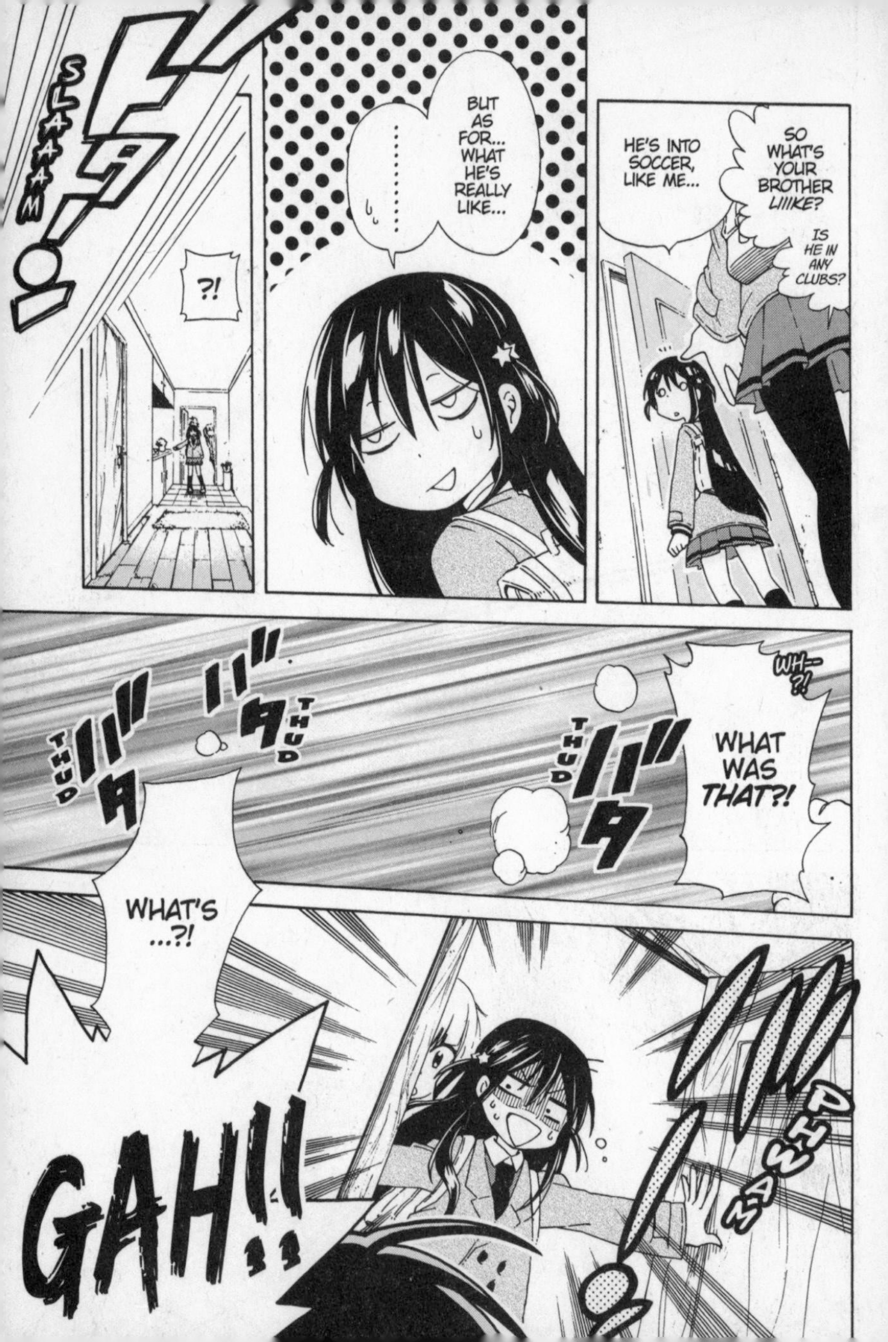
SO WHAT'S YOUR BROTHER LIIIKE?
IS HE IN ANY CLUBS?
HE'S INTO SOCCER, LIKE ME...
BUT AS FOR... WHAT HE'S REALLY LIKE...
......
SLAAAAM
?!
WH-?!
WHAT WAS THAT?!
THUD
THUD
THUD
WHAT'S ...?!
PHWAM
GAH!!

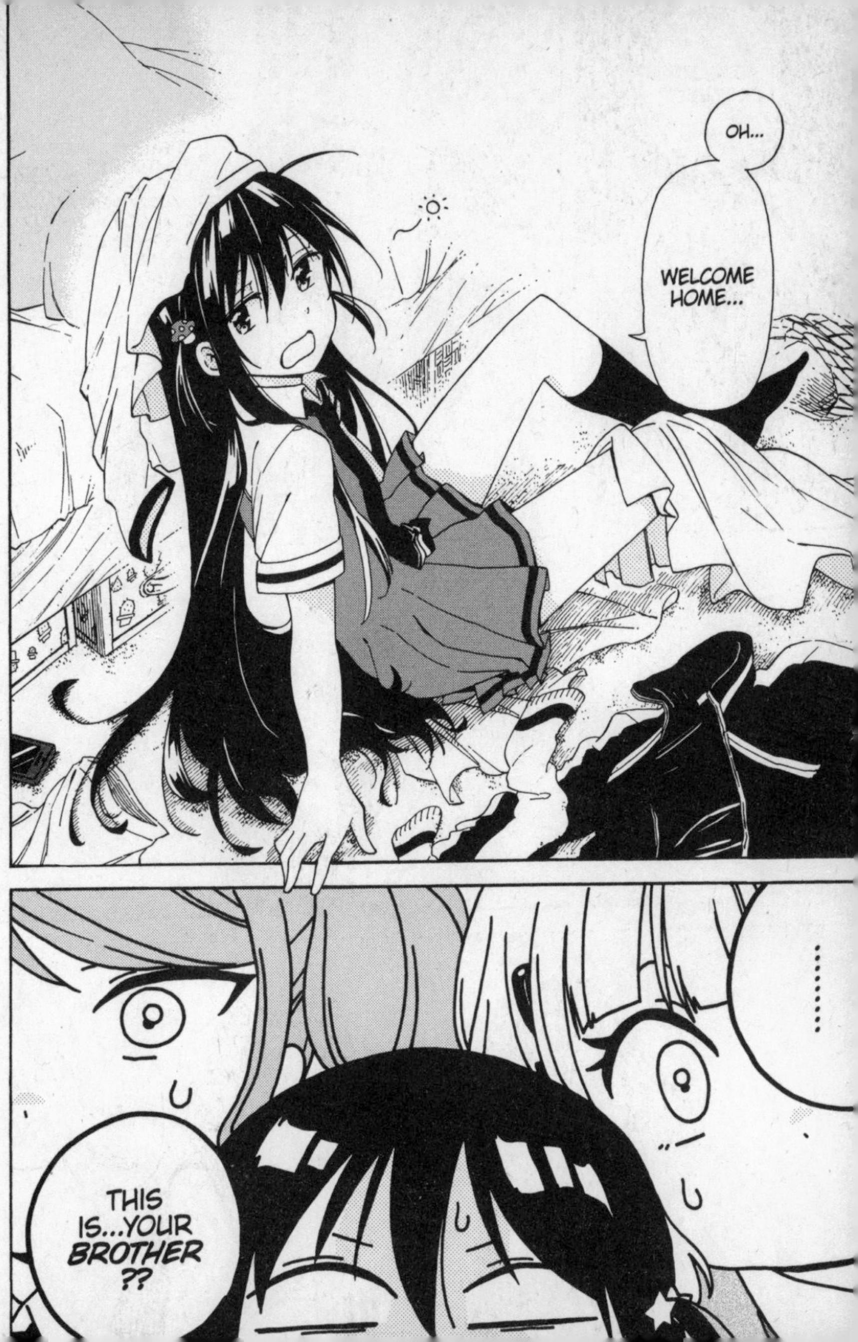
OH... WELCOME HOME...
......
THIS IS...YOUR BROTHER ??

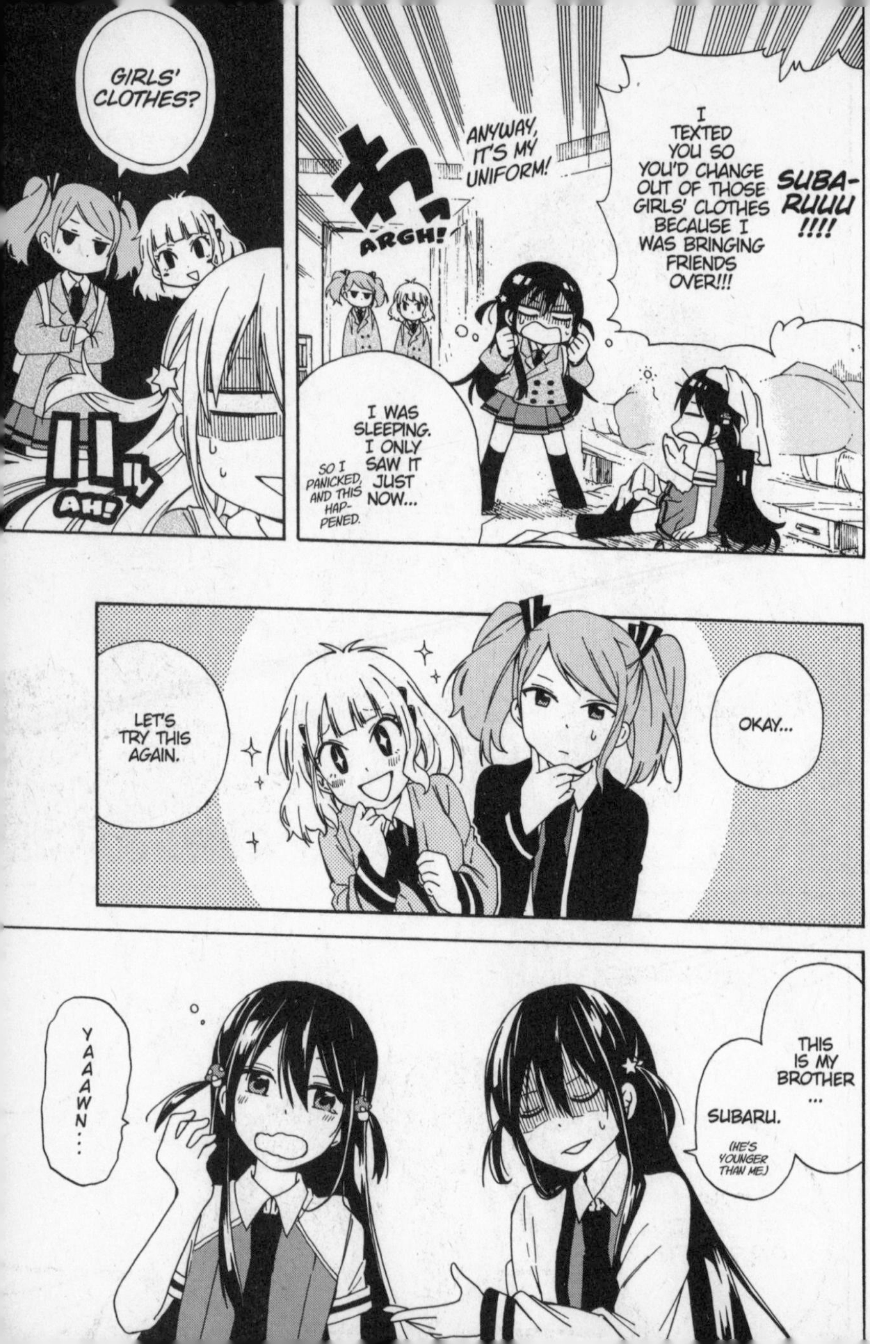
SUBA-RUUU!!!!
I TEXTED YOU SO YOU'D CHANGE OUT OF THOSE GIRLS' CLOTHES BECAUSE I WAS BRINGING FRIENDS OVER!!!
ANYWAY, IT'S MY UNIFORM!
ARGH!
I WAS SLEEPING. I ONLY SAW IT JUST NOW...
SO I PANICKED, AND THIS HAPPENED.
GIRLS' CLOTHES?
AH!
OKAY...
LET'S TRY THIS AGAIN.
THIS IS MY BROTHER... SUBARU.
(HE'S YOUNGER THAN ME)
YAAAAWN...

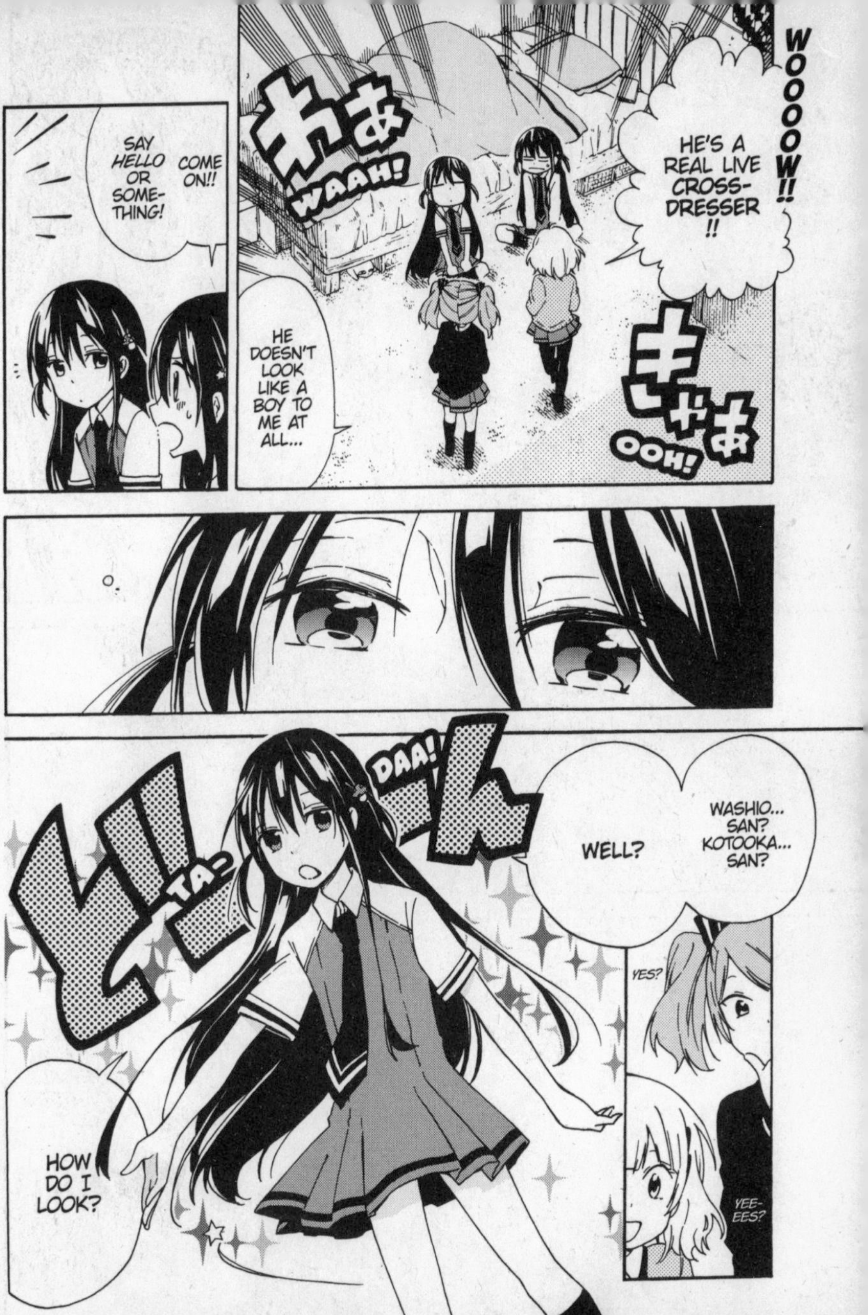
WOOOOOW!!
HE'S A REAL LIVE CROSS-DRESSER!!
わあ
WAAH!
きゃあ
OOH!
HE DOESN'T LOOK LIKE A BOY TO ME AT ALL...
COME ON!!
SAY HELLO OR SOMETHING!
WASHIO... SAN? KOTOOKA... SAN?
WELL?
ーん
DAA!
ど!!
TA-
YES?
YEEEES?
HOW DO I LOOK?

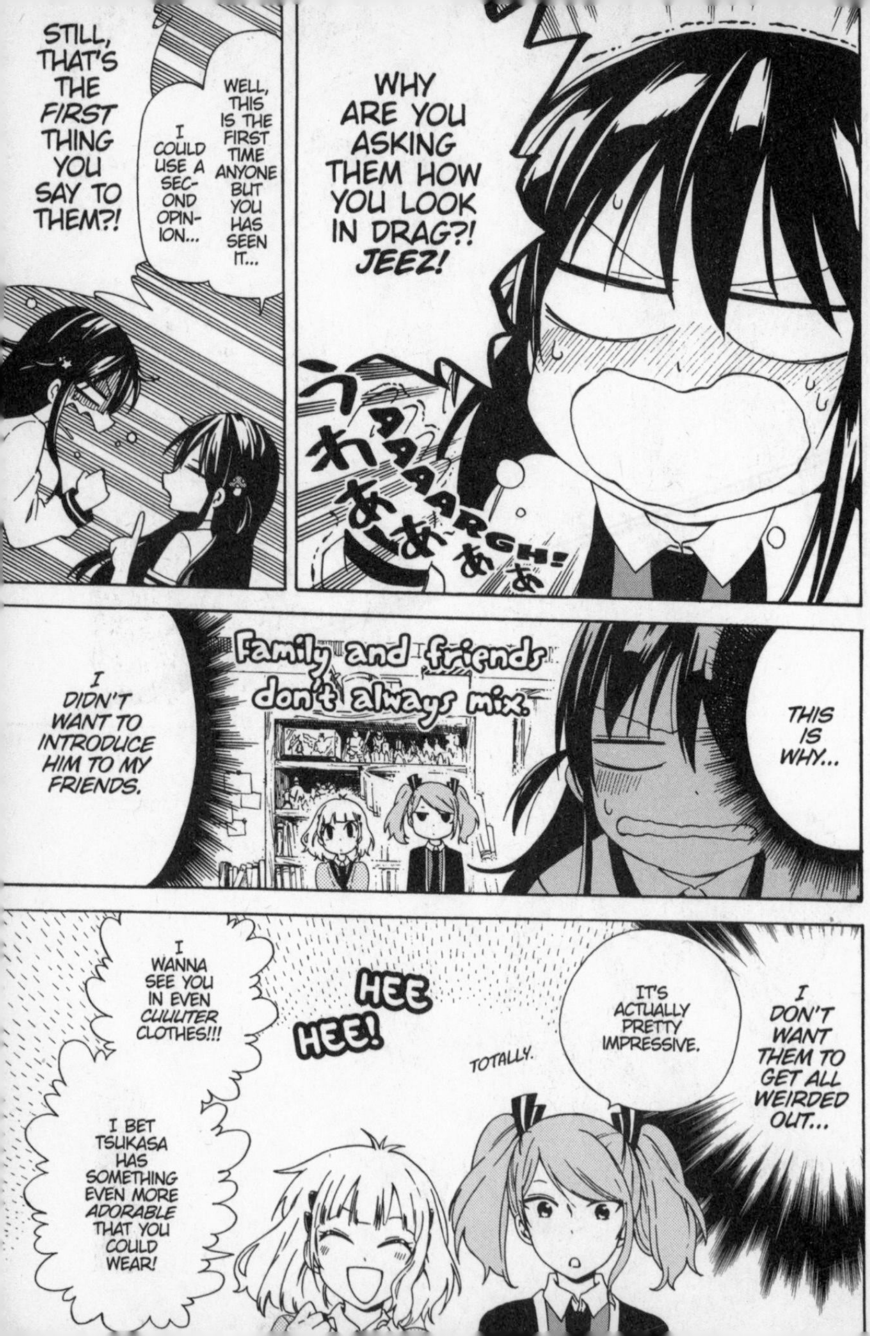
WHY ARE YOU ASKING THEM HOW YOU LOOK IN DRAG?! JEEZ!
AAAARGH!
WELL, THIS IS THE FIRST TIME ANYONE BUT YOU HAS SEEN IT...
I COULD USE A SECOND OPINION...
STILL, THAT'S THE FIRST THING YOU SAY TO THEM?!
THIS IS WHY...
Family and friends don't always mix.
I DIDN'T WANT TO INTRODUCE HIM TO MY FRIENDS.
I DON'T WANT THEM TO GET ALL WEIRDED OUT...
IT'S ACTUALLY PRETTY IMPRESSIVE.
TOTALLY.
HEE HEE!
I WANNA SEE YOU IN EVEN CUUUTER CLOTHES!!!
I BET TSUKASA HAS SOMETHING EVEN MORE ADORABLE THAT YOU COULD WEAR!

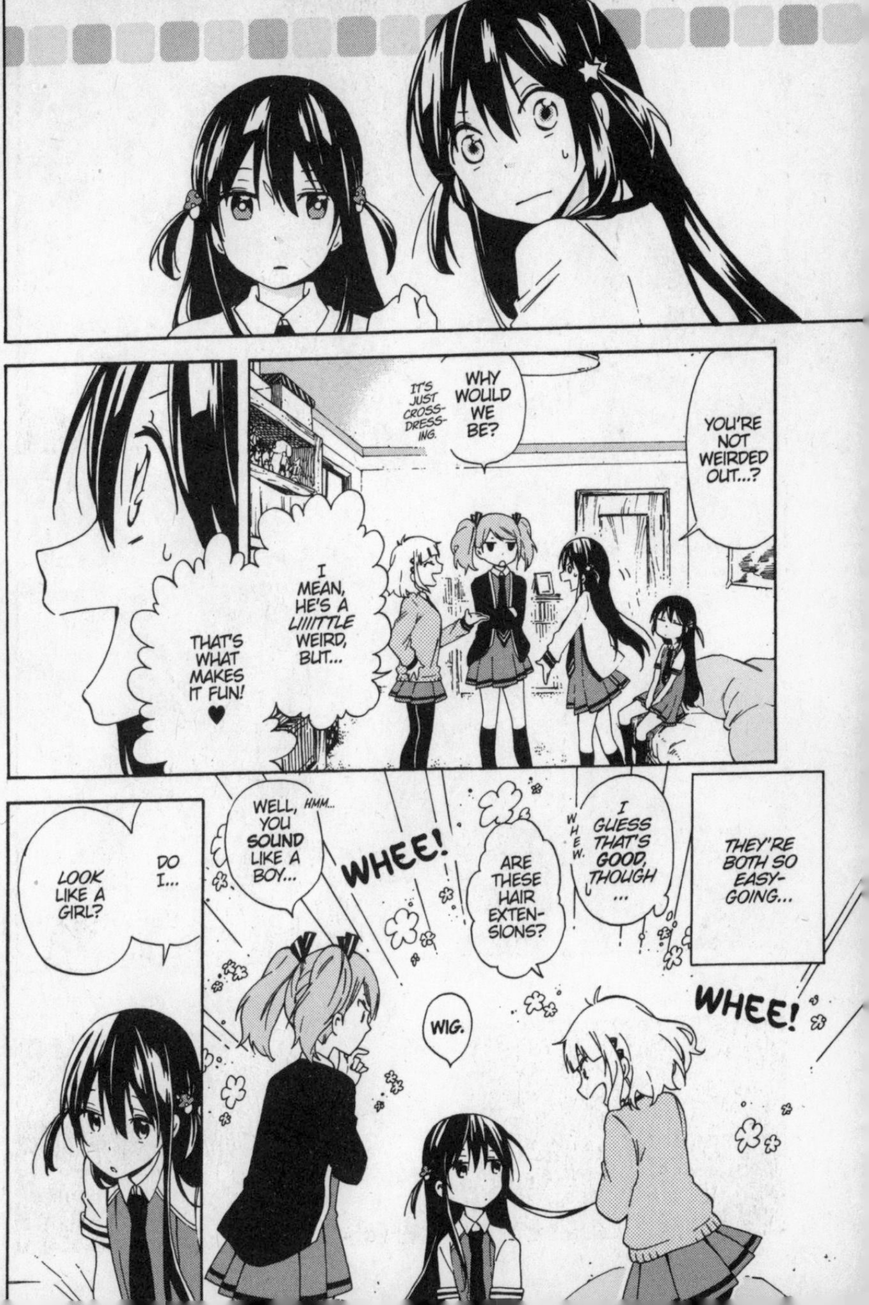
YOU'RE NOT WEIRDED OUT...?
WHY WOULD WE BE?
IT'S JUST CROSS-DRESSING.
I MEAN, HE'S A LIIIITTLE WEIRD, BUT...
THAT'S WHAT MAKES IT FUN! ♥
THEY'RE BOTH SO EASY-GOING...
I GUESS THAT'S GOOD, THOUGH...
WHEW.
WHEE!
ARE THESE HAIR EXTENSIONS?
WHEE!
WIG.
HMM...
WELL, YOU SOUND LIKE A BOY...
DO I...
LOOK LIKE A GIRL?

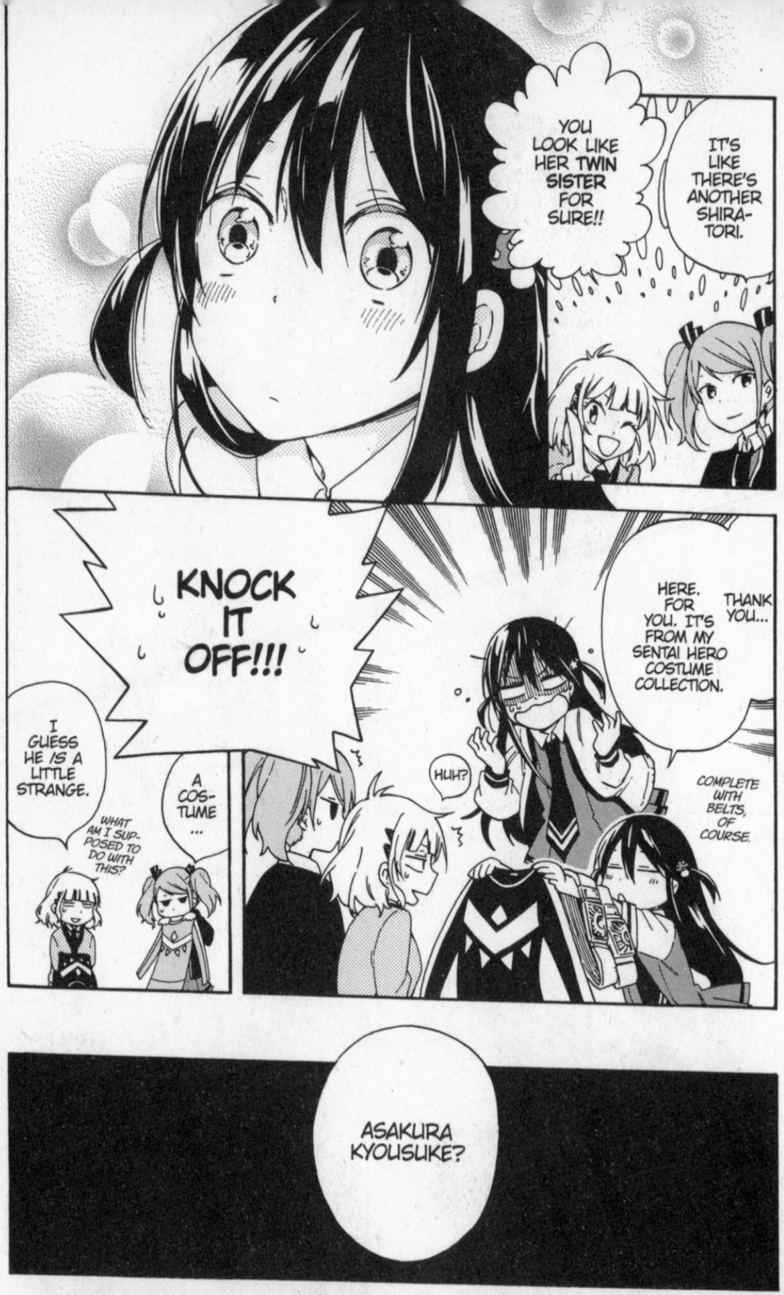
IT'S LIKE THERE'S ANOTHER SHIRATORI.
YOU LOOK LIKE HER TWIN SISTER FOR SURE!!
HERE. FOR YOU. IT'S FROM MY SENTAI HERO COSTUME COLLECTION.
THANK YOU...
COMPLETE WITH BELTS, OF COURSE.
HUH?
KNOCK IT OFF!!!
A COSTUME...
I GUESS HE IS A LITTLE STRANGE.
WHAT AM I SUPPOSED TO DO WITH THIS?
ASAKURA KYOUSUKE?

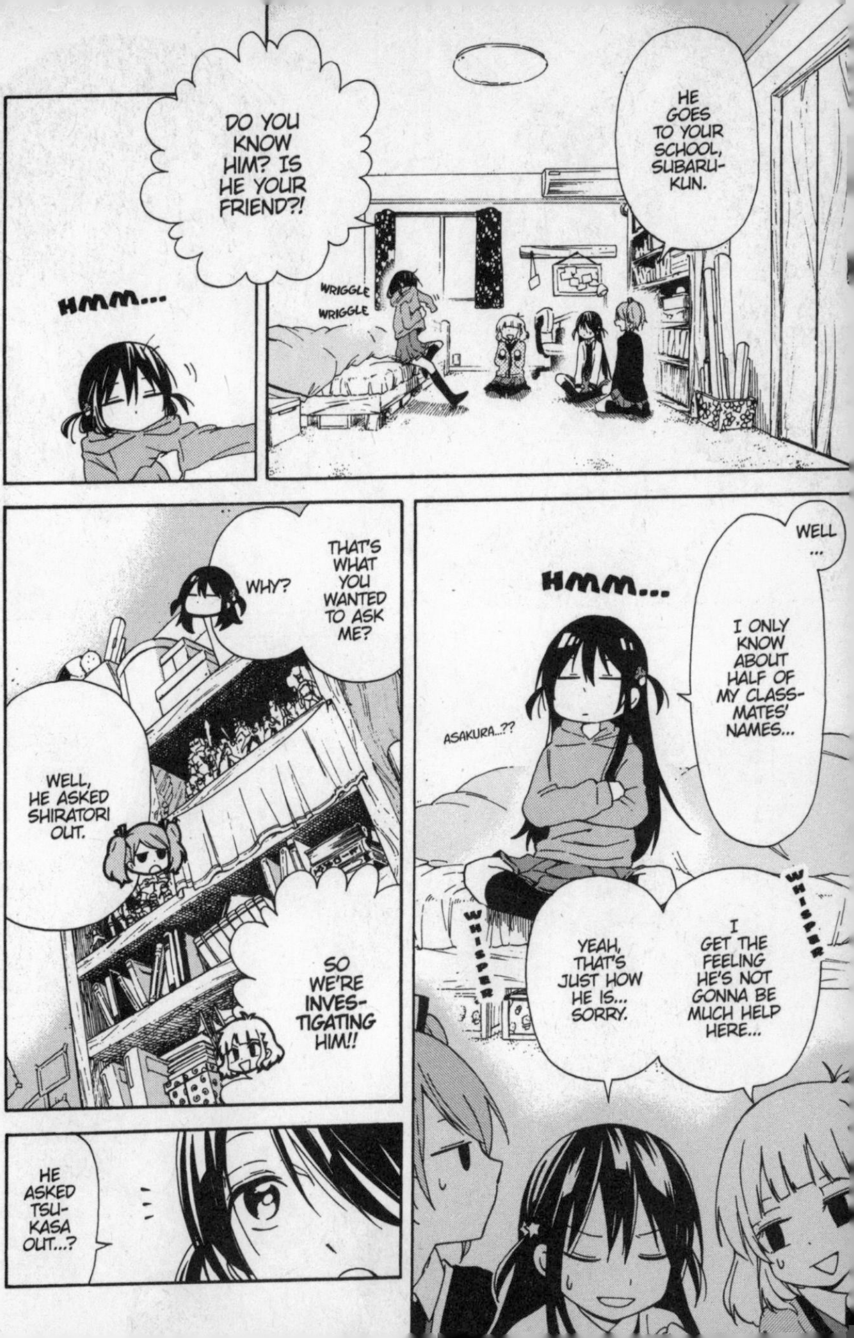
HE GOES TO YOUR SCHOOL, SUBARU-KUN.
DO YOU KNOW HIM? IS HE YOUR FRIEND?!
WRIGGLE WRIGGLE
HMM...
WELL ...
HMM...
I ONLY KNOW ABOUT HALF OF MY CLASS-MATES' NAMES...
ASAKURA...??
WHISPER
I GET THE FEELING HE'S NOT GONNA BE MUCH HELP HERE...
WHISPER
YEAH, THAT'S JUST HOW HE IS... SORRY.
WHY?
THAT'S WHAT YOU WANTED TO ASK ME?
WELL, HE ASKED SHIRATORI OUT.
SO WE'RE INVES-TIGATING HIM!!
HE ASKED TSU-KASA OUT...?

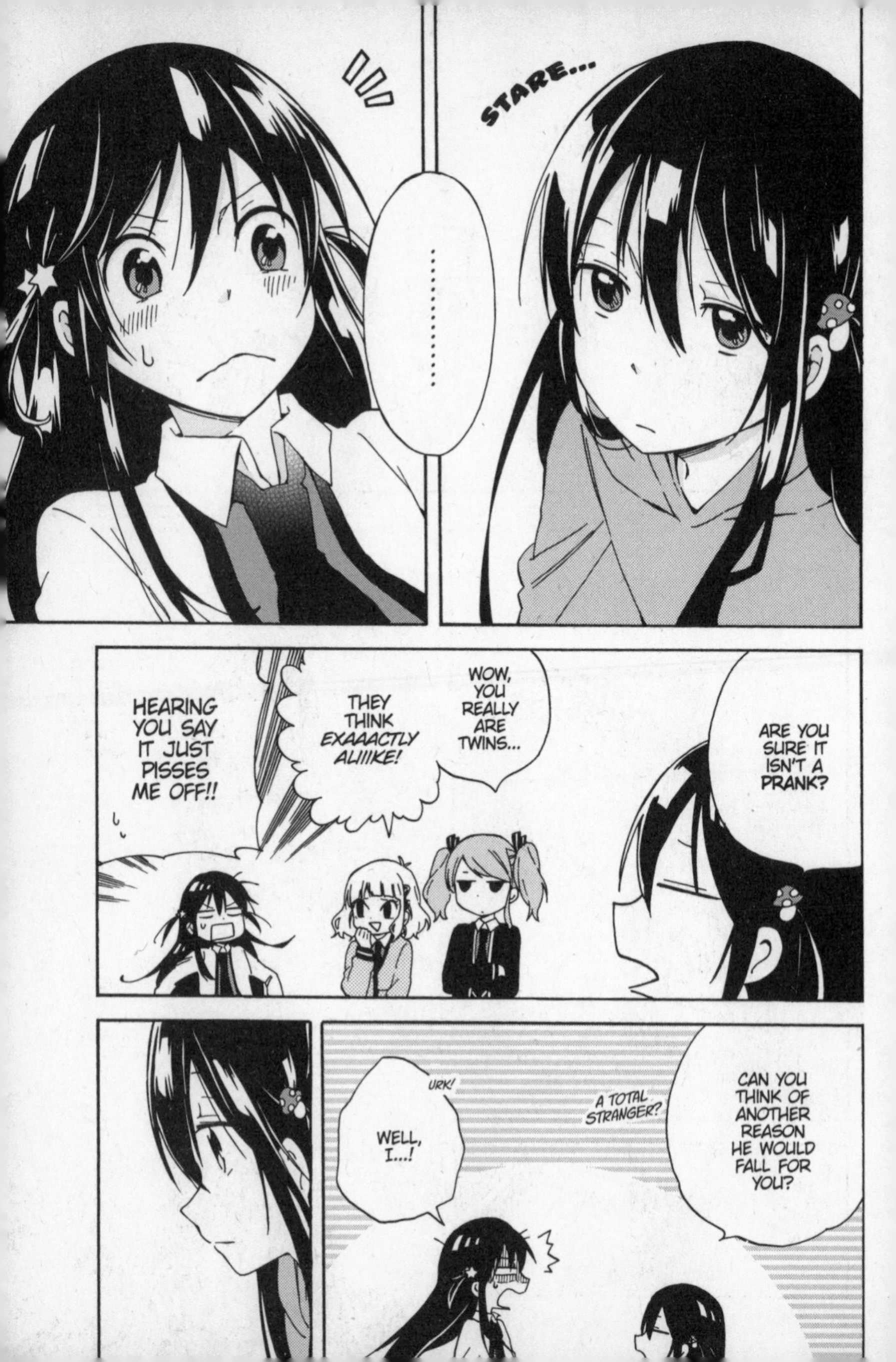
STARE...
......
ARE YOU SURE IT ISN'T A PRANK?
WOW, YOU REALLY ARE TWINS...
THEY THINK EXAAACTLY ALIIIKE!
HEARING YOU SAY IT JUST PISSES ME OFF!!
CAN YOU THINK OF ANOTHER REASON HE WOULD FALL FOR YOU?
A TOTAL STRANGER?
URK!
WELL, I...!

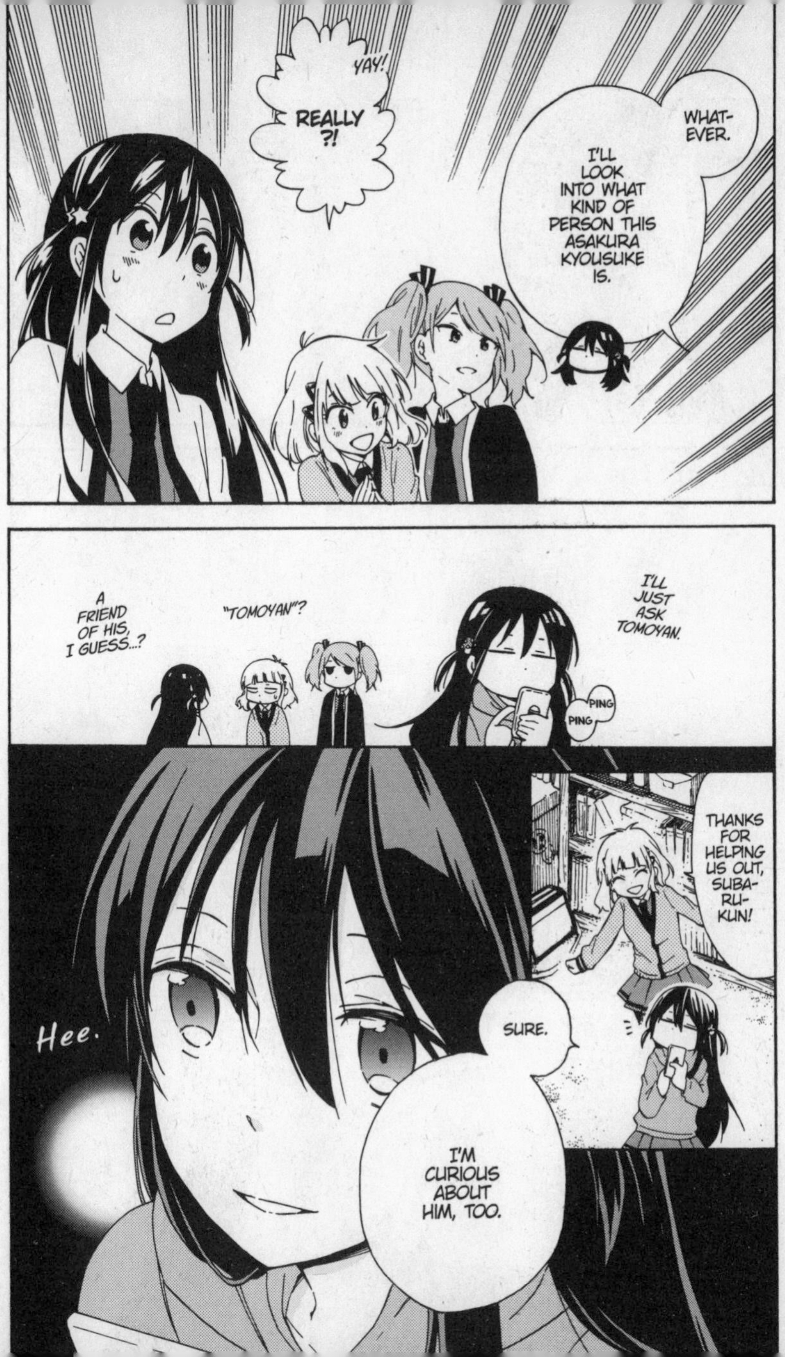
WHATEVER. I'LL LOOK INTO WHAT KIND OF PERSON THIS ASAKURA KYOUSUKE IS.
YAY!
REALLY?!
I'LL JUST ASK TOMOYAN.
PING
PING
"TOMOYAN"?
A FRIEND OF HIS, I GUESS...?
THANKS FOR HELPING US OUT, SUBARU-KUN!
SURE.
I'M CURIOUS ABOUT HIM, TOO.
Hee.

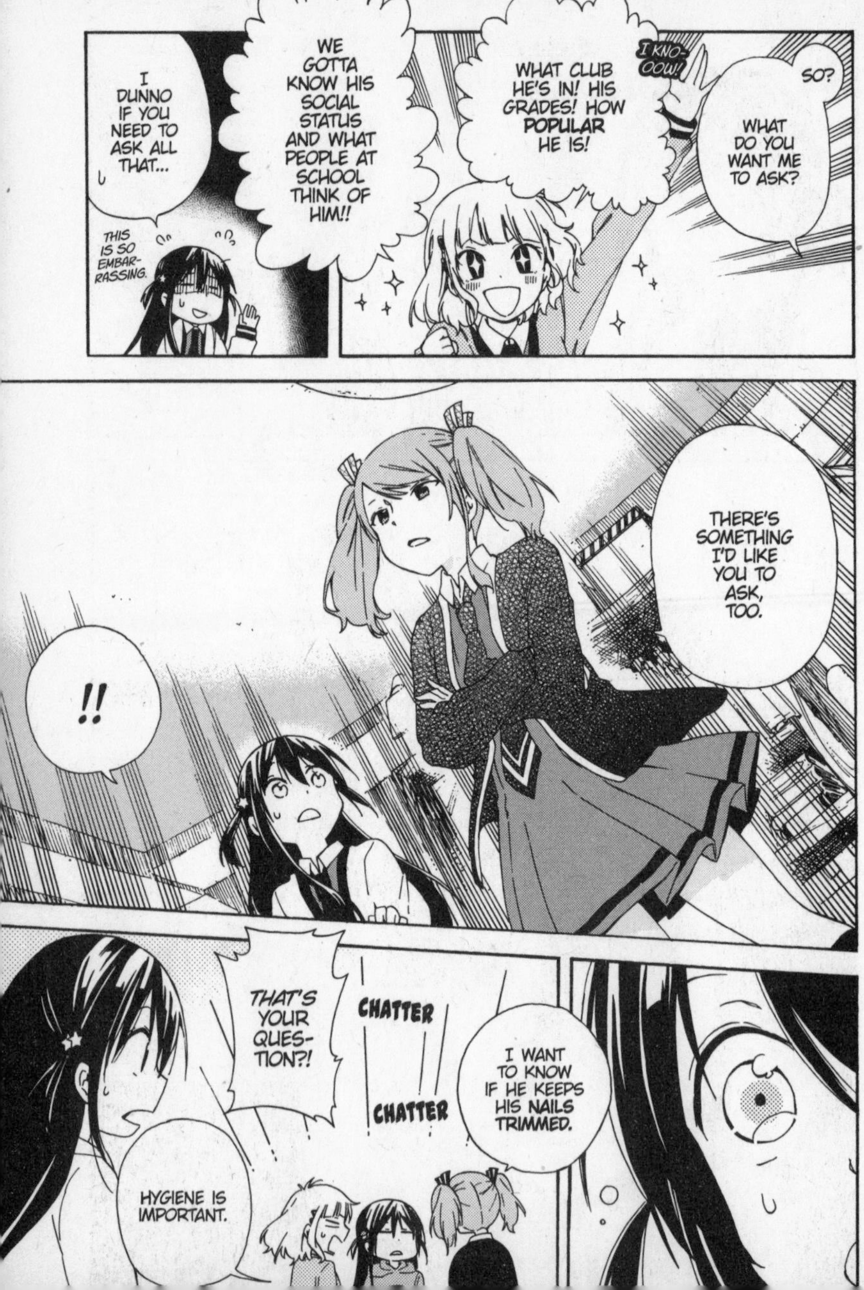
SO?
WHAT DO YOU WANT ME TO ASK?
I KNO-OOW!!
WHAT CLUB HE'S IN! HIS GRADES! HOW POPULAR HE IS!
WE GOTTA KNOW HIS SOCIAL STATUS AND WHAT PEOPLE AT SCHOOL THINK OF HIM!!
I DUNNO IF YOU NEED TO ASK ALL THAT...
THIS IS SO EMBARRASSING.
THERE'S SOMETHING I'D LIKE YOU TO ASK, TOO.
!!
I WANT TO KNOW IF HE KEEPS HIS NAILS TRIMMED.
CHATTER
CHATTER
THAT'S YOUR QUESTION?!
HYGIENE IS IMPORTANT.

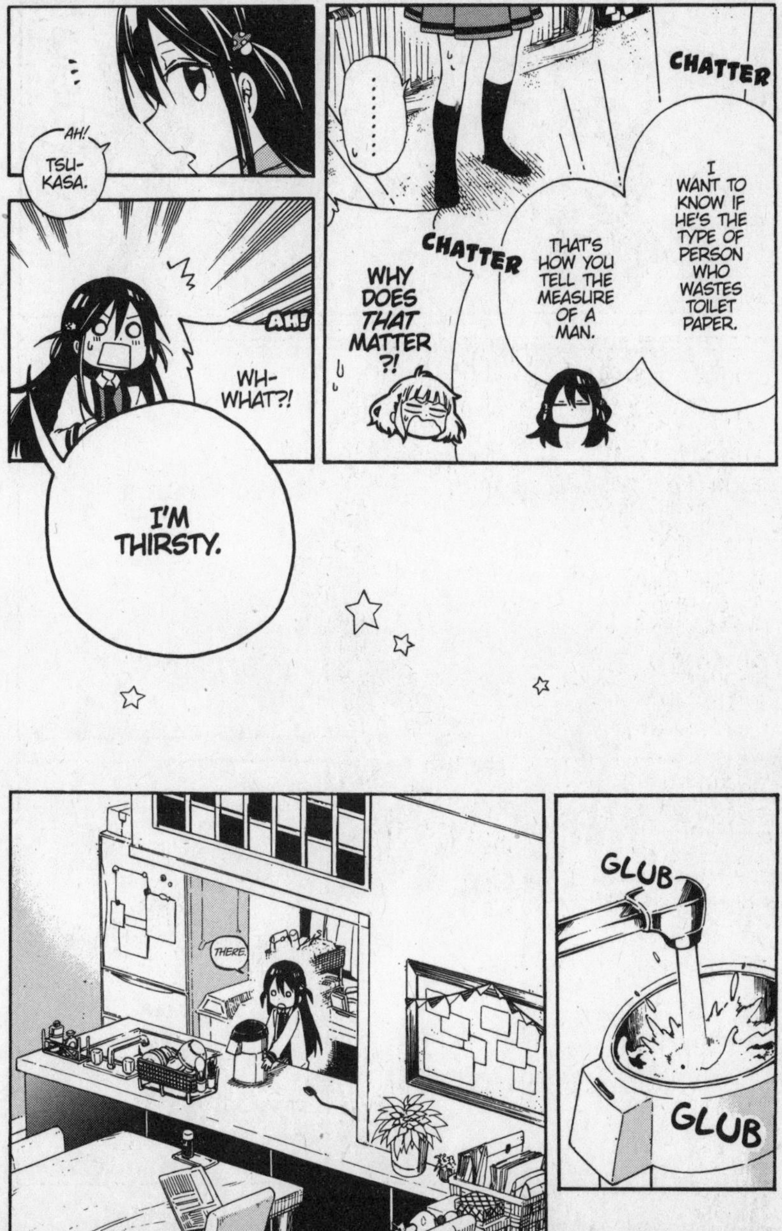
CHATTER
I WANT TO KNOW IF HE'S THE TYPE OF PERSON WHO WASTES TOILET PAPER.
THAT'S HOW YOU TELL THE MEASURE OF A MAN.
CHATTER
WHY DOES *THAT* MATTER?!
......
AH! TSU-KASA.
AH!
WH-WHAT?!
I'M THIRSTY.
GLUB
GLUB
THERE.

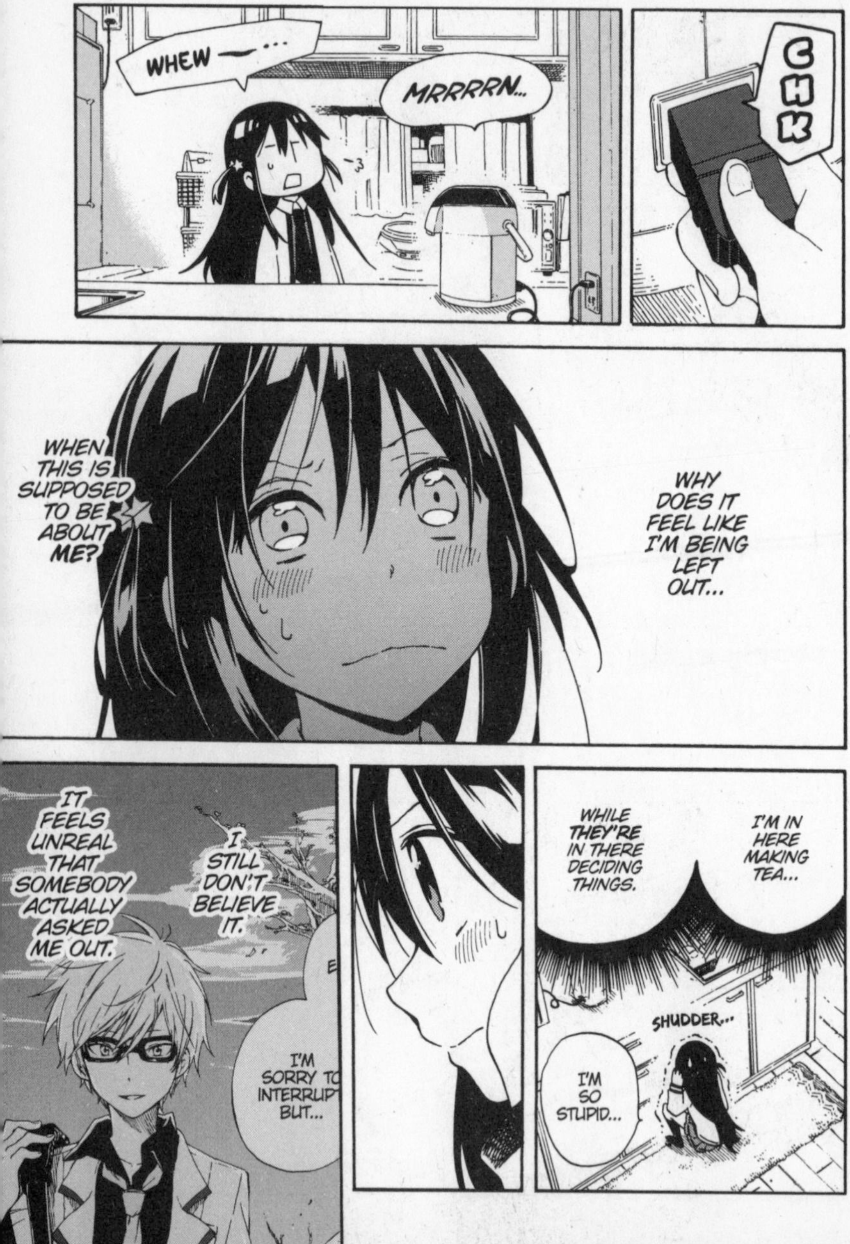
CHK
WHEW—...
MRRRRN...
WHY DOES IT FEEL LIKE I'M BEING LEFT OUT...
WHEN THIS IS SUPPOSED TO BE ABOUT ME?
I'M IN HERE MAKING TEA...
WHILE THEY'RE IN THERE DECIDING THINGS.
SHUDDER...
I'M SO STUPID...
I STILL DON'T BELIEVE IT.
IT FEELS UNREAL THAT SOMEBODY ACTUALLY ASKED ME OUT.
I'M SORRY TO INTERRUP BUT...

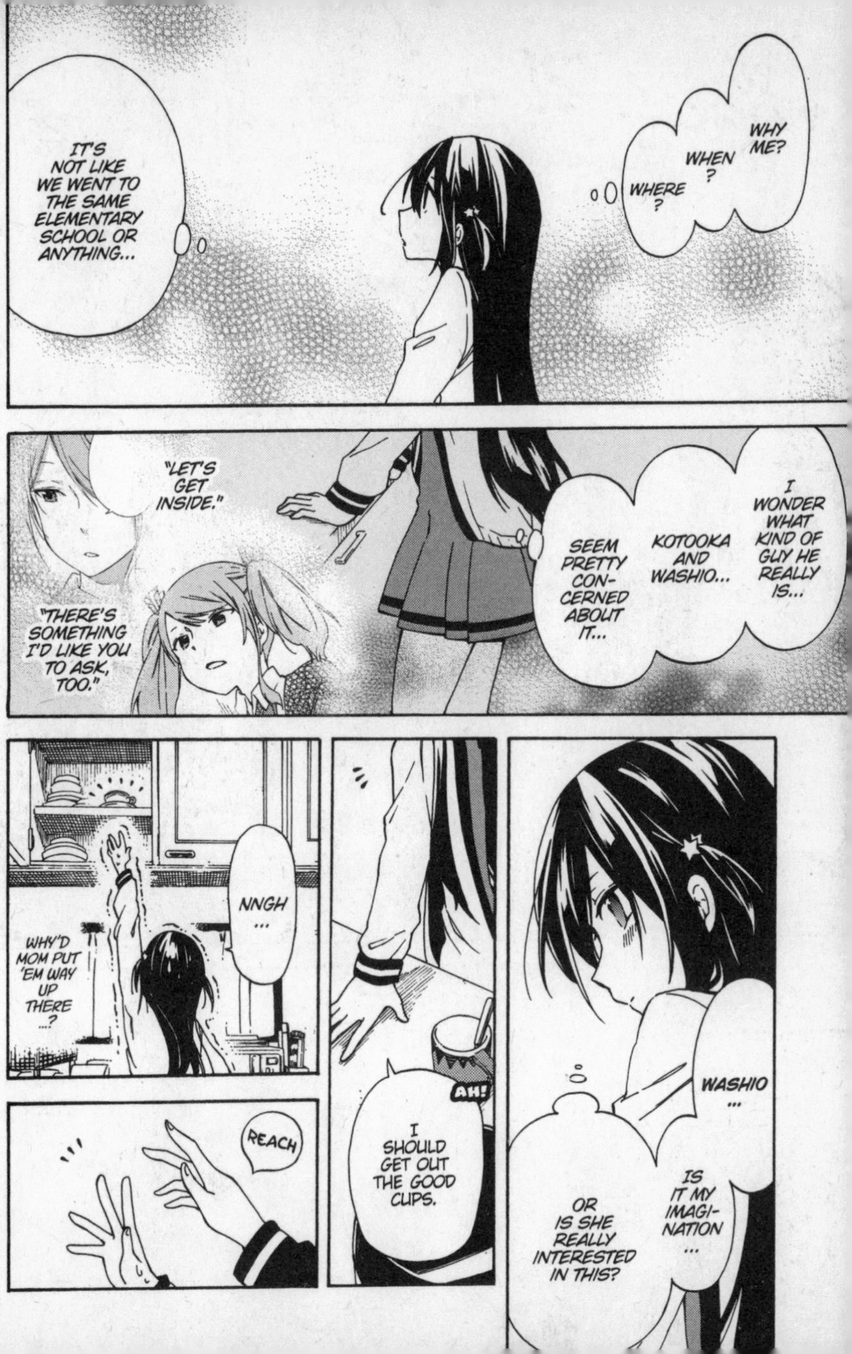

WHY ME?
WHEN?
WHERE?
IT'S NOT LIKE WE WENT TO THE SAME ELEMENTARY SCHOOL OR ANYTHING...
I WONDER WHAT KIND OF GUY HE REALLY IS...
KOTOOKA AND WASHIO...
SEEM PRETTY CON-CERNED ABOUT IT...
"LET'S GET INSIDE."
"THERE'S SOMETHING I'D LIKE YOU TO ASK, TOO."
WASHIO...
IS IT MY IMAGI-NATION...
OR IS SHE REALLY INTERESTED IN THIS?
AH!
I SHOULD GET OUT THE GOOD CUPS.
NNGH...
WHY'D MOM PUT 'EM WAY UP THERE...?
REACH

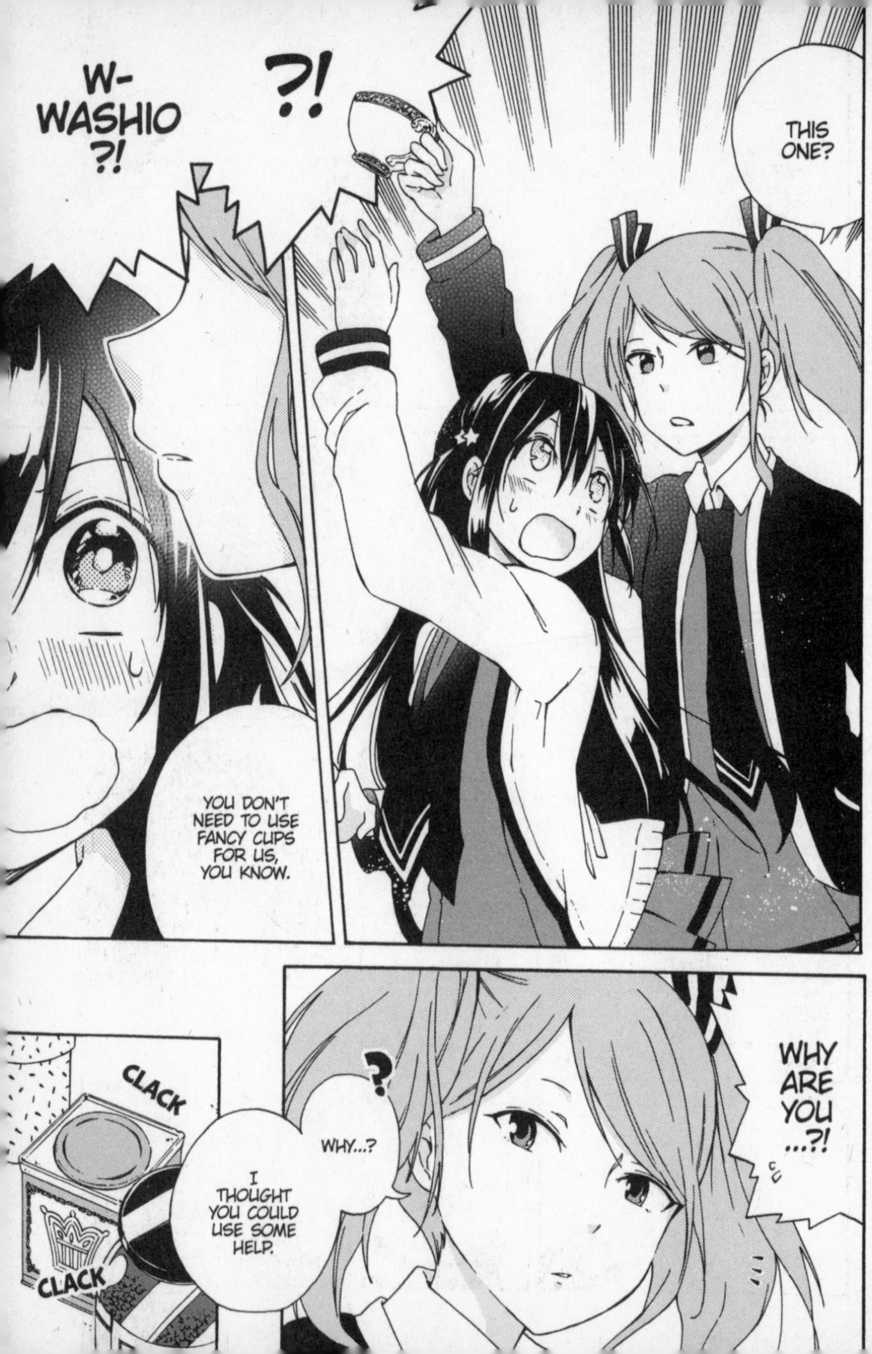
THIS ONE?
?!
W-WASHIO ?!
YOU DON'T NEED TO USE FANCY CUPS FOR US, YOU KNOW.
WHY ARE YOU ...?!
?
WHY...?
I THOUGHT YOU COULD USE SOME HELP.
CLACK
CLACK

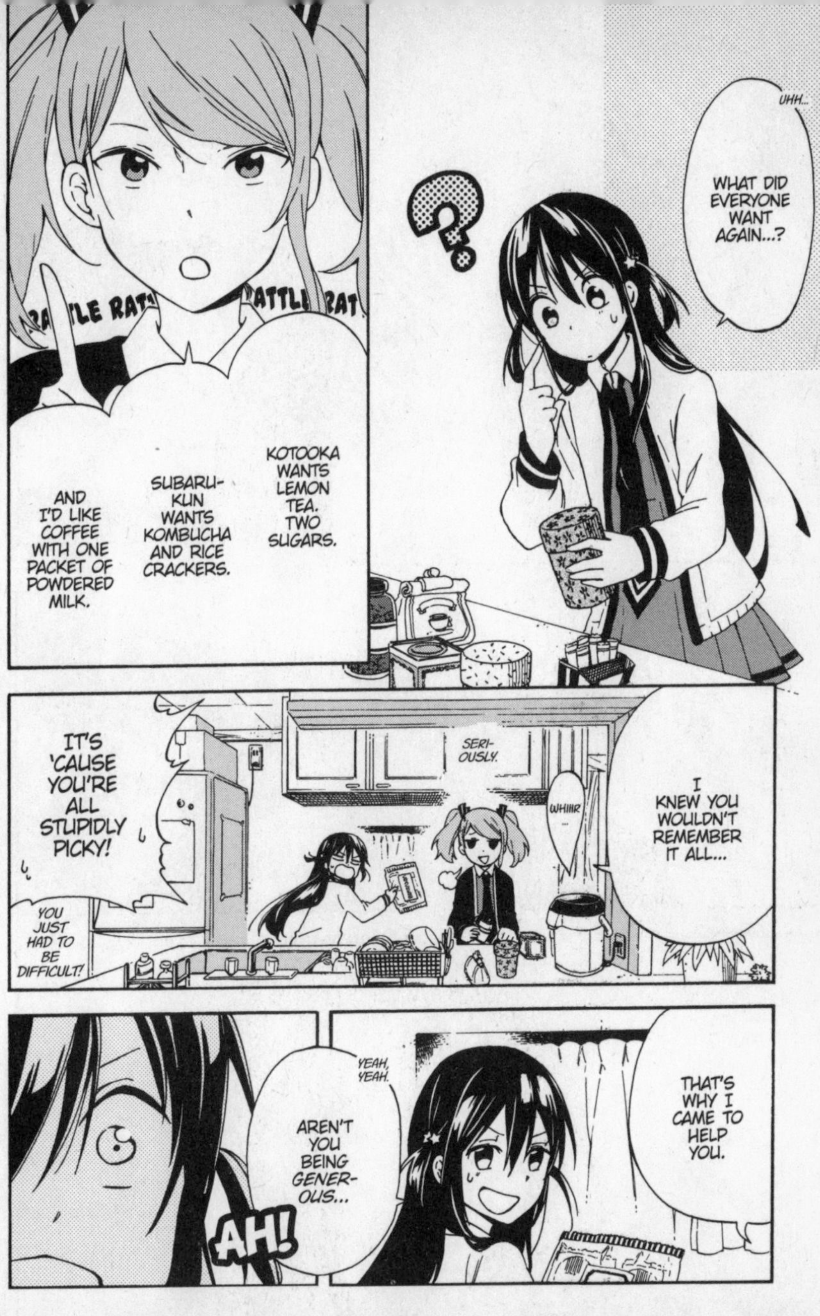
UHH...
WHAT DID EVERYONE WANT AGAIN...?
RATTLE RAT
RATTLE RAT
KOTOOKA WANTS LEMON TEA. TWO SUGARS.
SUBARU-KUN WANTS KOMBUCHA AND RICE CRACKERS.
AND I'D LIKE COFFEE WITH ONE PACKET OF POWDERED MILK.
I KNEW YOU WOULDN'T REMEMBER IT ALL...
WHIIIR...
SERI-OUSLY.
IT'S 'CAUSE YOU'RE ALL STUPIDLY PICKY!
YOU JUST HAD TO BE DIFFICULT!
THAT'S WHY I CAME TO HELP YOU.
YEAH, YEAH.
AREN'T YOU BEING GENER-OUS...
AH!

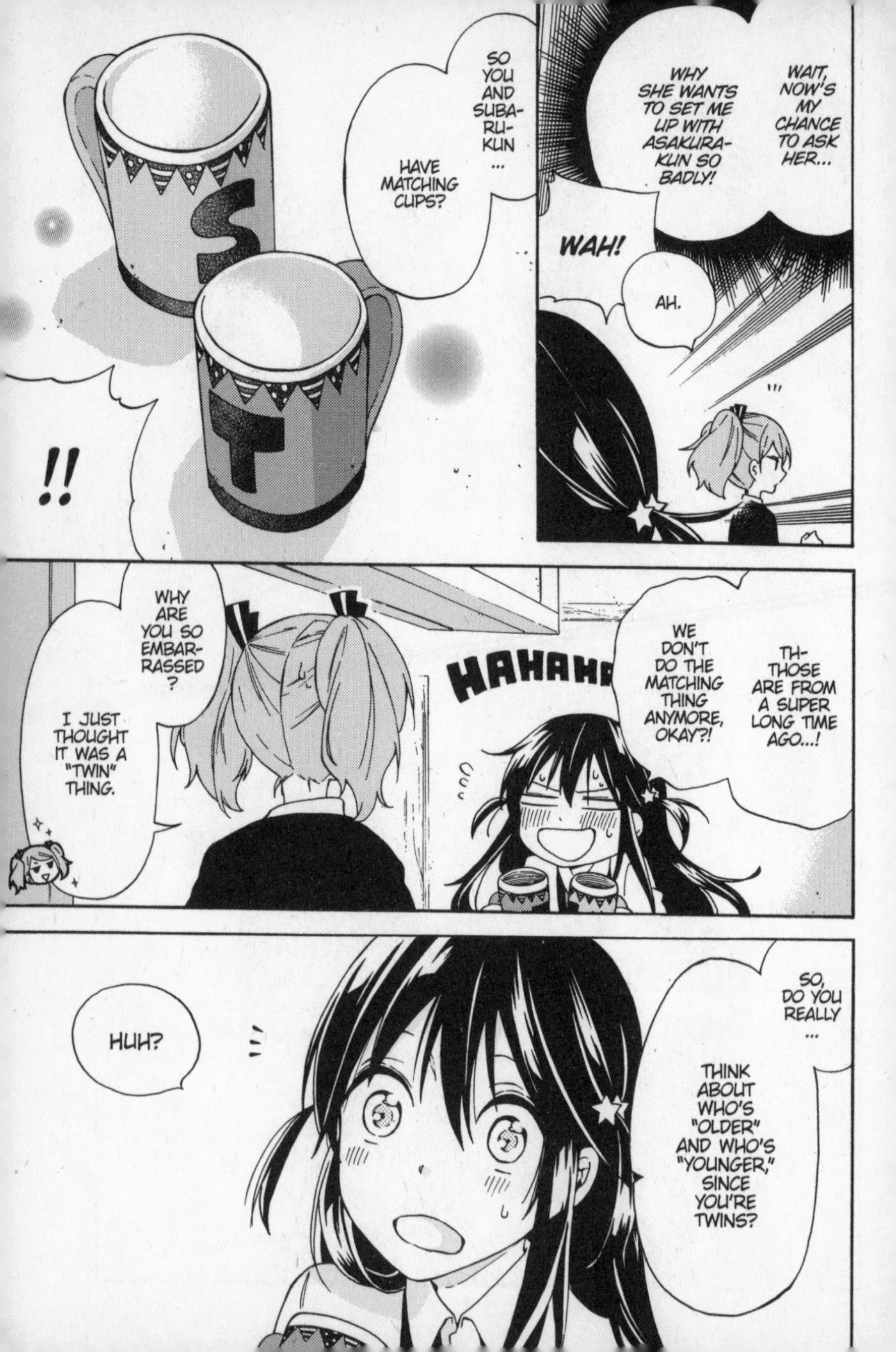
WAIT, NOW'S MY CHANCE TO ASK HER...
WHY SHE WANTS TO SET ME UP WITH ASAKURA-KUN SO BADLY!
WAH!
AH.
SO YOU AND SUBARU-KUN ...
HAVE MATCHING CUPS?
!!
TH-THOSE ARE FROM A SUPER LONG TIME AGO...!
WE DON'T DO THE MATCHING THING ANYMORE, OKAY?!
HAHAH
WHY ARE YOU SO EMBARRASSED?
I JUST THOUGHT IT WAS A "TWIN" THING.
SO, DO YOU REALLY ...
THINK ABOUT WHO'S "OLDER" AND WHO'S "YOUNGER," SINCE YOU'RE TWINS?
HUH?

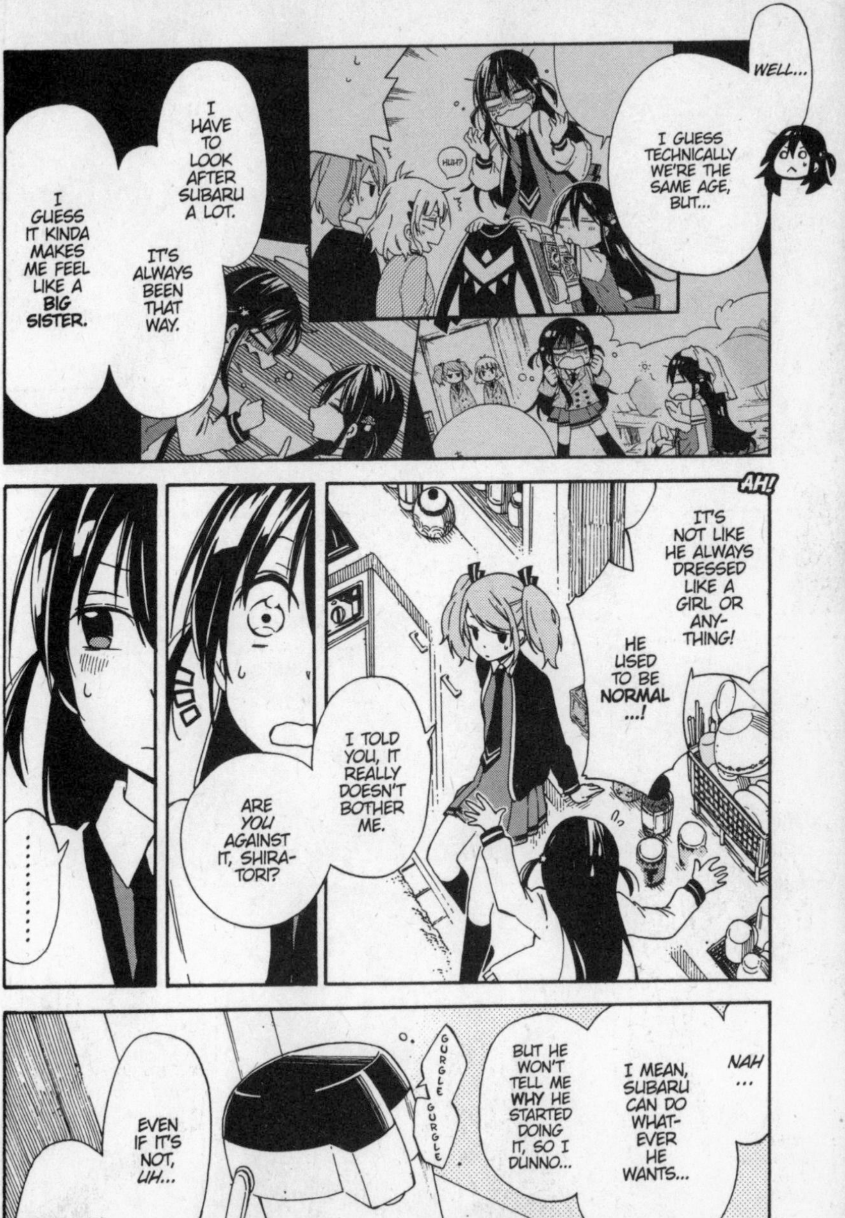
WELL...
I GUESS TECHNICALLY WE'RE THE SAME AGE, BUT...
HUH?
I HAVE TO LOOK AFTER SUBARU A LOT.
IT'S ALWAYS BEEN THAT WAY.
I GUESS IT KINDA MAKES ME FEEL LIKE A BIG SISTER.
AH!
IT'S NOT LIKE HE ALWAYS DRESSED LIKE A GIRL OR ANYTHING!
HE USED TO BE NORMAL...!
I TOLD YOU, IT REALLY DOESN'T BOTHER ME.
ARE YOU AGAINST IT, SHIRATORI?
....
NAH...
I MEAN, SUBARU CAN DO WHATEVER HE WANTS...
BUT HE WON'T TELL ME WHY HE STARTED DOING IT, SO I DUNNO...
GURGLE GURGLE
EVEN IF IT'S NOT, UH...
"NORMAL"...

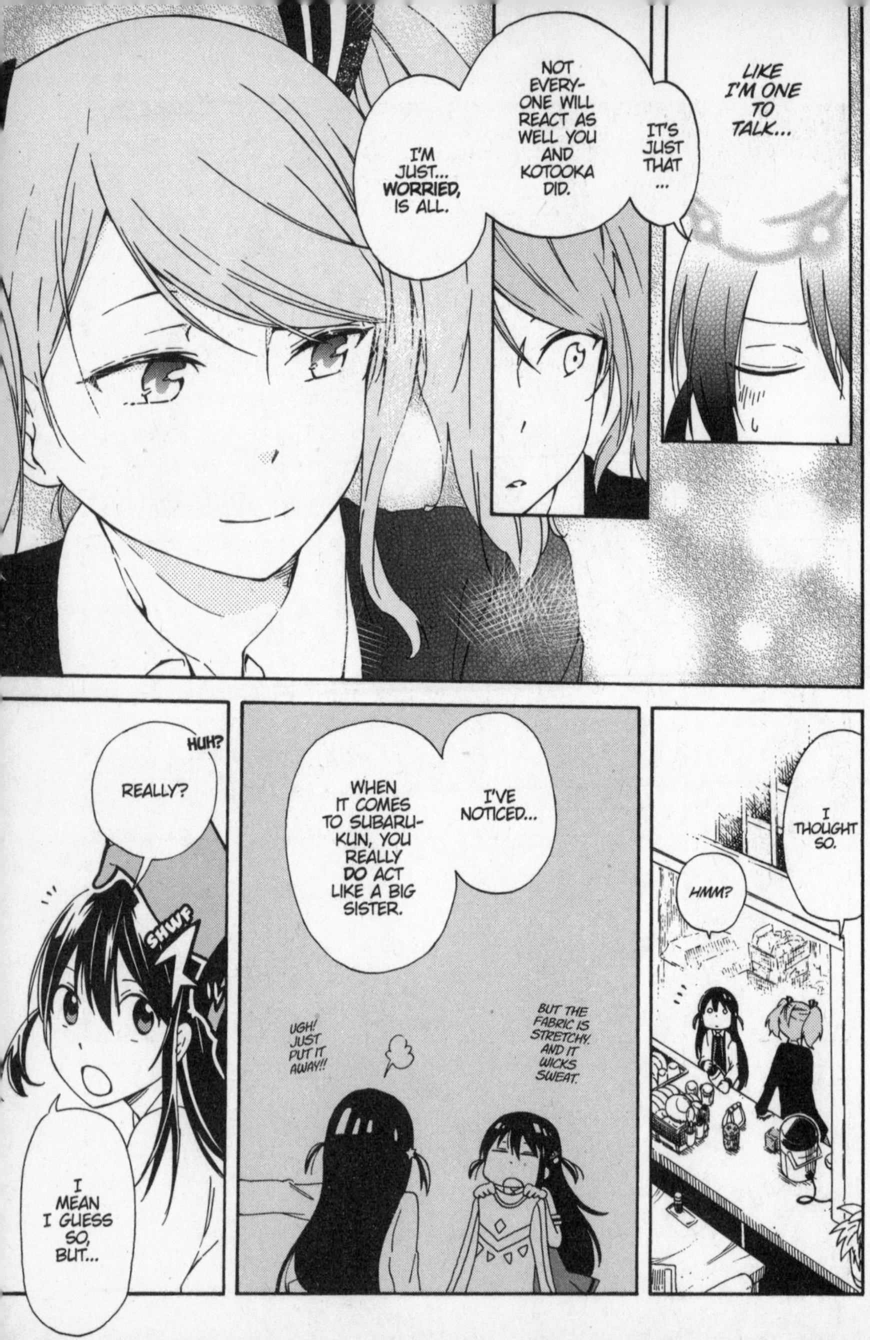
LIKE I'M ONE TO TALK...
IT'S JUST THAT...
NOT EVERY-ONE WILL REACT AS WELL YOU AND KOTOOKA DID.
I'M JUST... WORRIED, IS ALL.
I THOUGHT SO.
HMM?
I'VE NOTICED...
WHEN IT COMES TO SUBARU-KUN, YOU REALLY DO ACT LIKE A BIG SISTER.
BUT THE FABRIC IS STRETCHY. AND IT WICKS SWEAT.
UGH! JUST PUT IT AWAY!!
HUH?
REALLY?
SHWF
I MEAN I GUESS SO, BUT...

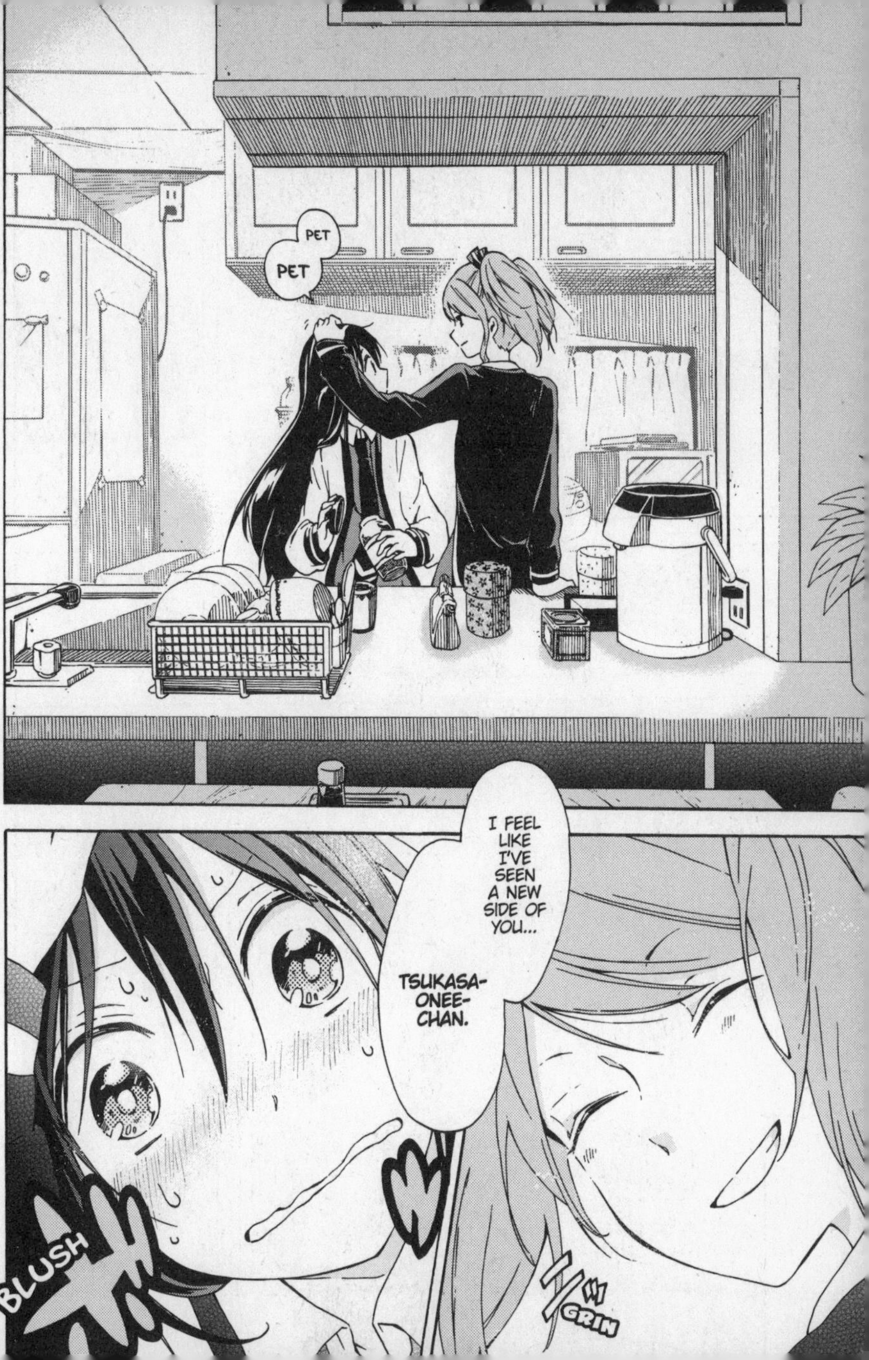
PET
PET
I FEEL LIKE I'VE SEEN A NEW SIDE OF YOU...
TSUKASA-ONEE-CHAN.
GRIN
BLUSH

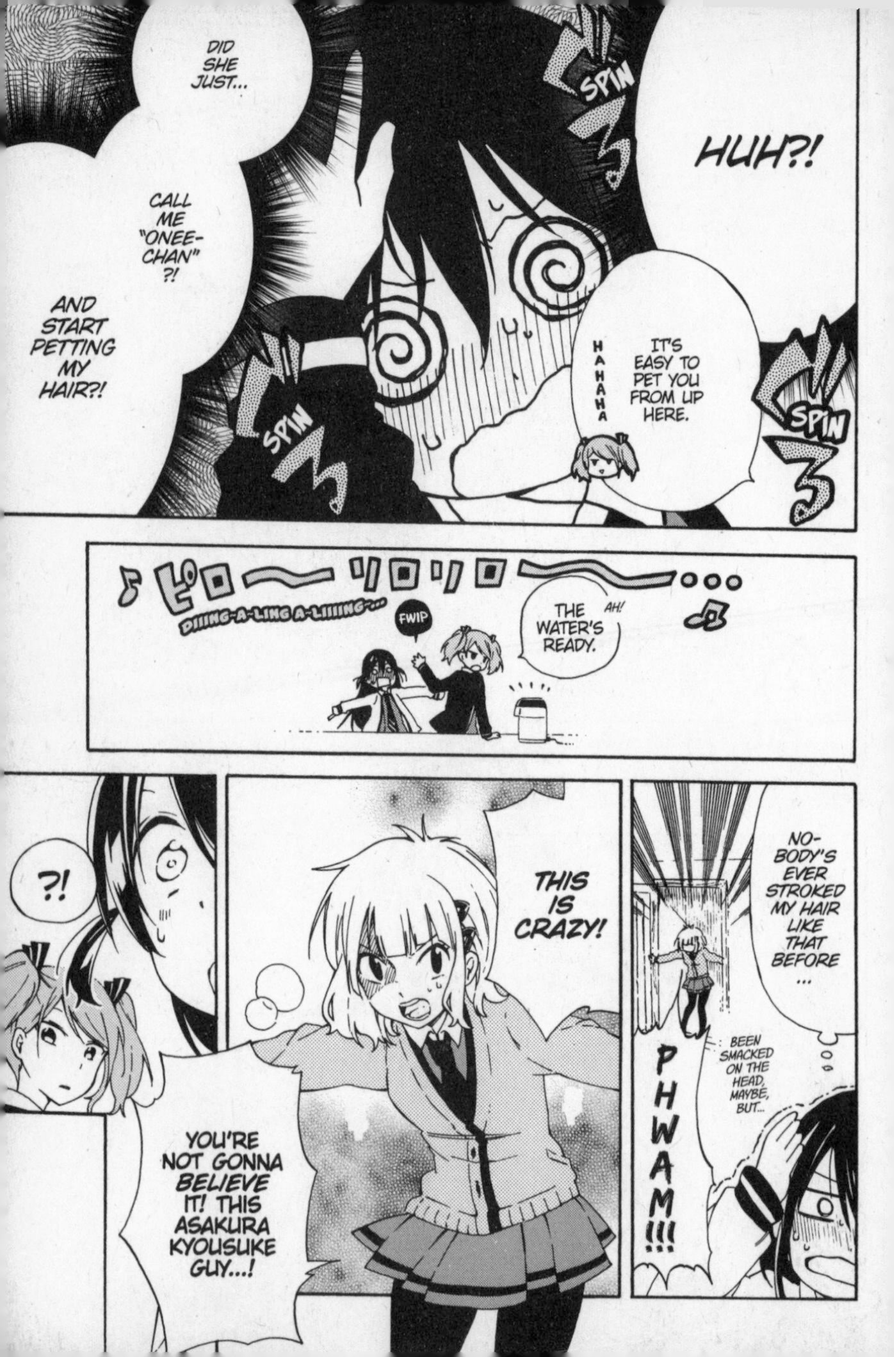
SPIN
HUH?!
SPIN
IT'S EASY TO PET YOU FROM UP HERE.
HAHAHA
DID SHE JUST...
CALL ME "ONEE-CHAN" ?!
AND START PETTING MY HAIR?!
SPIN
♪ピロ〜〜リロリロ〜〜〜…♫
DIIING-A-LING A-LIIIING~...
AH!
THE WATER'S READY.
FWIP
NO-BODY'S EVER STROKED MY HAIR LIKE THAT BEFORE...
BEEN SMACKED ON THE HEAD, MAYBE, BUT...
PHWAM!!!
THIS IS CRAZY!
YOU'RE NOT GONNA BELIEVE IT! THIS ASAKURA KYOUSUKE GUY...!
?!

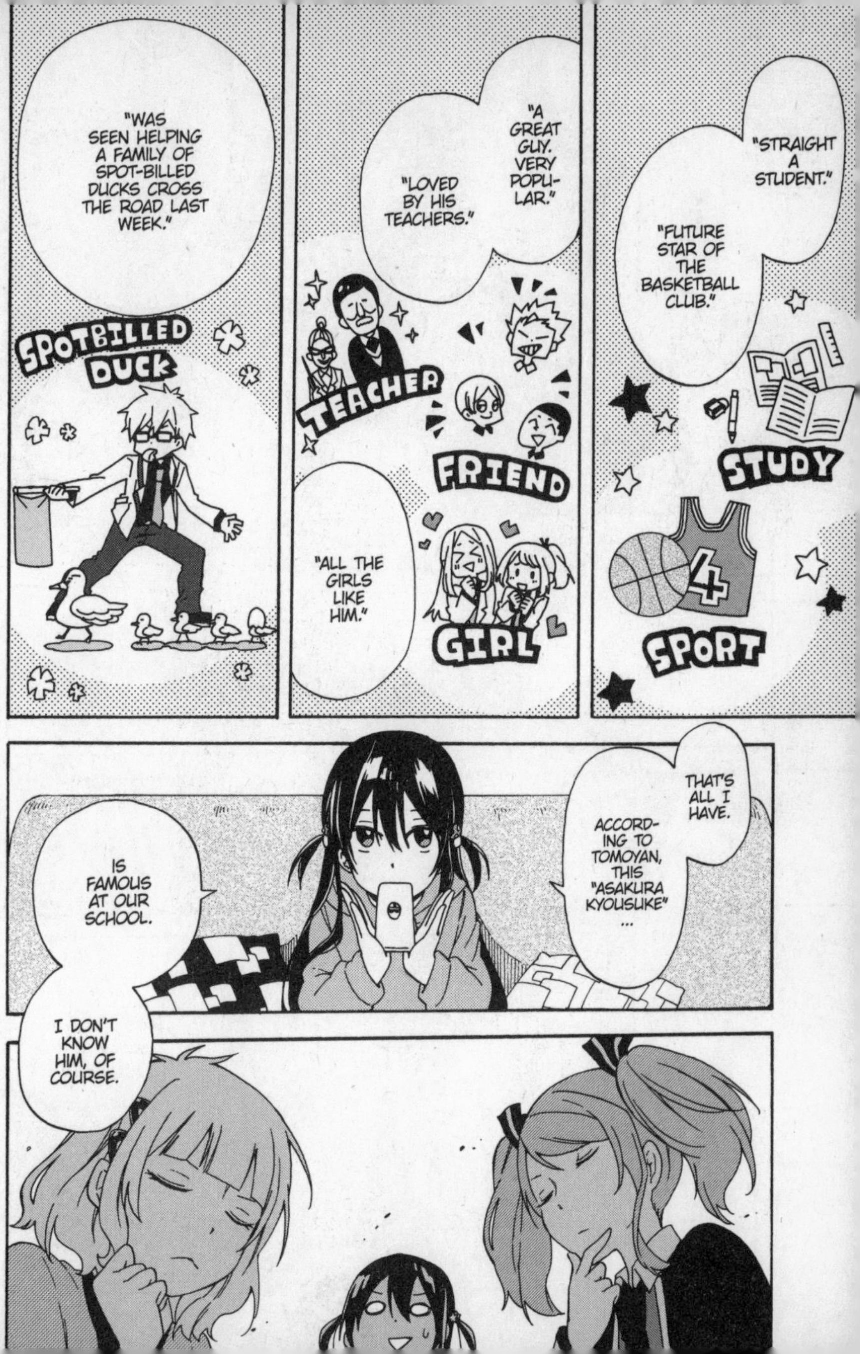
"STRAIGHT A STUDENT."
"FUTURE STAR OF THE BASKETBALL CLUB."
STUDY
SPORT
"A GREAT GUY. VERY POPULAR."
"LOVED BY HIS TEACHERS."
TEACHER
FRIEND
"ALL THE GIRLS LIKE HIM."
GIRL
"WAS SEEN HELPING A FAMILY OF SPOT-BILLED DUCKS CROSS THE ROAD LAST WEEK."
SPOTBILLED DUCK
THAT'S ALL I HAVE.
ACCORDING TO TOMOYAN, THIS "ASAKURA KYOUSUKE" ...
IS FAMOUS AT OUR SCHOOL.
I DON'T KNOW HIM, OF COURSE.

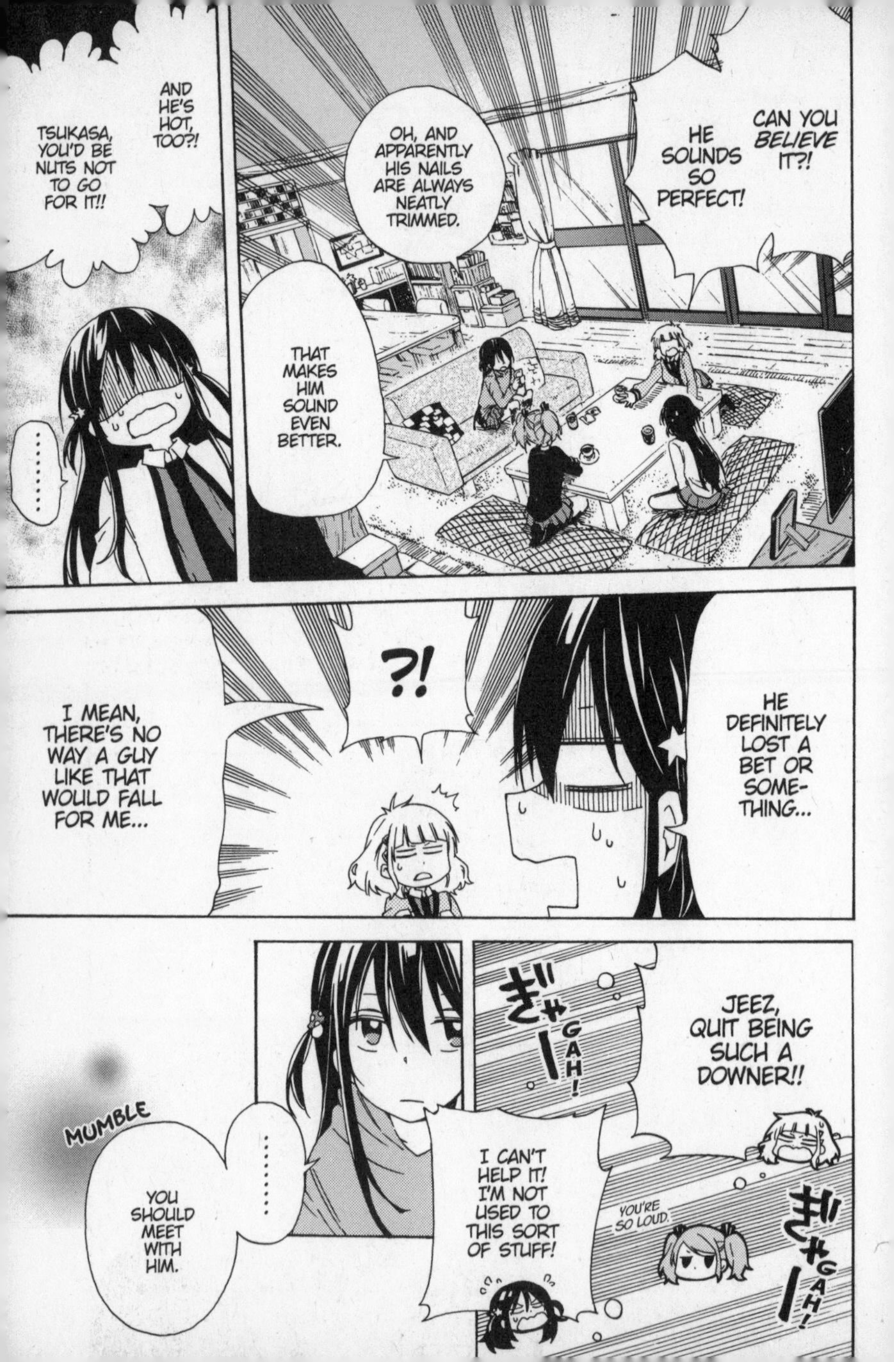
CAN YOU BELIEVE IT?!
HE SOUNDS SO PERFECT!
OH, AND APPARENTLY HIS NAILS ARE ALWAYS NEATLY TRIMMED.
THAT MAKES HIM SOUND EVEN BETTER.
AND HE'S HOT, TOO?!
TSUKASA, YOU'D BE NUTS NOT TO GO FOR IT!!
......
HE DEFINITELY LOST A BET OR SOME-THING...
?!
I MEAN, THERE'S NO WAY A GUY LIKE THAT WOULD FALL FOR ME...
JEEZ, QUIT BEING SUCH A DOWNER!!
ぎゃー GAH!
I CAN'T HELP IT! I'M NOT USED TO THIS SORT OF STUFF!
YOU'RE SO LOUD.
ぎゃー GAH!
......
MUMBLE
YOU SHOULD MEET WITH HIM.

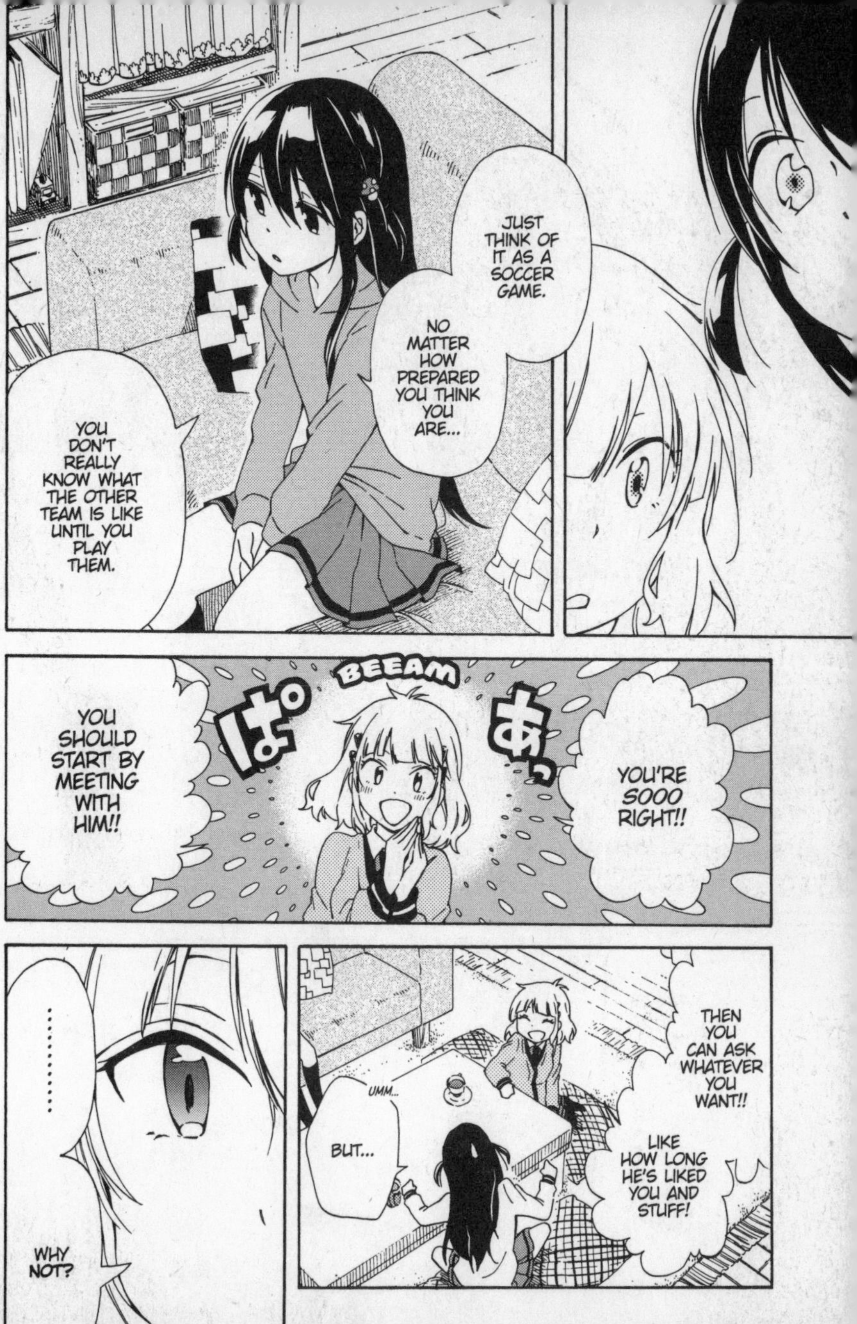
JUST THINK OF IT AS A SOCCER GAME.
NO MATTER HOW PREPARED YOU THINK YOU ARE...
YOU DON'T REALLY KNOW WHAT THE OTHER TEAM IS LIKE UNTIL YOU PLAY THEM.
BEEAM
ぱあっ
YOU'RE SOOO RIGHT!!
YOU SHOULD START BY MEETING WITH HIM!!
THEN YOU CAN ASK WHATEVER YOU WANT!!
LIKE HOW LONG HE'S LIKED YOU AND STUFF!
UMM...
BUT...
......
WHY NOT?

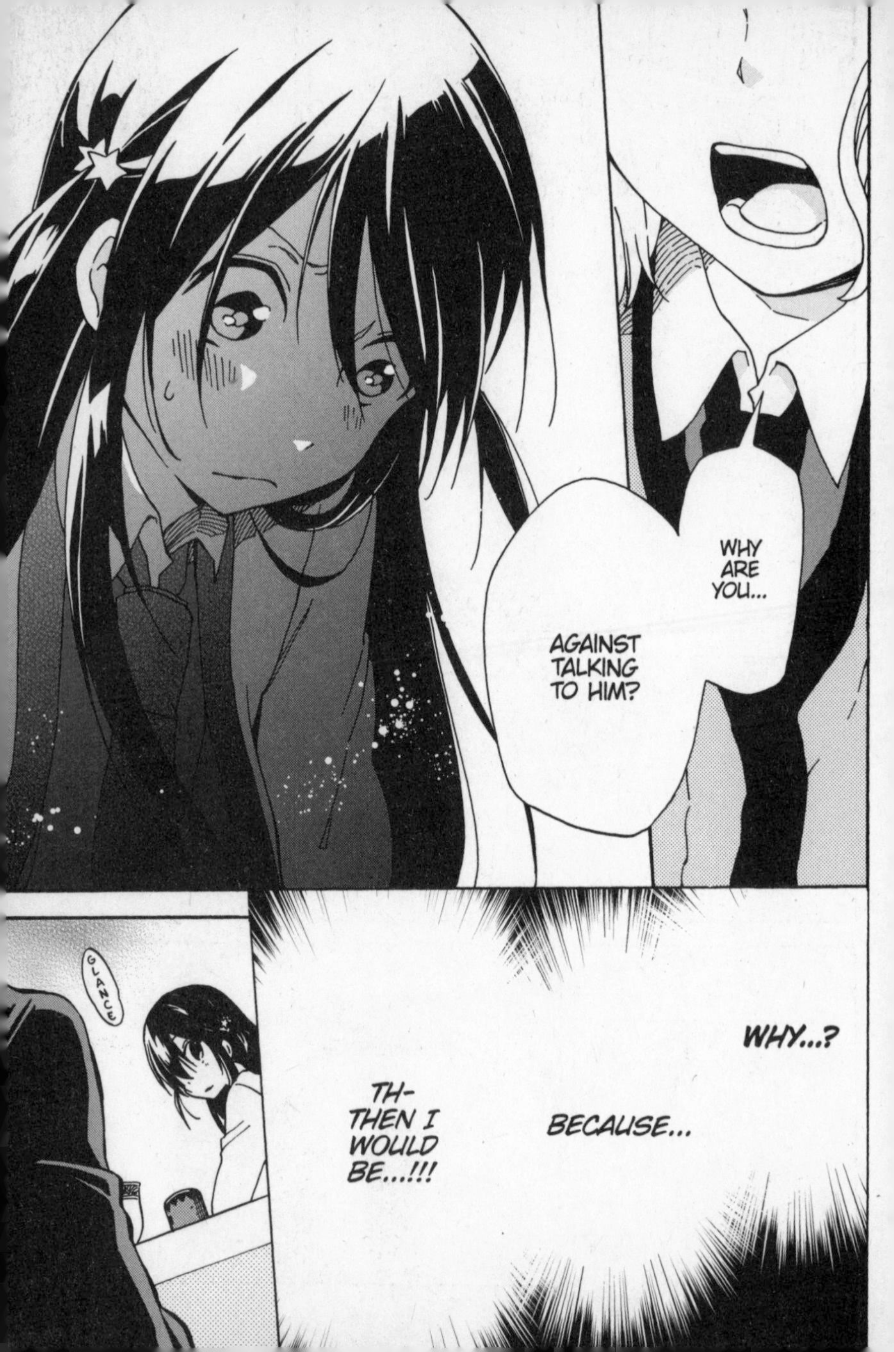
WHY ARE YOU...
AGAINST TALKING TO HIM?
WHY...?
BECAUSE...
TH-THEN I WOULD BE...!!!
GLANCE

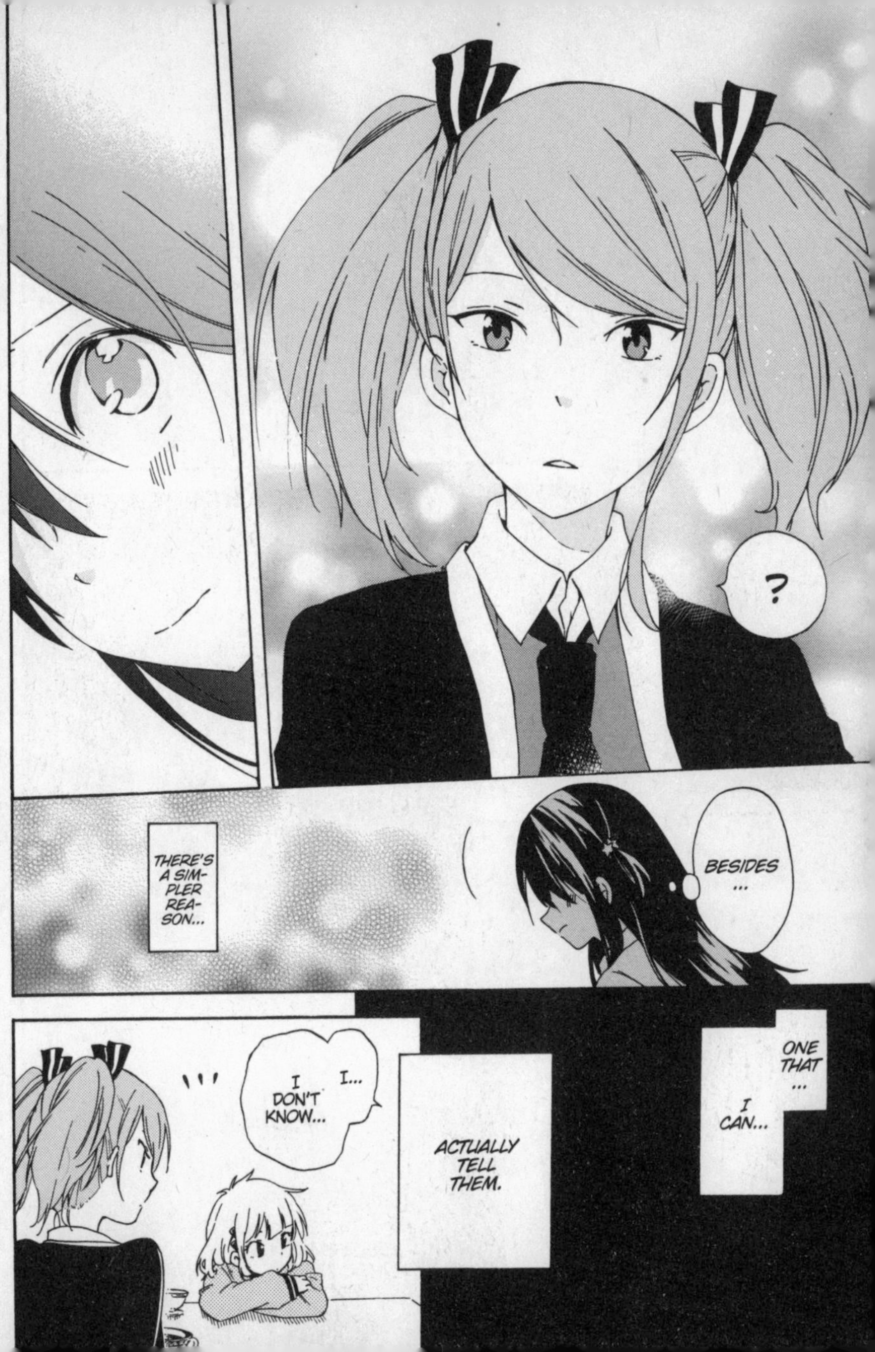
?
BESIDES ...
THERE'S A SIMPLER REASON...
ONE THAT ...
I CAN...
ACTUALLY TELL THEM.
I... I DON'T KNOW...

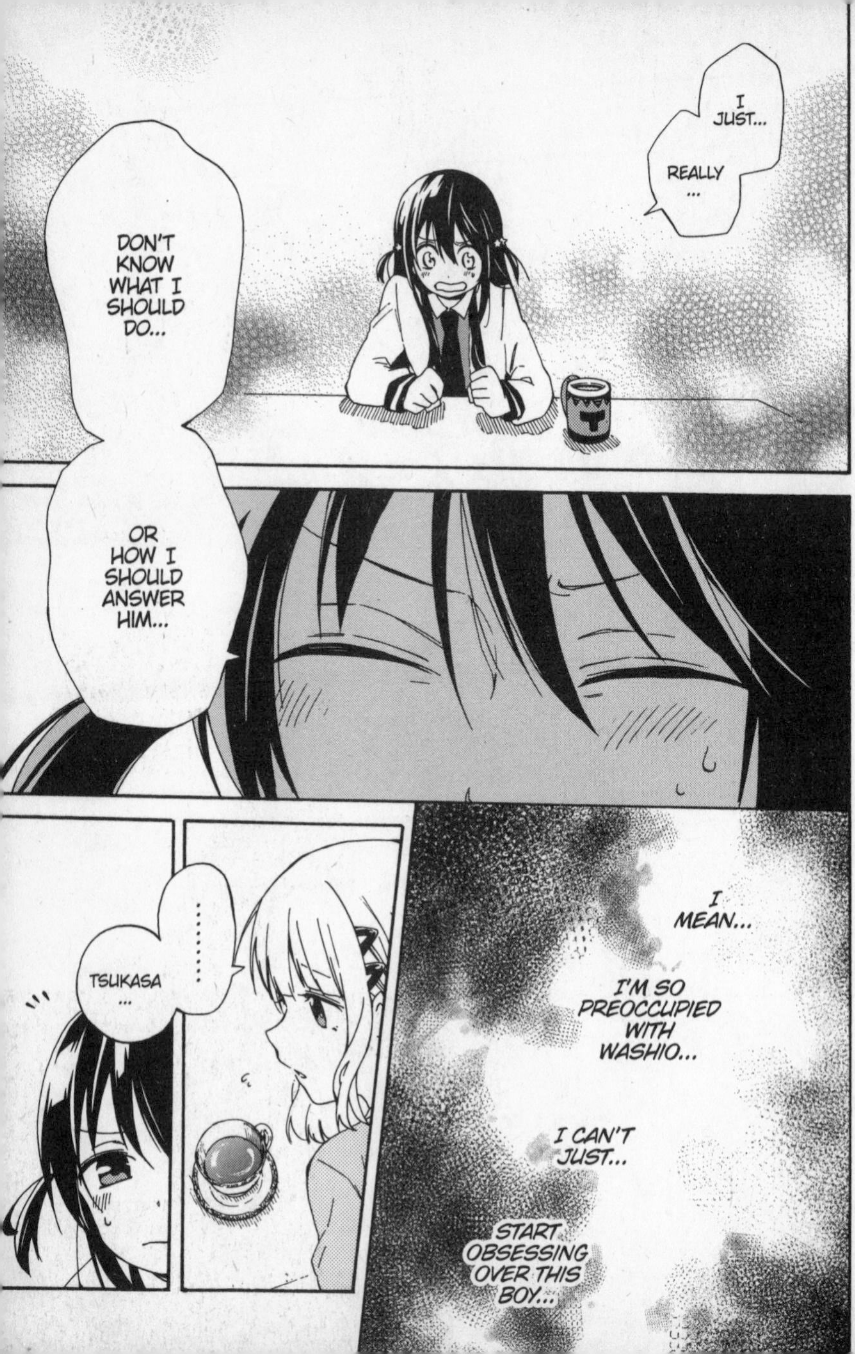
I JUST... REALLY...
DON'T KNOW WHAT I SHOULD DO...
OR HOW I SHOULD ANSWER HIM...
I MEAN...
I'M SO PREOCCUPIED WITH WASHIO...
I CAN'T JUST...
START OBSESSING OVER THIS BOY...
......
TSUKASA...

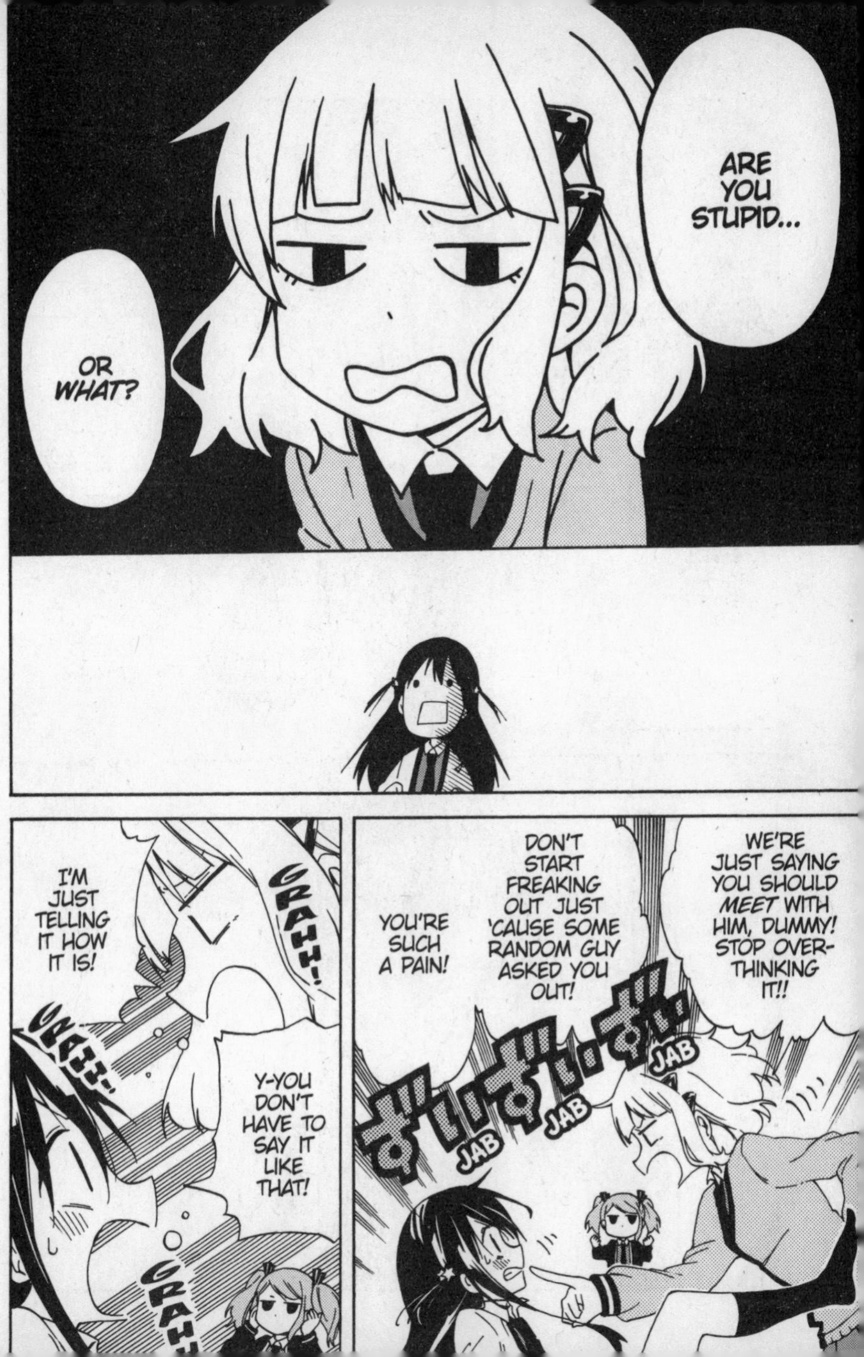
ARE YOU STUPID...
OR WHAT?
WE'RE JUST SAYING YOU SHOULD *MEET* WITH HIM, DUMMY! STOP OVER-THINKING IT!!
DON'T START FREAKING OUT JUST 'CAUSE SOME RANDOM GUY ASKED YOU OUT!
YOU'RE SUCH A PAIN!
JAB
JAB
JAB
GRAHH!
I'M JUST TELLING IT HOW IT IS!
Y-YOU DON'T HAVE TO SAY IT LIKE THAT!

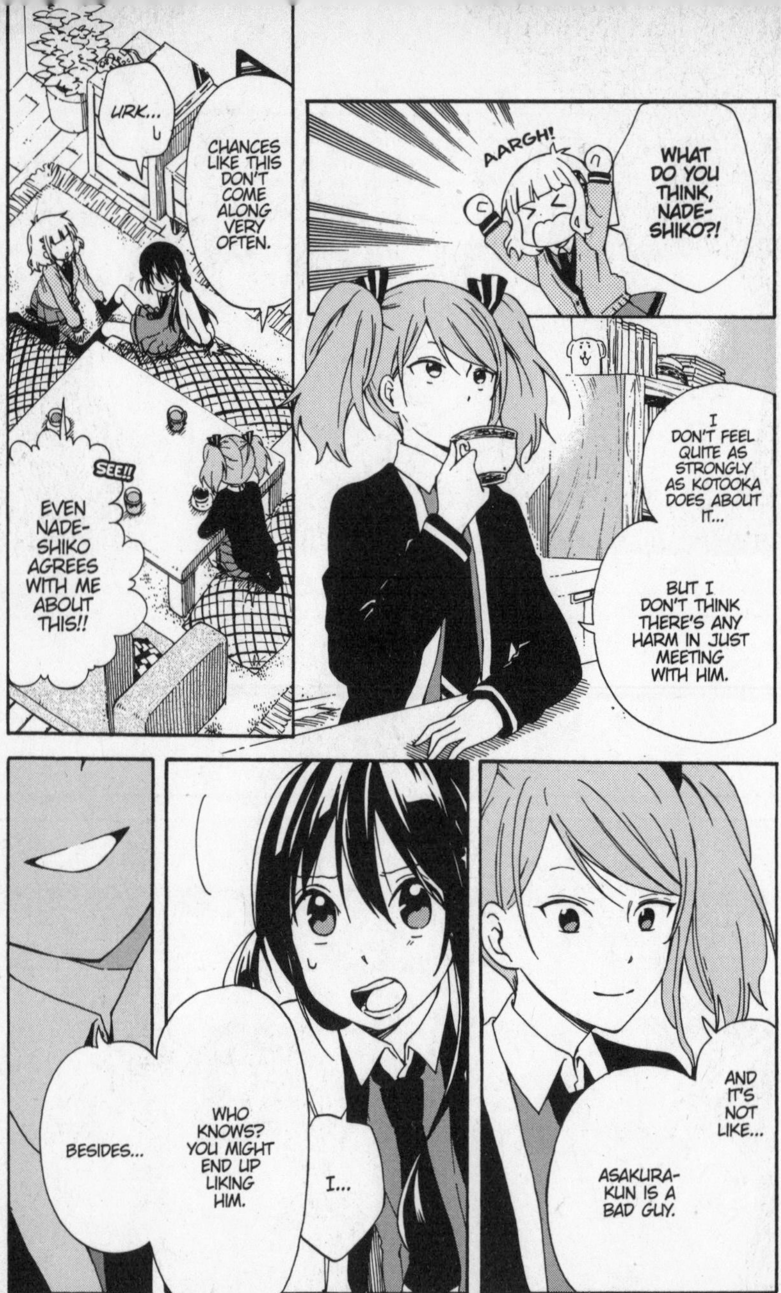

AARGH!
WHAT DO YOU THINK, NADE-SHIKO?!
I DON'T FEEL QUITE AS STRONGLY AS KOTOOKA DOES ABOUT IT...
BUT I DON'T THINK THERE'S ANY HARM IN JUST MEETING WITH HIM.
CHANCES LIKE THIS DON'T COME ALONG VERY OFTEN.
URK...
SEE!!
EVEN NADE-SHIKO AGREES WITH ME ABOUT THIS!!
AND IT'S NOT LIKE...
ASAKURA-KUN IS A BAD GUY.
WHO KNOWS? YOU MIGHT END UP LIKING HIM.
I...
BESIDES...

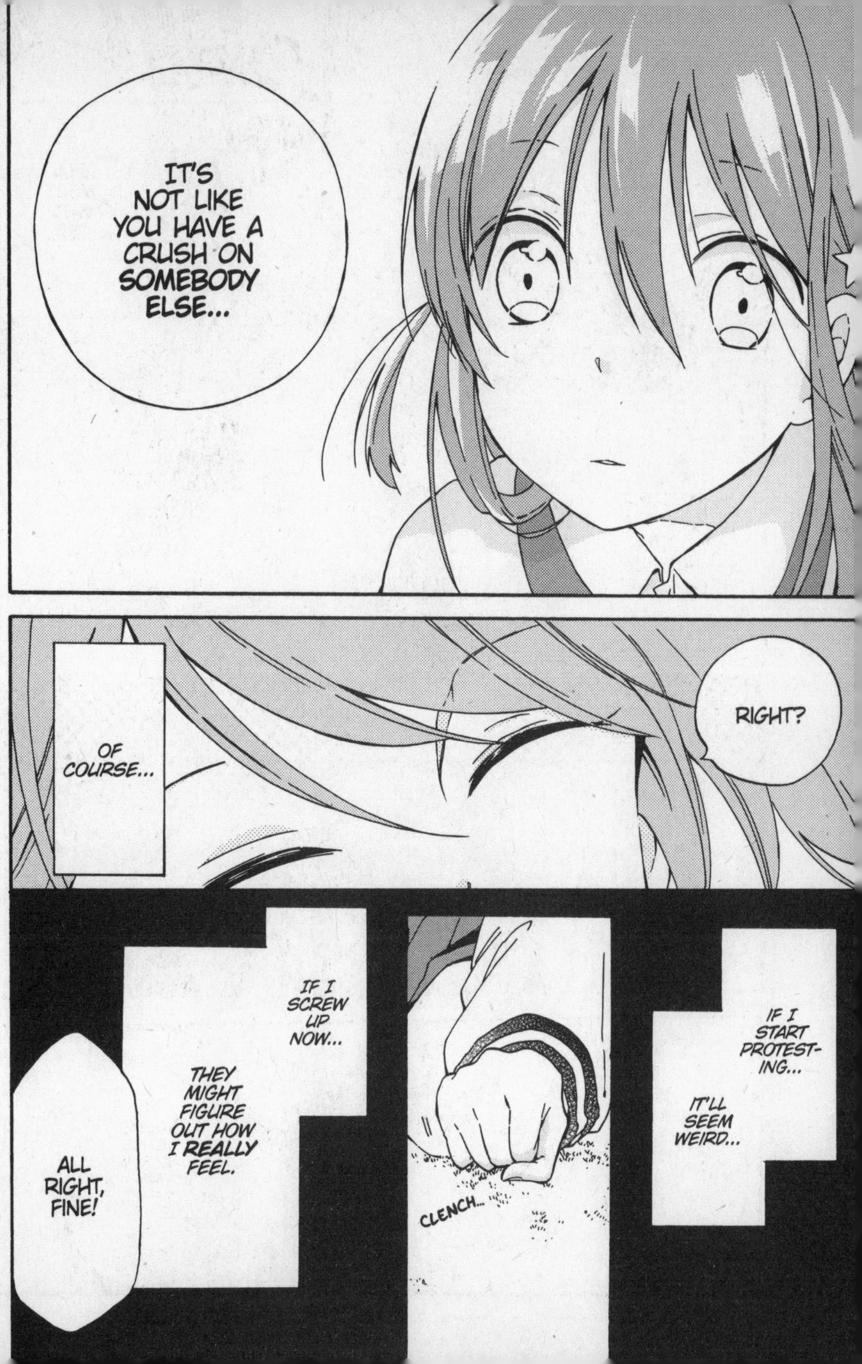
IT'S NOT LIKE YOU HAVE A CRUSH ON SOMEBODY ELSE...
RIGHT?
OF COURSE...
IF I START PROTEST-ING...
IT'LL SEEM WEIRD...
CLENCH...
IF I SCREW UP NOW...
THEY MIGHT FIGURE OUT HOW I REALLY FEEL.
ALL RIGHT, FINE!

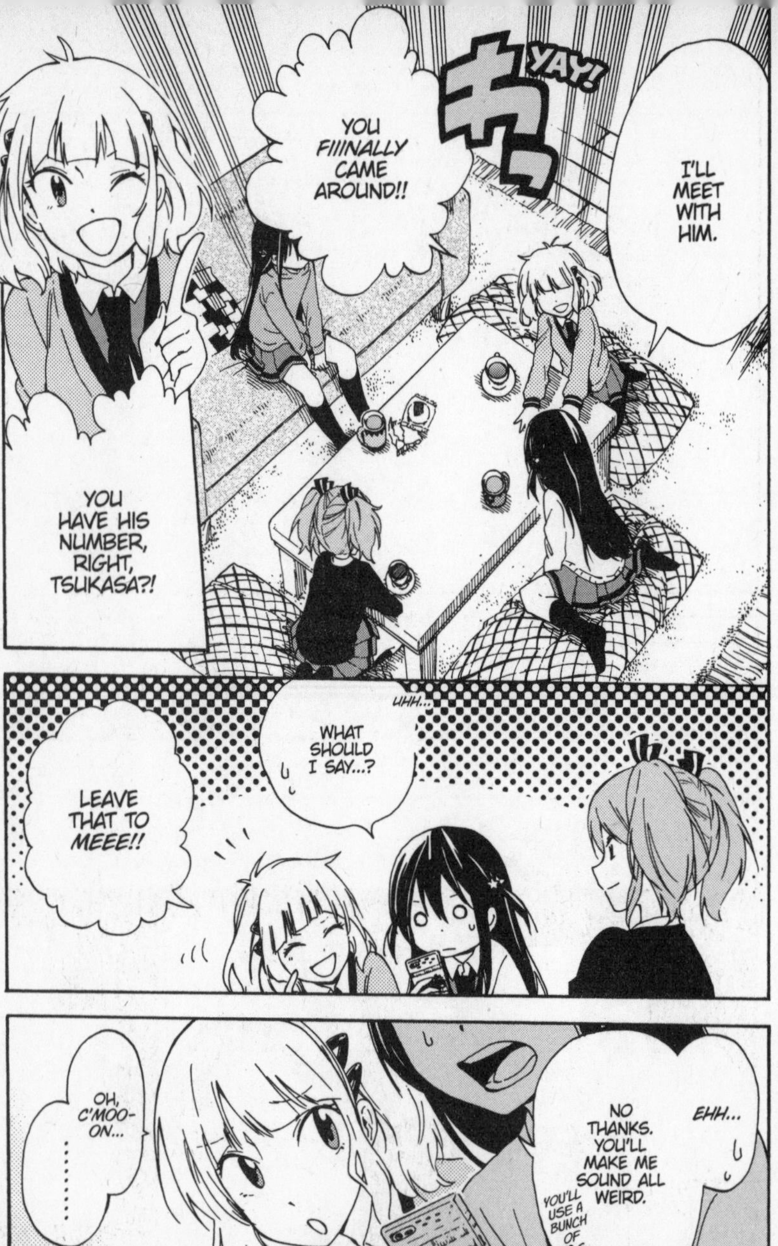
I'LL MEET WITH HIM.
YAY!
YOU FIIINALLY CAME AROUND!!
YOU HAVE HIS NUMBER, RIGHT, TSUKASA?!
UHH...
WHAT SHOULD I SAY...?
LEAVE THAT TO MEEE!!
EHH...
NO THANKS. YOU'LL MAKE ME SOUND ALL WEIRD.
YOU'LL USE A BUNCH OF ♥S AND STUFF.
OH, C'MOO-ON...
......

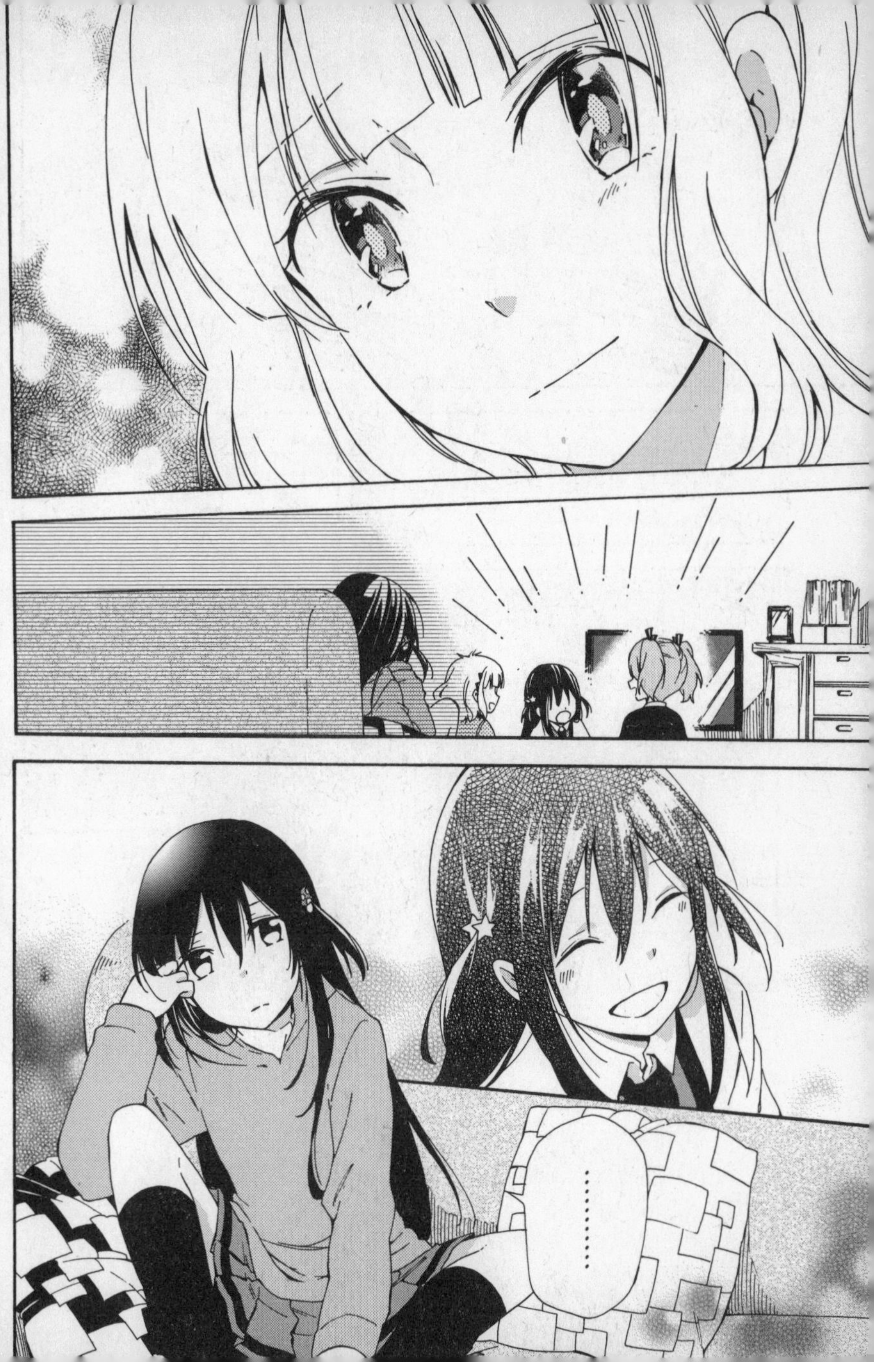
……

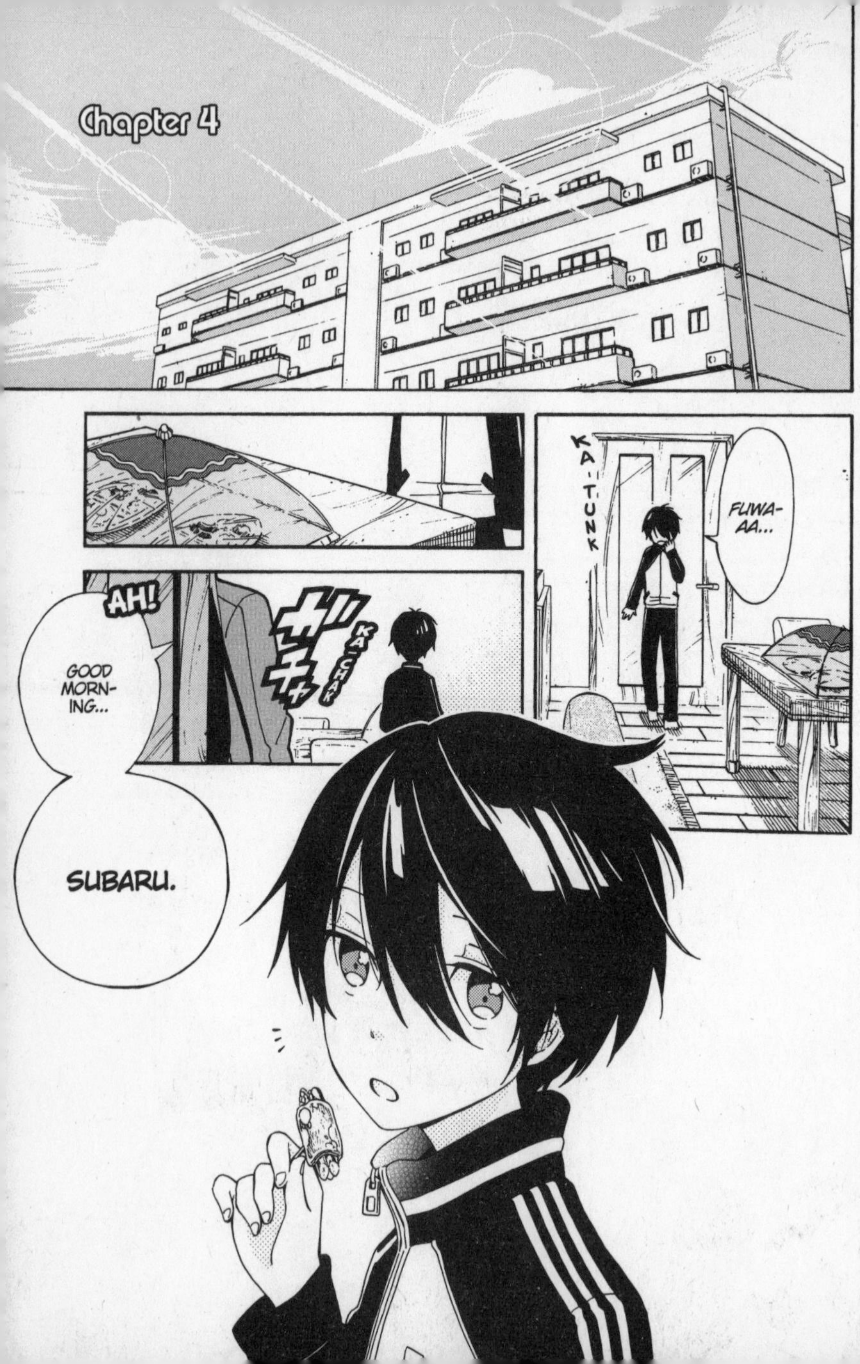
Chapter 4
KA-TUNK
FUWA-AA...
KA-CHAK
AH!
GOOD MORNING...
SUBARU.

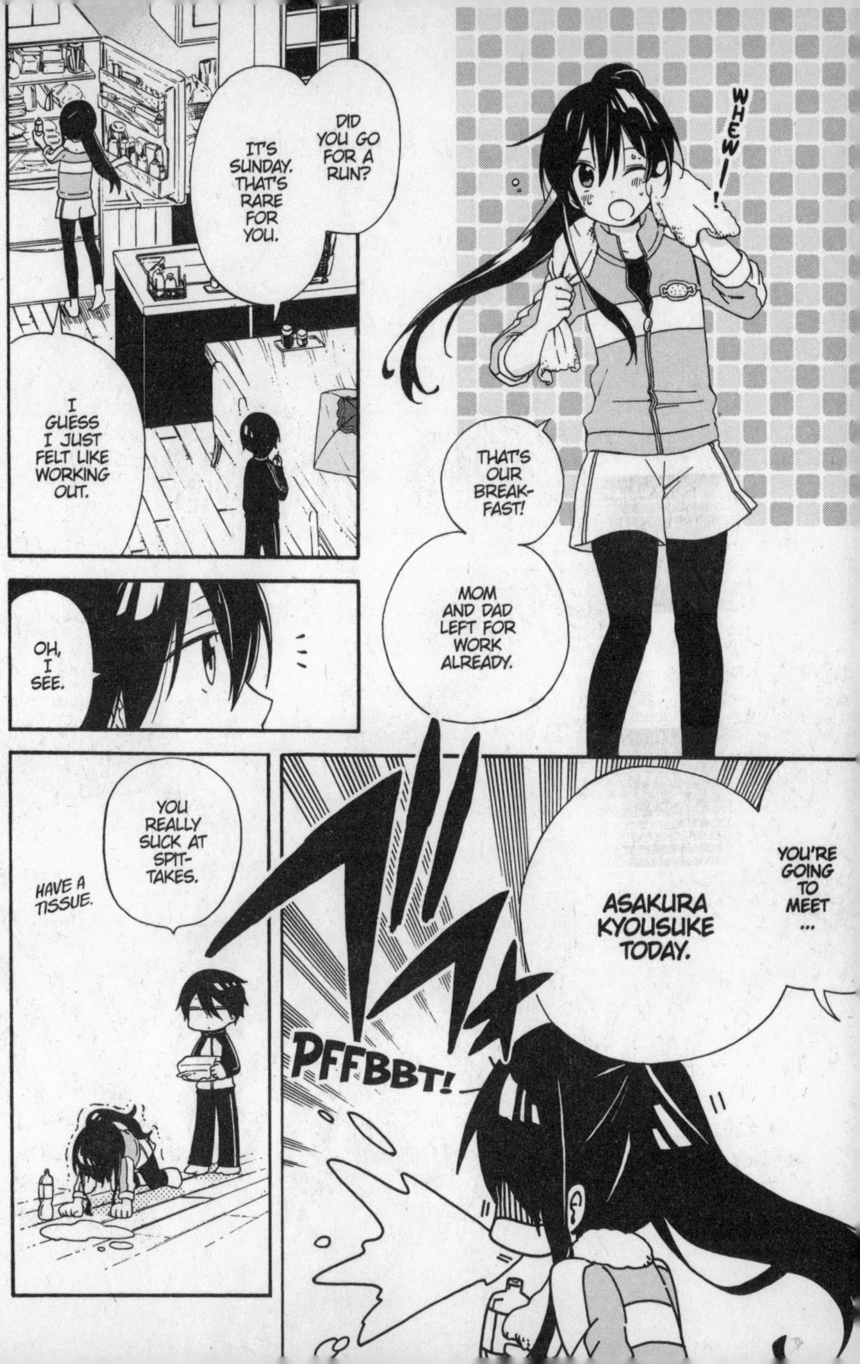
WHEW!
THAT'S OUR BREAK-FAST!
MOM AND DAD LEFT FOR WORK ALREADY.
DID YOU GO FOR A RUN?
IT'S SUNDAY. THAT'S RARE FOR YOU.
I GUESS I JUST FELT LIKE WORKING OUT.
OH, I SEE.
YOU'RE GOING TO MEET...
ASAKURA KYOUSUKE TODAY.
PFFBBT!
YOU REALLY SUCK AT SPIT-TAKES.
HAVE A TISSUE.

Chapter 4 ★ Advice

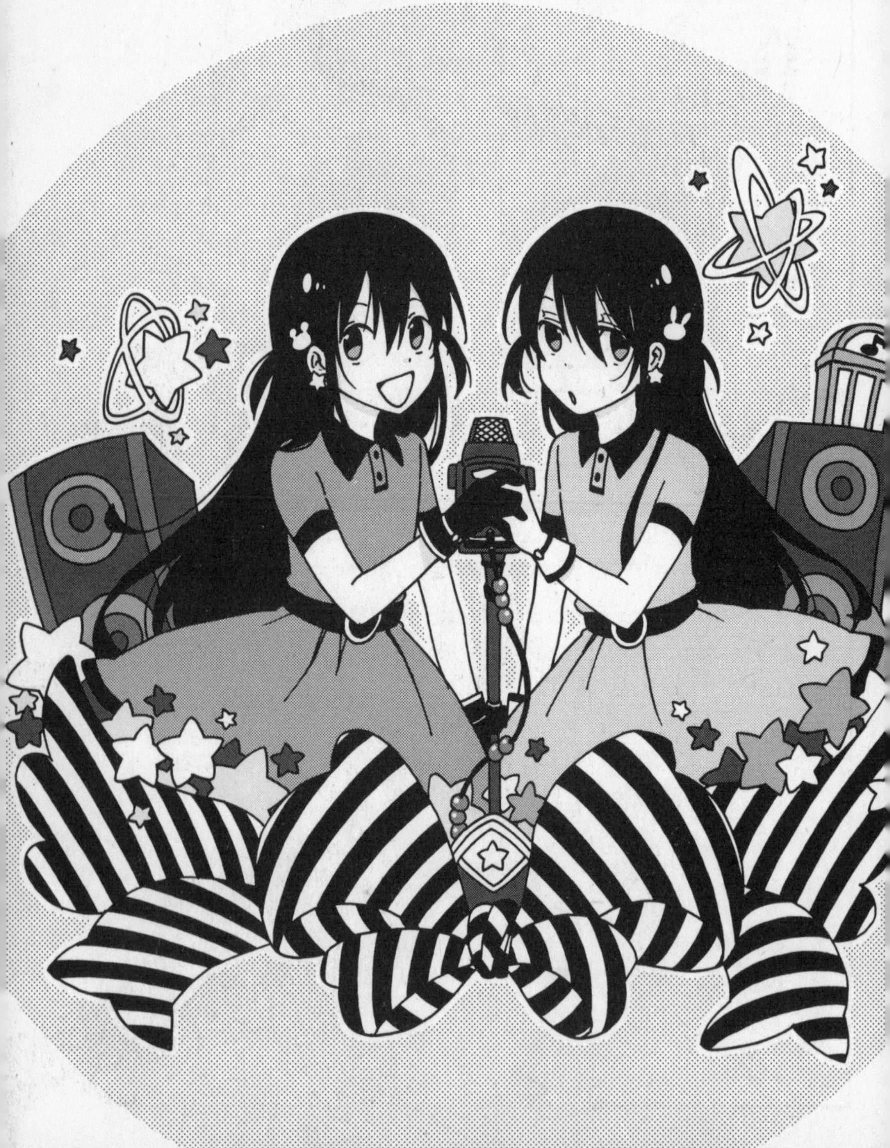

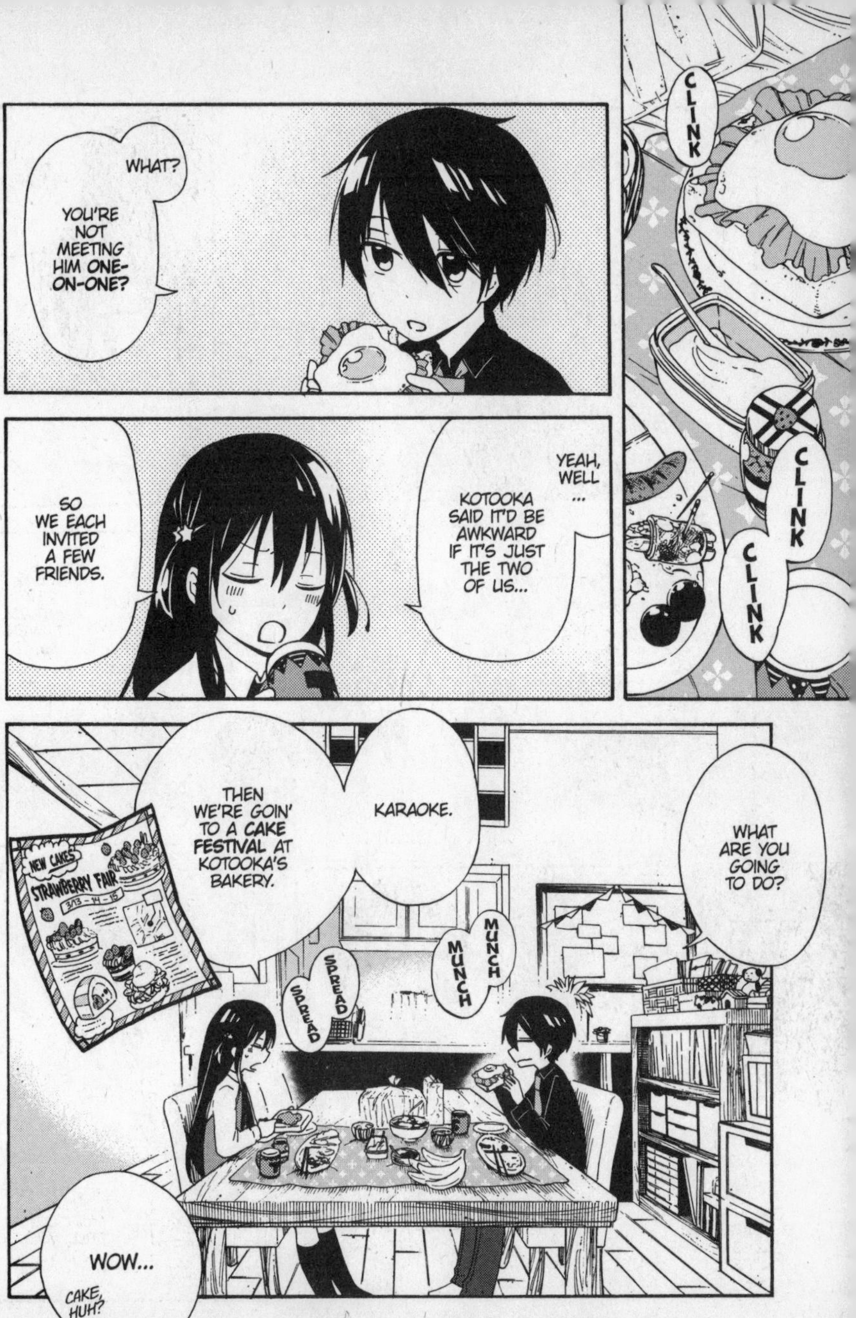
CLINK
CLINK
CLINK
WHAT?
YOU'RE NOT MEETING HIM ONE-ON-ONE?
YEAH, WELL...
KOTOOKA SAID IT'D BE AWKWARD IF IT'S JUST THE TWO OF US...
SO WE EACH INVITED A FEW FRIENDS.
WHAT ARE YOU GOING TO DO?
KARAOKE.
THEN WE'RE GOIN' TO A CAKE FESTIVAL AT KOTOOKA'S BAKERY.
MUNCH MUNCH
SPREAD SPREAD
NEW CAKES
STRAWBERRY FAIR
3/13 - 14 - 15
WOW...
CAKE, HUH?

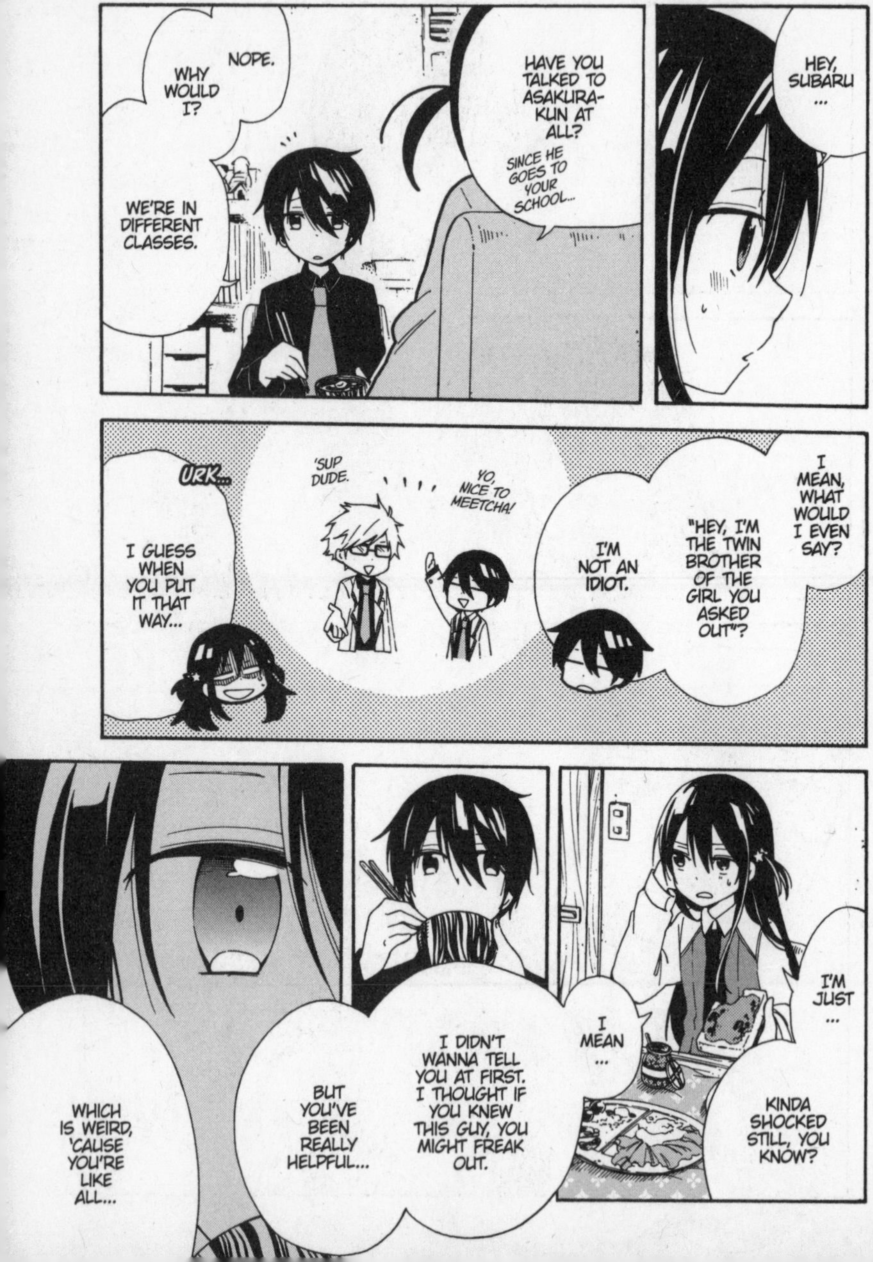
HEY, SUBARU ...
HAVE YOU TALKED TO ASAKURA-KUN AT ALL?
SINCE HE GOES TO YOUR SCHOOL...
NOPE.
WHY WOULD I?
WE'RE IN DIFFERENT CLASSES.
I MEAN, WHAT WOULD I EVEN SAY?
"HEY, I'M THE TWIN BROTHER OF THE GIRL YOU ASKED OUT"?
I'M NOT AN IDIOT.
YO, NICE TO MEETCHA!
'SUP DUDE.
URK...
I GUESS WHEN YOU PUT IT THAT WAY...
I'M JUST ...
KINDA SHOCKED STILL, YOU KNOW?
I MEAN ...
I DIDN'T WANNA TELL YOU AT FIRST. I THOUGHT IF YOU KNEW THIS GUY, YOU MIGHT FREAK OUT.
BUT YOU'VE BEEN REALLY HELPFUL...
WHICH IS WEIRD, 'CAUSE YOU'RE LIKE ALL...

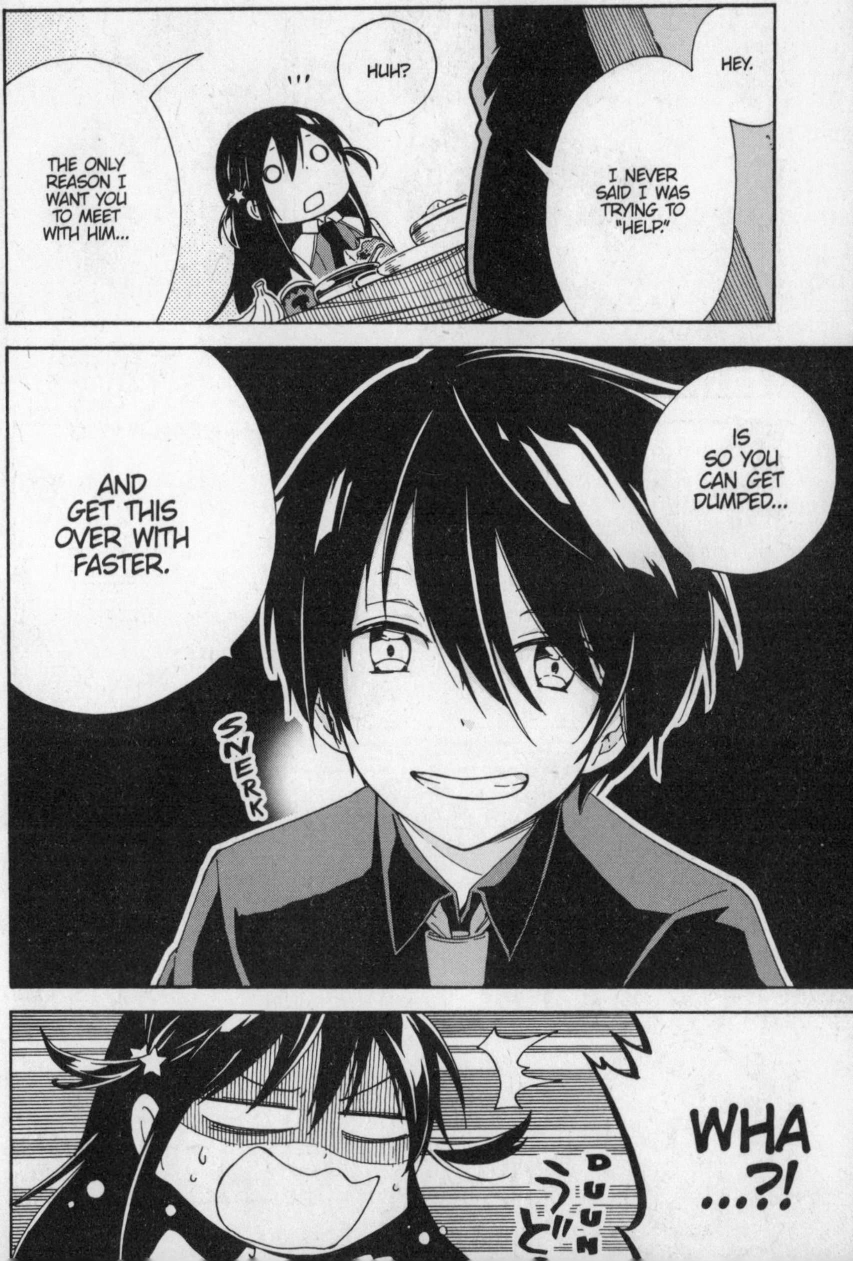
HEY.
I NEVER SAID I WAS TRYING TO "HELP."
HUH?
THE ONLY REASON I WANT YOU TO MEET WITH HIM...
IS SO YOU CAN GET DUMPED...
AND GET THIS OVER WITH FASTER.
SNERK
WHA ...?!
DUUN

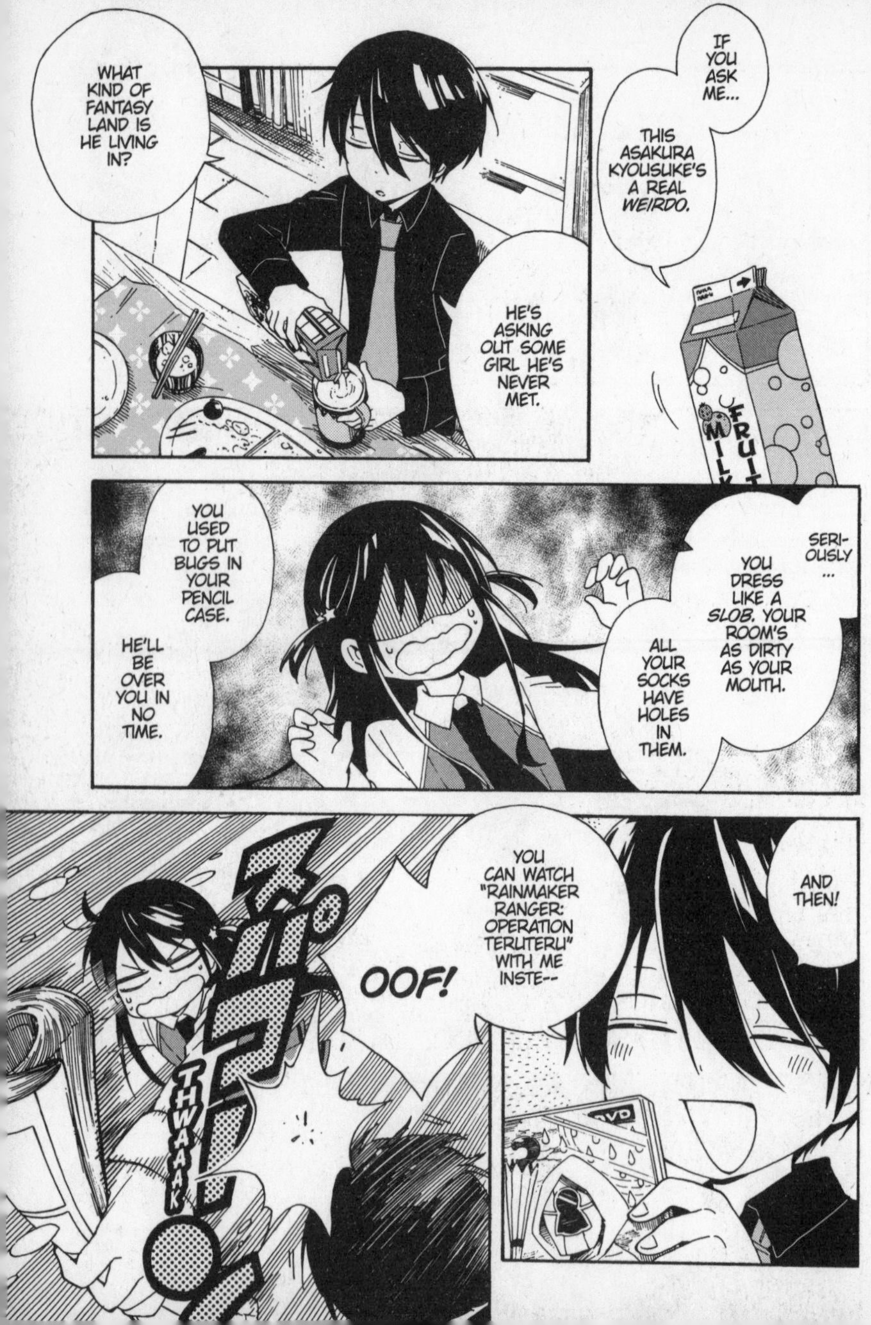

IF YOU ASK ME...
THIS ASAKURA KYOUSUKE'S A REAL *WEIRDO.*
HE'S ASKING OUT SOME GIRL HE'S NEVER MET.
WHAT KIND OF FANTASY LAND IS HE LIVING IN?
FRUIT MILK
SERI-OUSLY...
YOU DRESS LIKE A *SLOB.* YOUR ROOM'S AS DIRTY AS YOUR MOUTH.
ALL YOUR SOCKS HAVE HOLES IN THEM.
YOU USED TO PUT BUGS IN YOUR PENCIL CASE.
HE'LL BE OVER YOU IN NO TIME.
AND THEN!
YOU CAN WATCH "RAINMAKER RANGER: OPERATION TERUTERU" WITH ME INSTE--
DVD
THWAAAK
OOF!

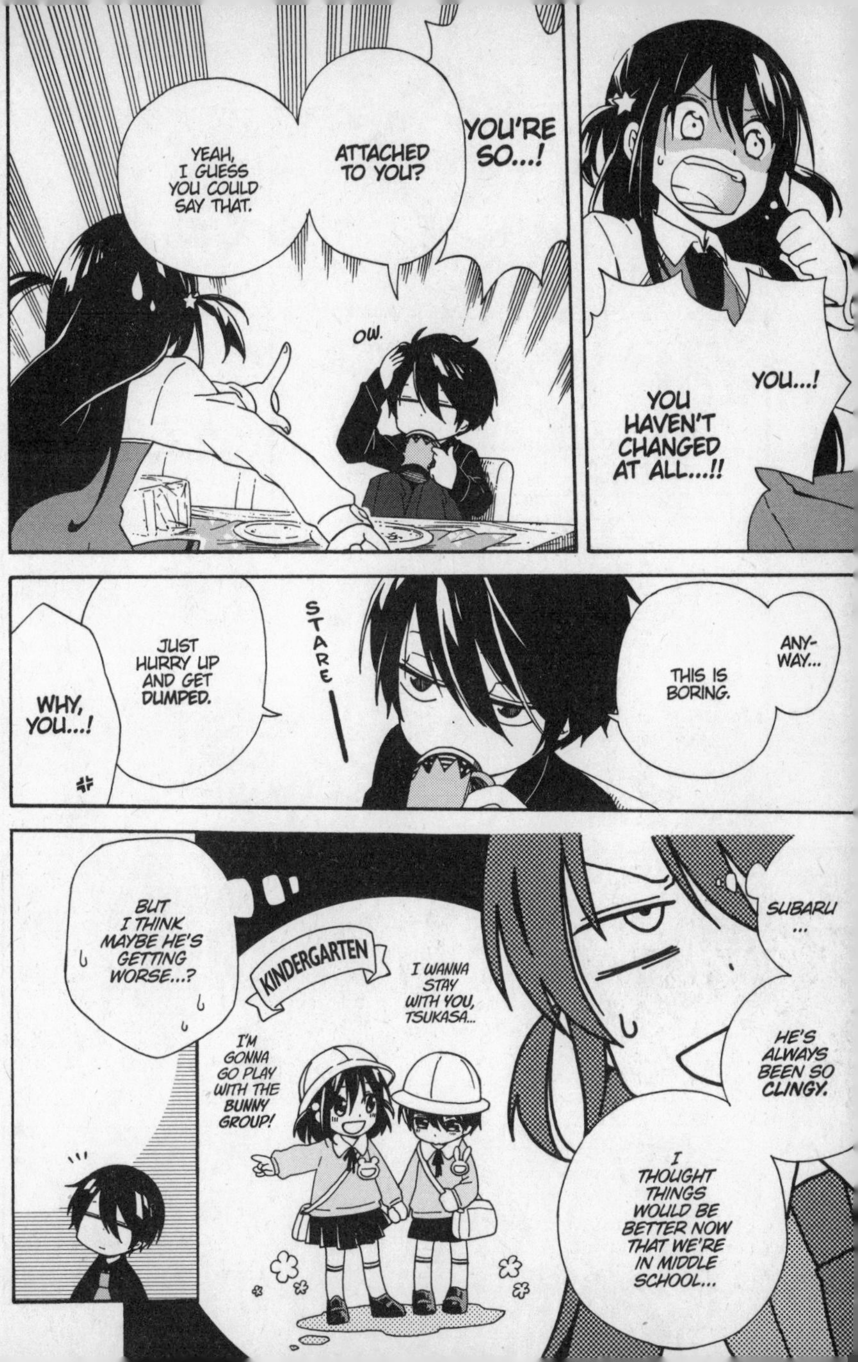
YOU...!
YOU HAVEN'T CHANGED AT ALL...!!
YOU'RE SO...!
ATTACHED TO YOU?
YEAH, I GUESS YOU COULD SAY THAT.
OW.
ANY-WAY...
THIS IS BORING.
STARE
JUST HURRY UP AND GET DUMPED.
WHY, YOU...!
SUBARU...
HE'S ALWAYS BEEN SO CLINGY.
I THOUGHT THINGS WOULD BE BETTER NOW THAT WE'RE IN MIDDLE SCHOOL...
I WANNA STAY WITH YOU, TSUKASA...
KINDERGARTEN
I'M GONNA GO PLAY WITH THE BUNNY GROUP!
BUT I THINK MAYBE HE'S GETTING WORSE...?

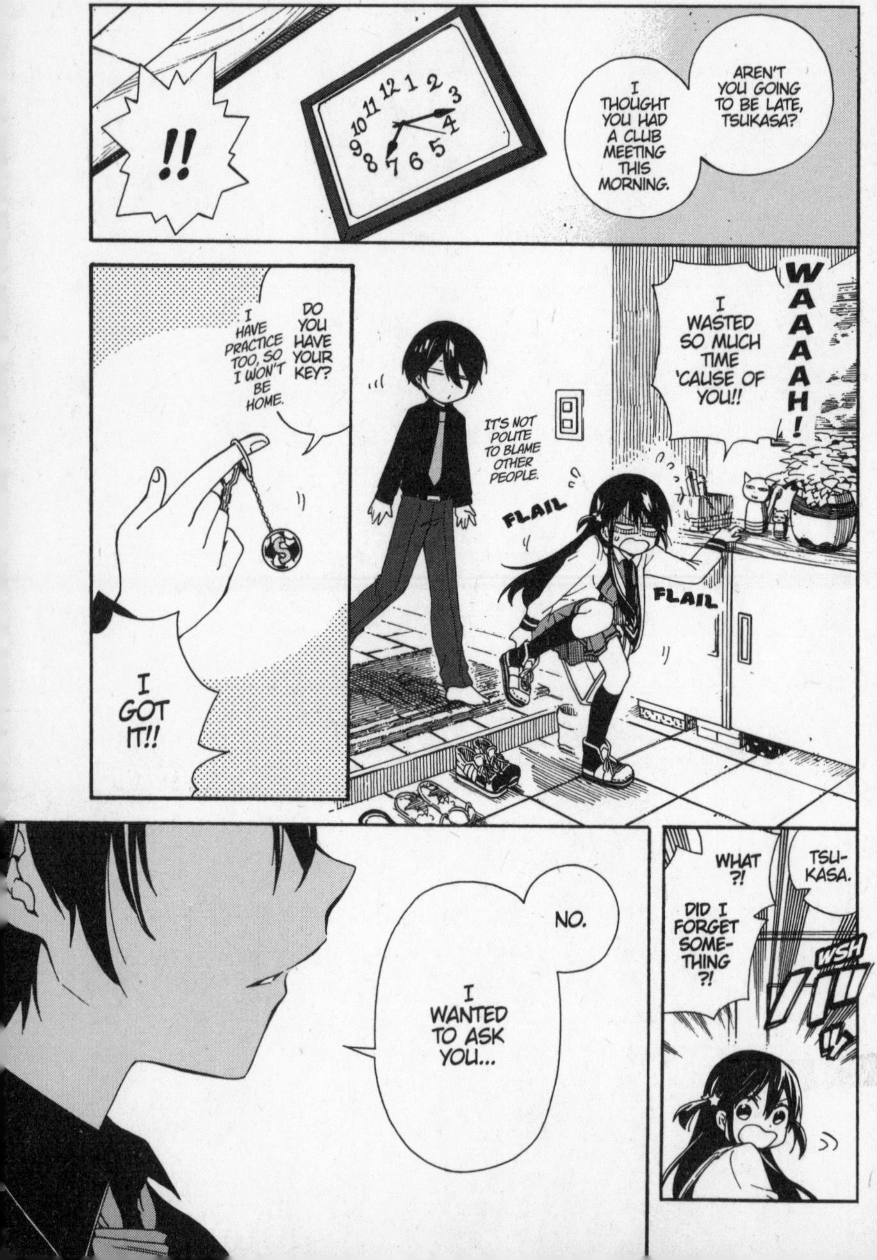
AREN'T YOU GOING TO BE LATE, TSUKASA?
I THOUGHT YOU HAD A CLUB MEETING THIS MORNING.
!!
WAAAAAH!
I WASTED SO MUCH TIME 'CAUSE OF YOU!!
IT'S NOT POLITE TO BLAME OTHER PEOPLE.
FLAIL
FLAIL
DO YOU HAVE YOUR KEY?
I HAVE PRACTICE TOO, SO I WON'T BE HOME.
I GOT IT!!
TSU-KASA.
WHAT?!
DID I FORGET SOME-THING?!
WSH
NO.
I WANTED TO ASK YOU...

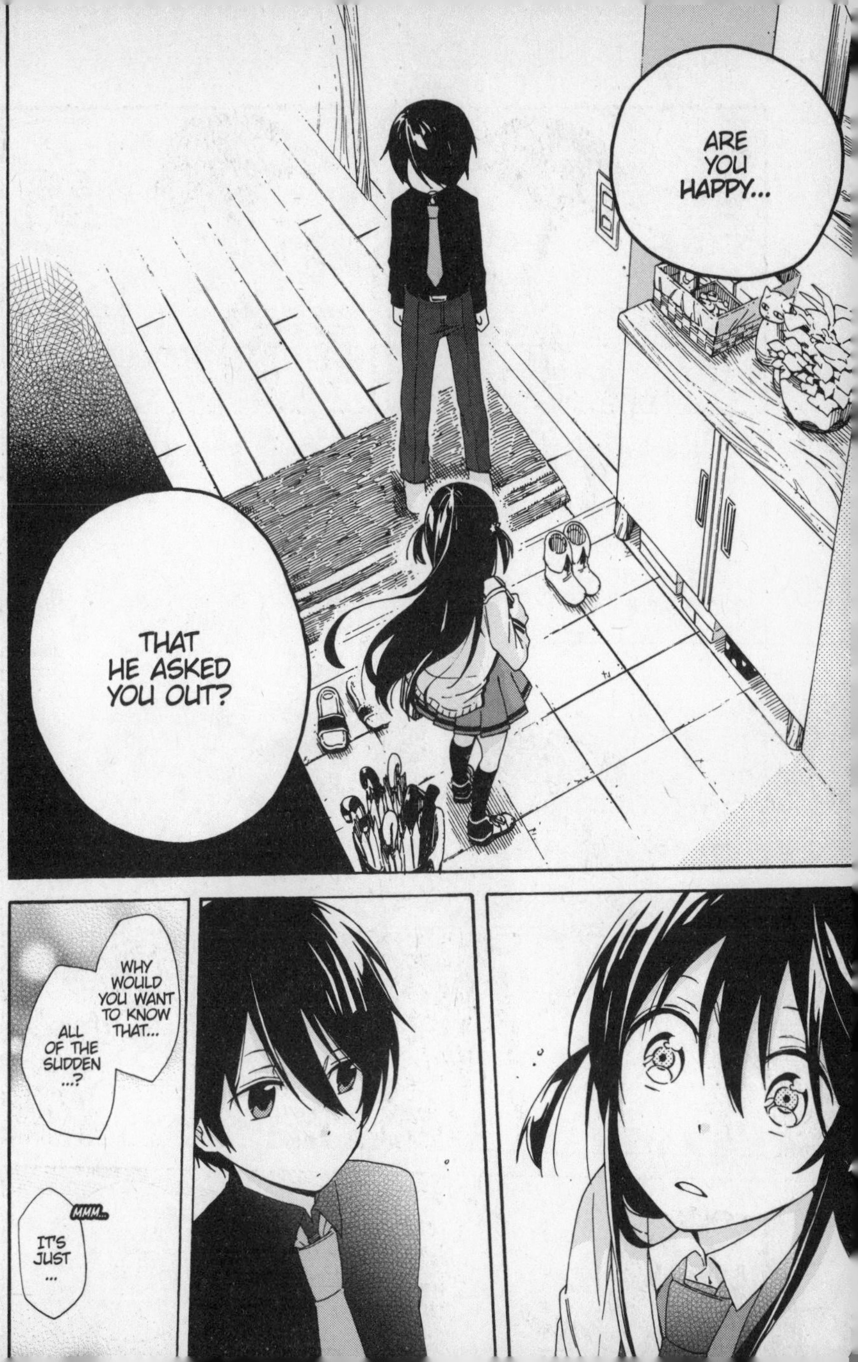
ARE YOU HAPPY...
THAT HE ASKED YOU OUT?
WHY WOULD YOU WANT TO KNOW THAT...
ALL OF THE SUDDEN ...?
MMM...
IT'S JUST ...

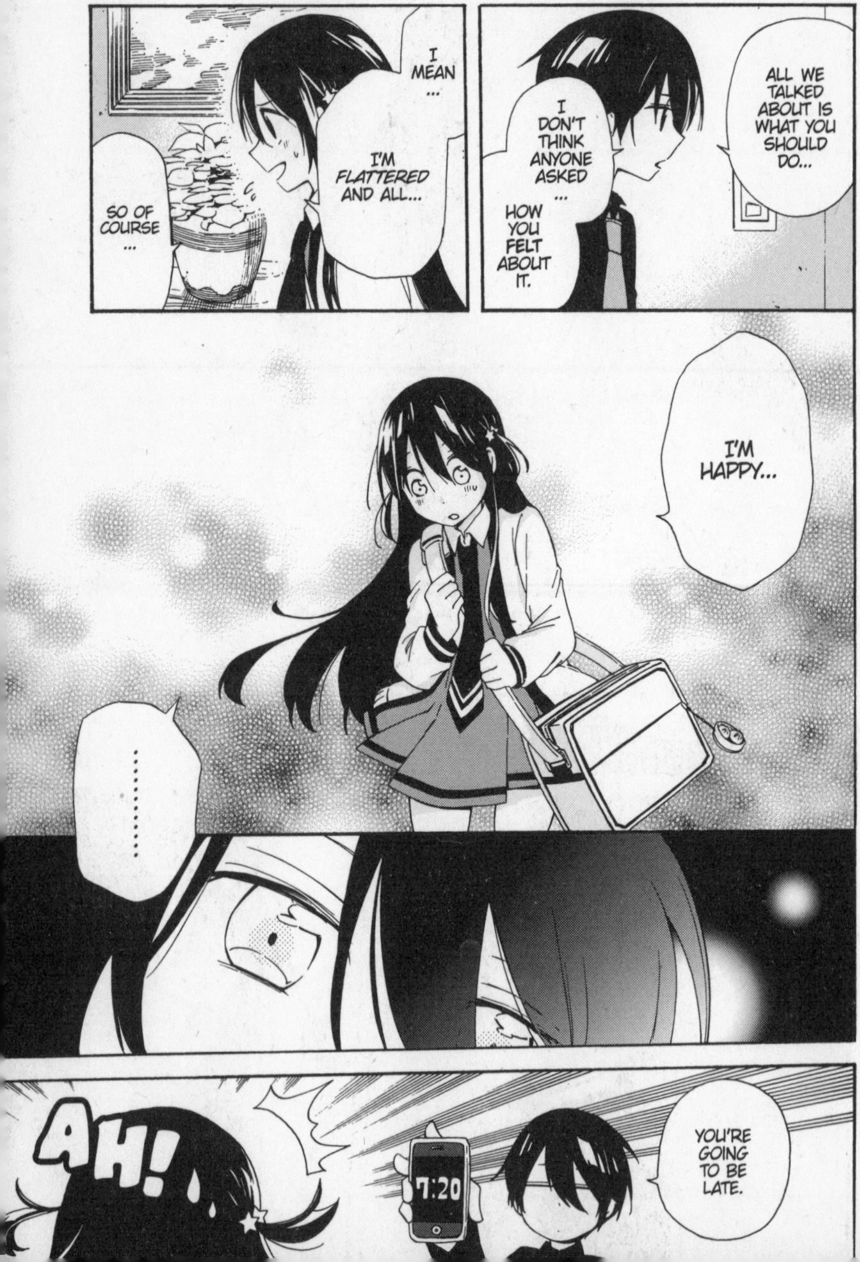
ALL WE TALKED ABOUT IS WHAT YOU SHOULD DO...
I DON'T THINK ANYONE ASKED ...
HOW YOU FELT ABOUT IT.
I MEAN ...
I'M FLATTERED AND ALL...
SO OF COURSE ...
I'M HAPPY...
....
YOU'RE GOING TO BE LATE.
7:20
AH!

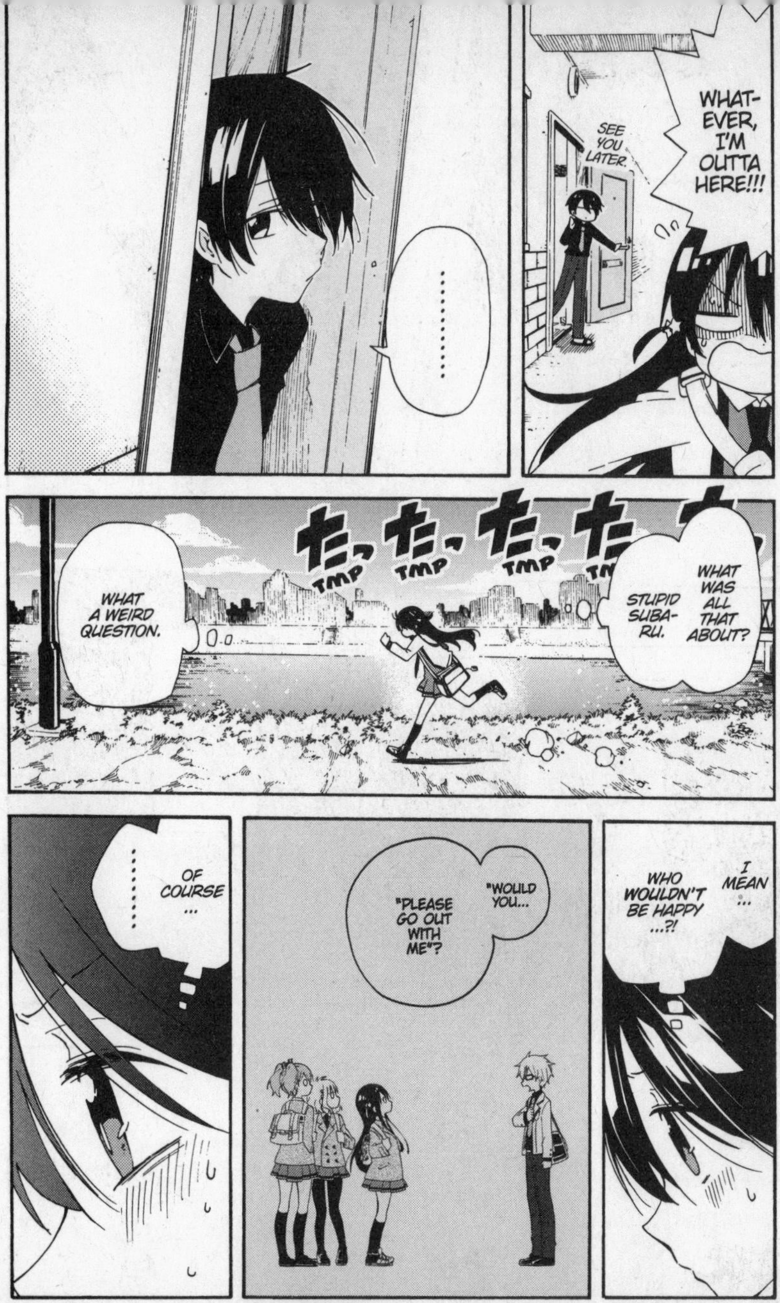
WHAT-EVER, I'M OUTTA HERE!!!
SEE YOU LATER.
......
WHAT WAS ALL THAT ABOUT?
STUPID SUBA-RU.
たっ たっ たっ たっ
TMP TMP TMP TMP
WHAT A WEIRD QUESTION.
I MEAN...
WHO WOULDN'T BE HAPPY...?!
"WOULD YOU...
"PLEASE GO OUT WITH ME"?
......
OF COURSE...

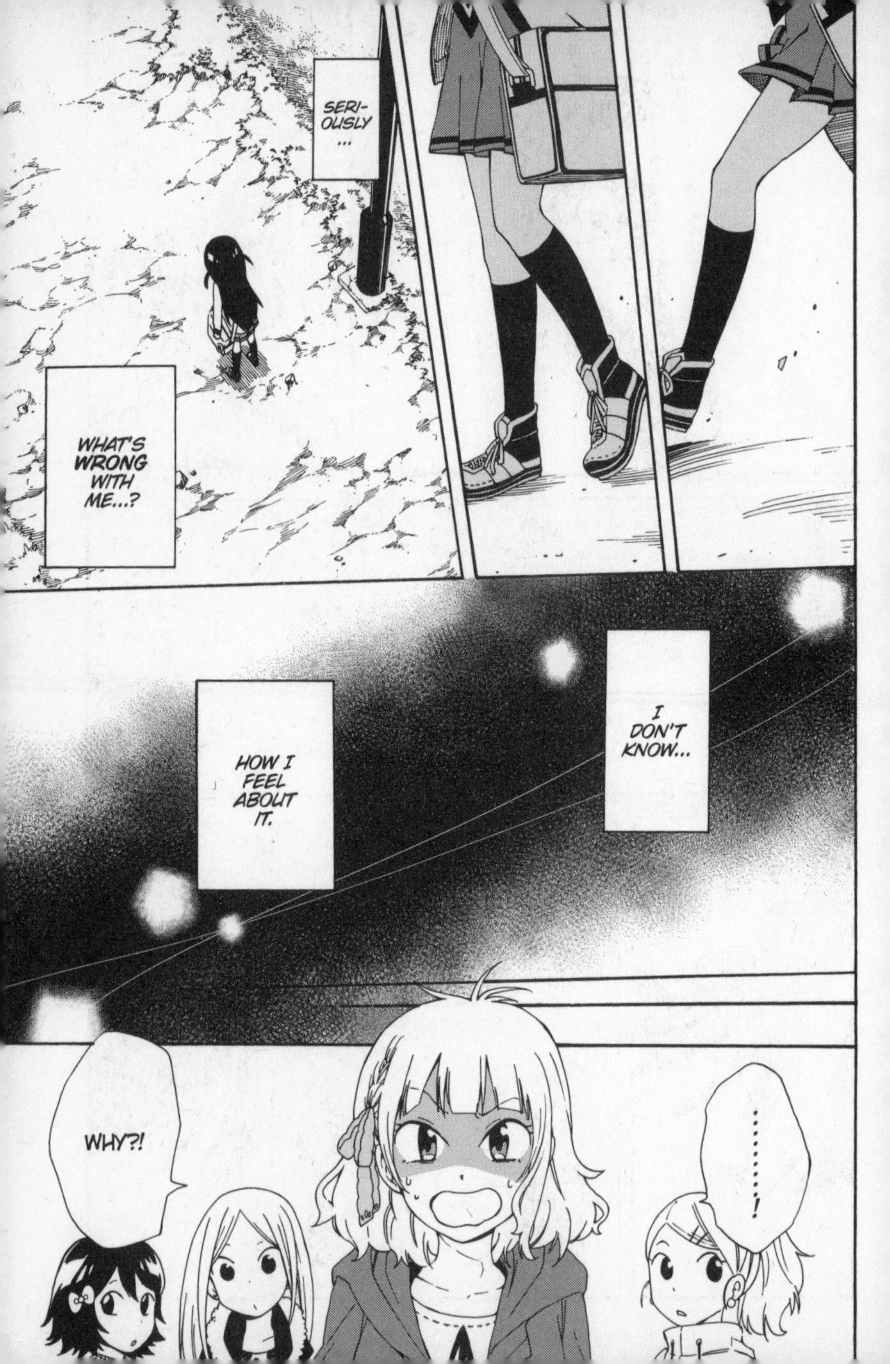
SERI-OUSLY...
WHAT'S WRONG WITH ME...?
I DON'T KNOW...
HOW I FEEL ABOUT IT.
.........!
WHY?!

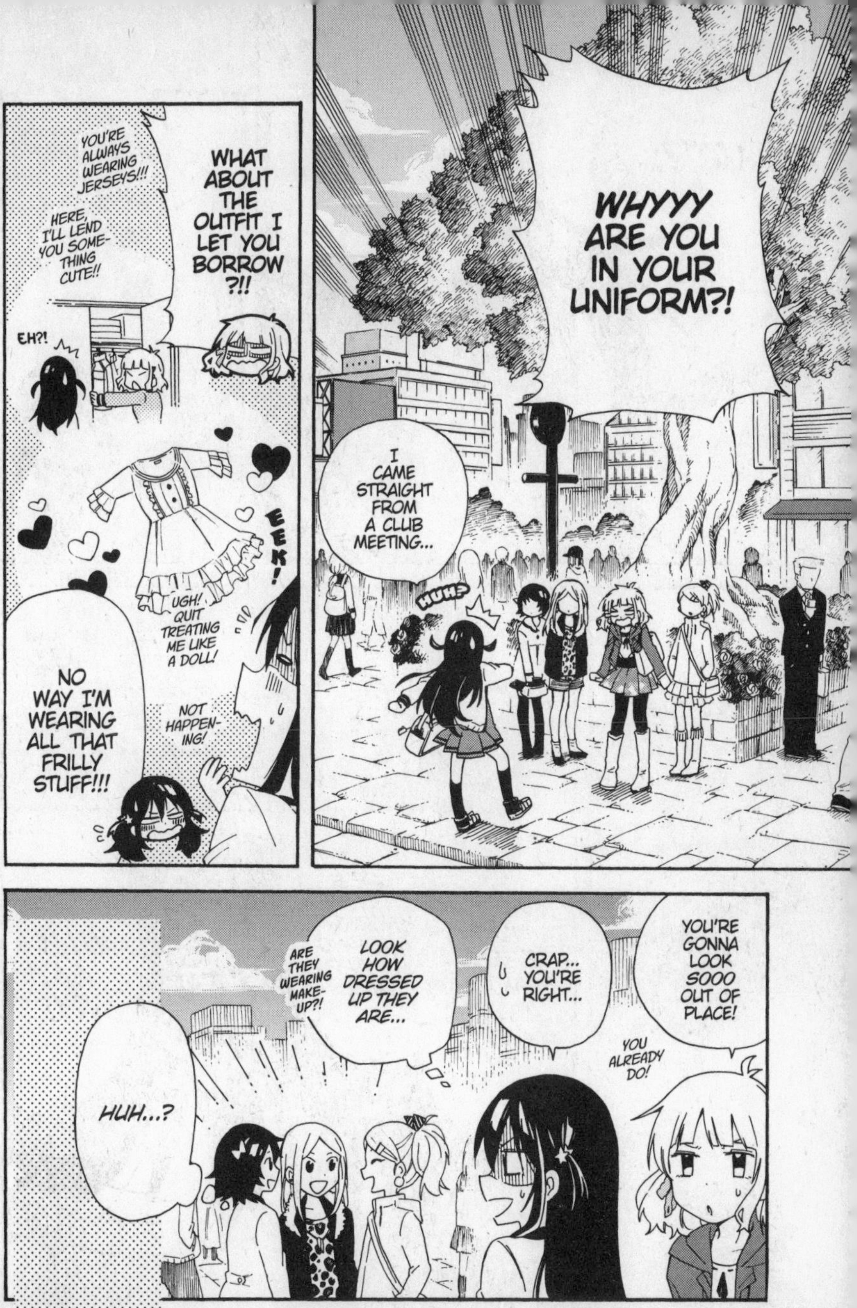
WHYYY ARE YOU IN YOUR UNIFORM?!
I CAME STRAIGHT FROM A CLUB MEETING...
HUH?
WHAT ABOUT THE OUTFIT I LET YOU BORROW ?!!
YOU'RE ALWAYS WEARING JERSEYS!!!
HERE, I'LL LEND YOU SOME-THING CUTE!!
EH?!
EEK!
UGH! QUIT TREATING ME LIKE A DOLL!
NOT HAPPEN-ING!
NO WAY I'M WEARING ALL THAT FRILLY STUFF!!!
YOU'RE GONNA LOOK SOOO OUT OF PLACE!
YOU ALREADY DO!
CRAP... YOU'RE RIGHT...
LOOK HOW DRESSED UP THEY ARE...
ARE THEY WEARING MAKE-UP?!
HUH...?

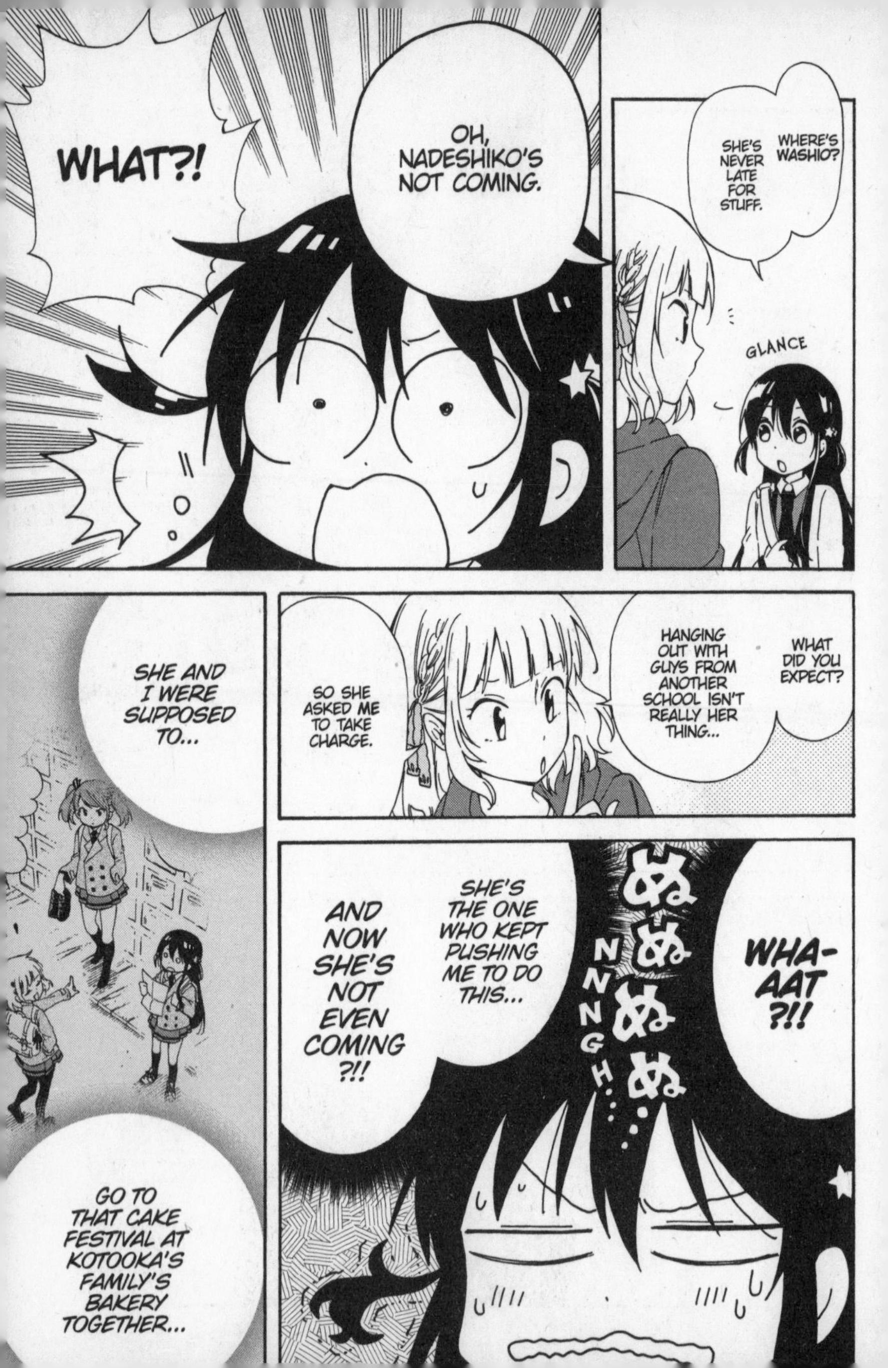

WHERE'S WASHIO?
SHE'S NEVER LATE FOR STUFF.
GLANCE
OH, NADESHIKO'S NOT COMING.
WHAT?!
WHAT DID YOU EXPECT?
HANGING OUT WITH GUYS FROM ANOTHER SCHOOL ISN'T REALLY HER THING...
SO SHE ASKED ME TO TAKE CHARGE.
WHA-AAT?!!
ぬぬぬぬ…
NNNGH...
SHE'S THE ONE WHO KEPT PUSHING ME TO DO THIS...
AND NOW SHE'S NOT EVEN COMING?!!
SHE AND I WERE SUPPOSED TO...
GO TO THAT CAKE FESTIVAL AT KOTOOKA'S FAMILY'S BAKERY TOGETHER...

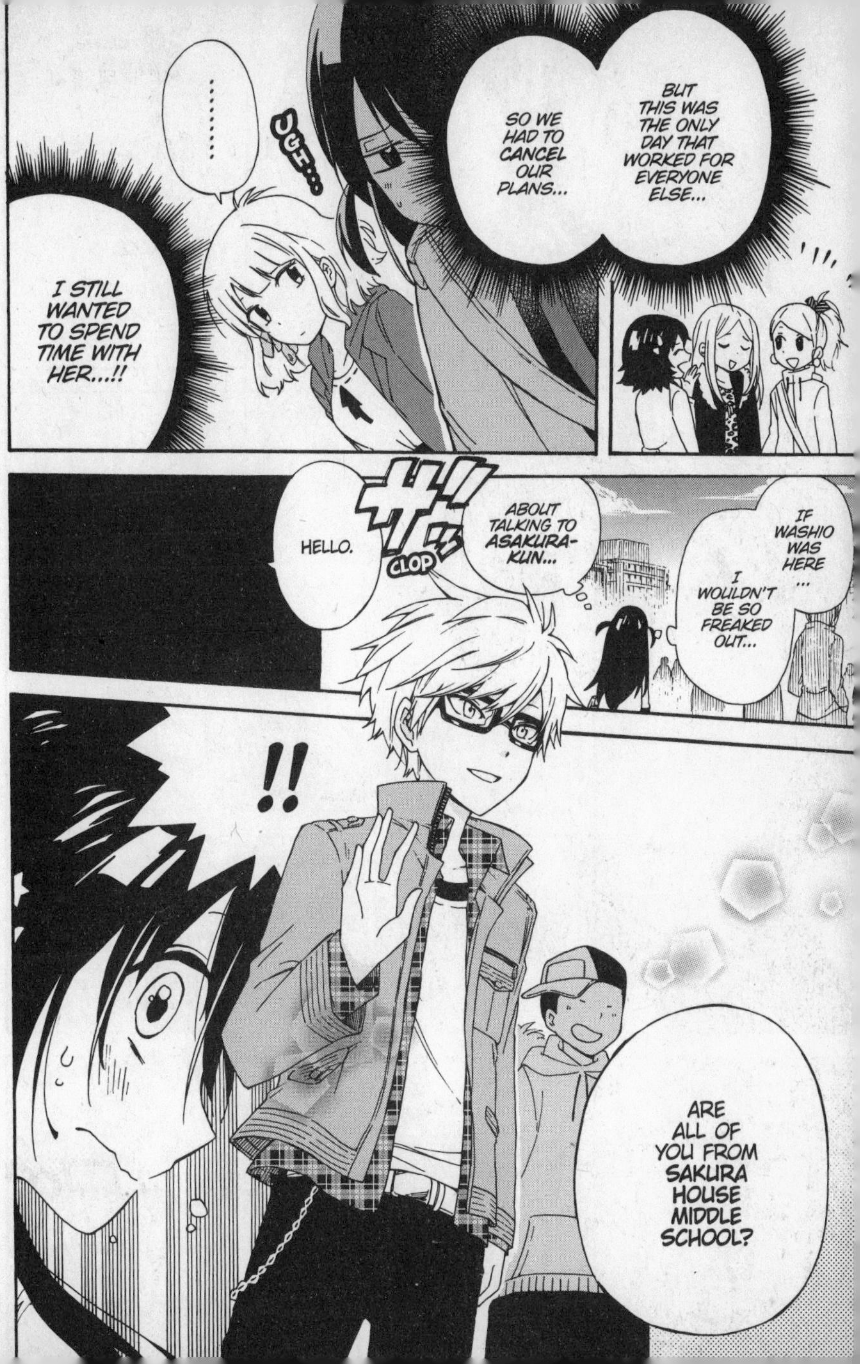
BUT THIS WAS THE ONLY DAY THAT WORKED FOR EVERYONE ELSE...
SO WE HAD TO CANCEL OUR PLANS...
UGH...
......
I STILL WANTED TO SPEND TIME WITH HER...!!
IF WASHIO WAS HERE...
I WOULDN'T BE SO FREAKED OUT...
ABOUT TALKING TO ASAKURA-KUN...
CLOP
HELLO.
ARE ALL OF YOU FROM SAKURA HOUSE MIDDLE SCHOOL?
!!

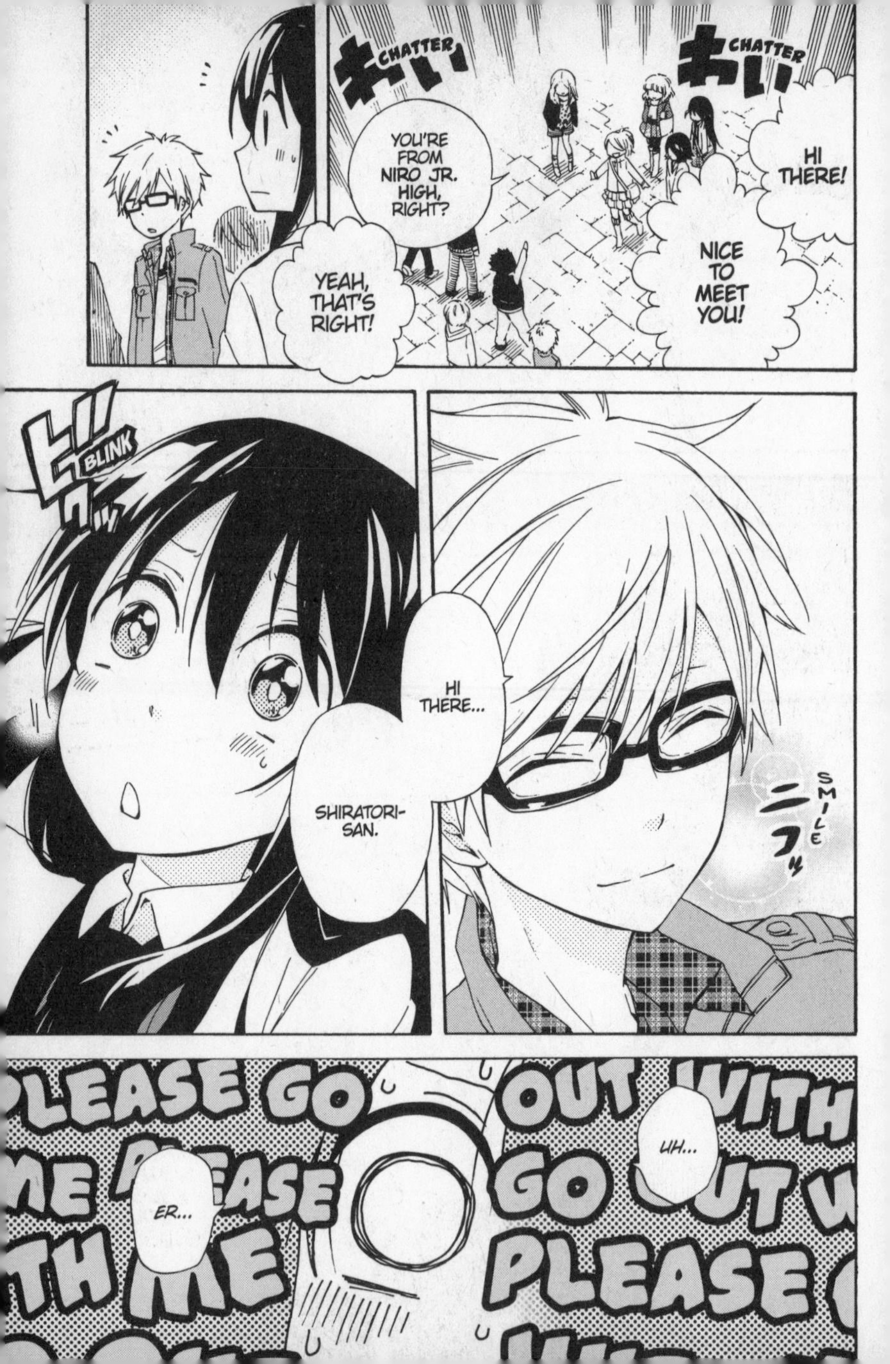
CHATTER
HI THERE!
CHATTER
YOU'RE FROM NIRO JR. HIGH, RIGHT?
NICE TO MEET YOU!
YEAH, THAT'S RIGHT!
SMILE
HI THERE...
SHIRATORI-SAN.
BLINK
PLEASE GO OUT WITH
PLEASE
UH...
ER...

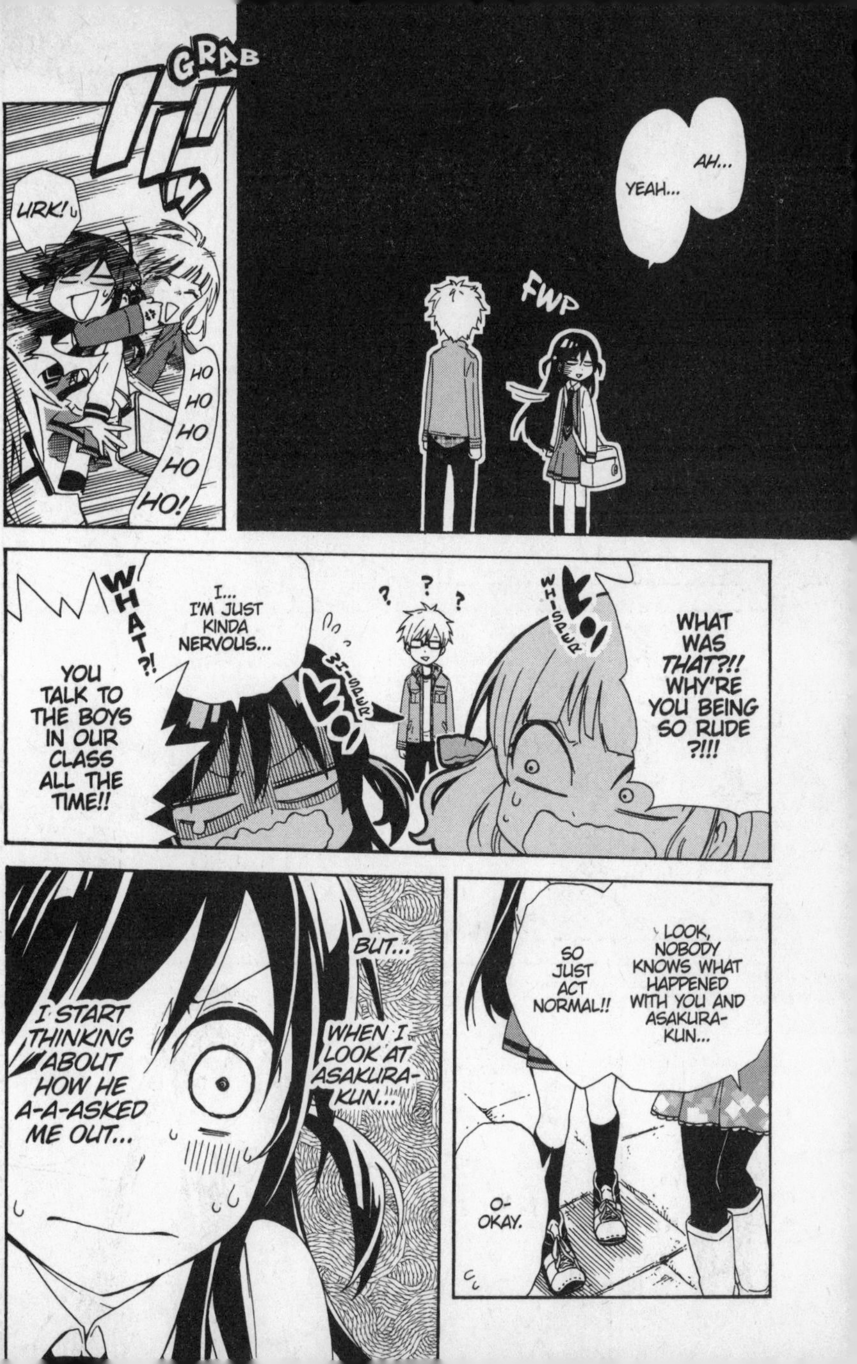
AH...
YEAH...
FWP
GRAB
URK!
HO HO HO HO HO!
WHISPER
WHAT WAS THAT?!! WHY'RE YOU BEING SO RUDE ?!!!
WHISPER
I... I'M JUST KINDA NERVOUS...
WHAT ?!
YOU TALK TO THE BOYS IN OUR CLASS ALL THE TIME!!
LOOK, NOBODY KNOWS WHAT HAPPENED WITH YOU AND ASAKURA-KUN...
SO JUST ACT NORMAL!!
O-OKAY.
BUT...
WHEN I LOOK AT ASAKURA-KUN...
I START THINKING ABOUT HOW HE A-A-ASKED ME OUT...

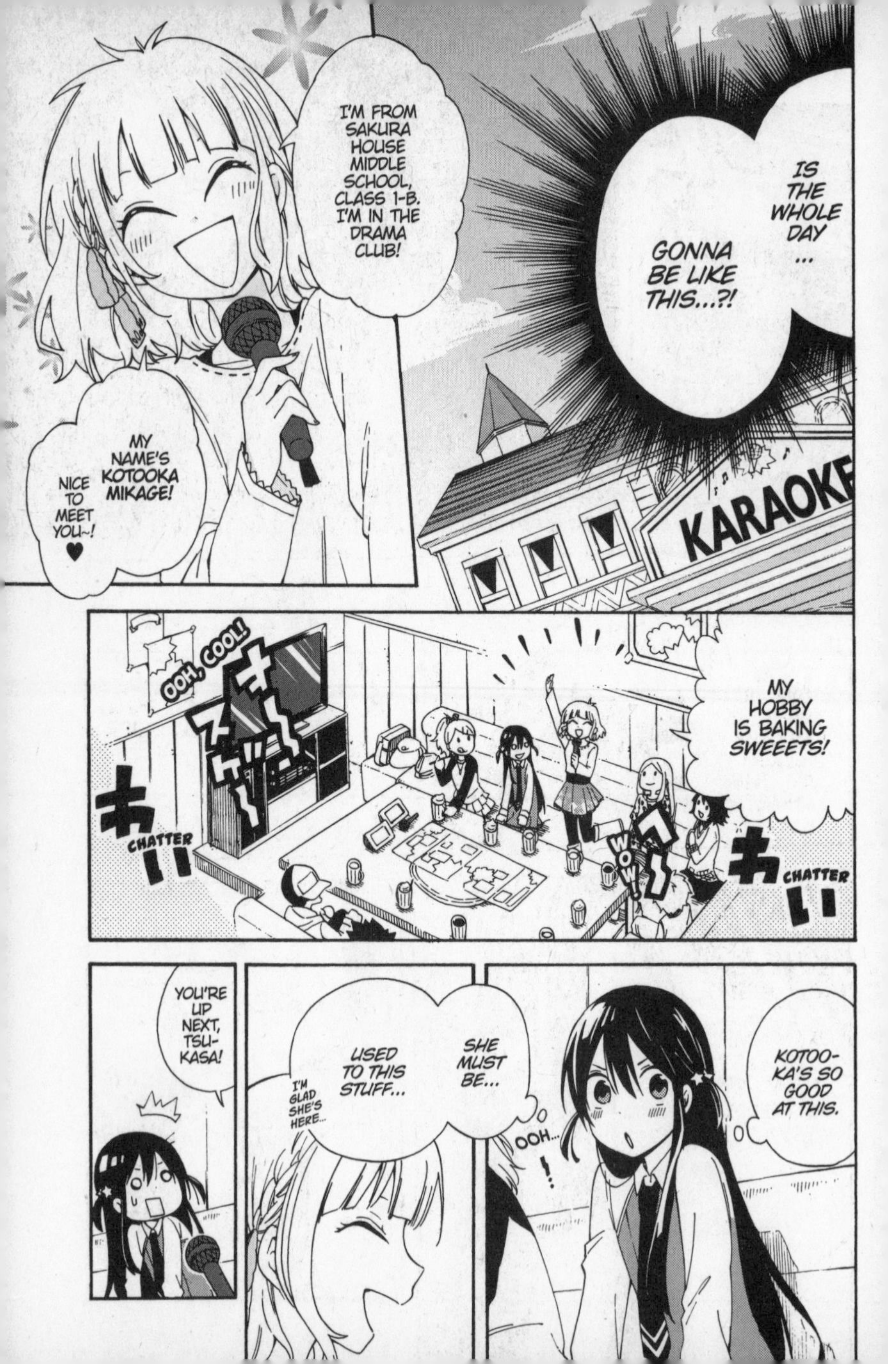
IS THE WHOLE DAY ...
GONNA BE LIKE THIS...?!
KARAOKE
I'M FROM SAKURA HOUSE MIDDLE SCHOOL, CLASS 1-B. I'M IN THE DRAMA CLUB!
MY NAME'S KOTOOKA MIKAGE!
NICE TO MEET YOU~! ♥
MY HOBBY IS BAKING SWEEETS!
CHATTER
WOW!
OOH, COOL!
CHATTER
KOTOOKA'S SO GOOD AT THIS.
OOH...!
SHE MUST BE...
USED TO THIS STUFF...
I'M GLAD SHE'S HERE...
YOU'RE UP NEXT, TSUKASA!

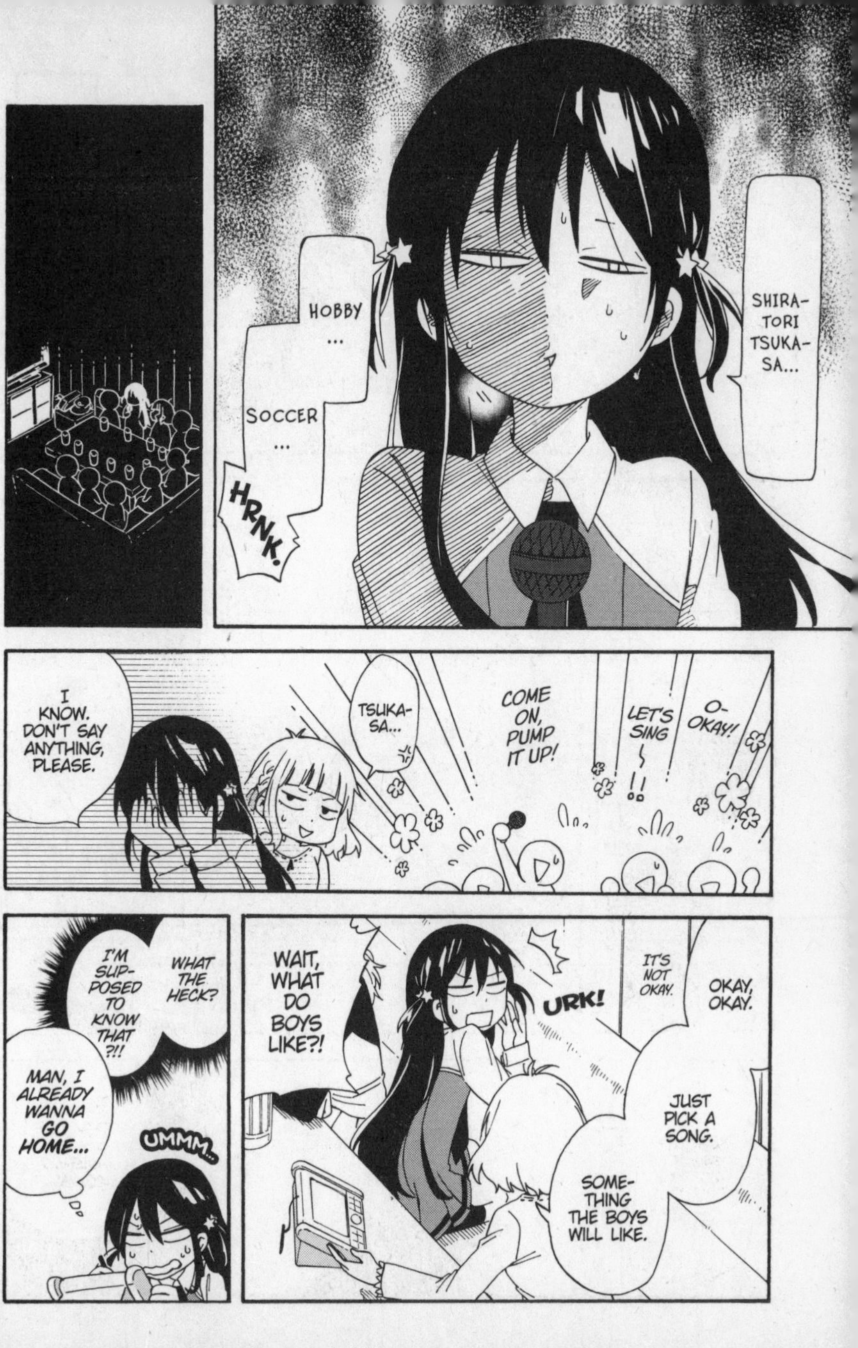
SHIRA-TORI TSUKA-SA...
HOBBY ...
SOCCER ...
HRNK!
O-OKAY!
LET'S SING~!!
COME ON, PUMP IT UP!
TSUKA-SA...
I KNOW. DON'T SAY ANYTHING, PLEASE.
OKAY, OKAY.
IT'S NOT OKAY.
URK!
WAIT, WHAT DO BOYS LIKE?!
JUST PICK A SONG.
SOME-THING THE BOYS WILL LIKE.
WHAT THE HECK?
I'M SUP-POSED TO KNOW THAT ?!!
MAN, I ALREADY WANNA GO HOME...
UMMM..

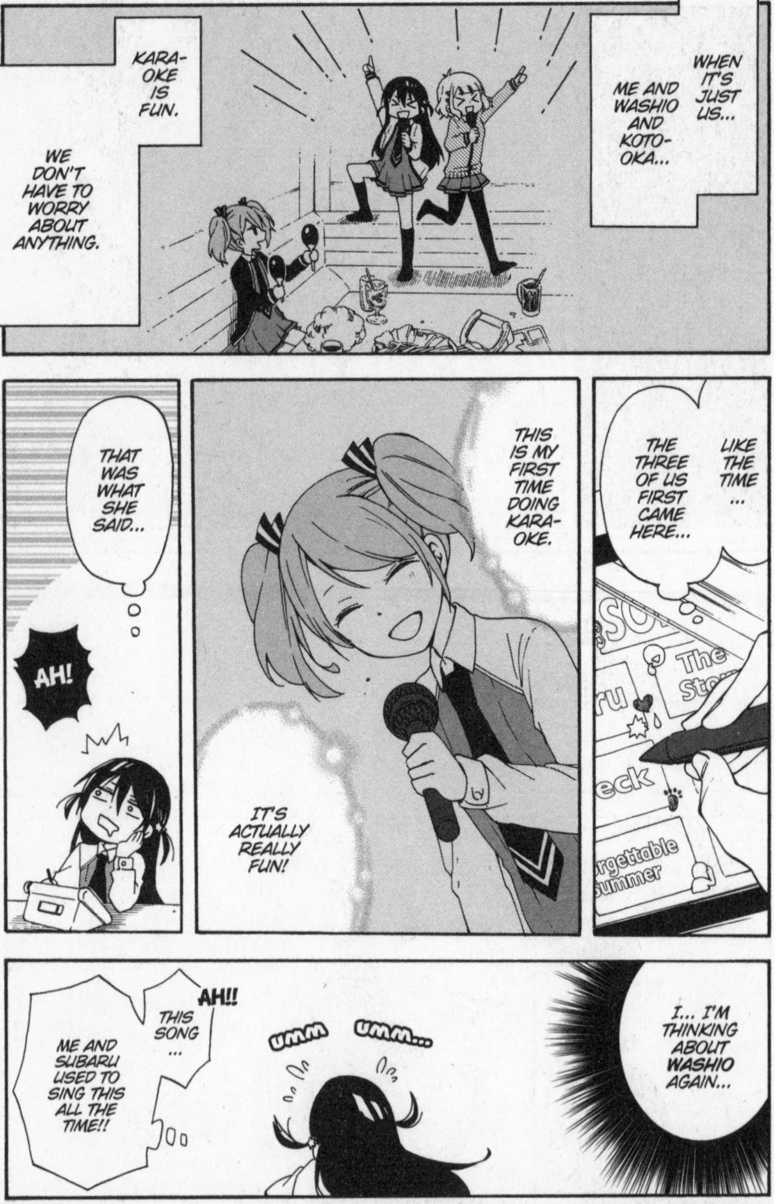
WHEN IT'S JUST US...
ME AND WASHIO AND KOTO-OKA...
KARA-OKE IS FUN.
WE DON'T HAVE TO WORRY ABOUT ANYTHING.
LIKE THE TIME...
THE THREE OF US FIRST CAME HERE...
THIS IS MY FIRST TIME DOING KARA-OKE.
IT'S ACTUALLY REALLY FUN!
THAT WAS WHAT SHE SAID...
AH!
I... I'M THINKING ABOUT WASHIO AGAIN...
UMM UMM...
AH!!
THIS SONG...
ME AND SUBARU USED TO SING THIS ALL THE TIME!!

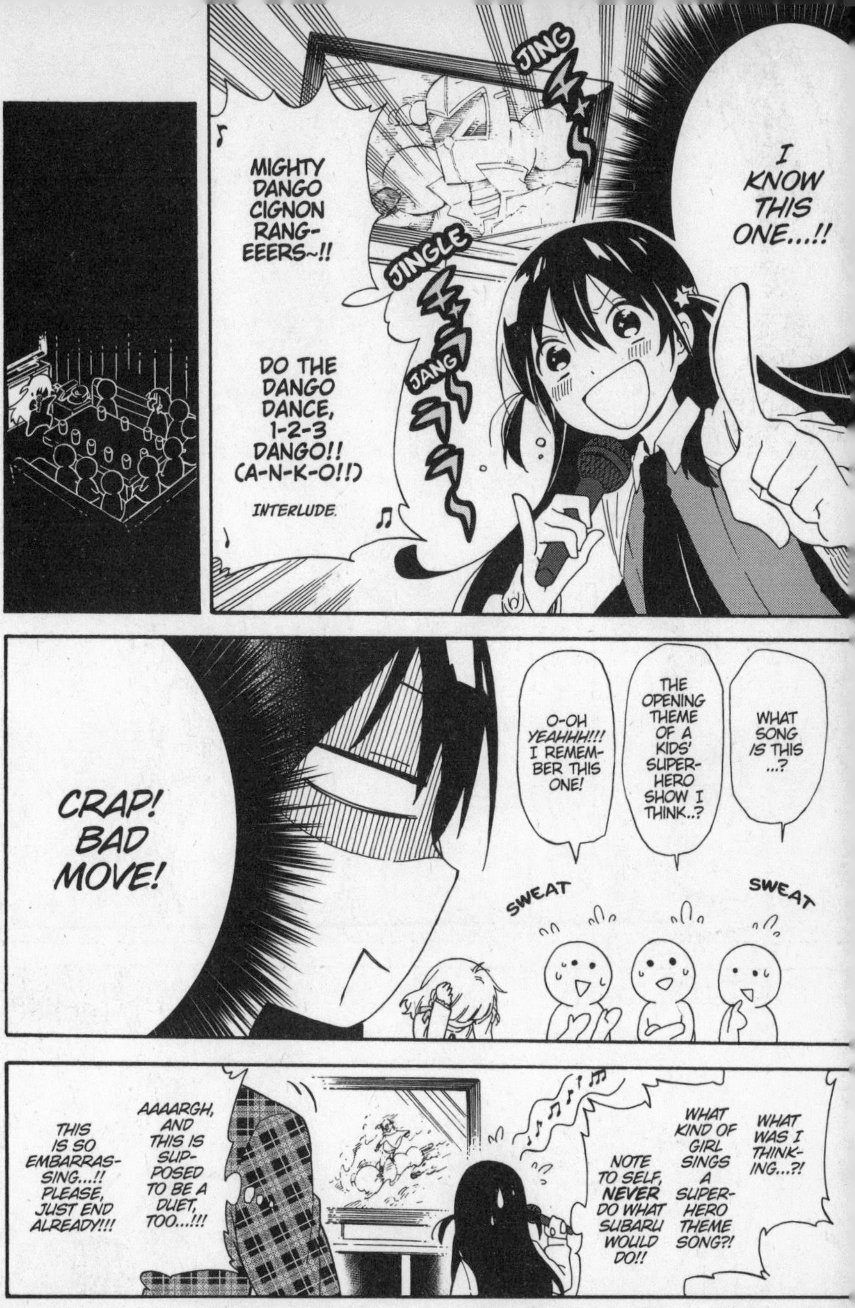
I KNOW THIS ONE...!!
JING
JINGLE
JANG
MIGHTY DANGO CIGNON RANG-EEERS~!!
DO THE DANGO DANCE, 1-2-3 DANGO!! (A-N-K-O!!)
INTERLUDE.
WHAT SONG IS THIS ...?
THE OPENING THEME OF A KIDS' SUPER-HERO SHOW I THINK..?
O-OH YEAHHH!!! I REMEM-BER THIS ONE!
SWEAT
SWEAT
CRAP! BAD MOVE!
WHAT WAS I THINK-ING...?!
WHAT KIND OF GIRL SINGS A SUPER-HERO THEME SONG?!
NOTE TO SELF, NEVER DO WHAT SUBARU WOULD DO!!
AAAARGH, AND THIS IS SUP-POSED TO BE A DUET, TOO...!!!
THIS IS SO EMBARRAS-SING...!! PLEASE, JUST END ALREADY!!!

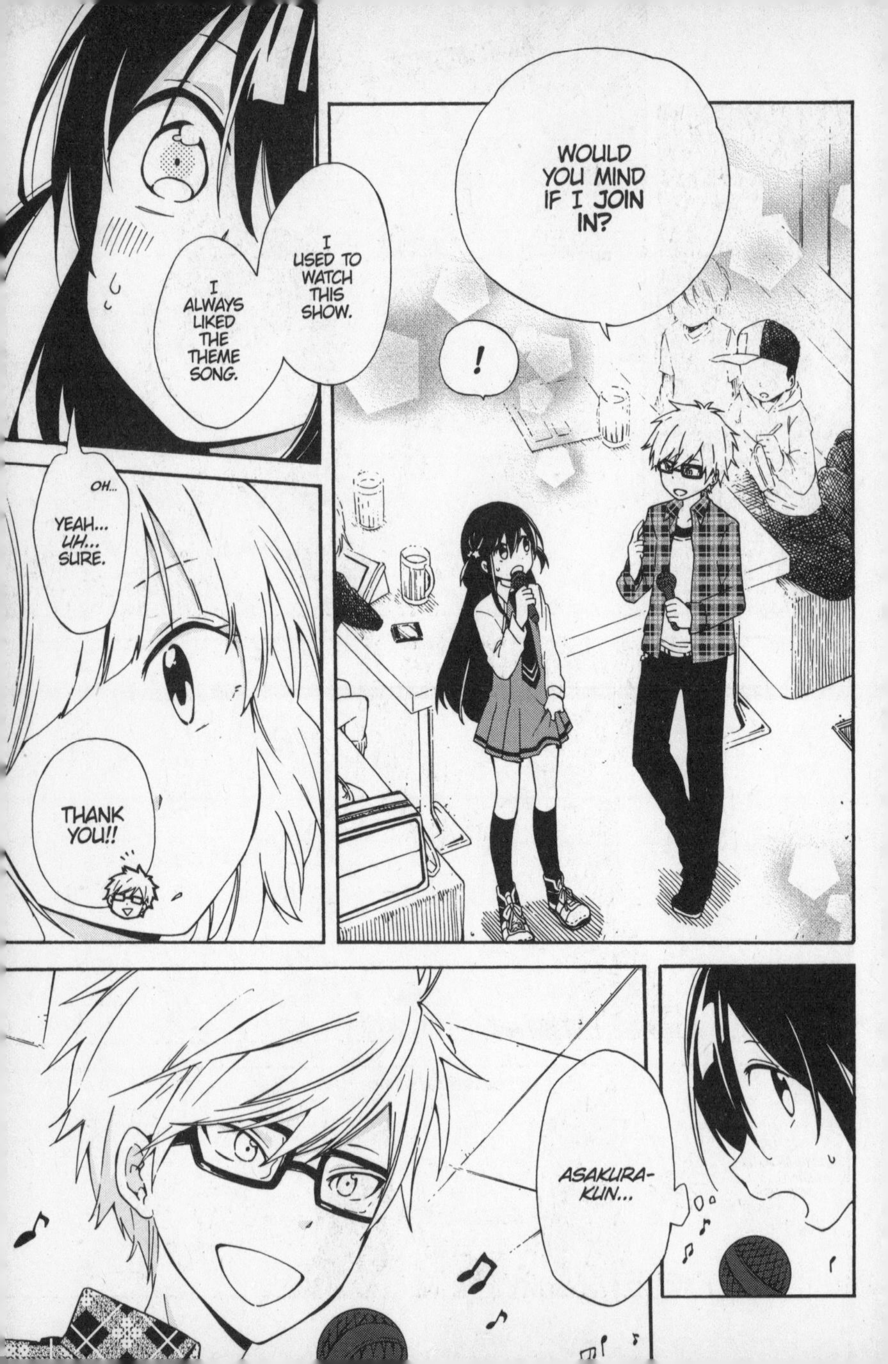
WOULD YOU MIND IF I JOIN IN?
!
I USED TO WATCH THIS SHOW.
I ALWAYS LIKED THE THEME SONG.
OH... YEAH... UH... SURE.
THANK YOU!!
ASAKURA-KUN...

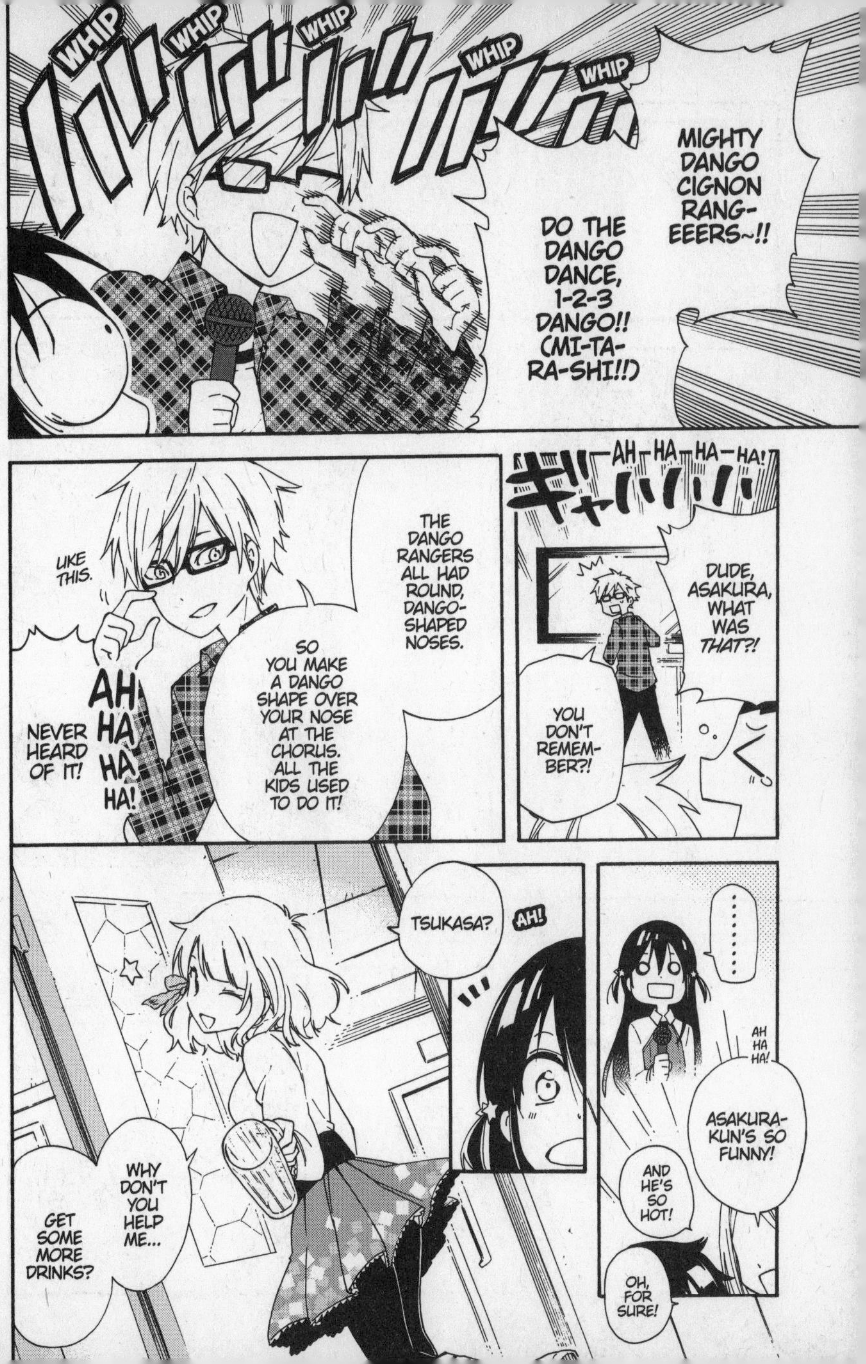

WHIP WHIP WHIP WHIP WHIP
MIGHTY DANGO CIGNON RANG-EEERS~!!
DO THE DANGO DANCE, 1-2-3 DANGO!! (MI-TA-RA-SHI!!)
AH-HA-HA-HA!
DUDE, ASAKURA, WHAT WAS THAT?!
YOU DON'T REMEMBER?!
THE DANGO RANGERS ALL HAD ROUND, DANGO-SHAPED NOSES.
SO YOU MAKE A DANGO SHAPE OVER YOUR NOSE AT THE CHORUS. ALL THE KIDS USED TO DO IT!
LIKE THIS.
AH HA HA HA!
NEVER HEARD OF IT!
......
AH HA HA!
ASAKURA-KUN'S SO FUNNY!
AND HE'S SO HOT!
OH, FOR SURE!
AH!
TSUKASA?
WHY DON'T YOU HELP ME...
GET SOME MORE DRINKS?

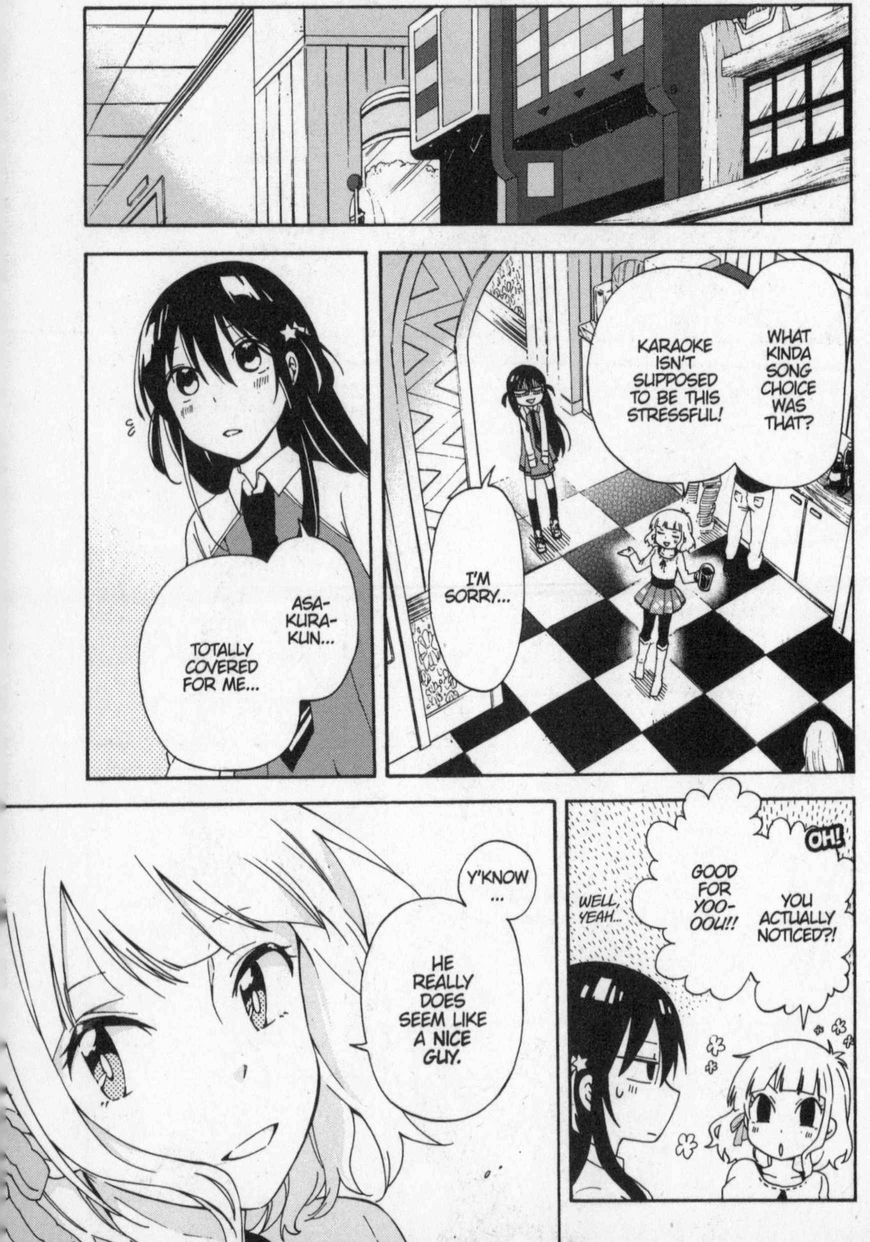
WHAT KINDA SONG CHOICE WAS THAT?
KARAOKE ISN'T SUPPOSED TO BE THIS STRESSFUL!
I'M SORRY...
ASA-KURA-KUN...
TOTALLY COVERED FOR ME...
OH!
YOU ACTUALLY NOTICED?!
GOOD FOR YOO-OOU!!
WELL, YEAH...
Y'KNOW...
HE REALLY DOES SEEM LIKE A NICE GUY.

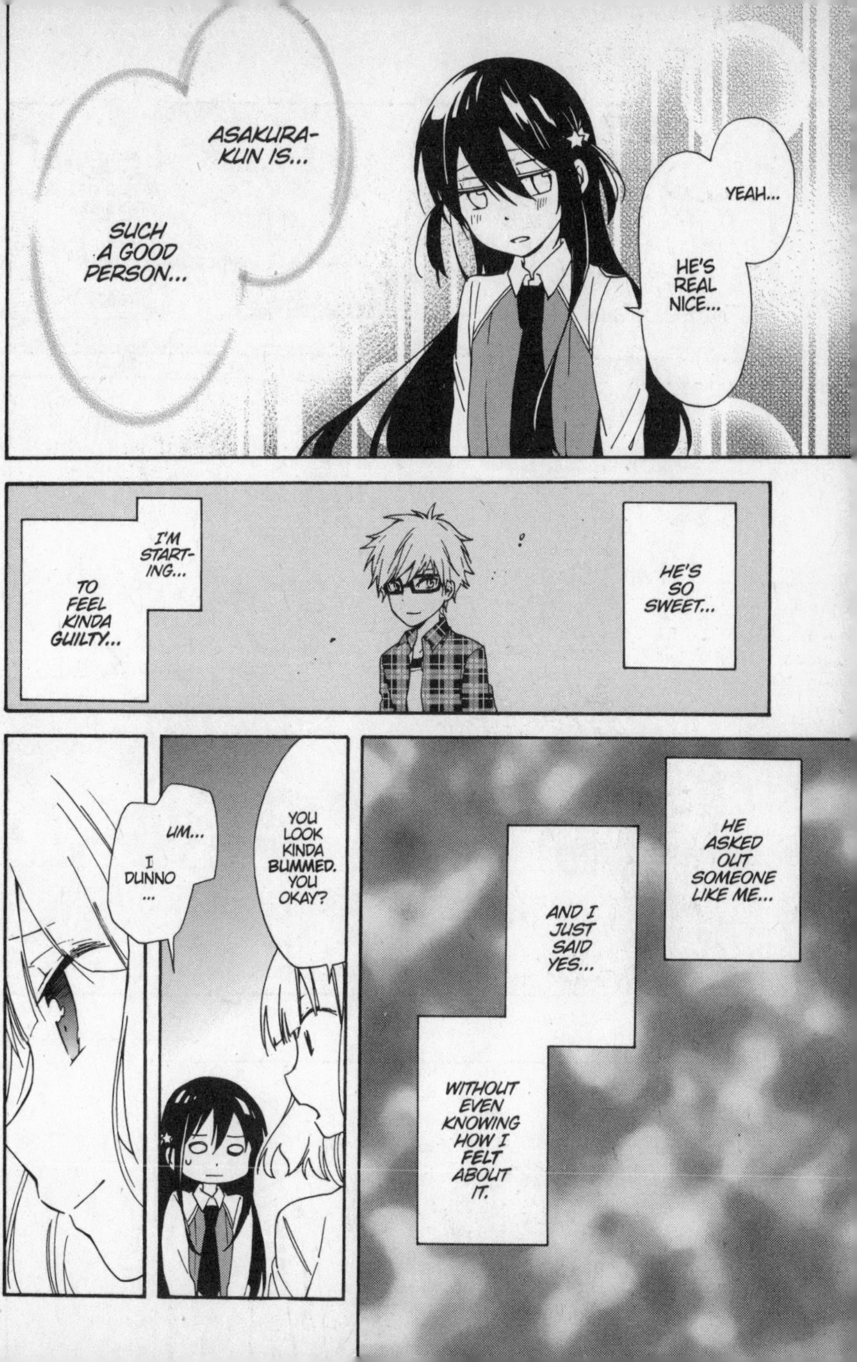
YEAH... HE'S REAL NICE...
ASAKURA-KUN IS...
SUCH A GOOD PERSON...
HE'S SO SWEET...
I'M STARTING... TO FEEL KINDA GUILTY...
HE ASKED OUT SOMEONE LIKE ME...
AND I JUST SAID YES...
WITHOUT EVEN KNOWING HOW I FELT ABOUT IT.
YOU LOOK KINDA BUMMED. YOU OKAY?
UM... I DUNNO...

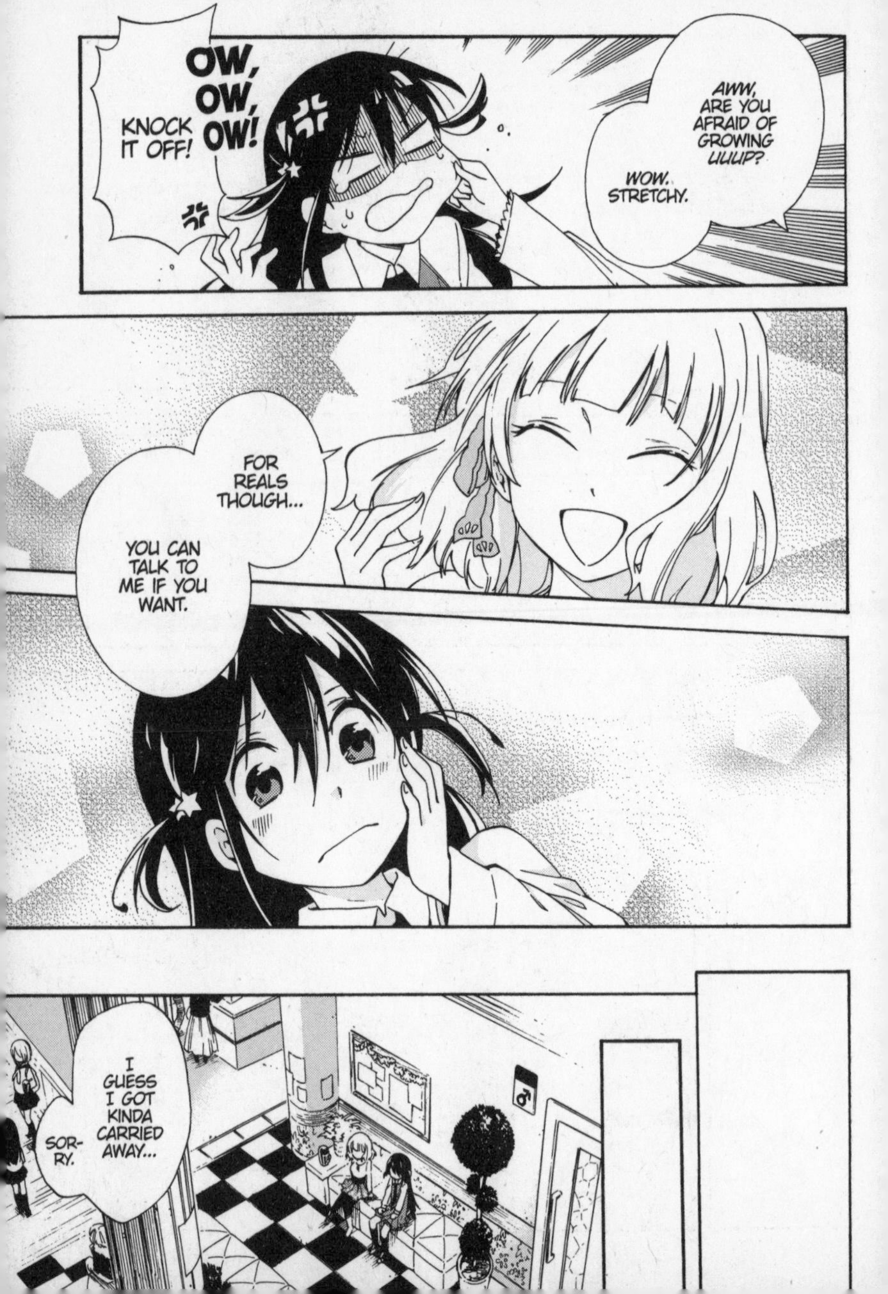
AWW, ARE YOU AFRAID OF GROWING UUUP?
WOW. STRETCHY.
OW, OW, OW!
KNOCK IT OFF!
FOR REALS THOUGH...
YOU CAN TALK TO ME IF YOU WANT.
I GUESS I GOT KINDA CARRIED AWAY...
SOR-RY.

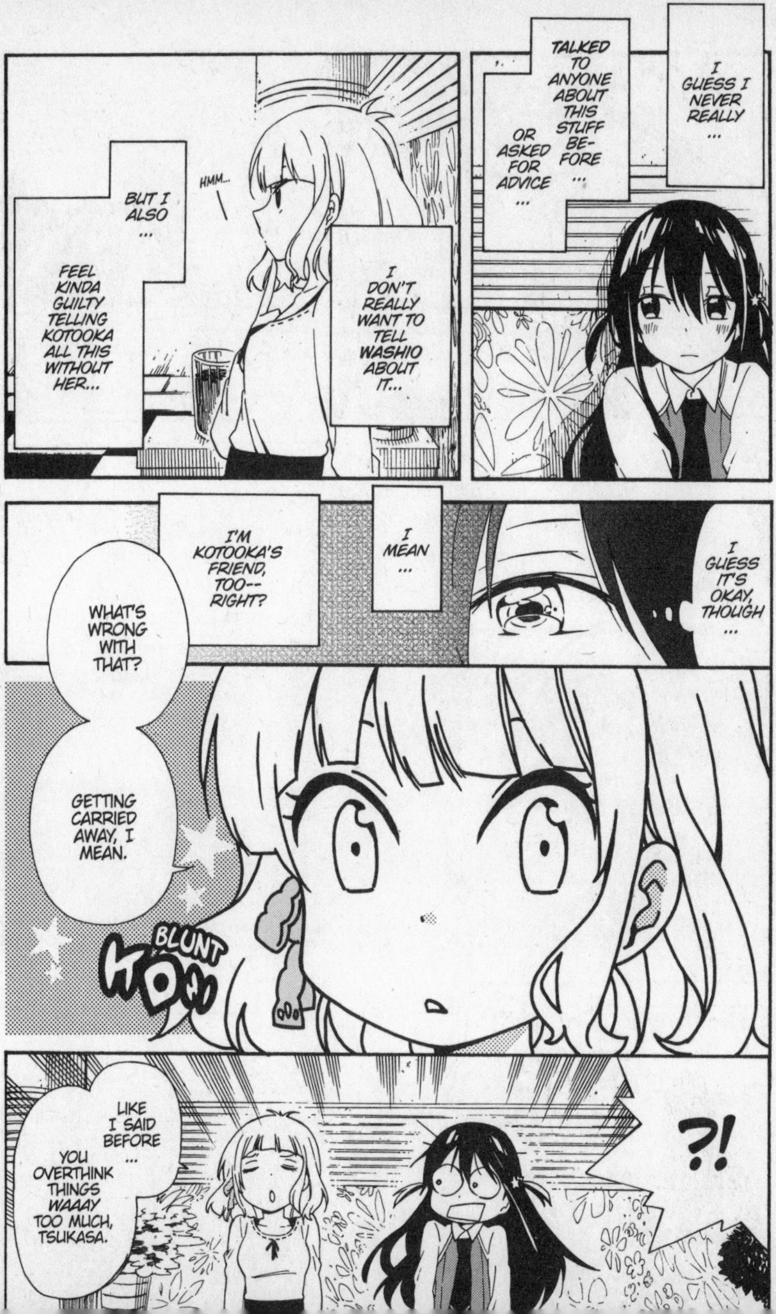
I GUESS I NEVER REALLY ...
TALKED TO ANYONE ABOUT THIS STUFF BEFORE ...
OR ASKED FOR ADVICE ...
I DON'T REALLY WANT TO TELL WASHIO ABOUT IT...
HMM...
BUT I ALSO ...
FEEL KINDA GUILTY TELLING KOTOOKA ALL THIS WITHOUT HER...
I GUESS IT'S OKAY, THOUGH ...
I MEAN ...
I'M KOTOOKA'S FRIEND, TOO-- RIGHT?
WHAT'S WRONG WITH THAT?
GETTING CARRIED AWAY, I MEAN.
BLUNT
?!
LIKE I SAID BEFORE ...
YOU OVERTHINK THINGS WAAAY TOO MUCH, TSUKASA.

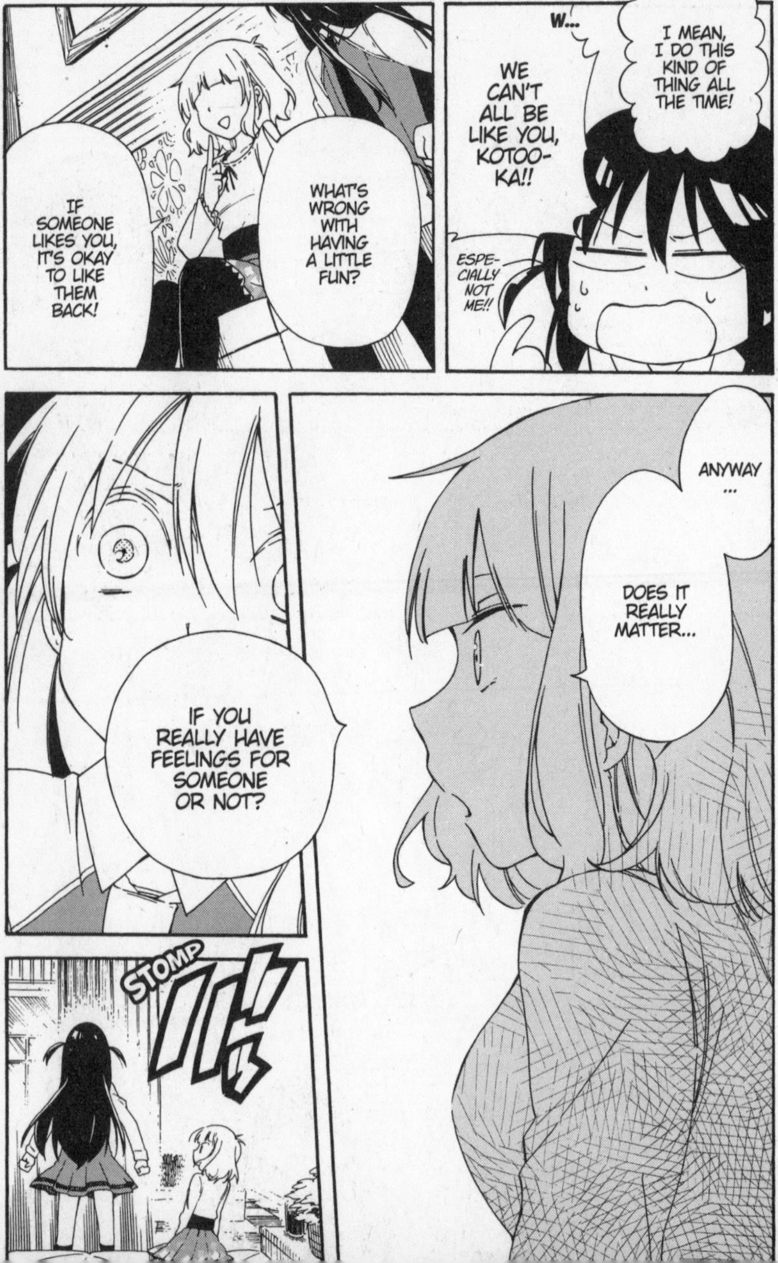
I MEAN, I DO THIS KIND OF THING ALL THE TIME!
W...
WE CAN'T ALL BE LIKE YOU, KOTOO-KA!!
ESPE-CIALLY NOT ME!!
WHAT'S WRONG WITH HAVING A LITTLE FUN?
IF SOMEONE LIKES YOU, IT'S OKAY TO LIKE THEM BACK!
ANYWAY...
DOES IT REALLY MATTER...
IF YOU REALLY HAVE FEELINGS FOR SOMEONE OR NOT?
STOMP

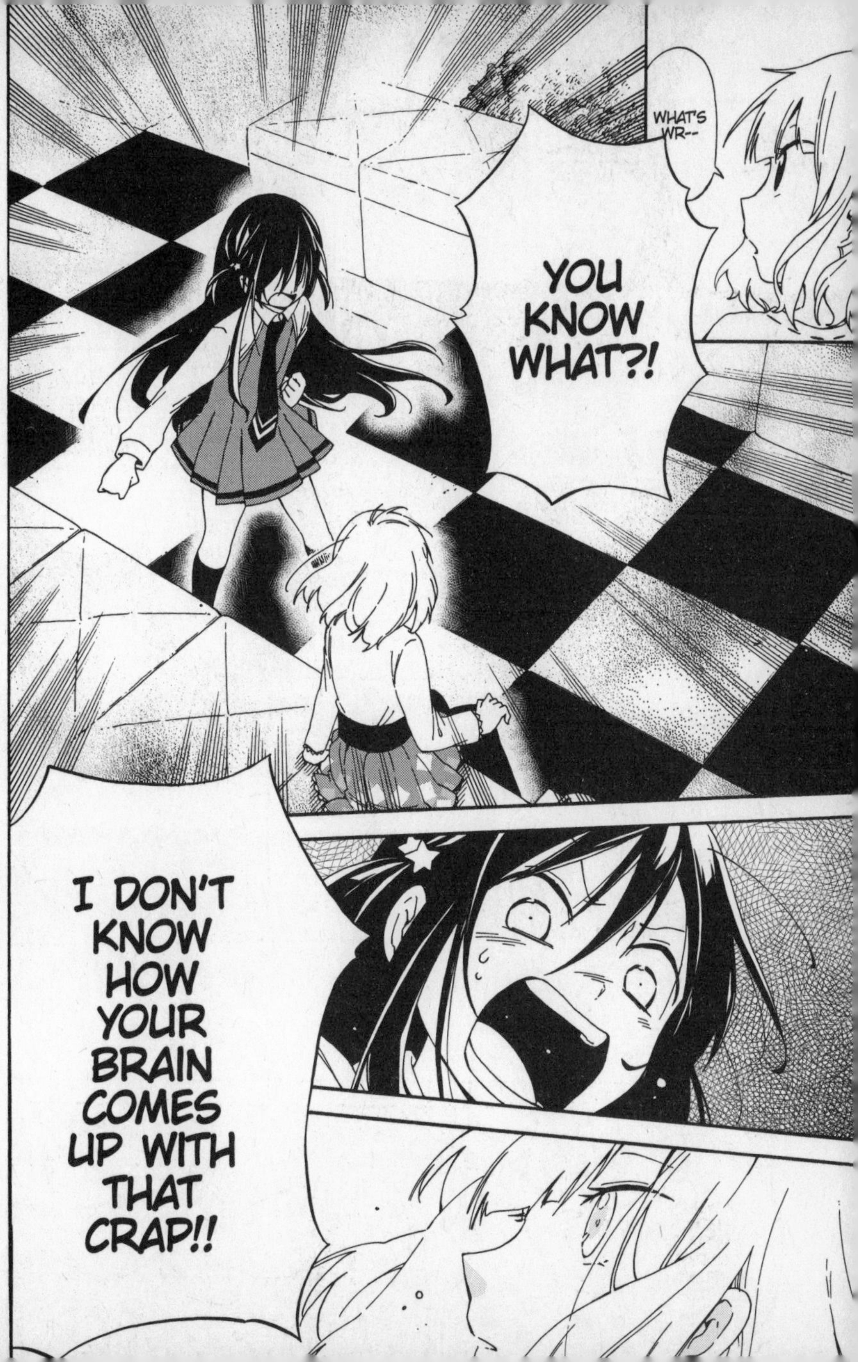
WHAT'S WR--
YOU KNOW WHAT?!
I DON'T KNOW HOW YOUR BRAIN COMES UP WITH THAT CRAP!!

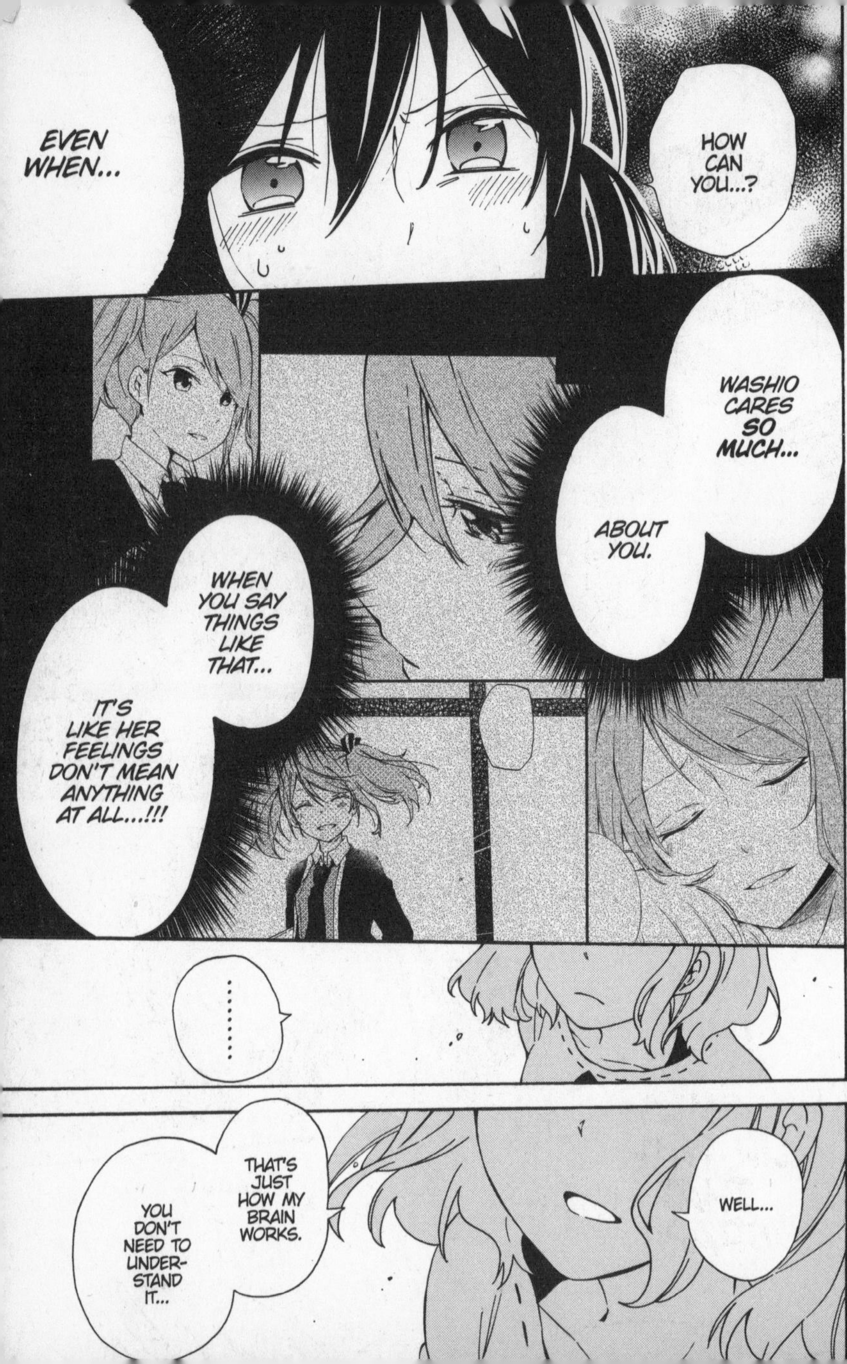
HOW CAN YOU...?
EVEN WHEN...
WASHIO CARES SO MUCH...
ABOUT YOU.
WHEN YOU SAY THINGS LIKE THAT...
IT'S LIKE HER FEELINGS DON'T MEAN ANYTHING AT ALL...!!!
......
WELL...
THAT'S JUST HOW MY BRAIN WORKS.
YOU DON'T NEED TO UNDER-STAND IT...

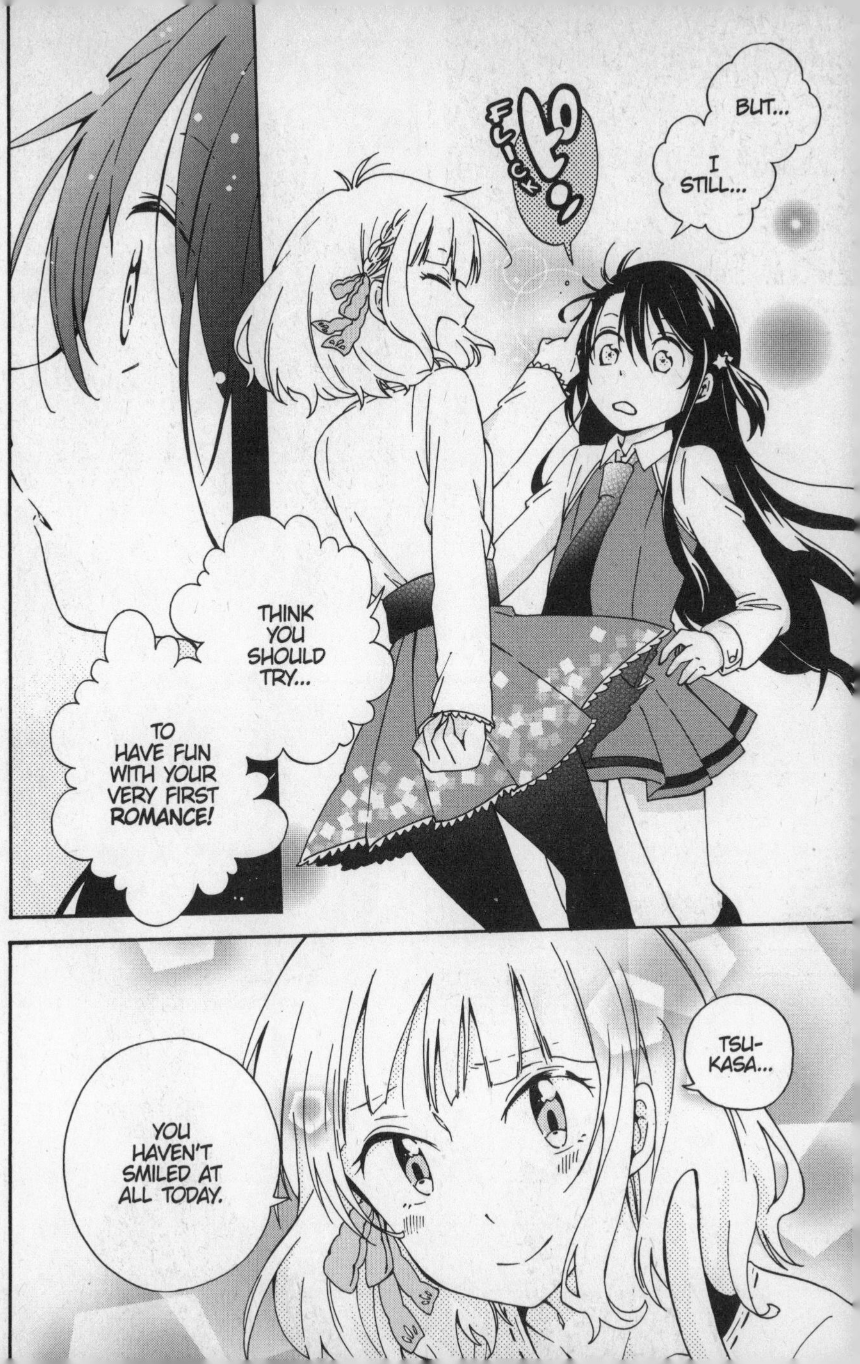
BUT... I STILL...
FLICK
THINK YOU SHOULD TRY...
TO HAVE FUN WITH YOUR VERY FIRST ROMANCE!
TSU-KASA...
YOU HAVEN'T SMILED AT ALL TODAY.

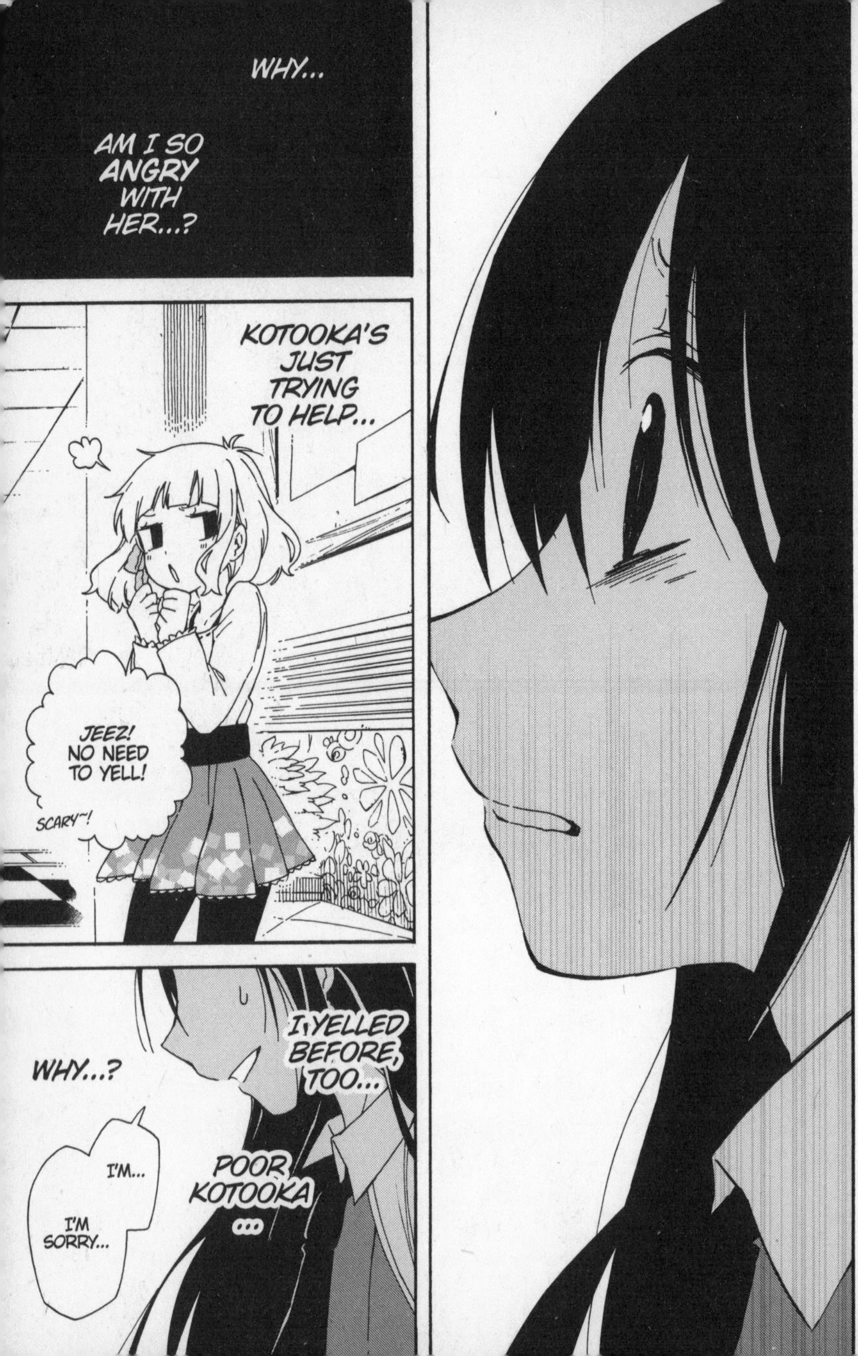
WHY...
AM I SO ANGRY WITH HER...?
KOTOOKA'S JUST TRYING TO HELP...
JEEZ! NO NEED TO YELL!
SCARY~!
I YELLED BEFORE, TOO...
WHY...?
POOR KOTOOKA...
I'M...
I'M SORRY...

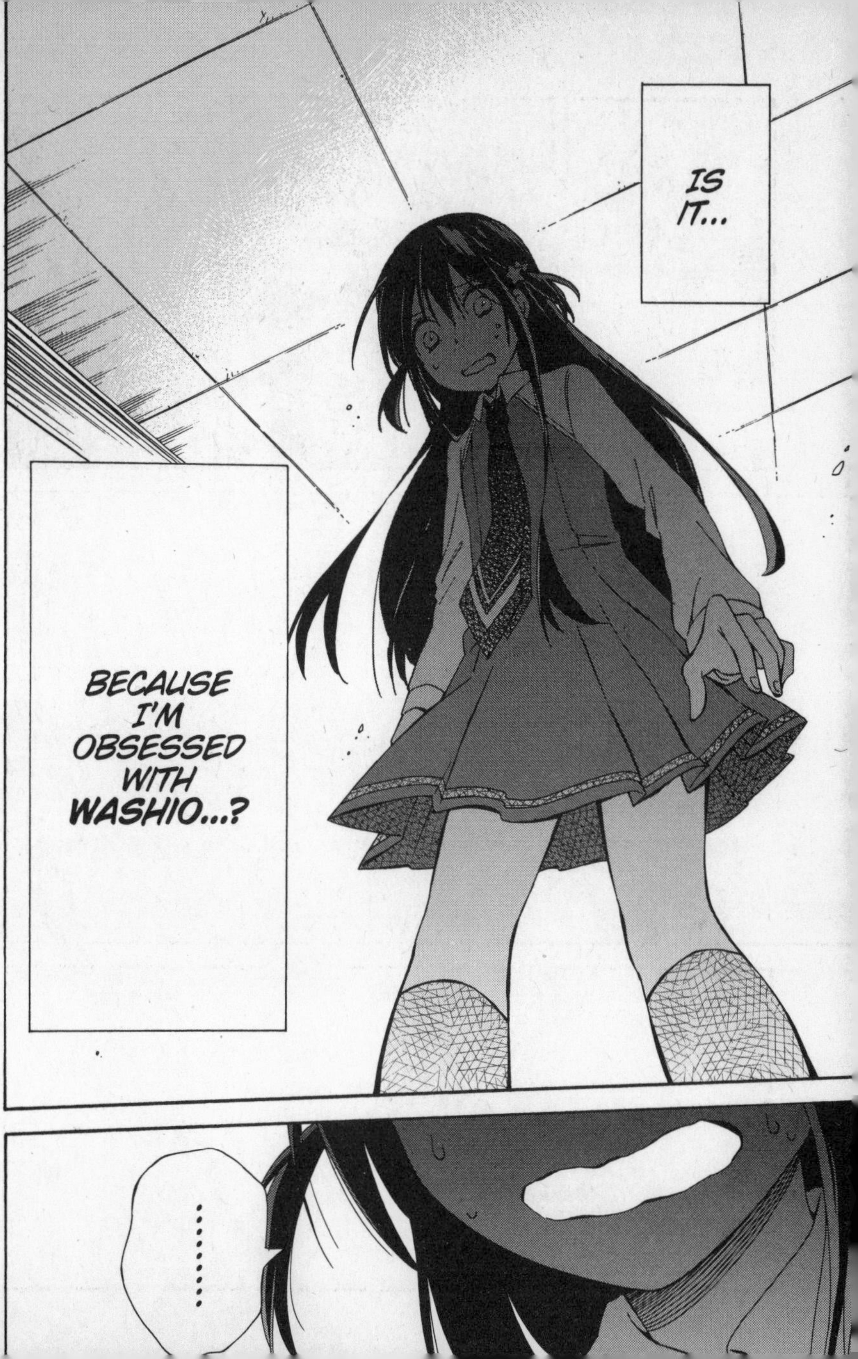
IS IT...
BECAUSE I'M OBSESSED WITH WASHIO...?
......

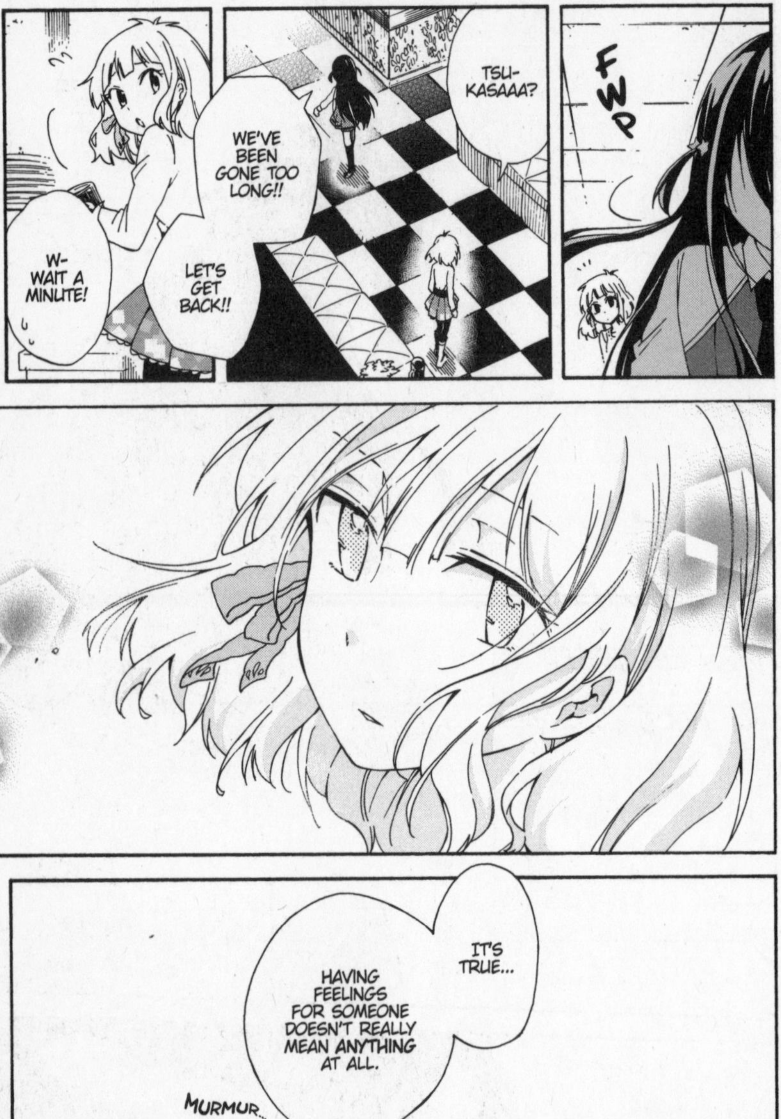
FWP
TSU-KASAAA?
WE'VE BEEN GONE TOO LONG!!
LET'S GET BACK!!
W-WAIT A MINUTE!
IT'S TRUE...
HAVING FEELINGS FOR SOMEONE DOESN'T REALLY MEAN ANYTHING AT ALL.
MURMUR...

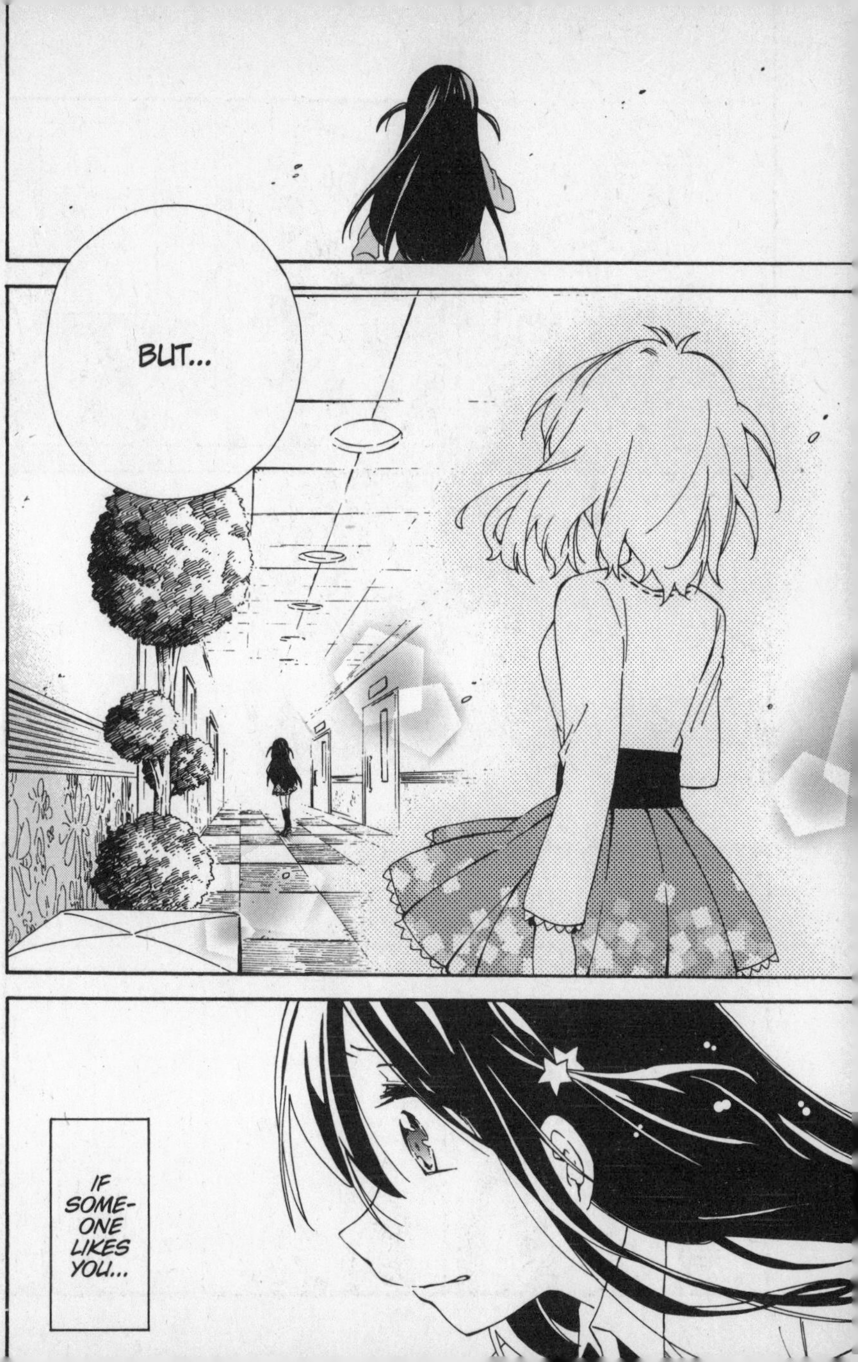
BUT...
IF SOMEONE LIKES YOU...

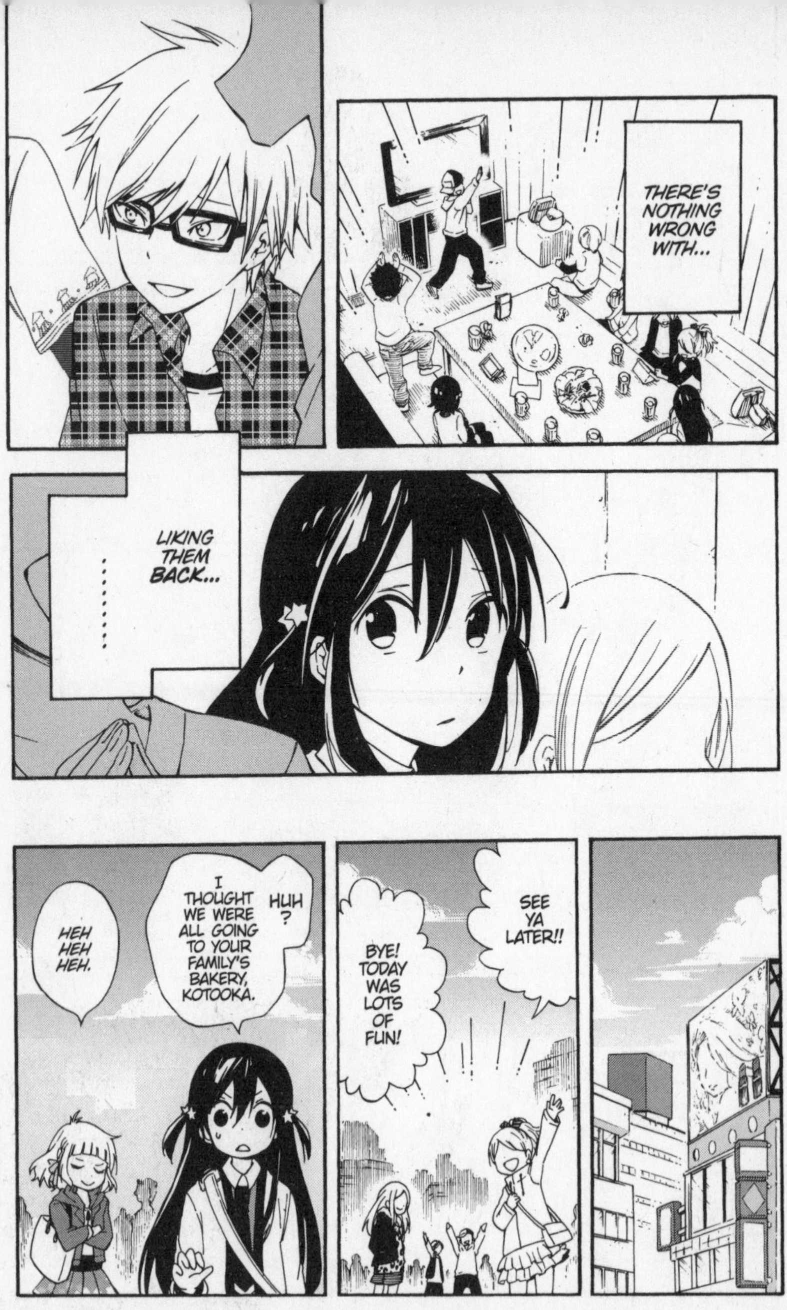
THERE'S NOTHING WRONG WITH...
LIKING THEM BACK...
......
SEE YA LATER!!
BYE! TODAY WAS LOTS OF FUN!
HUH?
I THOUGHT WE WERE ALL GOING TO YOUR FAMILY'S BAKERY, KOTOOKA.
HEH HEH HEH.

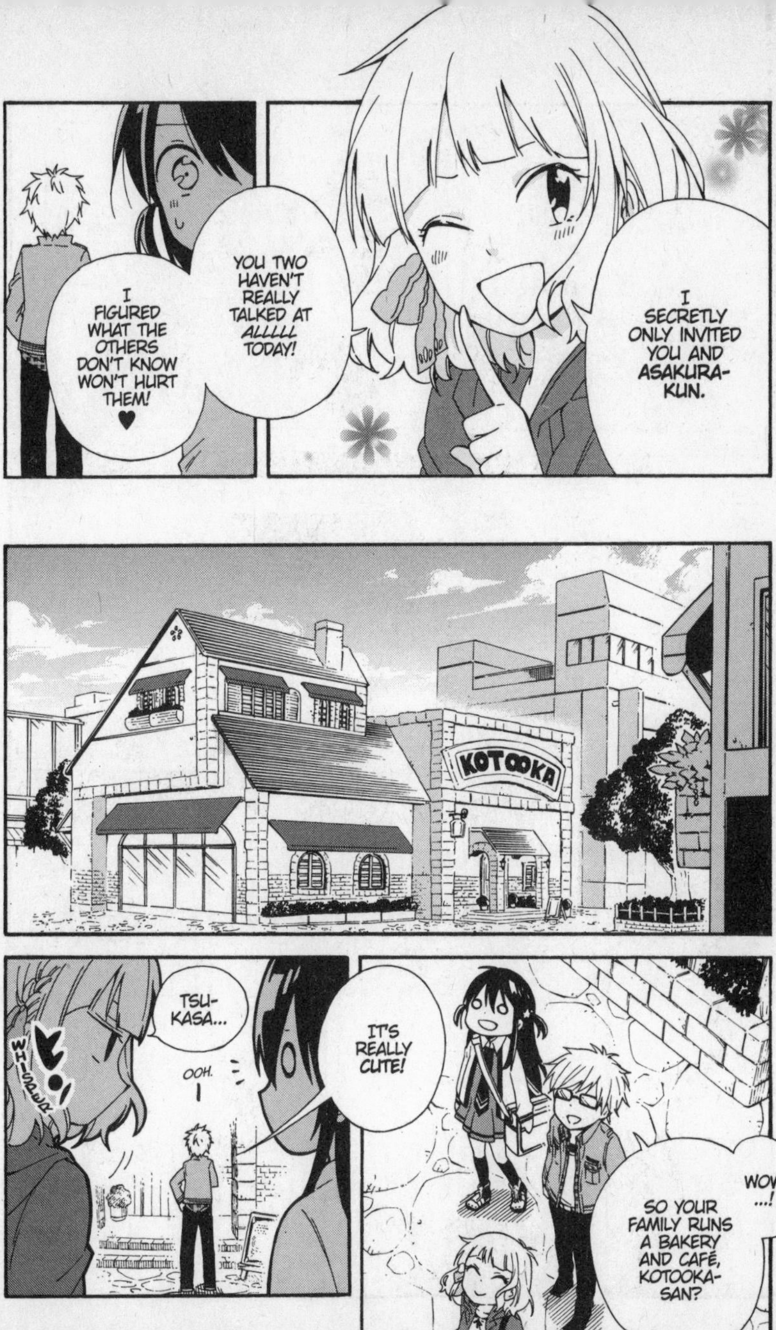
I SECRETLY ONLY INVITED YOU AND ASAKURA-KUN.
YOU TWO HAVEN'T REALLY TALKED AT ALLLLL TODAY!
I FIGURED WHAT THE OTHERS DON'T KNOW WON'T HURT THEM! ♥
KOTOOKA
WOW ...!
SO YOUR FAMILY RUNS A BAKERY AND CAFÉ, KOTOOKA-SAN?
IT'S REALLY CUTE!
TSU-KASA...
OOH.
WHISPER

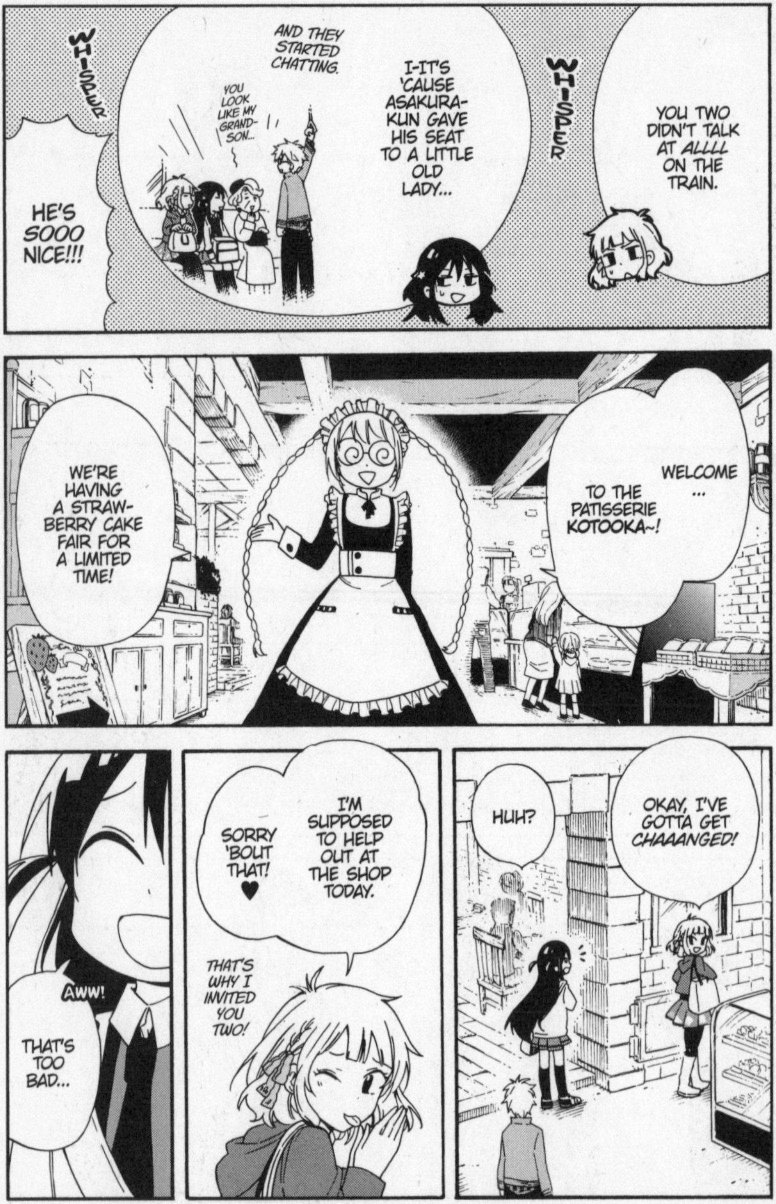
YOU TWO DIDN'T TALK AT ALLLL ON THE TRAIN.
WHISPER
I-IT'S 'CAUSE ASAKURA-KUN GAVE HIS SEAT TO A LITTLE OLD LADY...
AND THEY STARTED CHATTING.
YOU LOOK LIKE MY GRAND-SON...
WHISPER
HE'S SOOO NICE!!!
WELCOME ...
TO THE PATISSERIE KOTOOKA~!
WE'RE HAVING A STRAW-BERRY CAKE FAIR FOR A LIMITED TIME!
OKAY, I'VE GOTTA GET CHAAANGED!
HUH?
I'M SUPPOSED TO HELP OUT AT THE SHOP TODAY.
SORRY 'BOUT THAT! ♥
THAT'S WHY I INVITED YOU TWO!
AWW!
THAT'S TOO BAD...

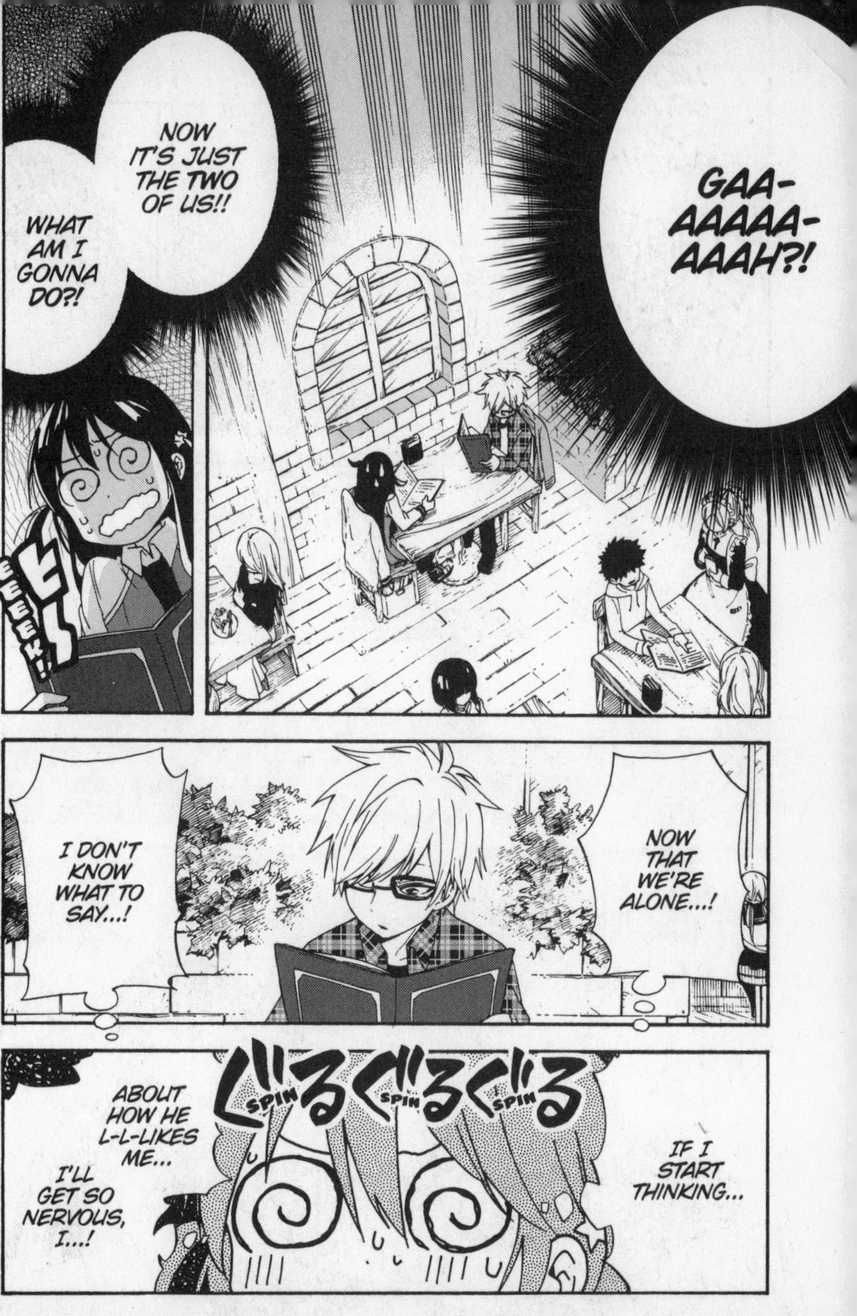
GAA-AAAAA-AAAH?!
NOW IT'S JUST THE TWO OF US!!
WHAT AM I GONNA DO?!
EEEEK!
NOW THAT WE'RE ALONE...!
I DON'T KNOW WHAT TO SAY...!
IF I START THINKING...
ぐるぐるぐる SPIN SPIN SPIN
ABOUT HOW HE L-L-LIKES ME...
I'LL GET SO NERVOUS, I...!

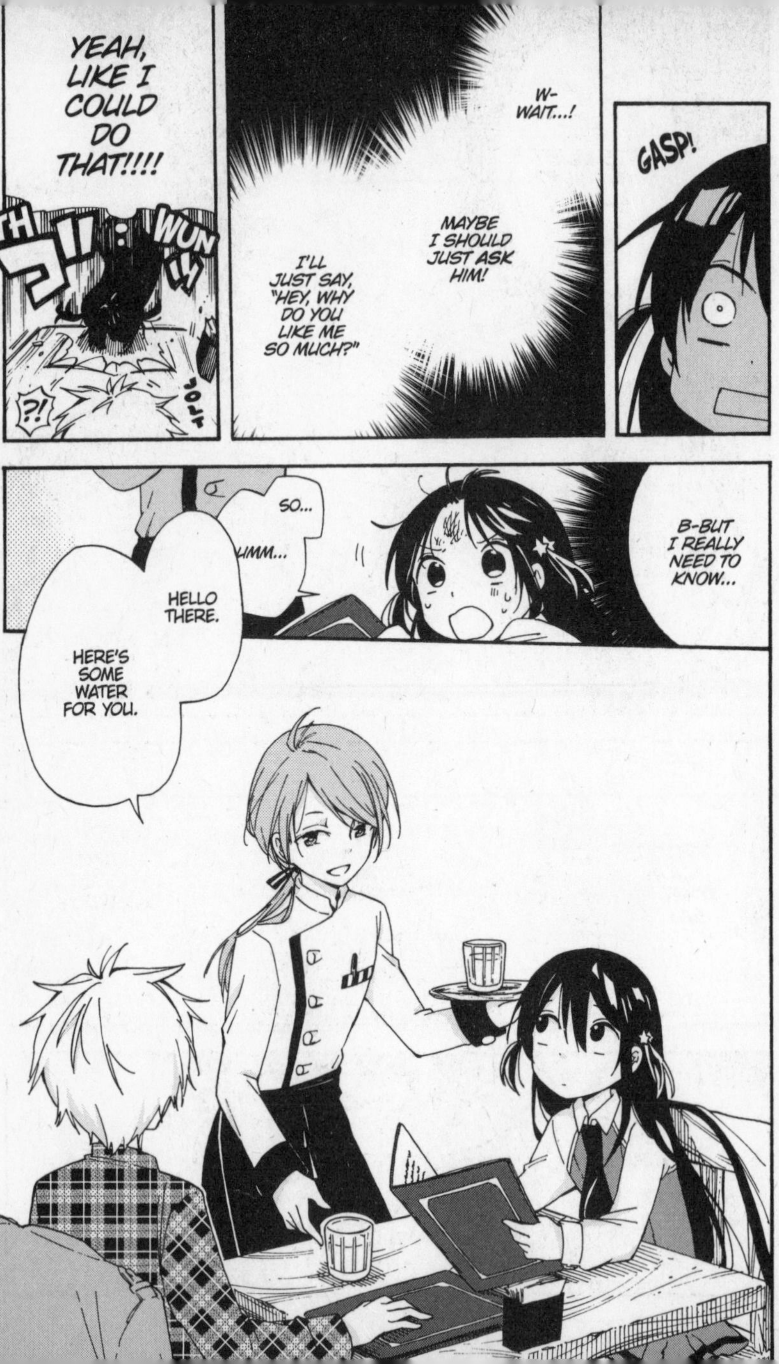
GASP!
W- WAIT...!
MAYBE I SHOULD JUST ASK HIM!
I'LL JUST SAY, "HEY, WHY DO YOU LIKE ME SO MUCH?"
YEAH, LIKE I COULD DO THAT!!!!
TH
WUN
JOLT
?!
B-BUT I REALLY NEED TO KNOW...
SO...
UMM...
HELLO THERE.
HERE'S SOME WATER FOR YOU.

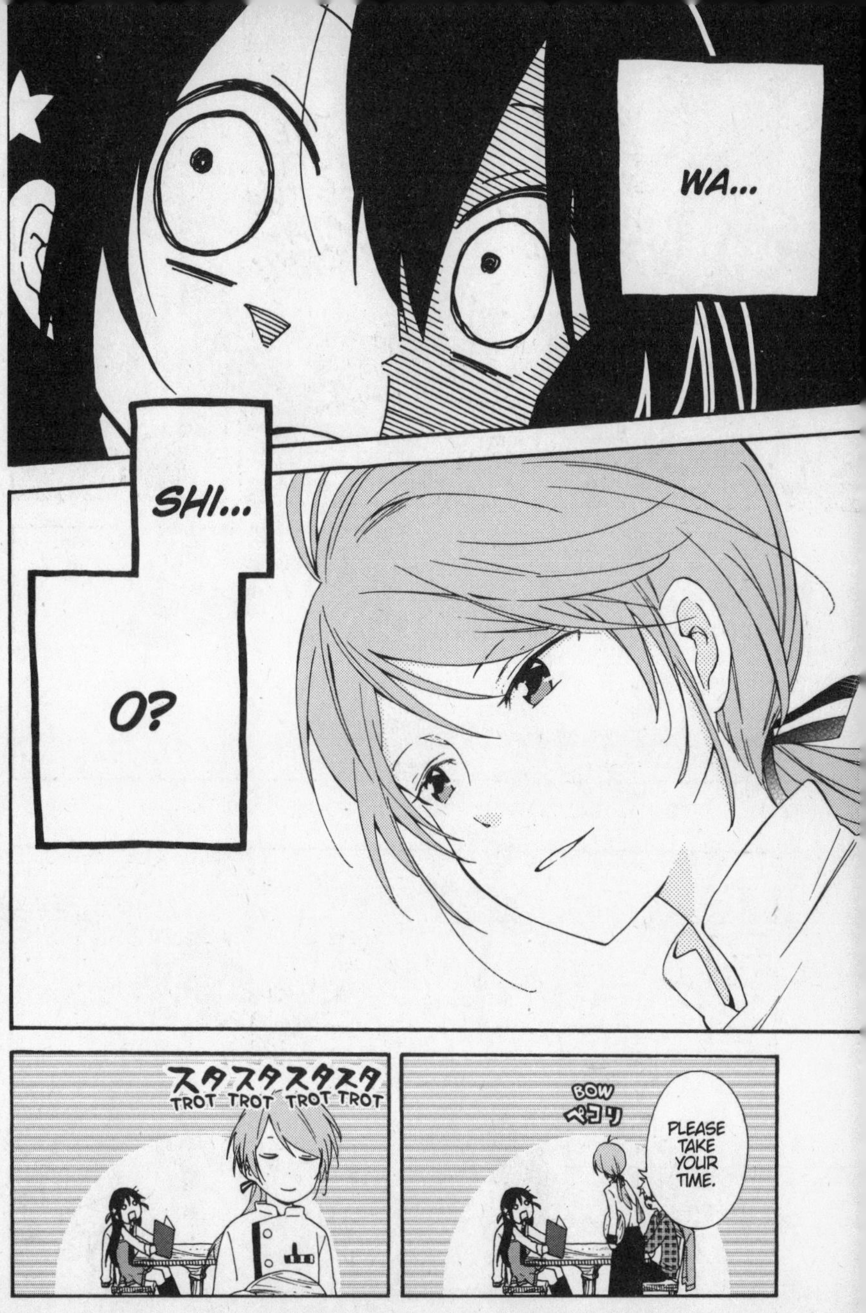
WA...
SHI...
O?
BOW
ペコリ
PLEASE TAKE YOUR TIME.
スタスタスタスタ
TROT TROT TROT TROT

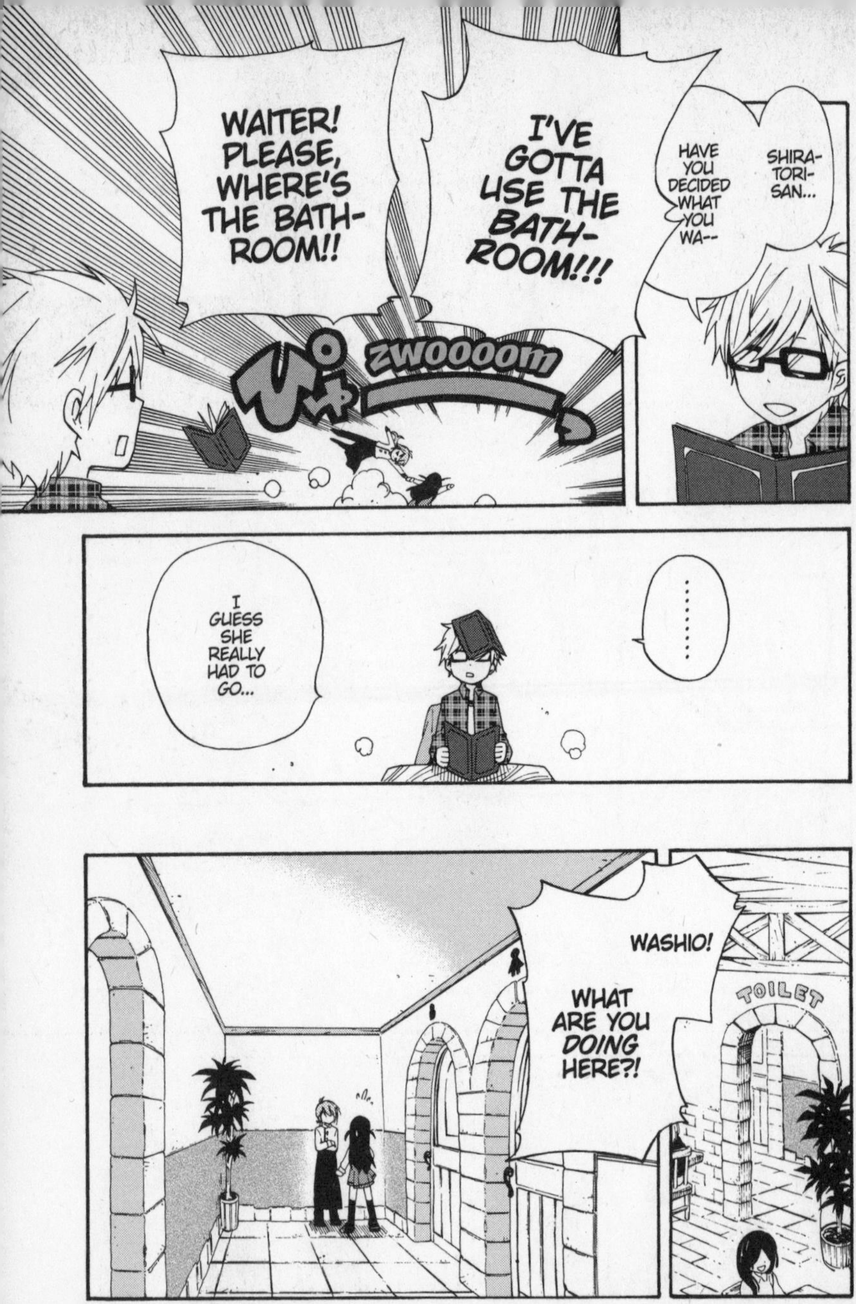
SHIRA-TORI-SAN...
HAVE YOU DECIDED WHAT YOU WA--
I'VE GOTTA USE THE BATH-ROOM!!!
WAITER! PLEASE, WHERE'S THE BATH-ROOM!!
ZWOOOOM
ぴゅ
......
I GUESS SHE REALLY HAD TO GO...
TOILET
WASHIO!
WHAT ARE YOU DOING HERE?!

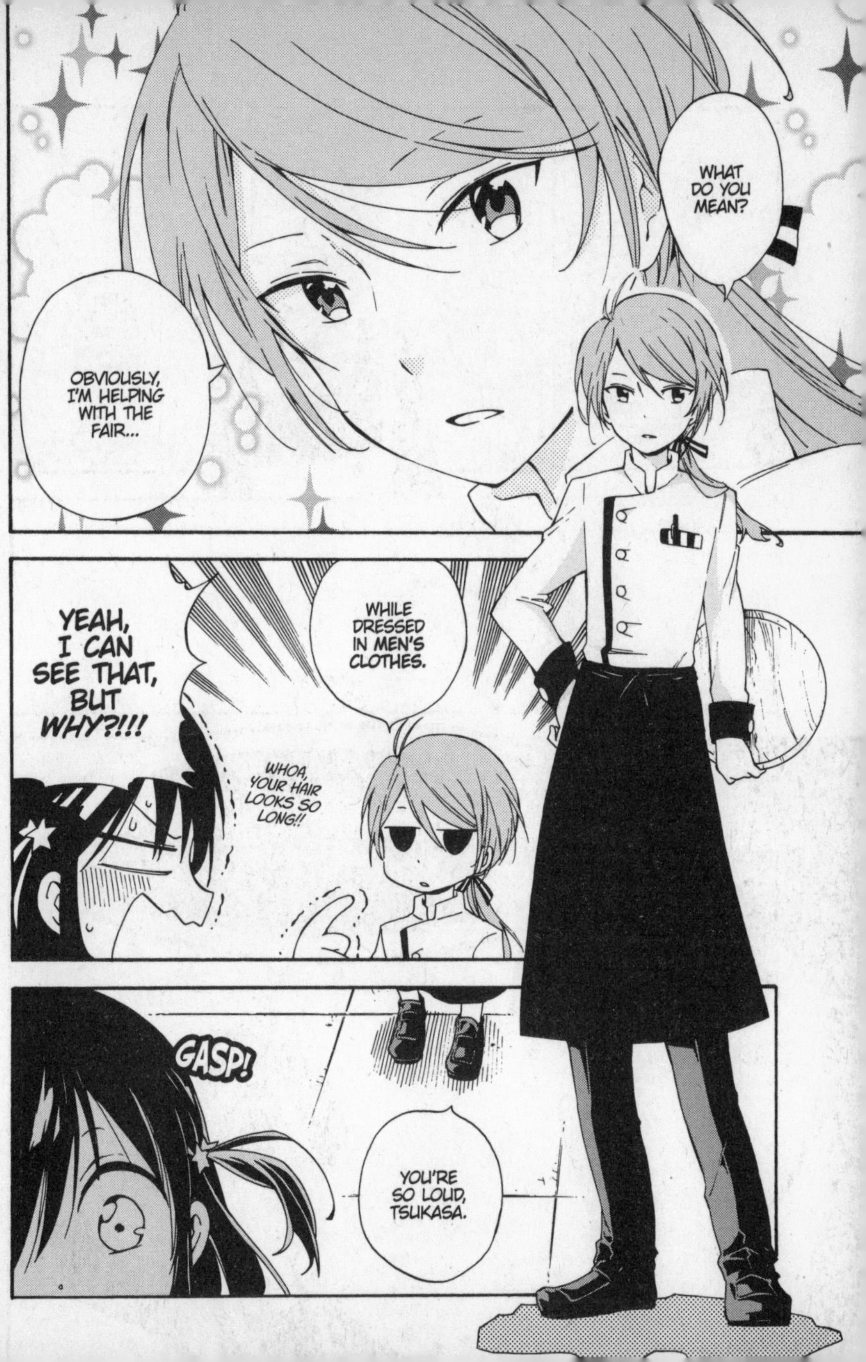
WHAT DO YOU MEAN?
OBVIOUSLY, I'M HELPING WITH THE FAIR...
WHILE DRESSED IN MEN'S CLOTHES.
YEAH, I CAN SEE THAT, BUT WHY?!!!
WHOA, YOUR HAIR LOOKS SO LONG!!
YOU'RE SO LOUD, TSUKASA.
GASP!

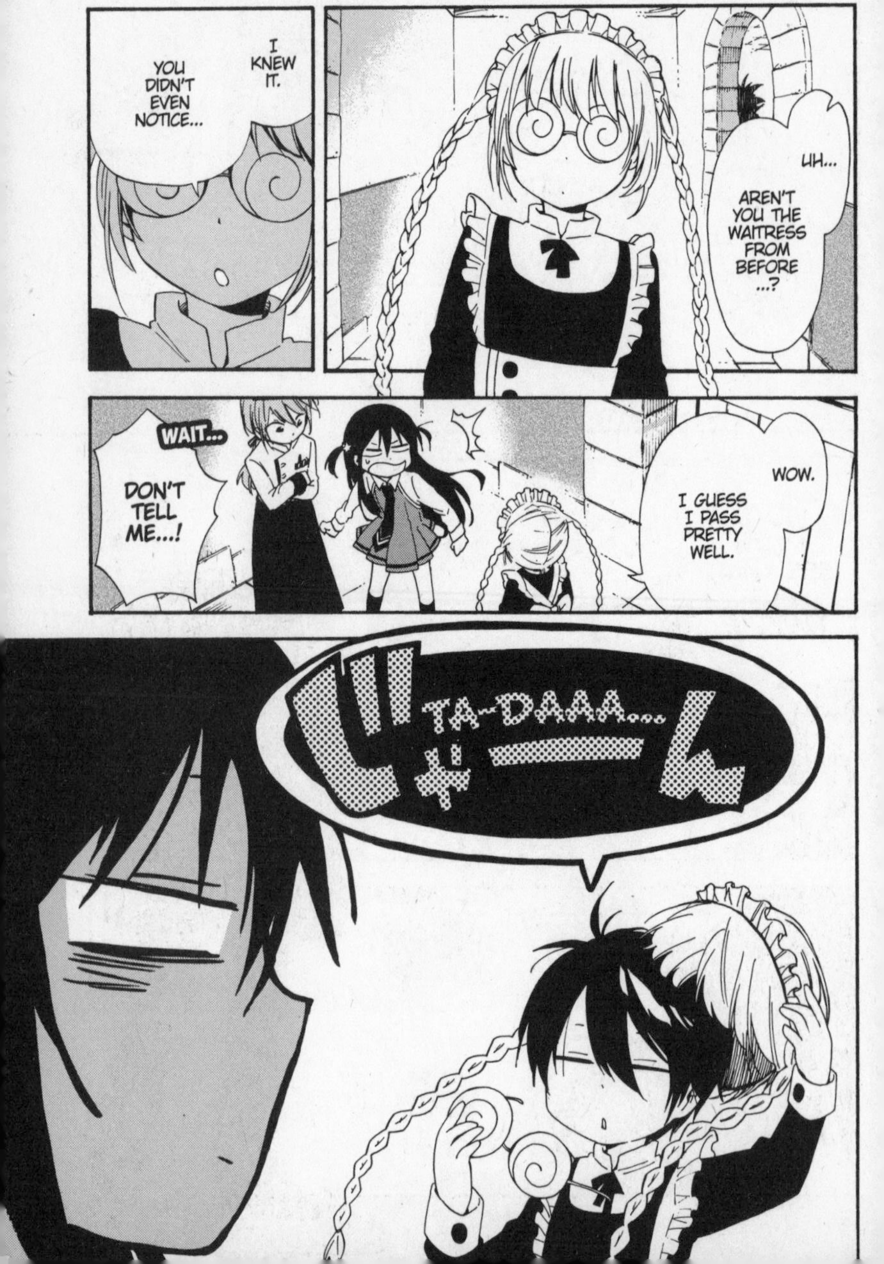
UH...
AREN'T YOU THE WAITRESS FROM BEFORE ...?
I KNEW IT.
YOU DIDN'T EVEN NOTICE...
WOW.
I GUESS I PASS PRETTY WELL.
WAIT...
DON'T TELL ME...!
TA-DAAA...
じゃーん

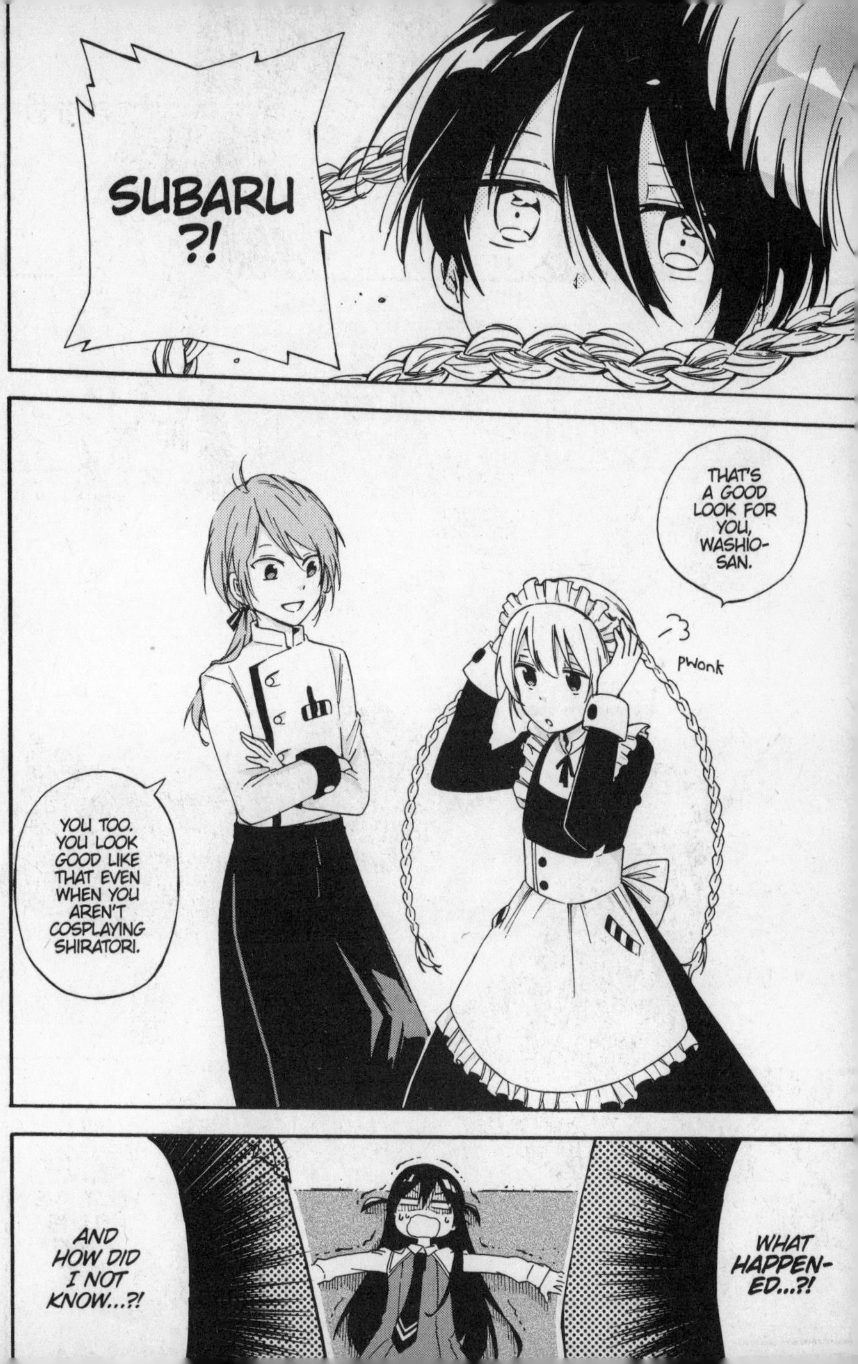
SUBARU ?!
THAT'S A GOOD LOOK FOR YOU, WASHIO-SAN.
PWONK
YOU TOO. YOU LOOK GOOD LIKE THAT EVEN WHEN YOU AREN'T COSPLAYING SHIRATORI.
WHAT HAPPEN-ED...?!
AND HOW DID I NOT KNOW...?!

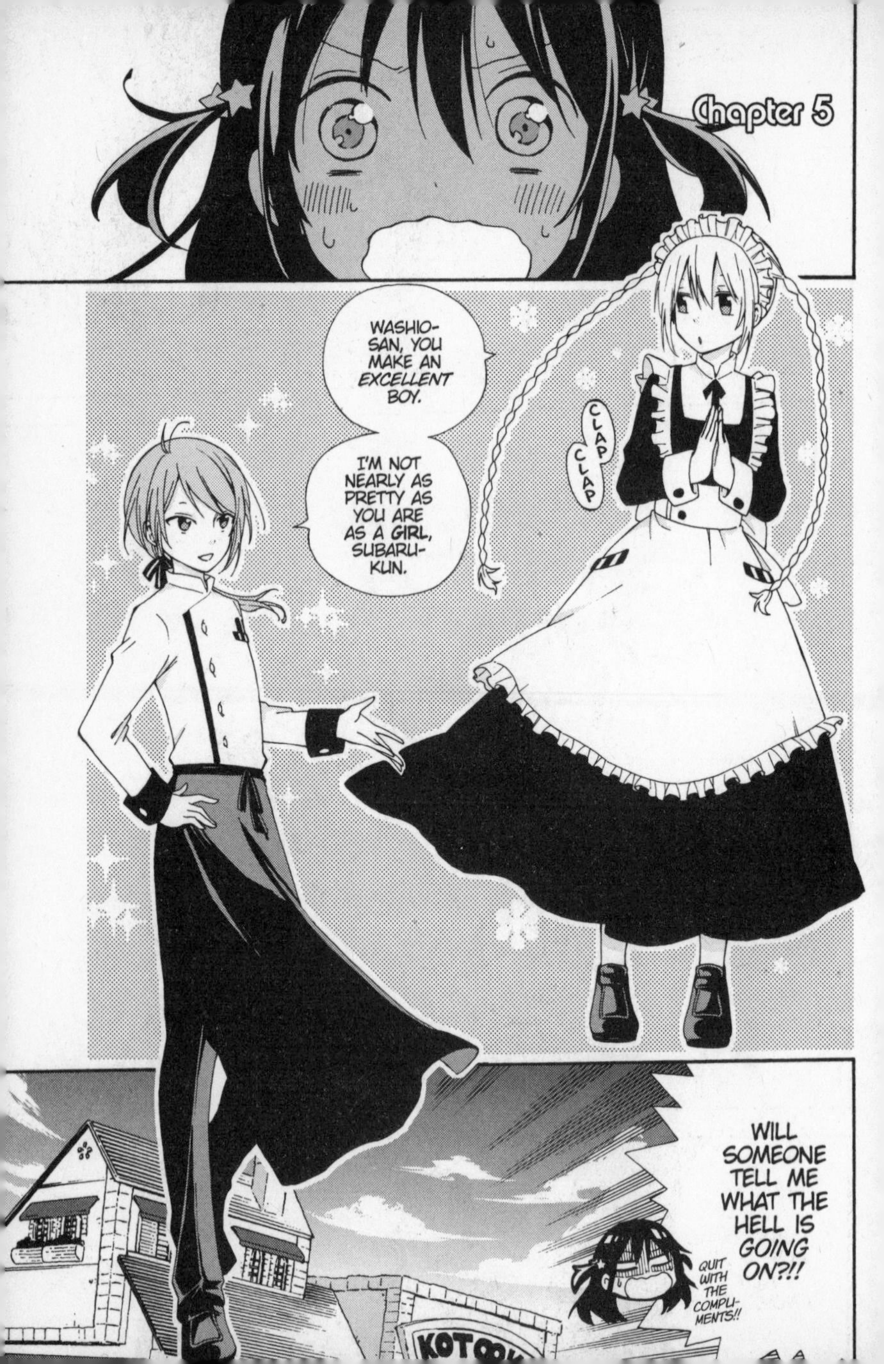
Chapter 5
WASHIO-SAN, YOU MAKE AN EXCELLENT BOY.
CLAP CLAP
I'M NOT NEARLY AS PRETTY AS YOU ARE AS A GIRL, SUBARU-KUN.
WILL SOMEONE TELL ME WHAT THE HELL IS GOING ON?!!
QUIT WITH THE COMPLI-MENTS!!

Chapter 5 ★ Nameless

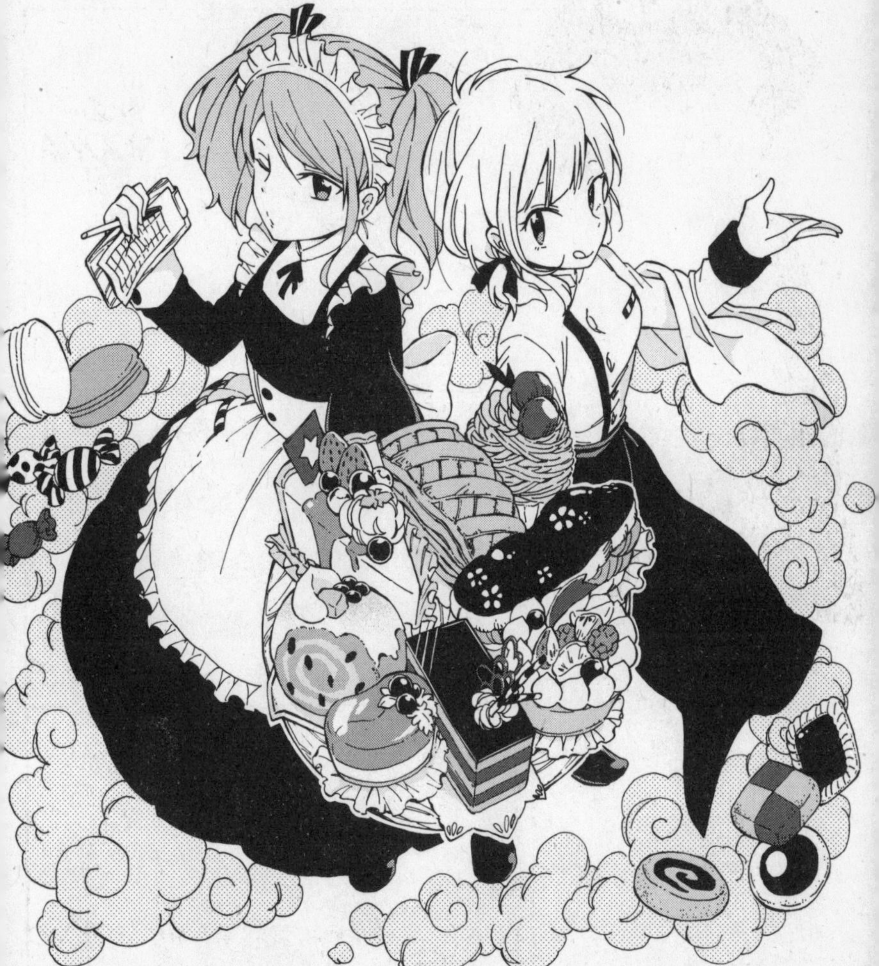

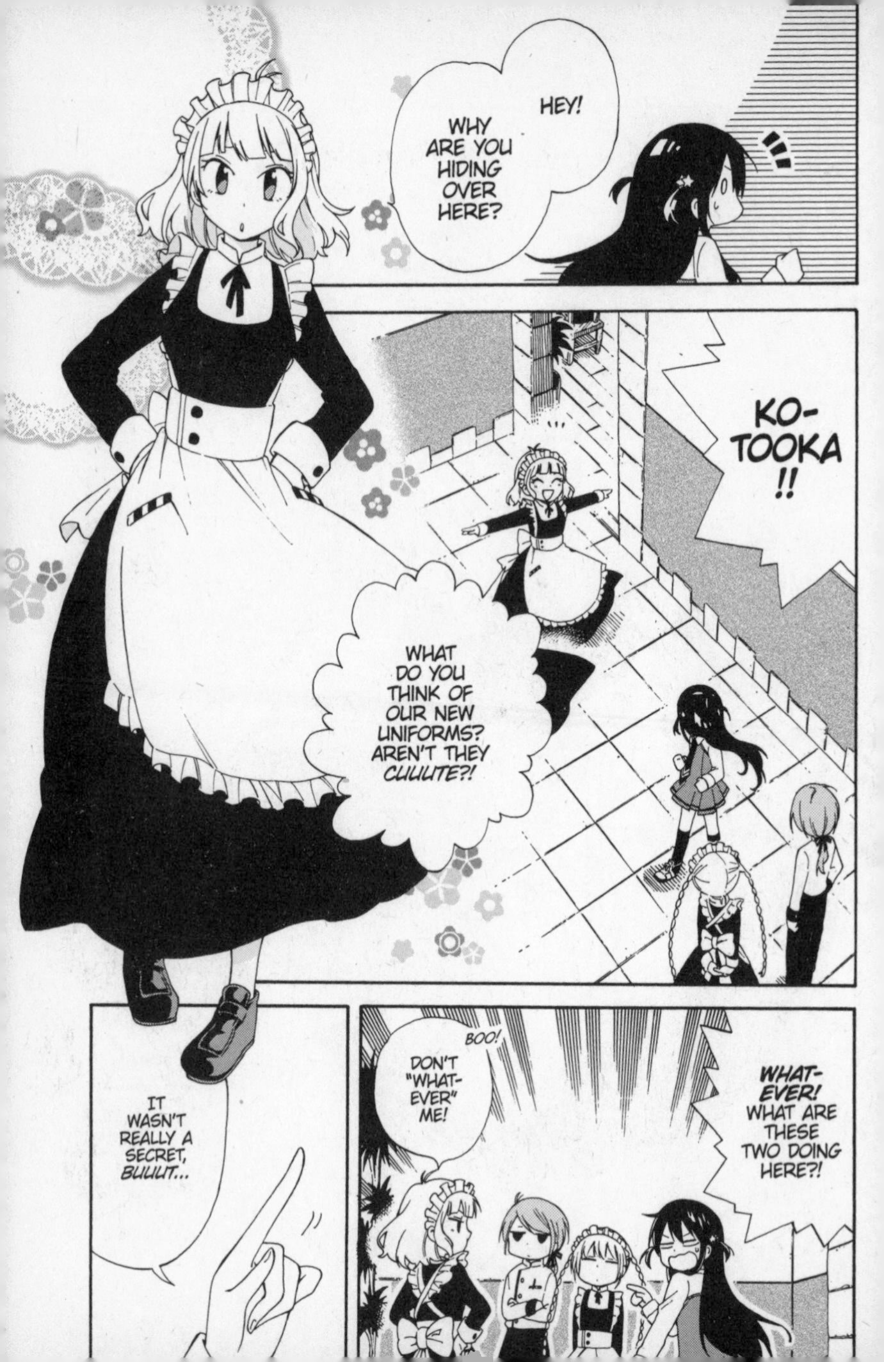
HEY!
WHY ARE YOU HIDING OVER HERE?
KO-TOOKA!!
WHAT DO YOU THINK OF OUR NEW UNIFORMS? AREN'T THEY *CUUUTE?!*
WHAT-EVER! WHAT ARE THESE TWO DOING HERE?!
BOO!
DON'T "WHAT-EVER" ME!
IT WASN'T REALLY A SECRET, *BUUUT...*

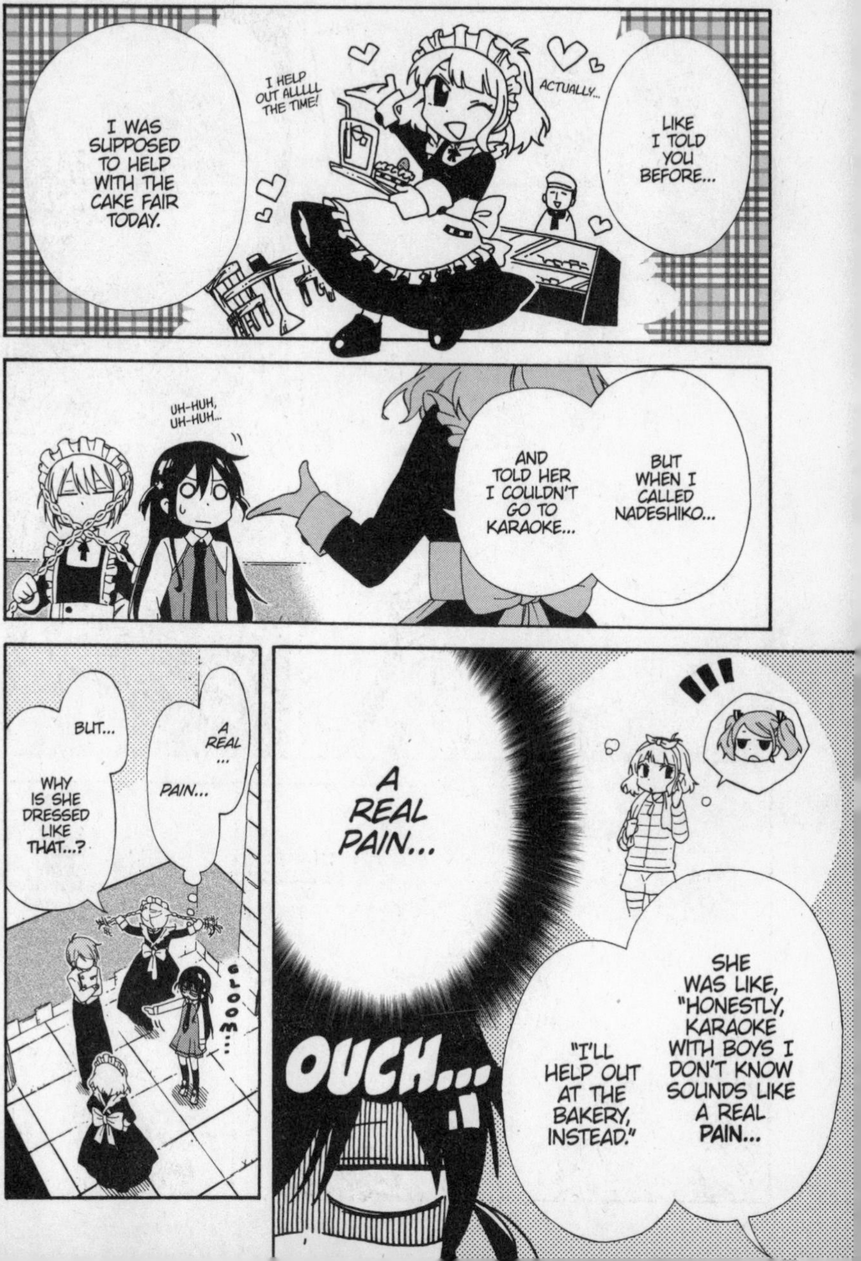
LIKE I TOLD YOU BEFORE...
ACTUALLY...
I HELP OUT ALLLLL THE TIME!
I WAS SUPPOSED TO HELP WITH THE CAKE FAIR TODAY.
BUT WHEN I CALLED NADESHIKO...
AND TOLD HER I COULDN'T GO TO KARAOKE...
UH-HUH, UH-HUH...
SHE WAS LIKE, "HONESTLY, KARAOKE WITH BOYS I DON'T KNOW SOUNDS LIKE A REAL PAIN...
"I'LL HELP OUT AT THE BAKERY, INSTEAD."
A REAL PAIN...
OUCH...
A REAL ... PAIN...
BUT... WHY IS SHE DRESSED LIKE THAT...?
GLOOM...

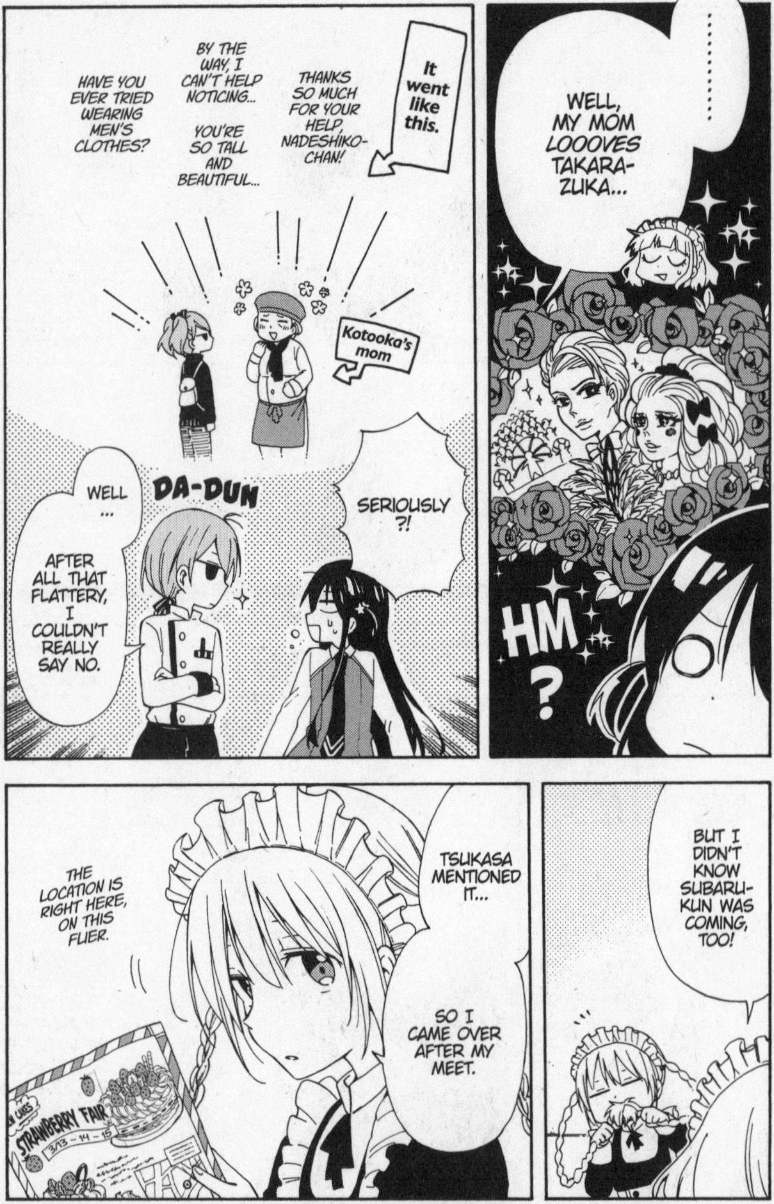
......
WELL, MY MOM LOOOVES TAKARAZUKA...
HM?
It went like this.
THANKS SO MUCH FOR YOUR HELP, NADESHIKO-CHAN!
BY THE WAY, I CAN'T HELP NOTICING... YOU'RE SO TALL AND BEAUTIFUL...
HAVE YOU EVER TRIED WEARING MEN'S CLOTHES?
Kotooka's mom
SERIOUSLY?!
DA-DUN
WELL... AFTER ALL THAT FLATTERY, I COULDN'T REALLY SAY NO.
BUT I DIDN'T KNOW SUBARU-KUN WAS COMING, TOO!
TSUKASA MENTIONED IT...
SO I CAME OVER AFTER MY MEET.
THE LOCATION IS RIGHT HERE, ON THIS FLIER.
STRAWBERRY FAIR
3/13 - 14 - 15

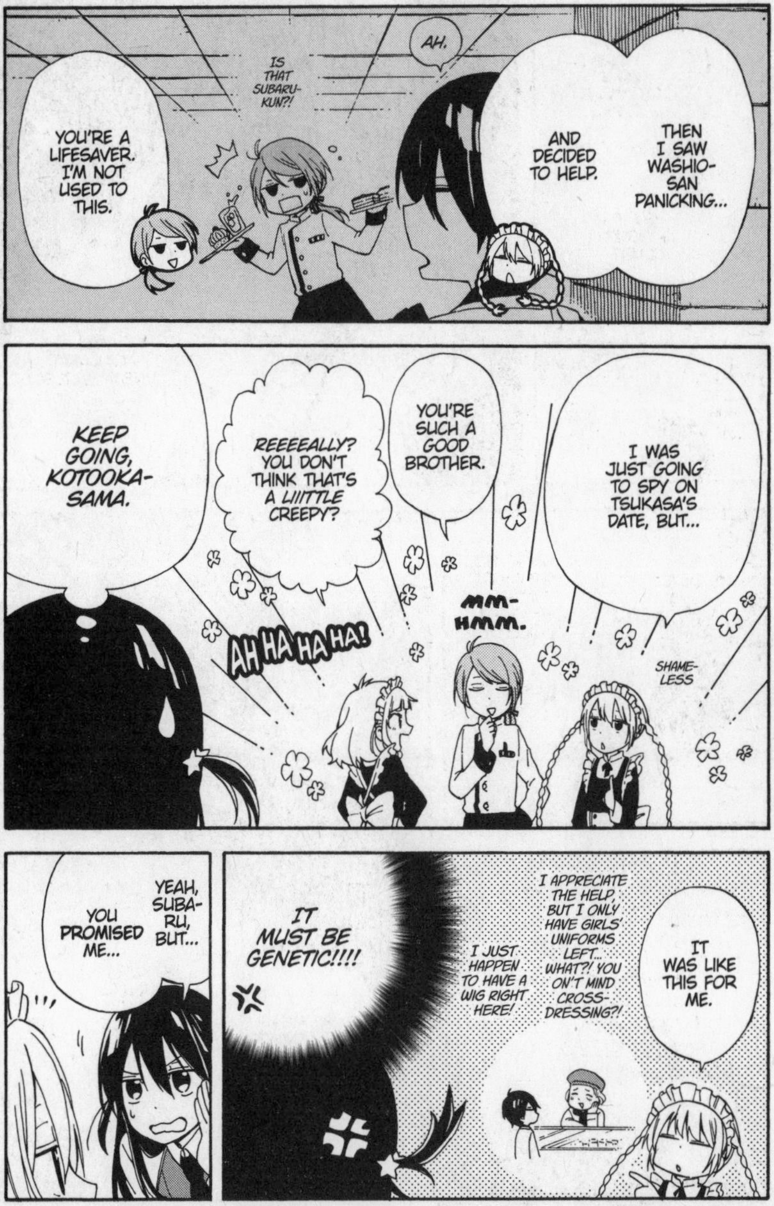
THEN I SAW WASHIO-SAN PANICKING...
AND DECIDED TO HELP.
AH.
IS THAT SUBARU-KUN?!
YOU'RE A LIFESAVER. I'M NOT USED TO THIS.
I WAS JUST GOING TO SPY ON TSUKASA'S DATE, BUT...
SHAME-LESS
MM-HMM.
YOU'RE SUCH A GOOD BROTHER.
REEEEALLY? YOU DON'T THINK THAT'S A LIIITTLE CREEPY?
AH HA HA HA!
KEEP GOING, KOTOOKA-SAMA.
IT WAS LIKE THIS FOR ME.
I APPRECIATE THE HELP, BUT I ONLY HAVE GIRLS' UNIFORMS LEFT... WHAT?! YOU ON'T MIND CROSS-DRESSING?!
I JUST HAPPEN TO HAVE A WIG RIGHT HERE!
IT MUST BE GENETIC!!!!
YEAH, SUBA-RU, BUT...
YOU PROMISED ME...

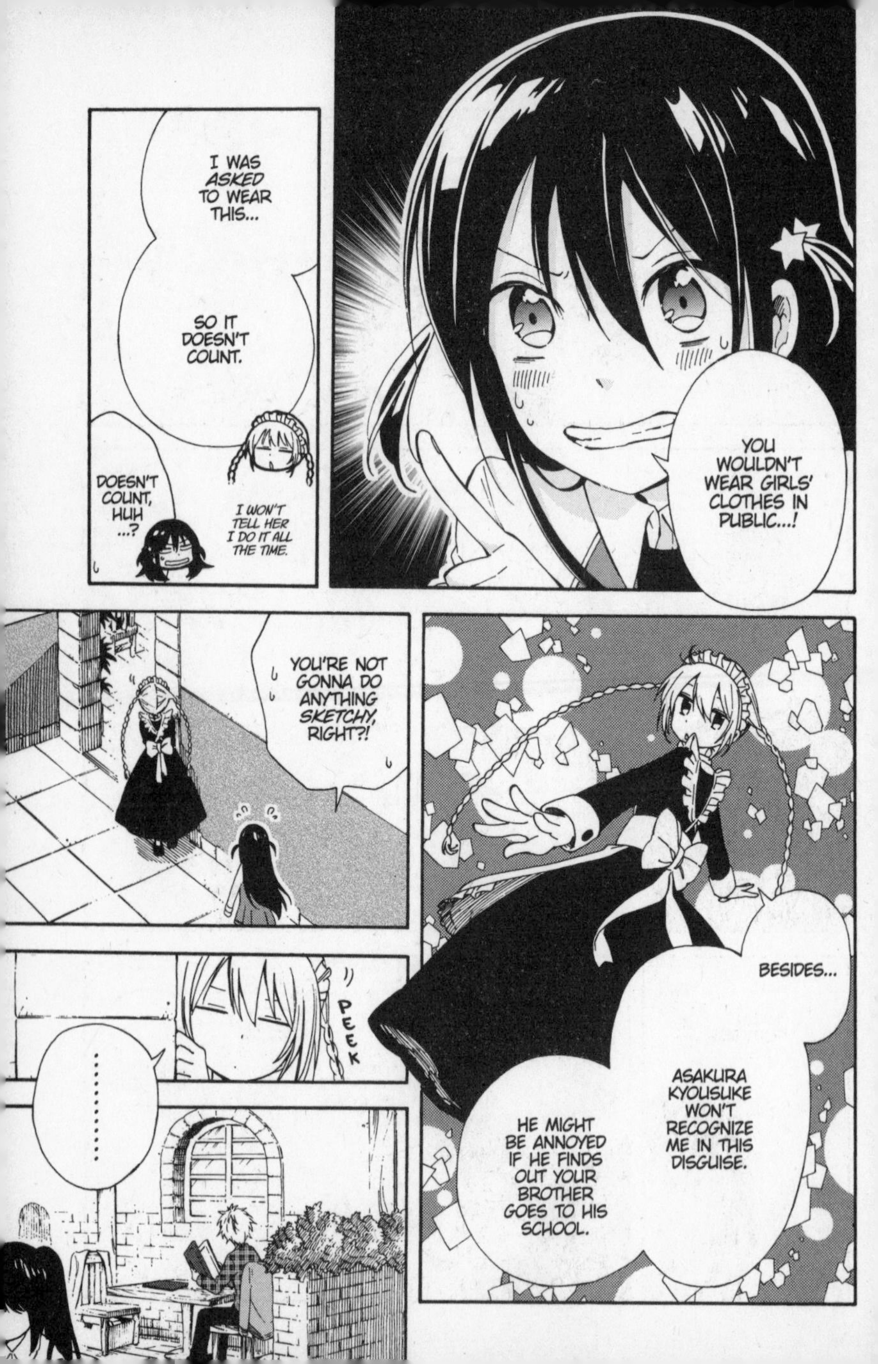
YOU WOULDN'T WEAR GIRLS' CLOTHES IN PUBLIC...!
I WAS ASKED TO WEAR THIS...
SO IT DOESN'T COUNT.
DOESN'T COUNT, HUH ...?
I WON'T TELL HER I DO IT ALL THE TIME.
BESIDES...
ASAKURA KYOUSUKE WON'T RECOGNIZE ME IN THIS DISGUISE.
HE MIGHT BE ANNOYED IF HE FINDS OUT YOUR BROTHER GOES TO HIS SCHOOL.
YOU'RE NOT GONNA DO ANYTHING SKETCHY, RIGHT?!
PEEK
....

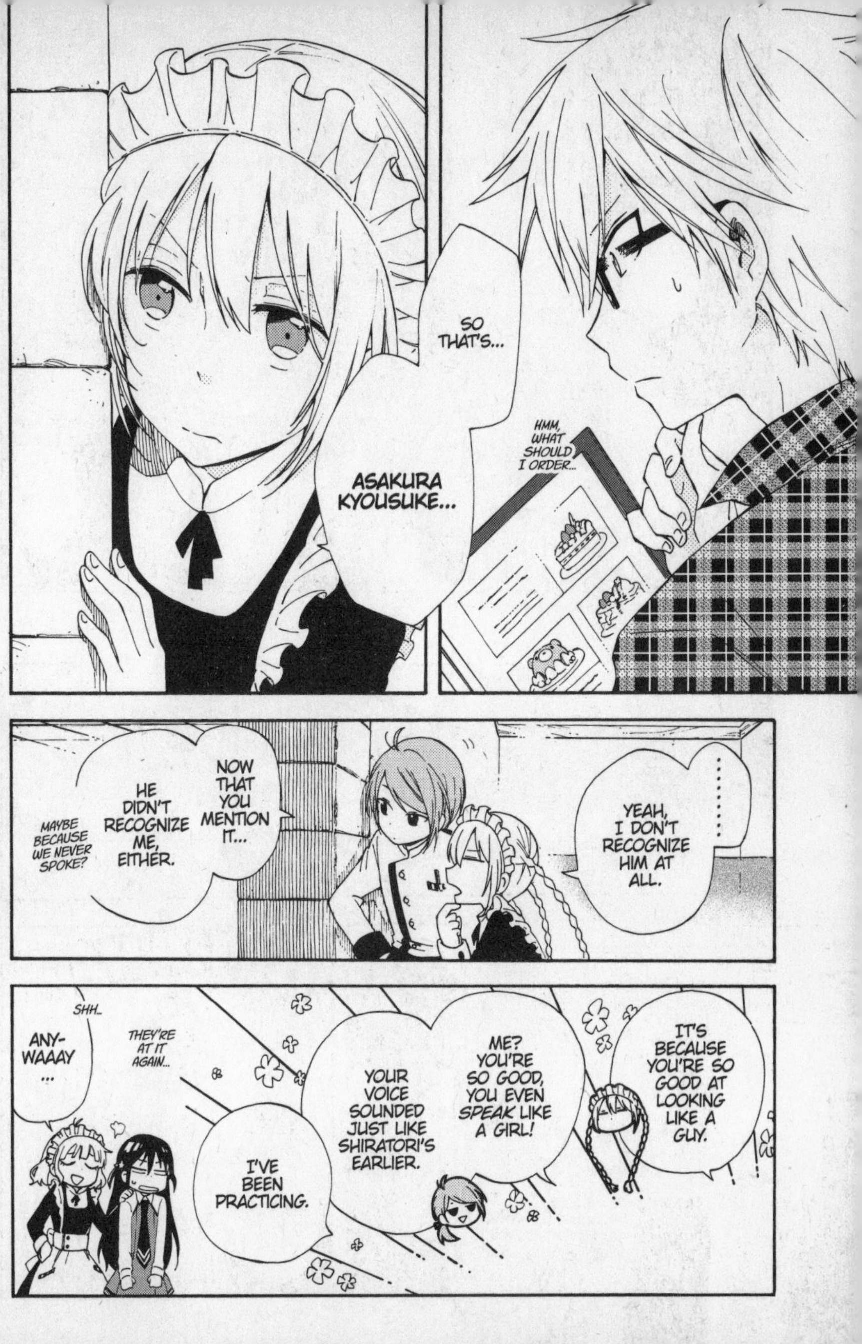
HMM, WHAT SHOULD I ORDER...
SO THAT'S... ASAKURA KYOUSUKE...
......
YEAH, I DON'T RECOGNIZE HIM AT ALL.
NOW THAT YOU MENTION IT...
HE DIDN'T RECOGNIZE ME, EITHER.
MAYBE BECAUSE WE NEVER SPOKE?
IT'S BECAUSE YOU'RE SO GOOD AT LOOKING LIKE A GUY.
ME? YOU'RE SO GOOD, YOU EVEN *SPEAK* LIKE A GIRL!
YOUR VOICE SOUNDED JUST LIKE SHIRATORI'S EARLIER.
I'VE BEEN PRACTICING.
THEY'RE AT IT AGAIN...
SHH...
ANY-WAAAY ...

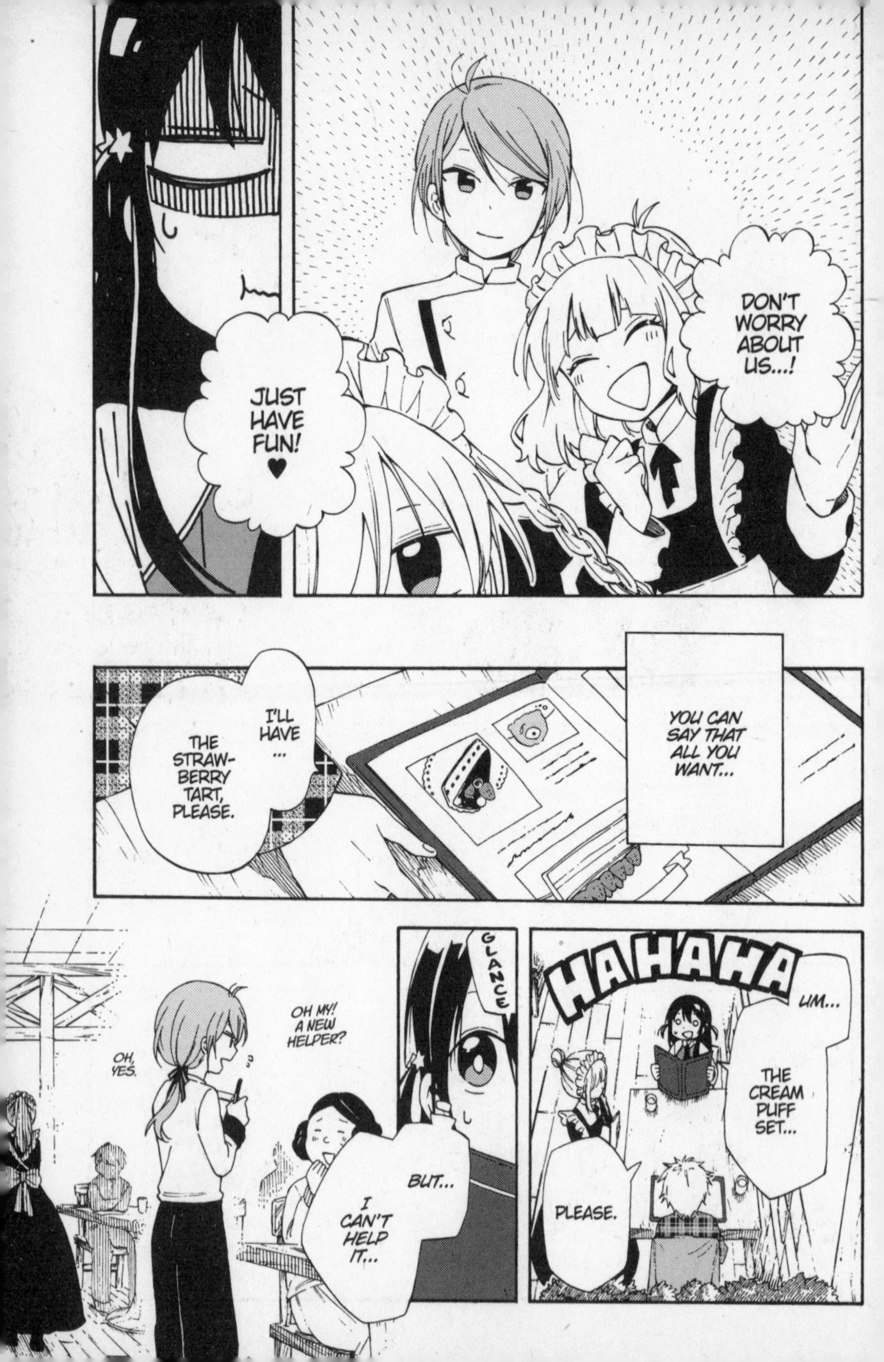
DON'T WORRY ABOUT US...!
JUST HAVE FUN! ♥
YOU CAN SAY THAT ALL YOU WANT...
I'LL HAVE ...
THE STRAWBERRY TART, PLEASE.
HAHAHA
UM...
THE CREAM PUFF SET...
PLEASE.
GLANCE
BUT...
I CAN'T HELP IT...
OH MY! A NEW HELPER?
OH, YES.

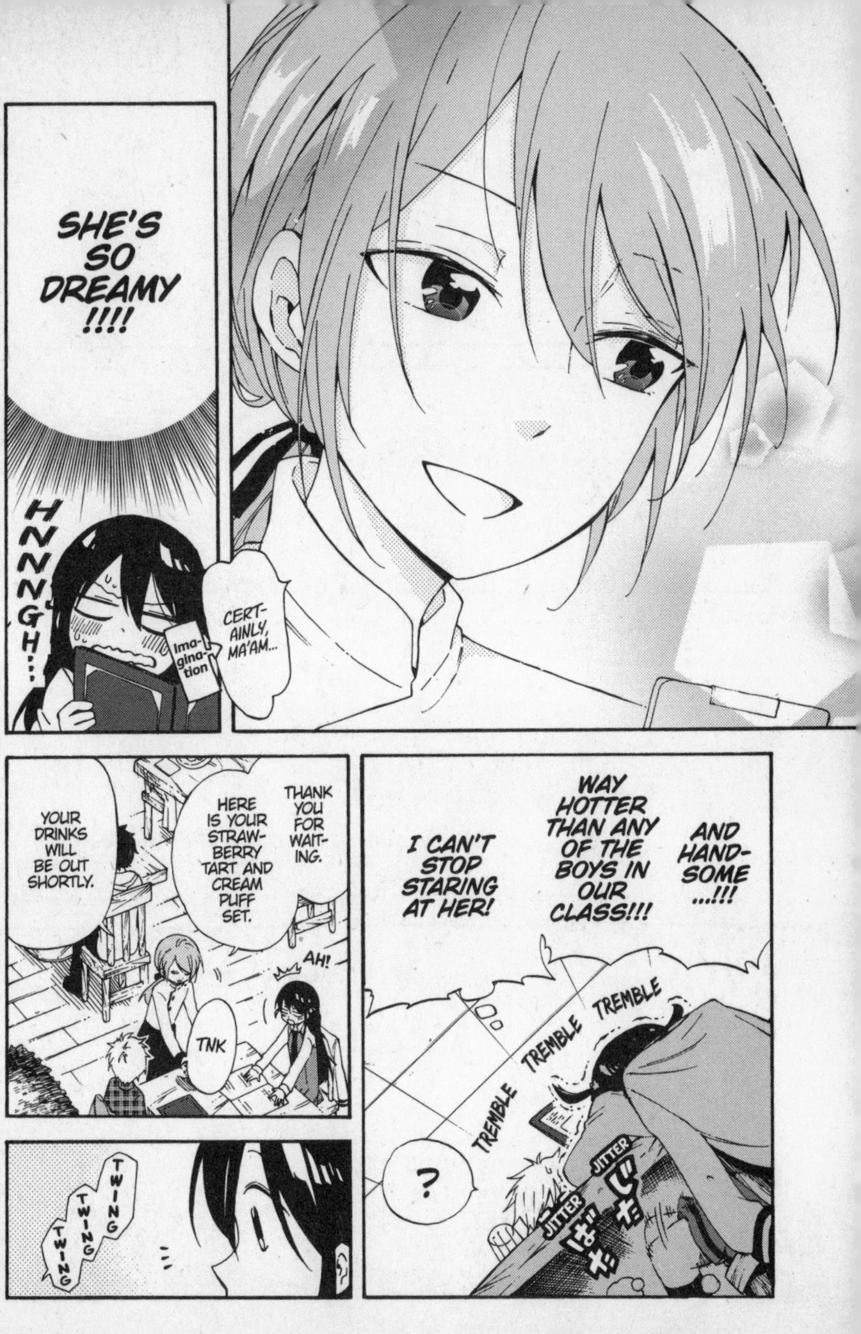
CERTAINLY, MA'AM...
Imagination
SHE'S SO DREAMY!!!!
HNNNNGH...
AND HANDSOME...!!!
WAY HOTTER THAN ANY OF THE BOYS IN OUR CLASS!!!
I CAN'T STOP STARING AT HER!
TREMBLE
TREMBLE
TREMBLE
?
JITTER
JITTER
THANK YOU FOR WAITING.
HERE IS YOUR STRAWBERRY TART AND CREAM PUFF SET.
YOUR DRINKS WILL BE OUT SHORTLY.
AH!
TNK
TWING
TWING
TWING

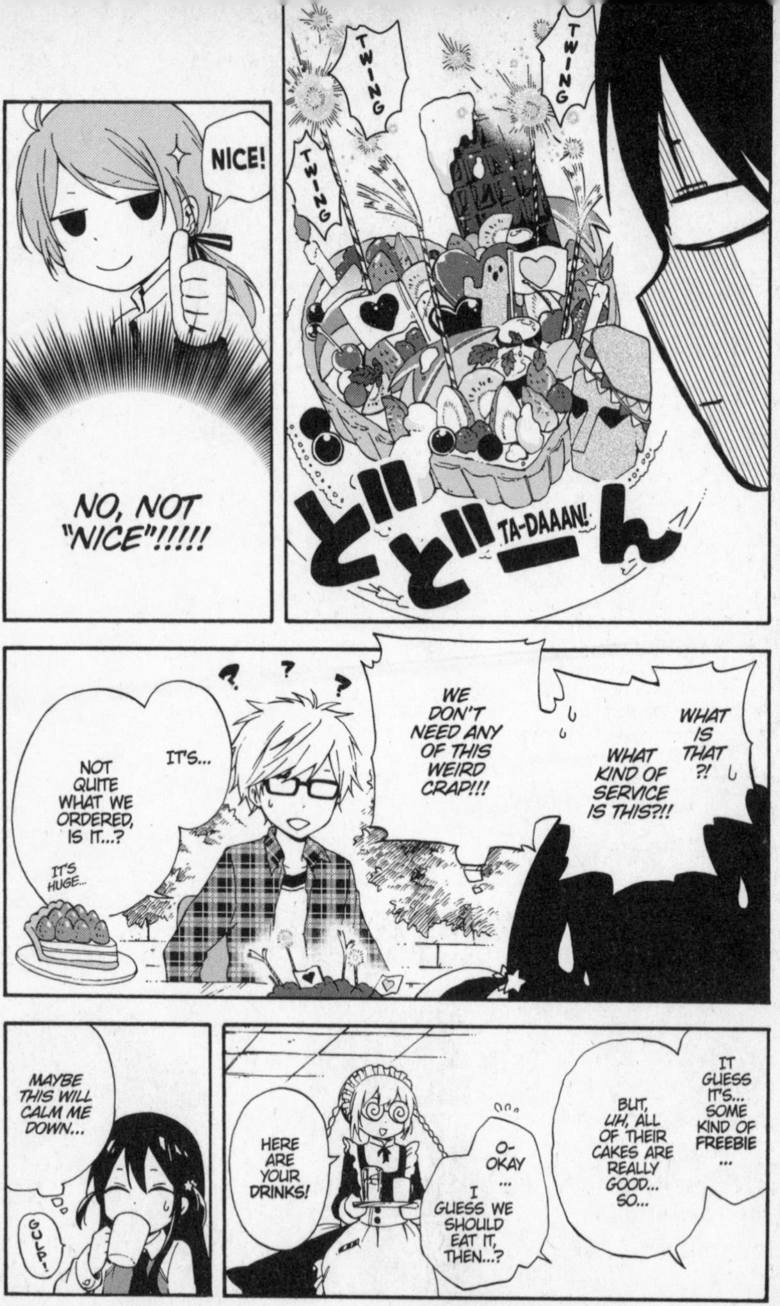
TWING
TWING
TWING
どどーん
TA-DAAN!
NICE!
NO, NOT "NICE"!!!!!
WHAT IS THAT?!
WHAT KIND OF SERVICE IS THIS?!!
WE DON'T NEED ANY OF THIS WEIRD CRAP!!!
IT'S...
NOT QUITE WHAT WE ORDERED, IS IT...?
IT'S HUGE...
IT GUESS IT'S... SOME KIND OF FREEBIE ...
BUT, UH, ALL OF THEIR CAKES ARE REALLY GOOD... SO...
O-OKAY ... I GUESS WE SHOULD EAT IT, THEN...?
HERE ARE YOUR DRINKS!
MAYBE THIS WILL CALM ME DOWN...
GULP!

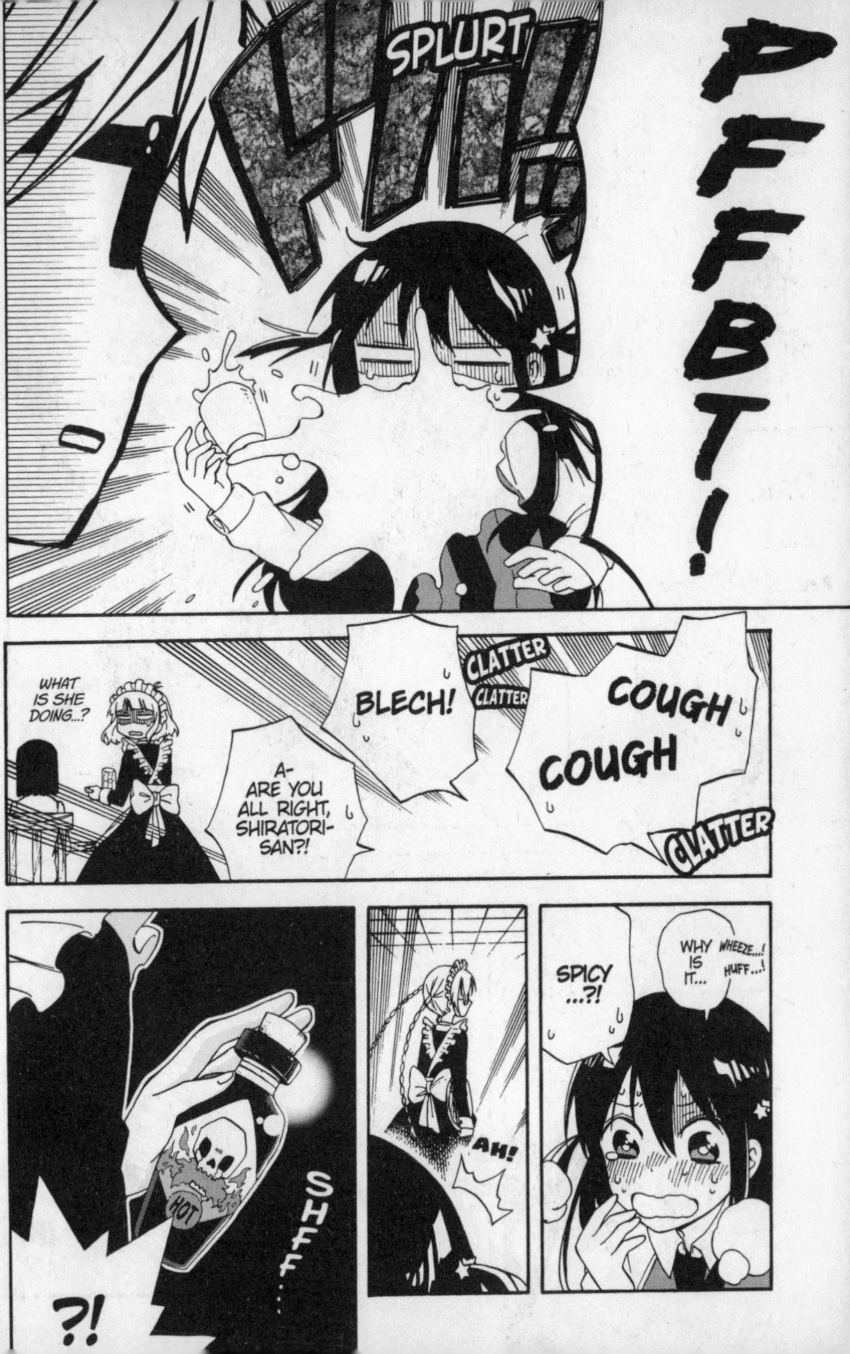
PFFBT!
SPLURT
COUGH COUGH
CLATTER
CLATTER
CLATTER
BLECH!
A- ARE YOU ALL RIGHT, SHIRATORI-SAN?!
WHAT IS SHE DOING...?
WHY IS IT...
WHEEZE...! HUFF...!
SPICY...?!
AH!
SHFF...
?!

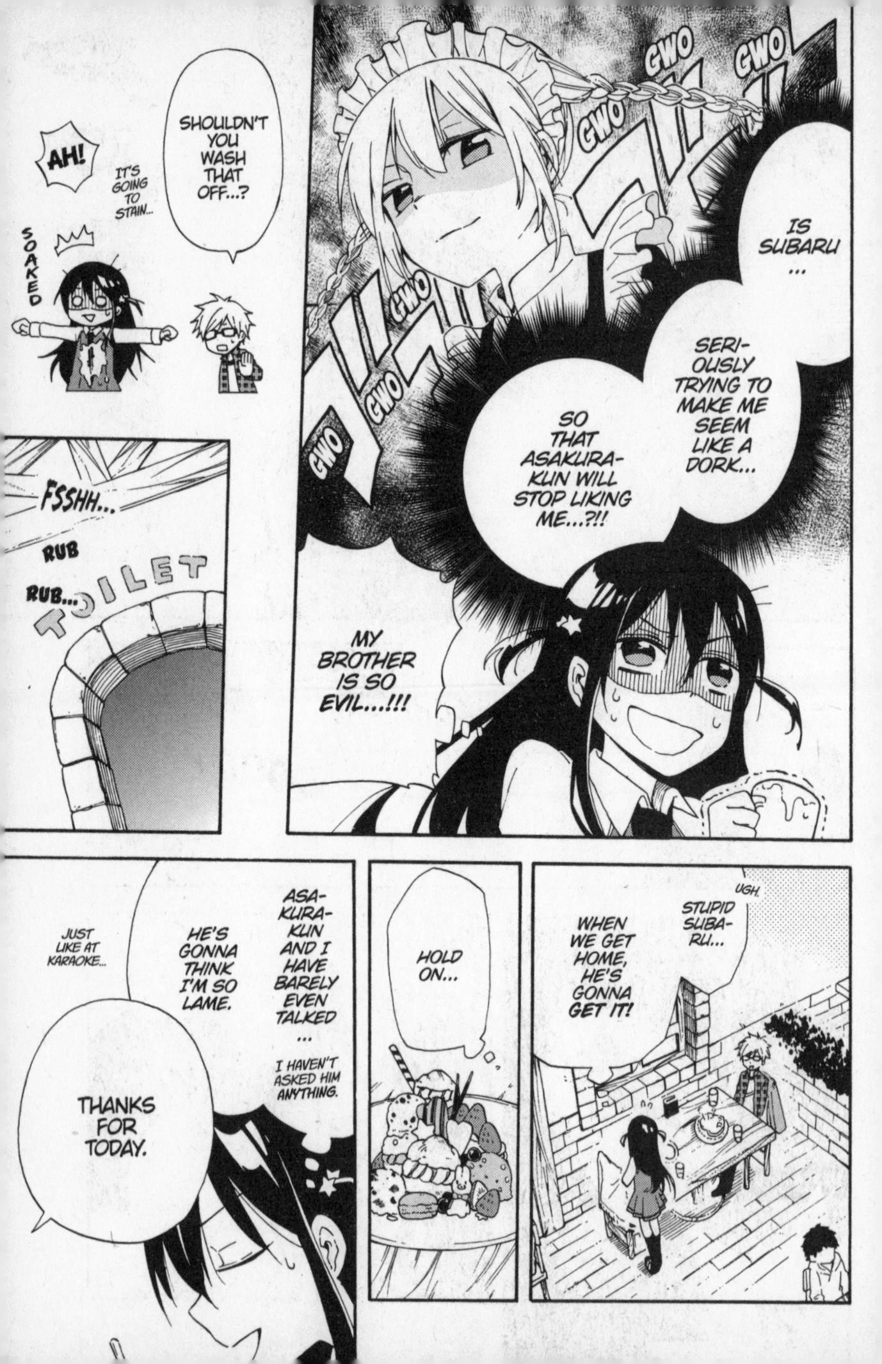
GWO GWO GWO
GWO GWO GWO GWO
IS SUBARU...
SERIOUSLY TRYING TO MAKE ME SEEM LIKE A DORK...
SO THAT ASAKURA-KUN WILL STOP LIKING ME...?!!
MY BROTHER IS SO EVIL...!!!
SHOULDN'T YOU WASH THAT OFF...?
AH!
IT'S GOING TO STAIN...
SOAKED
FSSHH...
RUB
RUB...
TOILET
UGH.
STUPID SUBARU...
WHEN WE GET HOME, HE'S GONNA GET IT!
HOLD ON...
ASAKURA-KUN AND I HAVE BARELY EVEN TALKED...
I HAVEN'T ASKED HIM ANYTHING.
HE'S GONNA THINK I'M SO LAME.
JUST LIKE AT KARAOKE...
THANKS FOR TODAY.

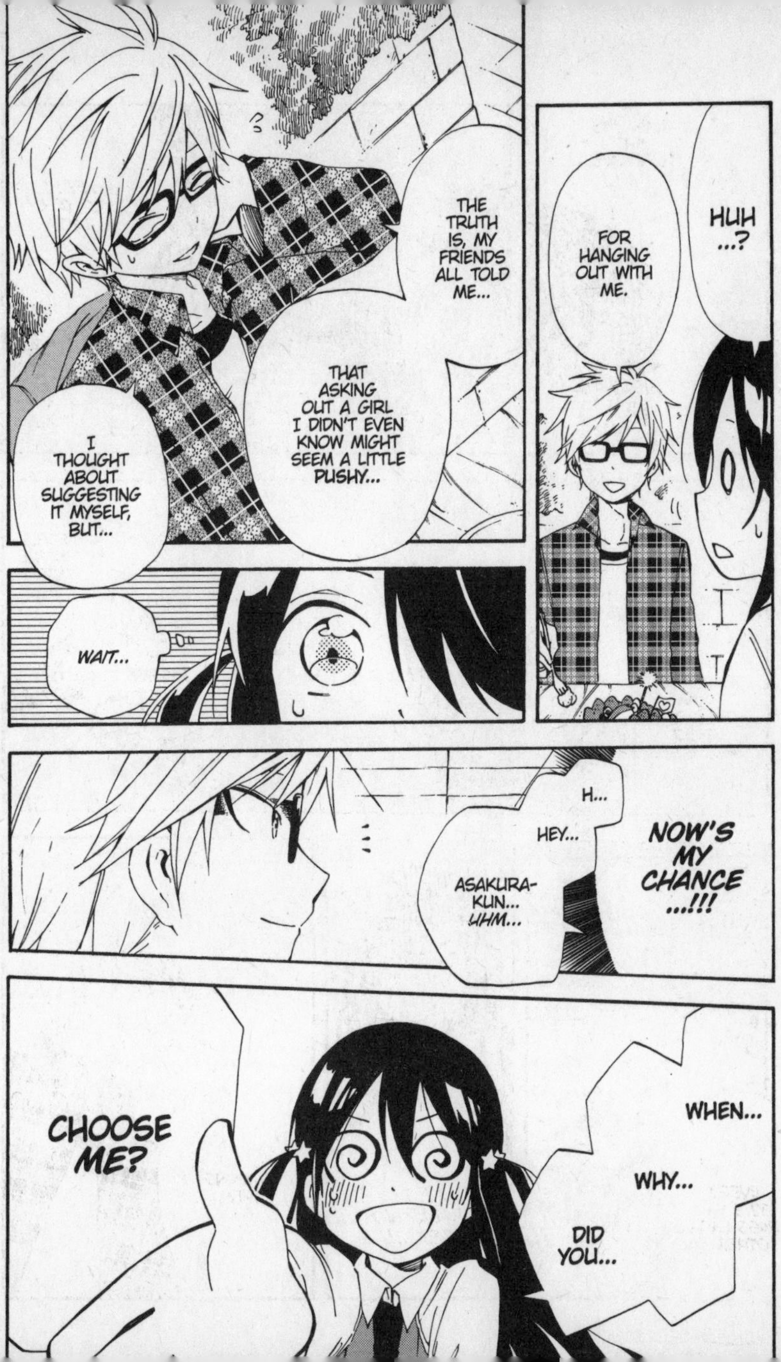
HUH ...?
FOR HANGING OUT WITH ME.
THE TRUTH IS, MY FRIENDS ALL TOLD ME...
THAT ASKING OUT A GIRL I DIDN'T EVEN KNOW MIGHT SEEM A LITTLE PUSHY...
I THOUGHT ABOUT SUGGESTING IT MYSELF, BUT...
WAIT...
NOW'S MY CHANCE ...!!!
H...
HEY...
ASAKURA-KUN... UHM...
WHEN...
WHY...
DID YOU...
CHOOSE ME?

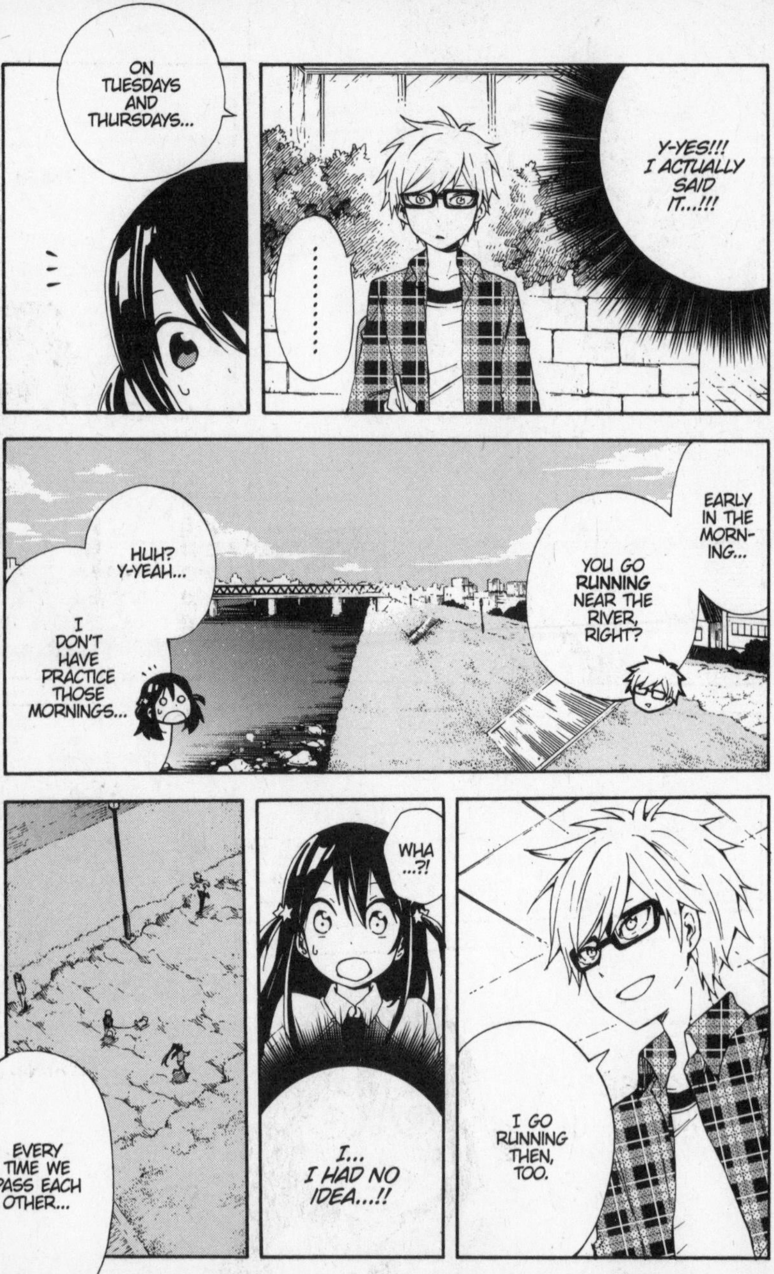

Y-YES!!! I ACTUALLY SAID IT...!!!
......
ON TUESDAYS AND THURSDAYS...
EARLY IN THE MORNING...
YOU GO RUNNING NEAR THE RIVER, RIGHT?
HUH? Y-YEAH...
I DON'T HAVE PRACTICE THOSE MORNINGS...
I GO RUNNING THEN, TOO.
WHA ...?!
I... I HAD NO IDEA...!!
EVERY TIME WE PASS EACH OTHER...

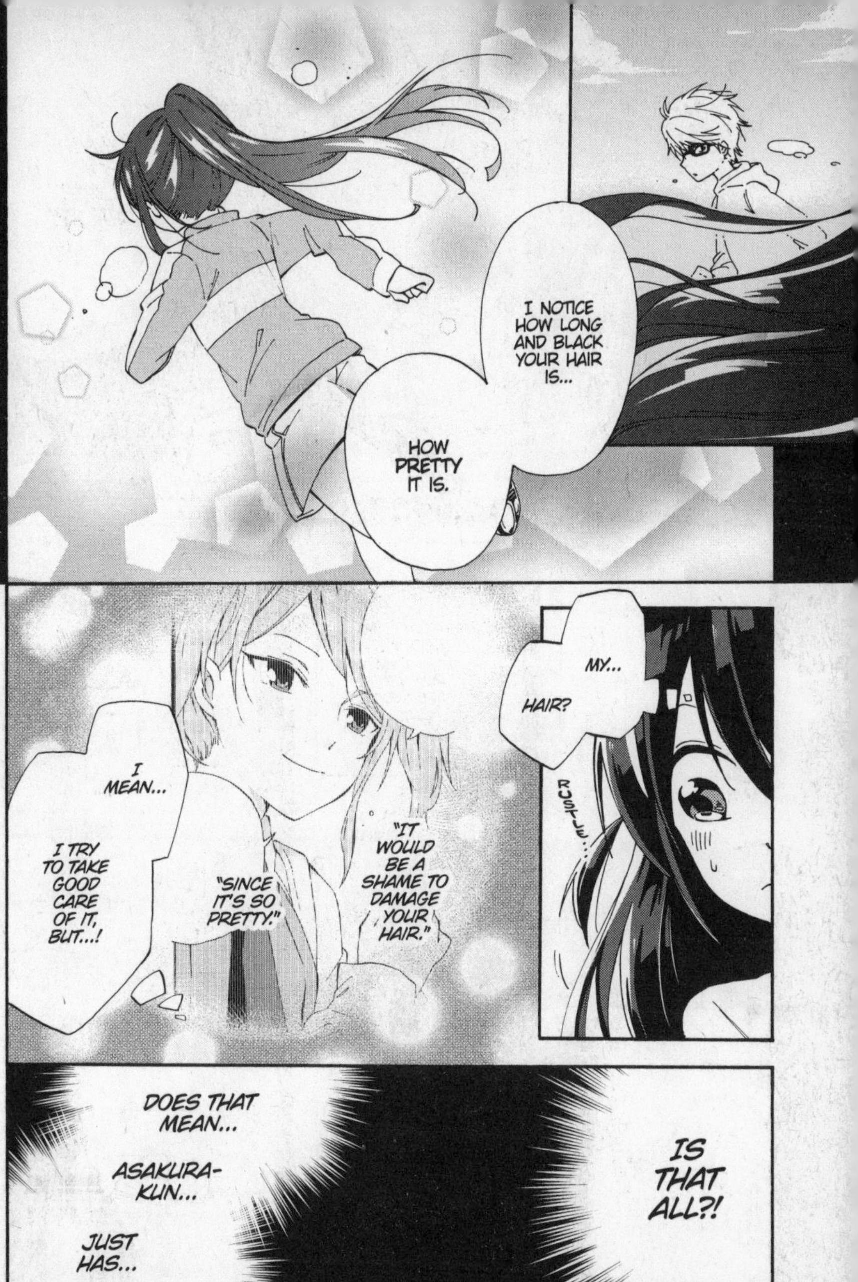
I NOTICE HOW LONG AND BLACK YOUR HAIR IS...
HOW PRETTY IT IS.
MY...
HAIR?
RUSTLE...
"IT WOULD BE A SHAME TO DAMAGE YOUR HAIR."
"SINCE IT'S SO PRETTY."
I MEAN...
I TRY TO TAKE GOOD CARE OF IT, BUT...!
DOES THAT MEAN...
ASAKURA-KUN...
JUST HAS...
IS THAT ALL?!

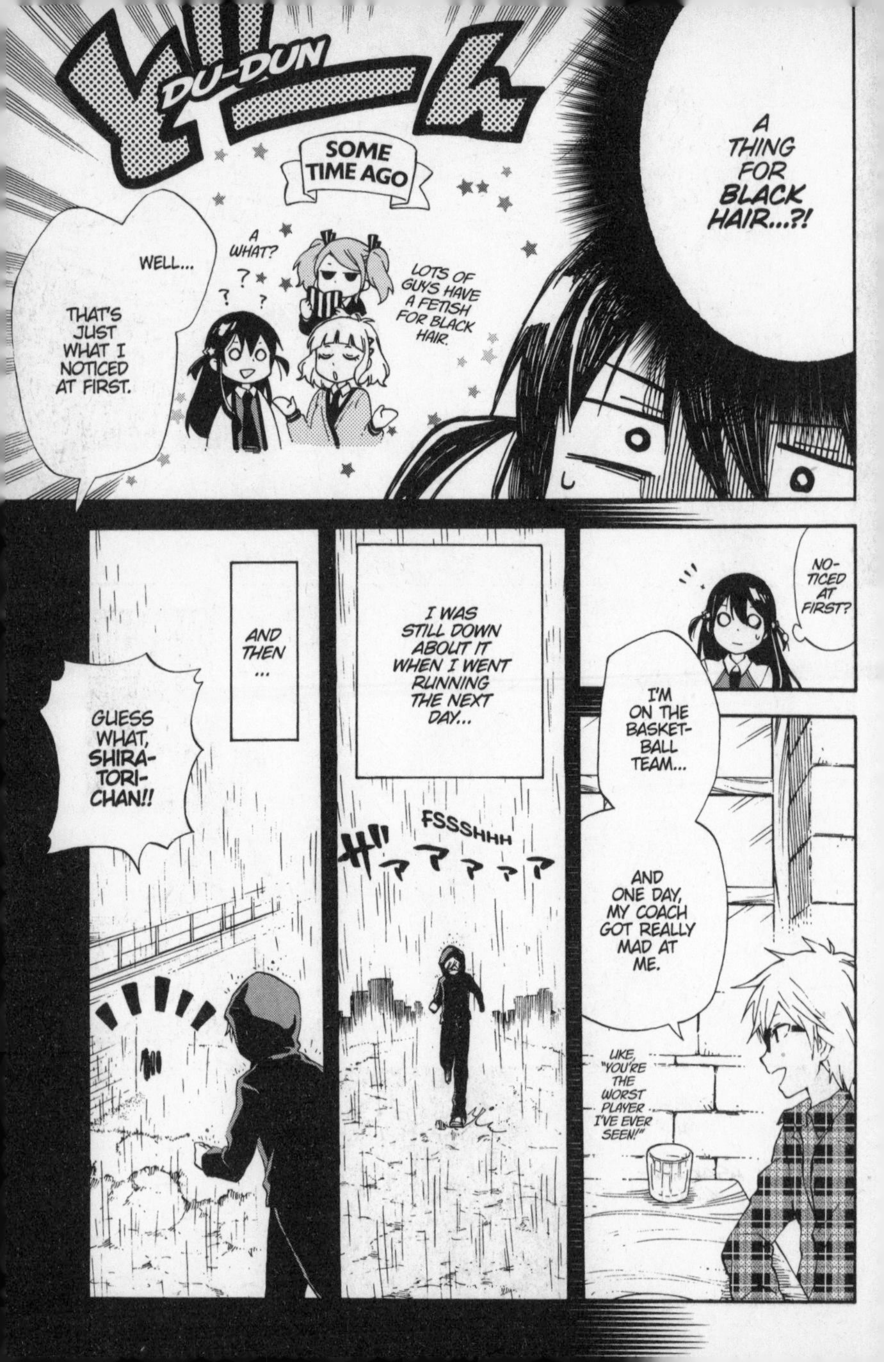
A THING FOR BLACK HAIR...?!
DU-DUN
SOME TIME AGO
LOTS OF GUYS HAVE A FETISH FOR BLACK HAIR.
A WHAT?
WELL...
THAT'S JUST WHAT I NOTICED AT FIRST.
NO-TICED AT FIRST?
I'M ON THE BASKET-BALL TEAM...
AND ONE DAY, MY COACH GOT REALLY MAD AT ME.
LIKE, "YOU'RE THE WORST PLAYER I'VE EVER SEEN!"
I WAS STILL DOWN ABOUT IT WHEN I WENT RUNNING THE NEXT DAY...
FSSSHHH
AND THEN...
GUESS WHAT, SHIRA-TORI-CHAN!!

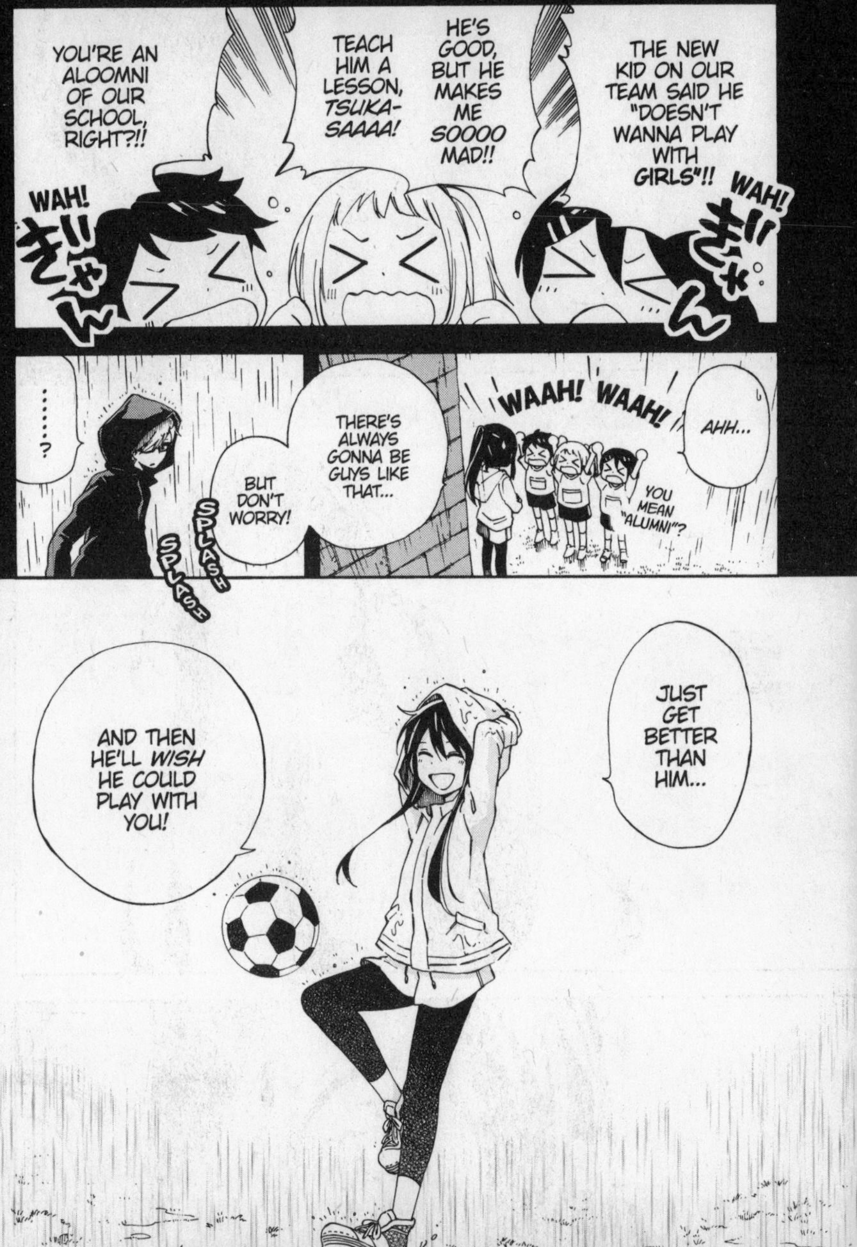
THE NEW KID ON OUR TEAM SAID HE "DOESN'T WANNA PLAY WITH GIRLS"!!
WAH!
ぎゃん
HE'S GOOD, BUT HE MAKES ME SOOOO MAD!!
TEACH HIM A LESSON, TSUKA-SAAAA!
YOU'RE AN ALOOMNI OF OUR SCHOOL, RIGHT?!!
WAH!
ぎゃん
AHH...
YOU MEAN "ALUMNI"?
WAAH! WAAH!
THERE'S ALWAYS GONNA BE GUYS LIKE THAT...
BUT DON'T WORRY!
......?
SPLASH
SPLASH
JUST GET BETTER THAN HIM...
AND THEN HE'LL *WISH* HE COULD PLAY WITH YOU!

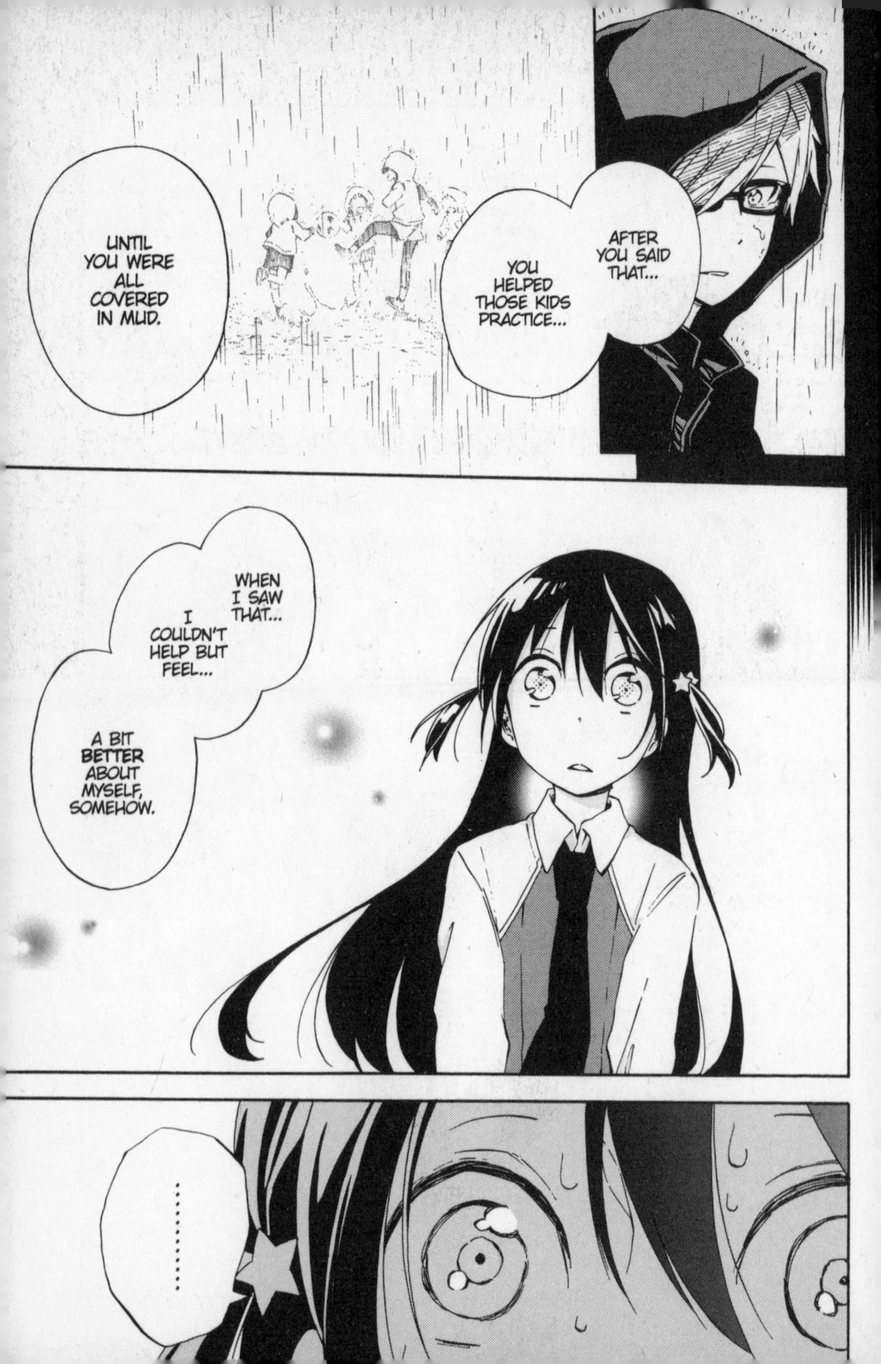
AFTER YOU SAID THAT...
YOU HELPED THOSE KIDS PRACTICE...
UNTIL YOU WERE ALL COVERED IN MUD.
WHEN I SAW THAT...
I COULDN'T HELP BUT FEEL...
A BIT BETTER ABOUT MYSELF, SOMEHOW.
....

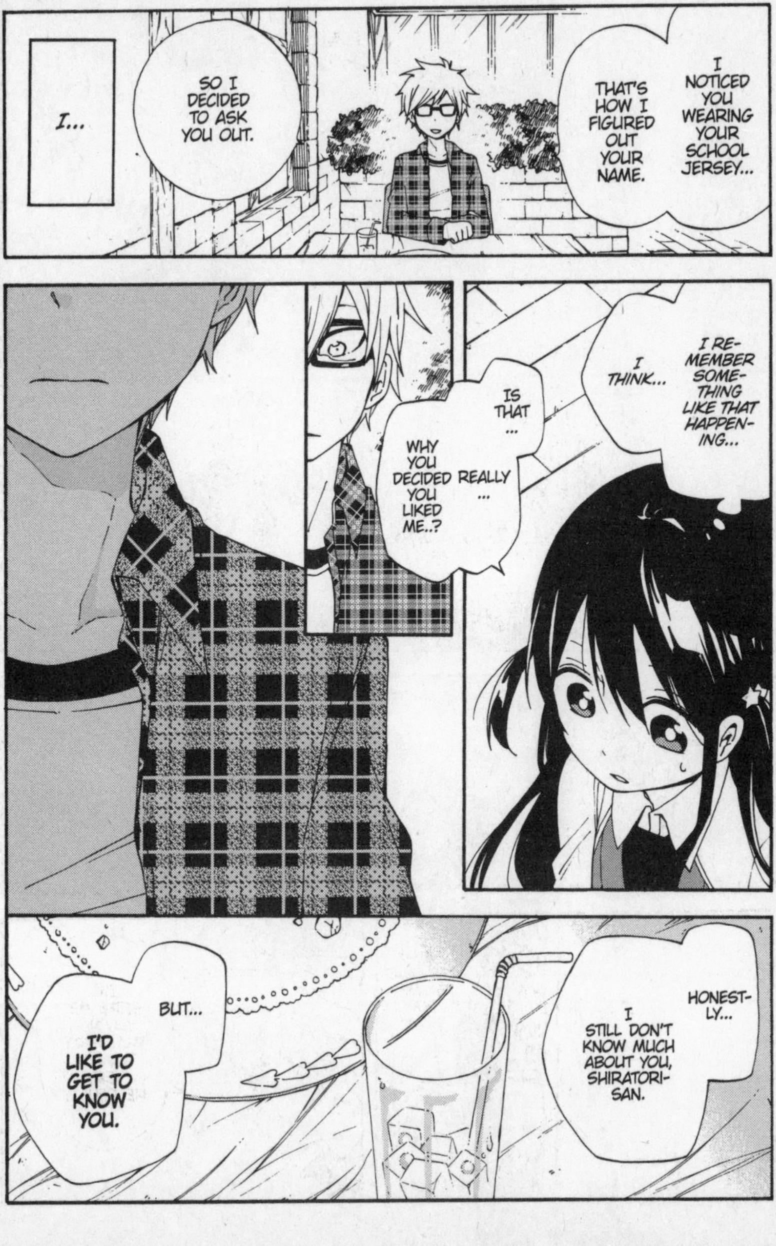
I NOTICED YOU WEARING YOUR SCHOOL JERSEY...
THAT'S HOW I FIGURED OUT YOUR NAME.
SO I DECIDED TO ASK YOU OUT.
I...
I REMEMBER SOMETHING LIKE THAT HAPPENING...
I THINK...
IS THAT...
REALLY...
WHY YOU DECIDED YOU LIKED ME..?
HONESTLY...
I STILL DON'T KNOW MUCH ABOUT YOU, SHIRATORI-SAN.
BUT...
I'D LIKE TO GET TO KNOW YOU.

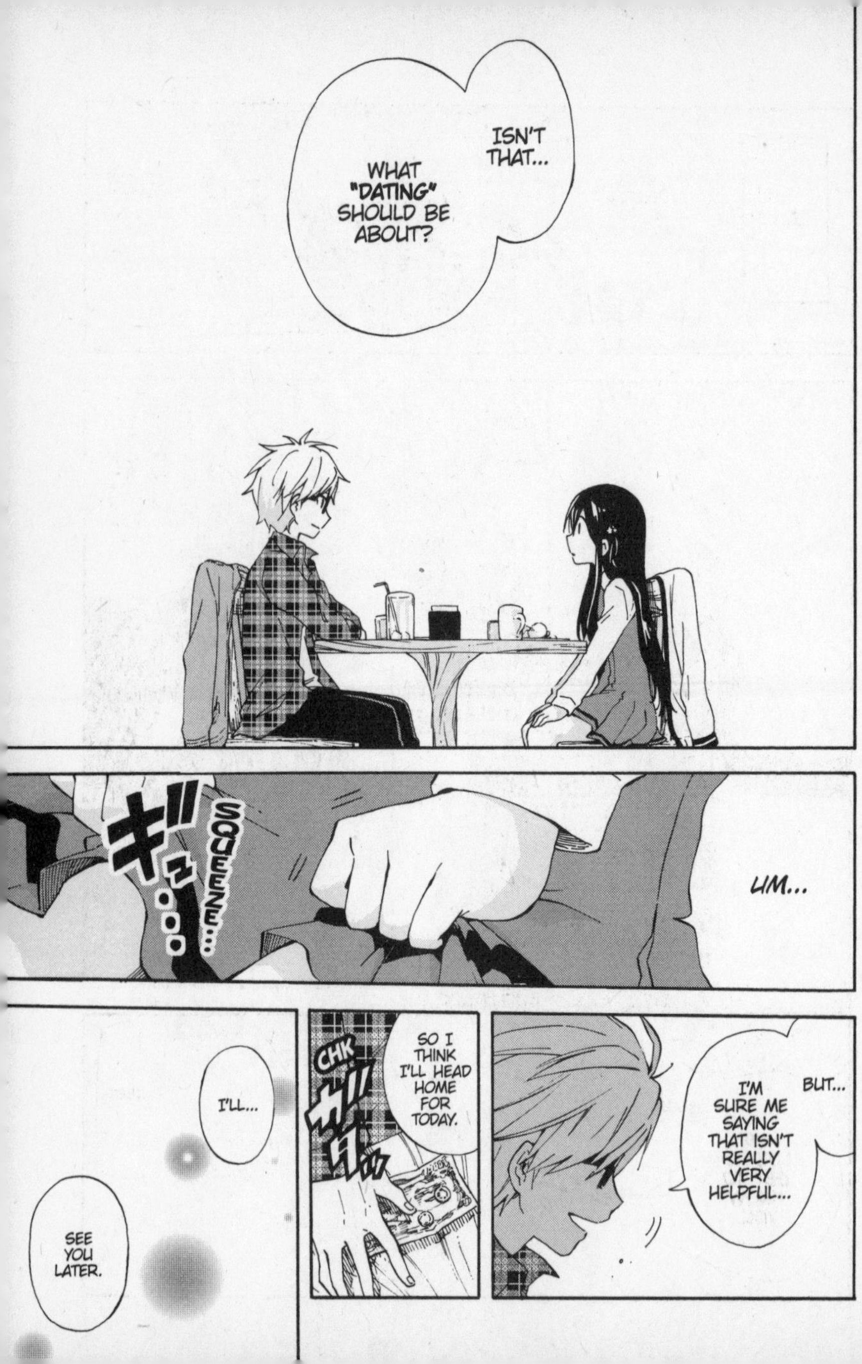
ISN'T THAT...
WHAT "DATING" SHOULD BE ABOUT?
UM...
SQUEEZE...
BUT...
I'M SURE ME SAYING THAT ISN'T REALLY VERY HELPFUL...
SO I THINK I'LL HEAD HOME FOR TODAY.
CHK
I'LL...
SEE YOU LATER.

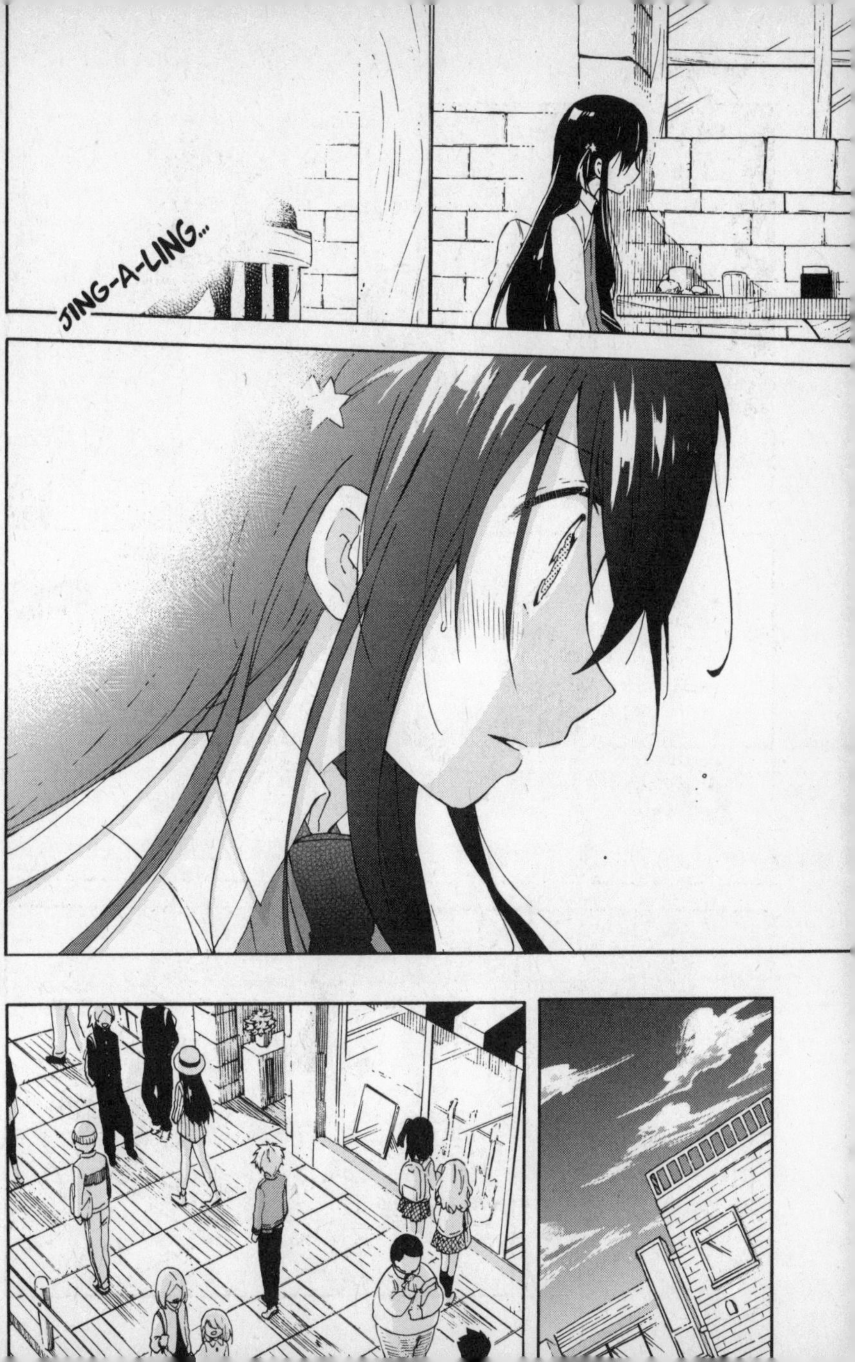
JING-A-LING...

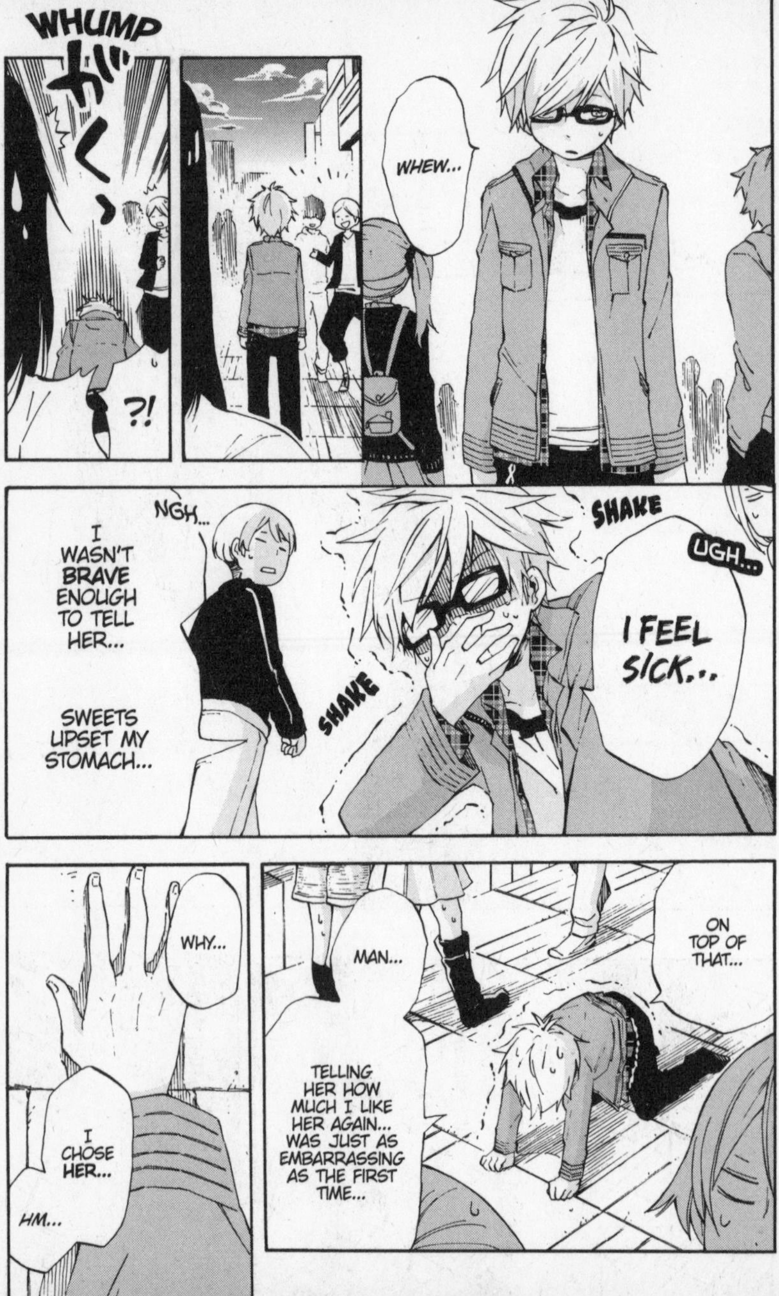
WHEW...
WHUMP
がく
?!
UGH...
I FEEL SICK...
SHAKE
SHAKE
NGH...
I WASN'T BRAVE ENOUGH TO TELL HER...
SWEETS UPSET MY STOMACH...
ON TOP OF THAT...
MAN...
TELLING HER HOW MUCH I LIKE HER AGAIN... WAS JUST AS EMBARRASSING AS THE FIRST TIME...
WHY...
I CHOSE HER...
HM...

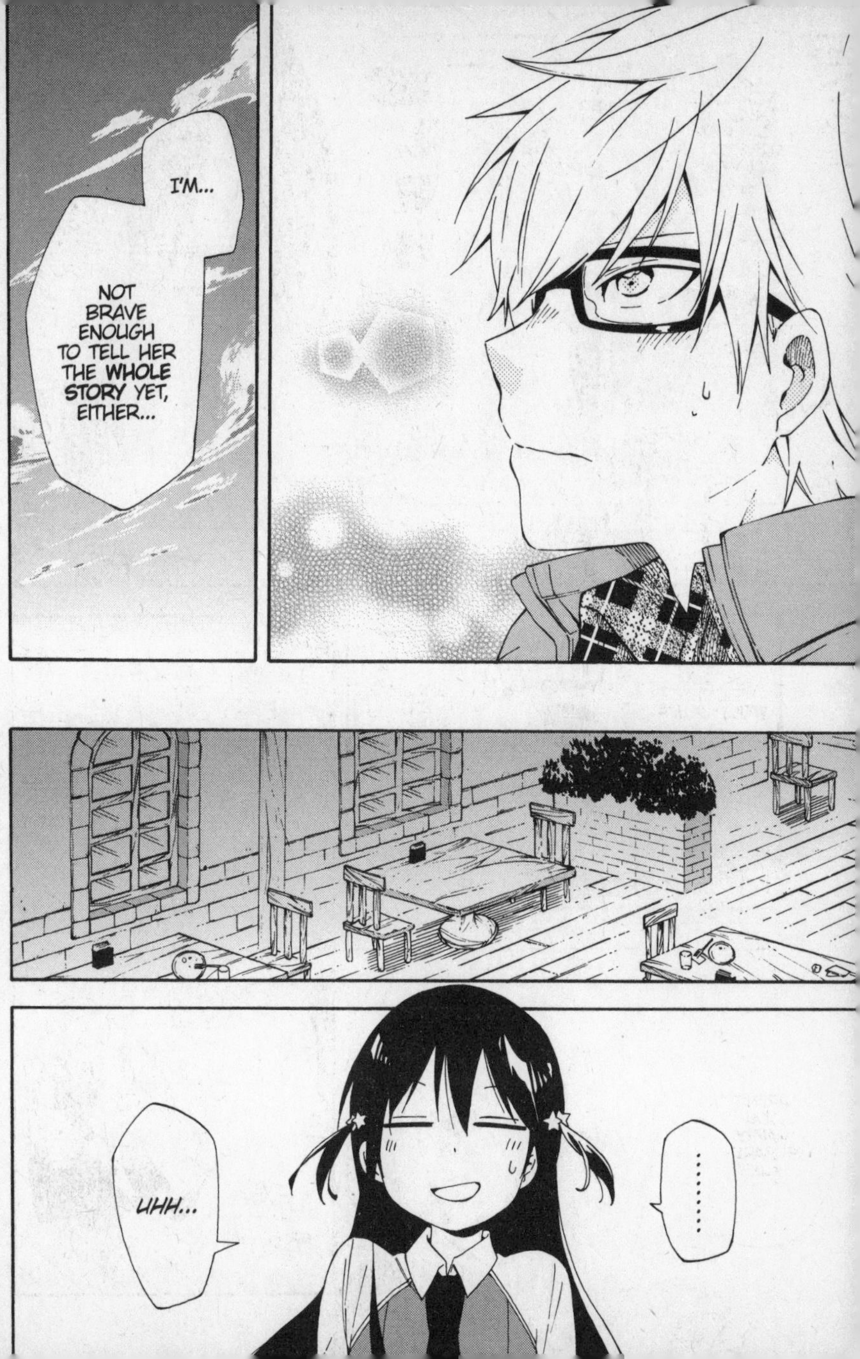
I'M...
NOT BRAVE ENOUGH TO TELL HER THE WHOLE STORY YET, EITHER...
....
UHH...

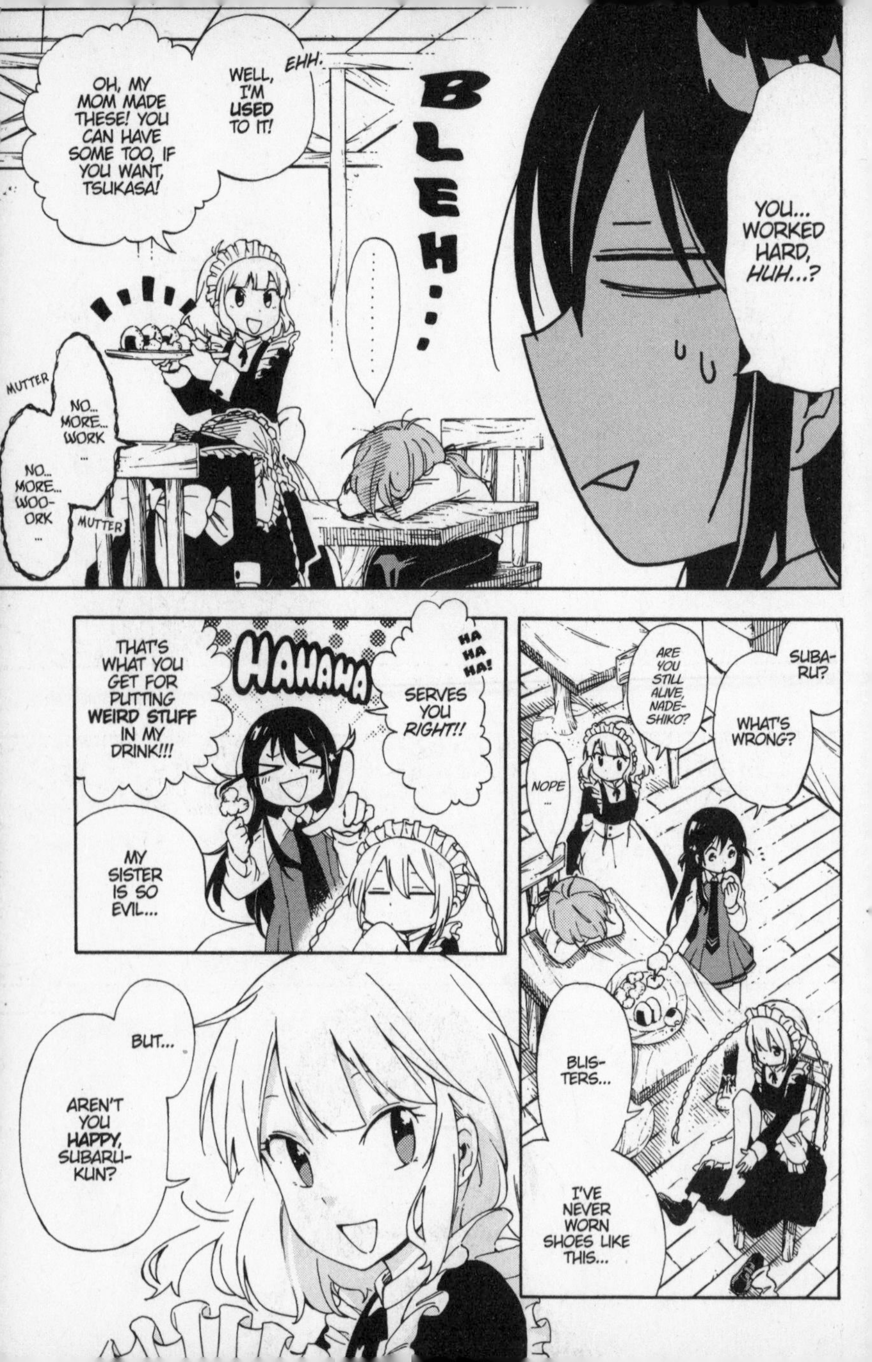
YOU... WORKED HARD, HUH...?
BLEH...
EHH.
WELL, I'M USED TO IT!
OH, MY MOM MADE THESE! YOU CAN HAVE SOME TOO, IF YOU WANT, TSUKASA!
......
NO... MORE... WORK ... NO... MORE... WOO-ORK ...
MUTTER
MUTTER
SUBA-RU? WHAT'S WRONG?
ARE YOU STILL ALIVE, NADE-SHIKO?
NOPE ...
BLIS-TERS...
I'VE NEVER WORN SHOES LIKE THIS...
HA HA HA!
SERVES YOU RIGHT!!
HAHAHA
THAT'S WHAT YOU GET FOR PUTTING WEIRD STUFF IN MY DRINK!!!
MY SISTER IS SO EVIL...
BUT...
AREN'T YOU HAPPY, SUBARU-KUN?

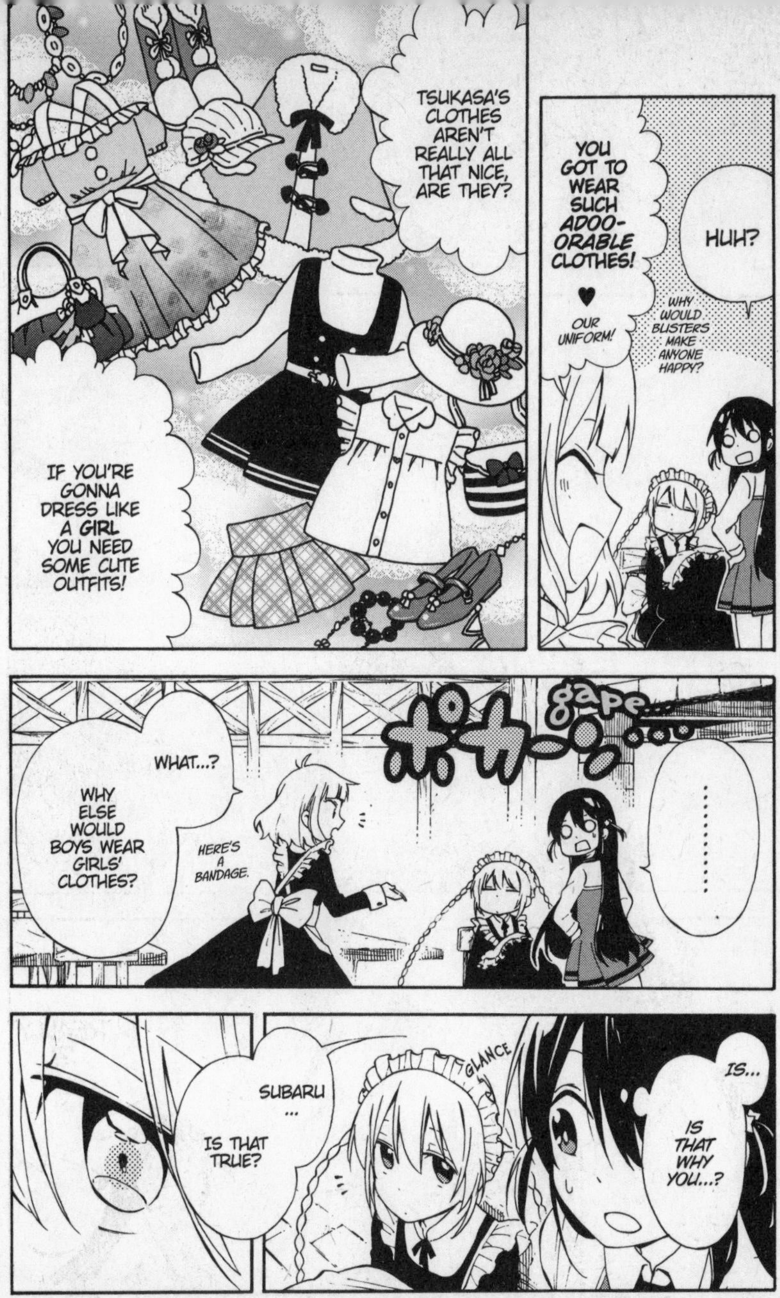
YOU GOT TO WEAR SUCH ADOO-ORABLE CLOTHES! ♥
OUR UNIFORM!
HUH?
WHY WOULD BLUSTERS MAKE ANYONE HAPPY?
TSUKASA'S CLOTHES AREN'T REALLY ALL THAT NICE, ARE THEY?
IF YOU'RE GONNA DRESS LIKE A GIRL YOU NEED SOME CUTE OUTFITS!
gape...
......
WHAT...?
WHY ELSE WOULD BOYS WEAR GIRLS' CLOTHES?
HERE'S A BANDAGE.
IS...
IS THAT WHY YOU...?
GLANCE
SUBARU ...
IS THAT TRUE?

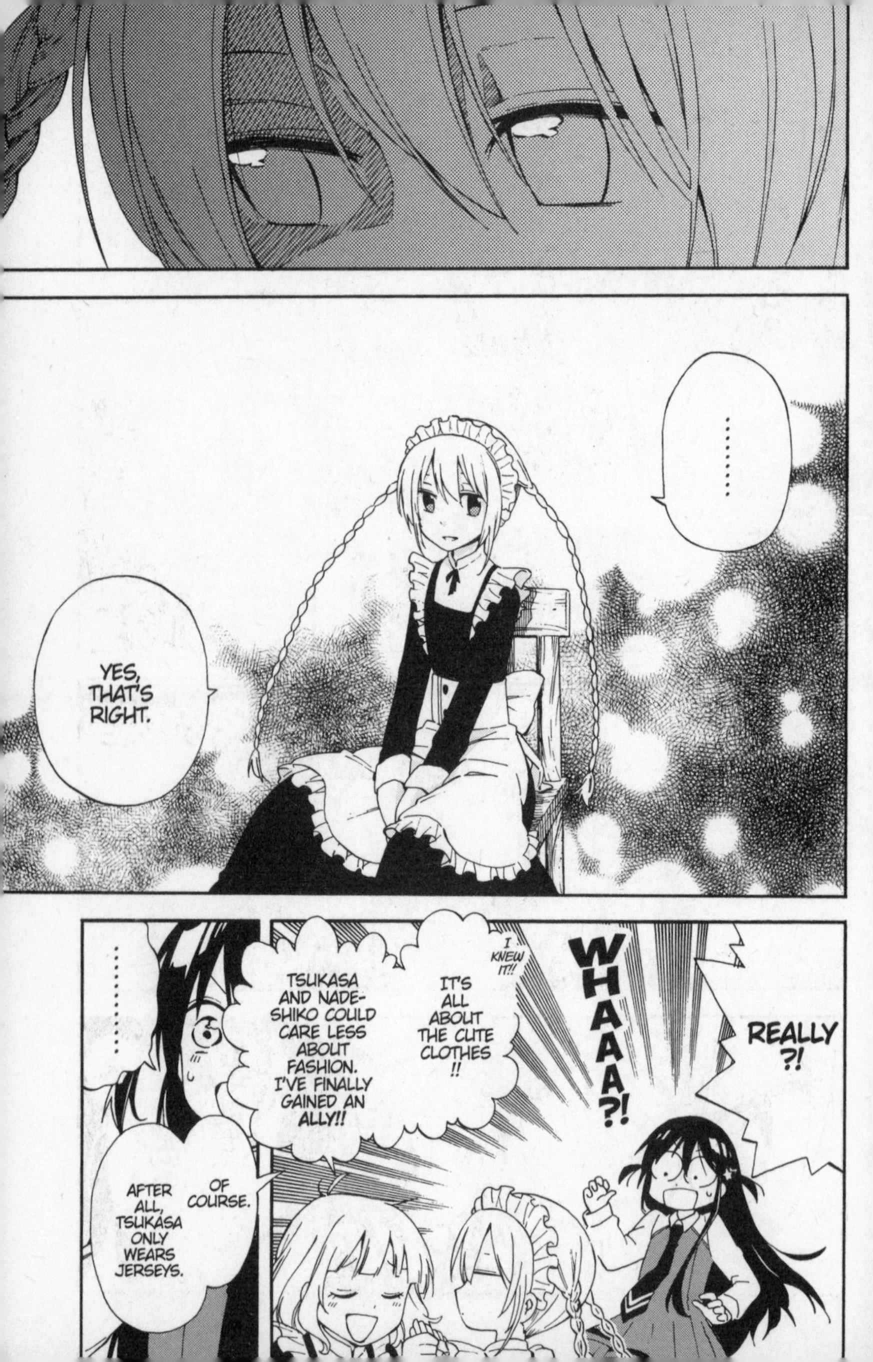
......
YES, THAT'S RIGHT.
REALLY?!
WHAAA?!
I KNEW IT!!
IT'S ALL ABOUT THE CUTE CLOTHES!!
TSUKASA AND NADE-SHIKO COULD CARE LESS ABOUT FASHION. I'VE FINALLY GAINED AN ALLY!!
......
OF COURSE.
AFTER ALL, TSUKASA ONLY WEARS JERSEYS.

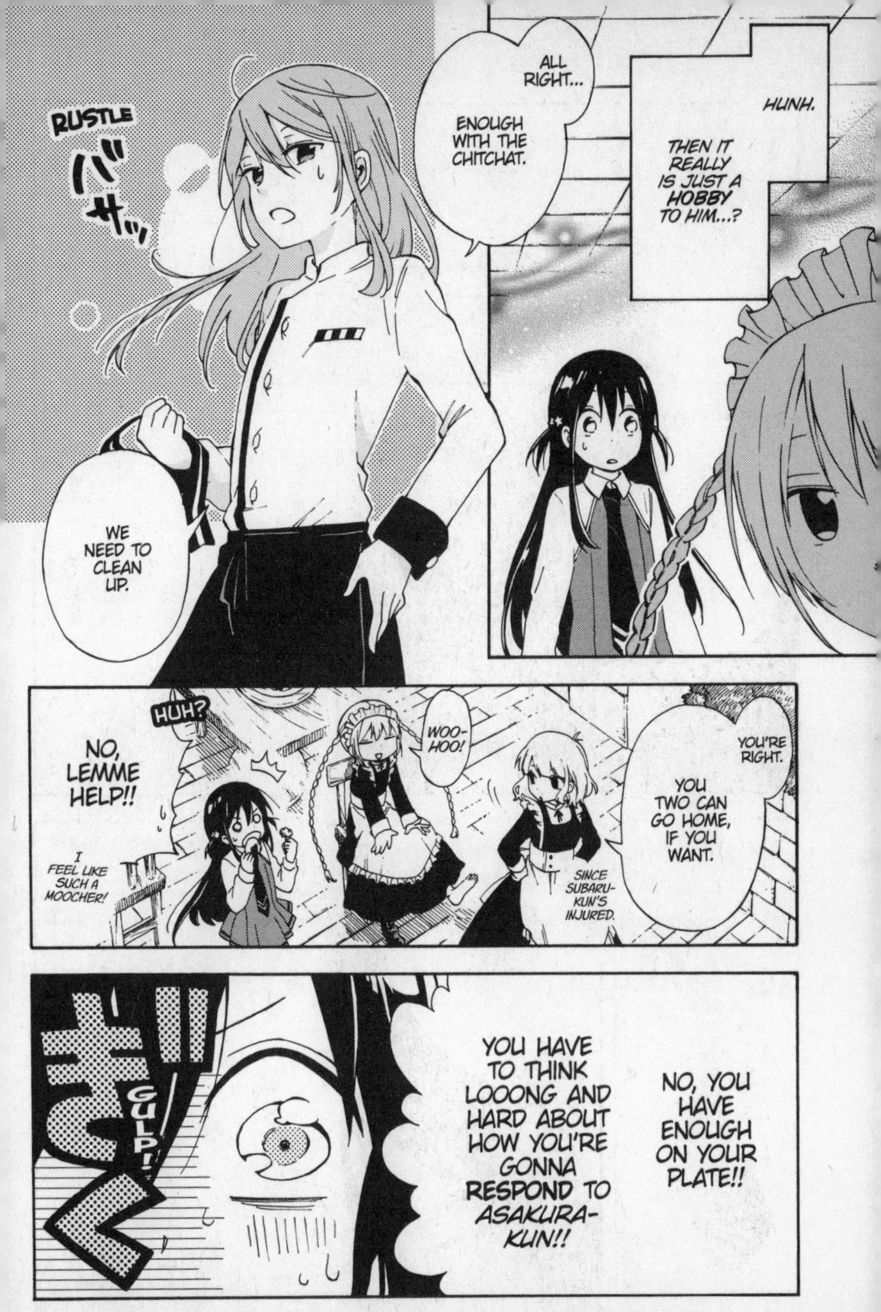
HUNH.
THEN IT REALLY IS JUST A HOBBY TO HIM...?
ALL RIGHT...
ENOUGH WITH THE CHITCHAT.
RUSTLE
バサッ
WE NEED TO CLEAN UP.
YOU'RE RIGHT.
YOU TWO CAN GO HOME, IF YOU WANT.
SINCE SUBARU-KUN'S INJURED.
WOO-HOO!
HUH?
NO, LEMME HELP!!
I FEEL LIKE SUCH A MOOCHER!
NO, YOU HAVE ENOUGH ON YOUR PLATE!!
YOU HAVE TO THINK LOOONG AND HARD ABOUT HOW YOU'RE GONNA RESPOND TO ASAKURA-KUN!!
GULP!

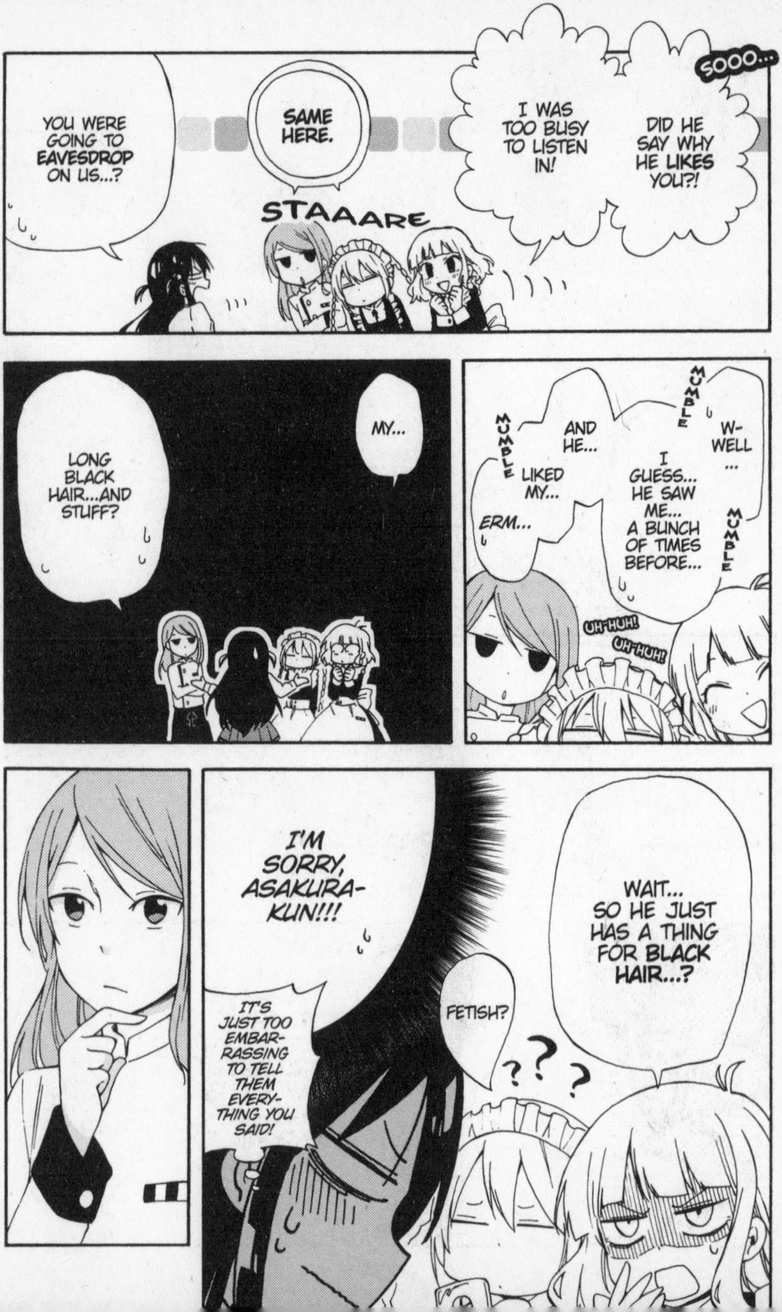
SOOO...
DID HE SAY WHY HE LIKES YOU?!
I WAS TOO BUSY TO LISTEN IN!
SAME HERE.
STAAARE
YOU WERE GOING TO EAVESDROP ON US...?
MUMBLE
W-WELL...
I GUESS... HE SAW ME... A BUNCH OF TIMES BEFORE...
MUMBLE
AND HE... LIKED MY...
MUMBLE
ERM...
UH-HUH!
UH-HUH!
MY...
LONG BLACK HAIR...AND STUFF?
WAIT... SO HE JUST HAS A THING FOR BLACK HAIR...?
I'M SORRY, ASAKURA-KUN!!!
FETISH?
IT'S JUST TOO EMBARRASSING TO TELL THEM EVERYTHING YOU SAID!

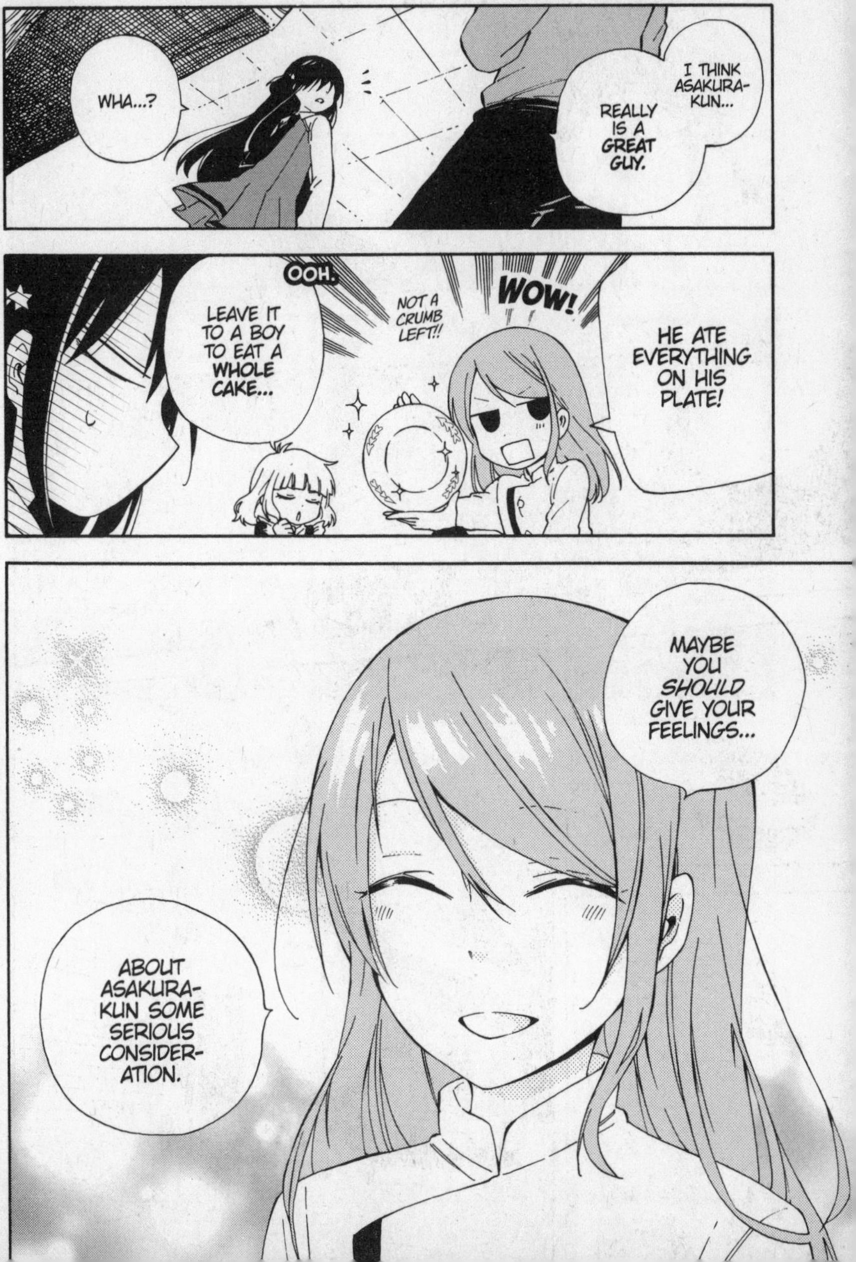
I THINK ASAKURA-KUN... REALLY IS A GREAT GUY.
WHA...?
HE ATE EVERYTHING ON HIS PLATE!
WOW!
NOT A CRUMB LEFT!!
OOH.
LEAVE IT TO A BOY TO EAT A WHOLE CAKE...
MAYBE YOU SHOULD GIVE YOUR FEELINGS...
ABOUT ASAKURA-KUN SOME SERIOUS CONSIDERATION.

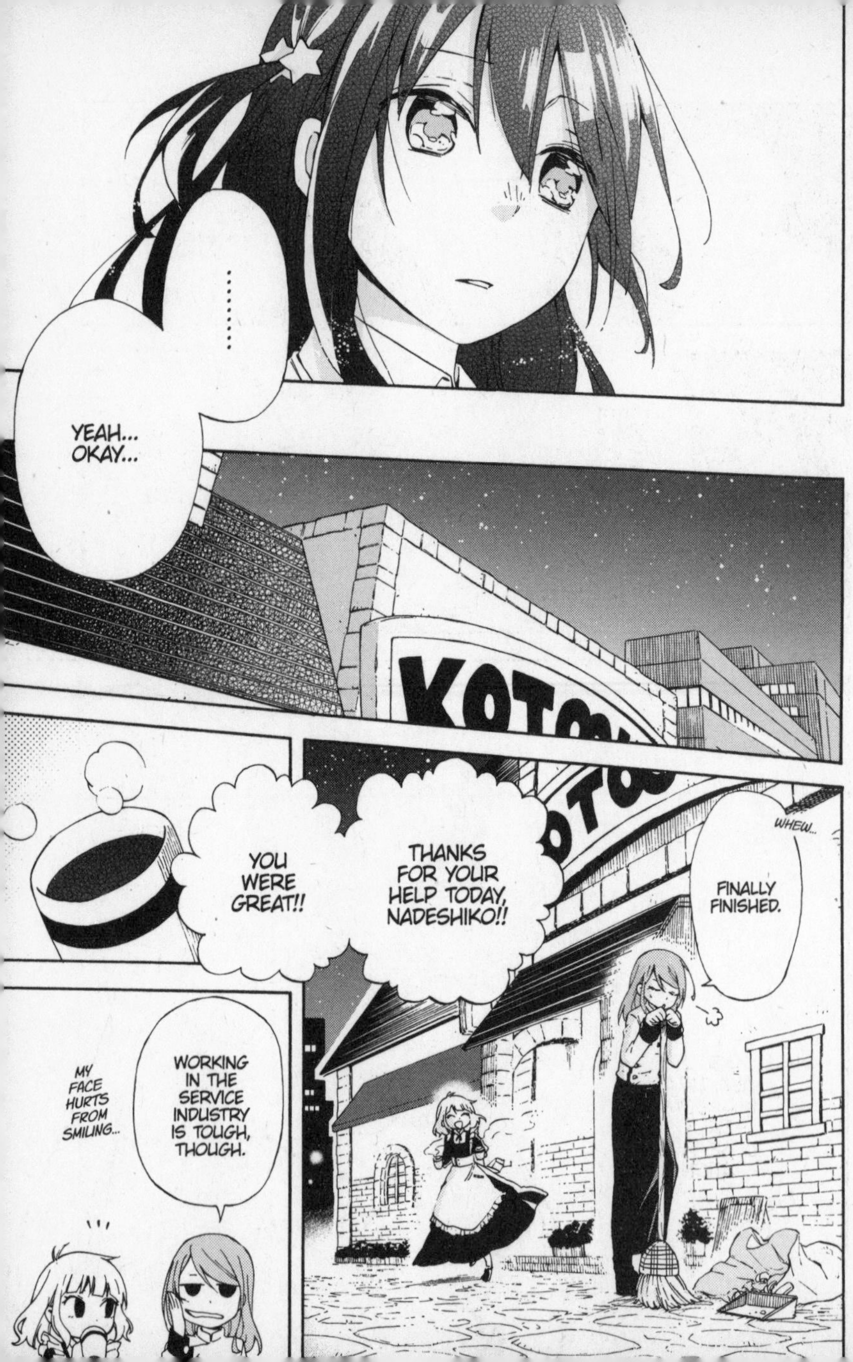
......
YEAH... OKAY...
WHEW...
FINALLY FINISHED.
THANKS FOR YOUR HELP TODAY, NADESHIKO!!
YOU WERE GREAT!!
WORKING IN THE SERVICE INDUSTRY IS TOUGH, THOUGH.
MY FACE HURTS FROM SMILING...

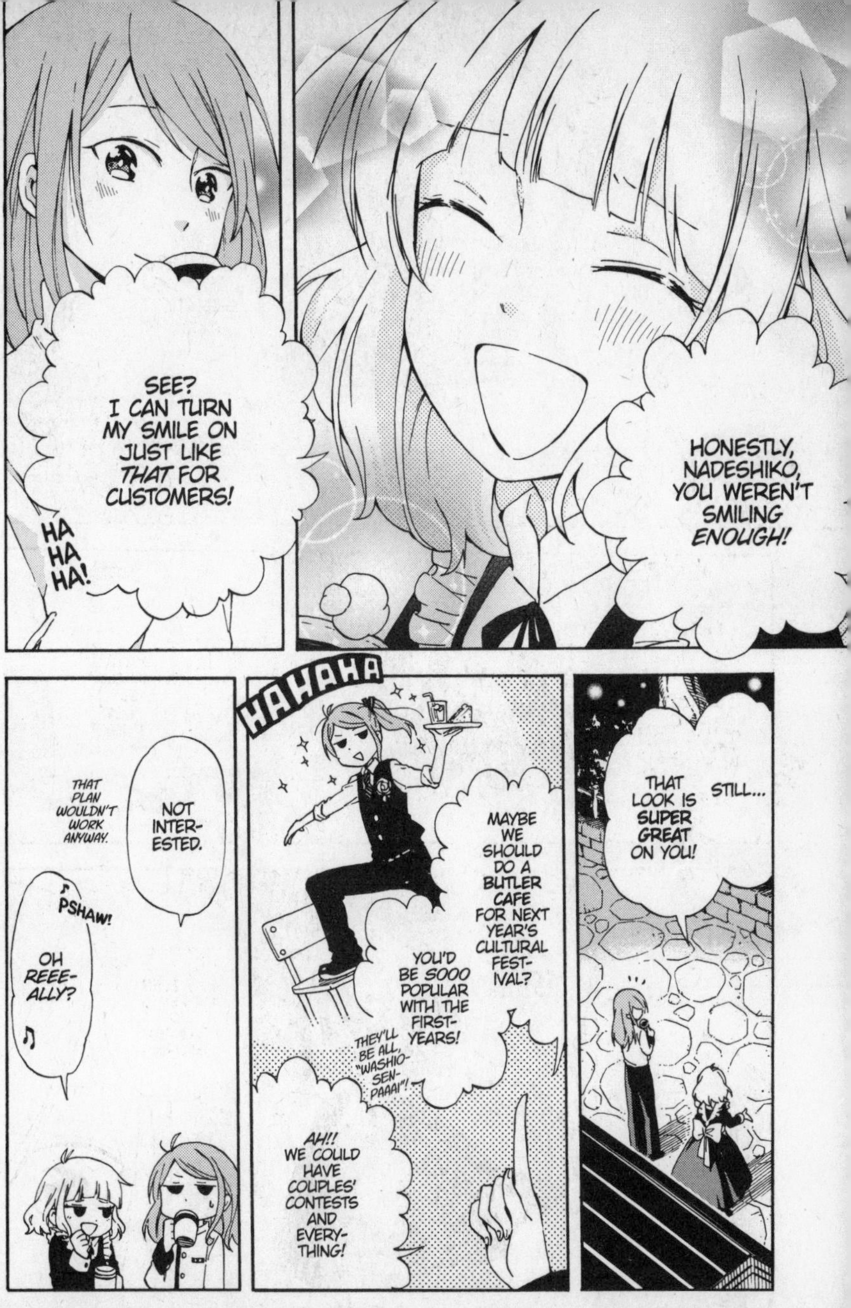
HONESTLY, NADESHIKO, YOU WEREN'T SMILING ENOUGH!
SEE? I CAN TURN MY SMILE ON JUST LIKE THAT FOR CUSTOMERS!
HA HA HA!
STILL...
THAT LOOK IS SUPER GREAT ON YOU!
HAHAHA
MAYBE WE SHOULD DO A BUTLER CAFE FOR NEXT YEAR'S CULTURAL FESTIVAL?
YOU'D BE SOOO POPULAR WITH THE FIRST-YEARS!
THEY'LL BE ALL, "WASHIO-SENPAAAI"!
AH!! WE COULD HAVE COUPLES' CONTESTS AND EVERYTHING!
NOT INTERESTED.
THAT PLAN WOULDN'T WORK ANYWAY.
♪ PSHAW!
OH REEE-ALLY? ♪

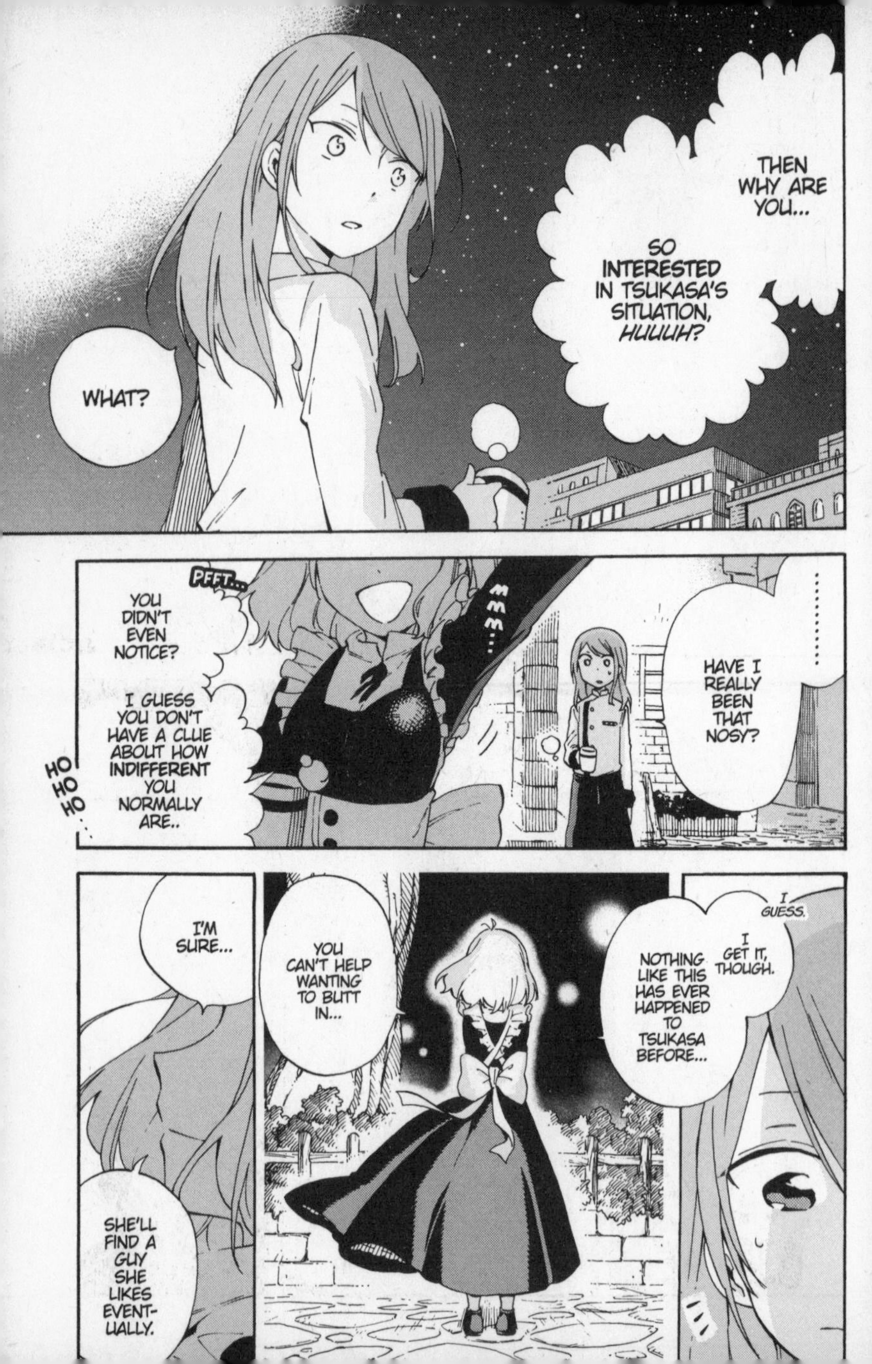
THEN WHY ARE YOU...
SO INTERESTED IN TSUKASA'S SITUATION, *HUUUH?*
WHAT?
......
HAVE I REALLY BEEN THAT NOSY?
PFFT...
MMM...
YOU DIDN'T EVEN NOTICE?
I GUESS YOU DON'T HAVE A CLUE ABOUT HOW INDIFFERENT YOU NORMALLY ARE..
HO HO HO..
I GUESS.
I GET IT, THOUGH.
NOTHING LIKE THIS HAS EVER HAPPENED TO TSUKASA BEFORE...
YOU CAN'T HELP WANTING TO BUTT IN...
I'M SURE...
SHE'LL FIND A GUY SHE LIKES EVENT-UALLY.

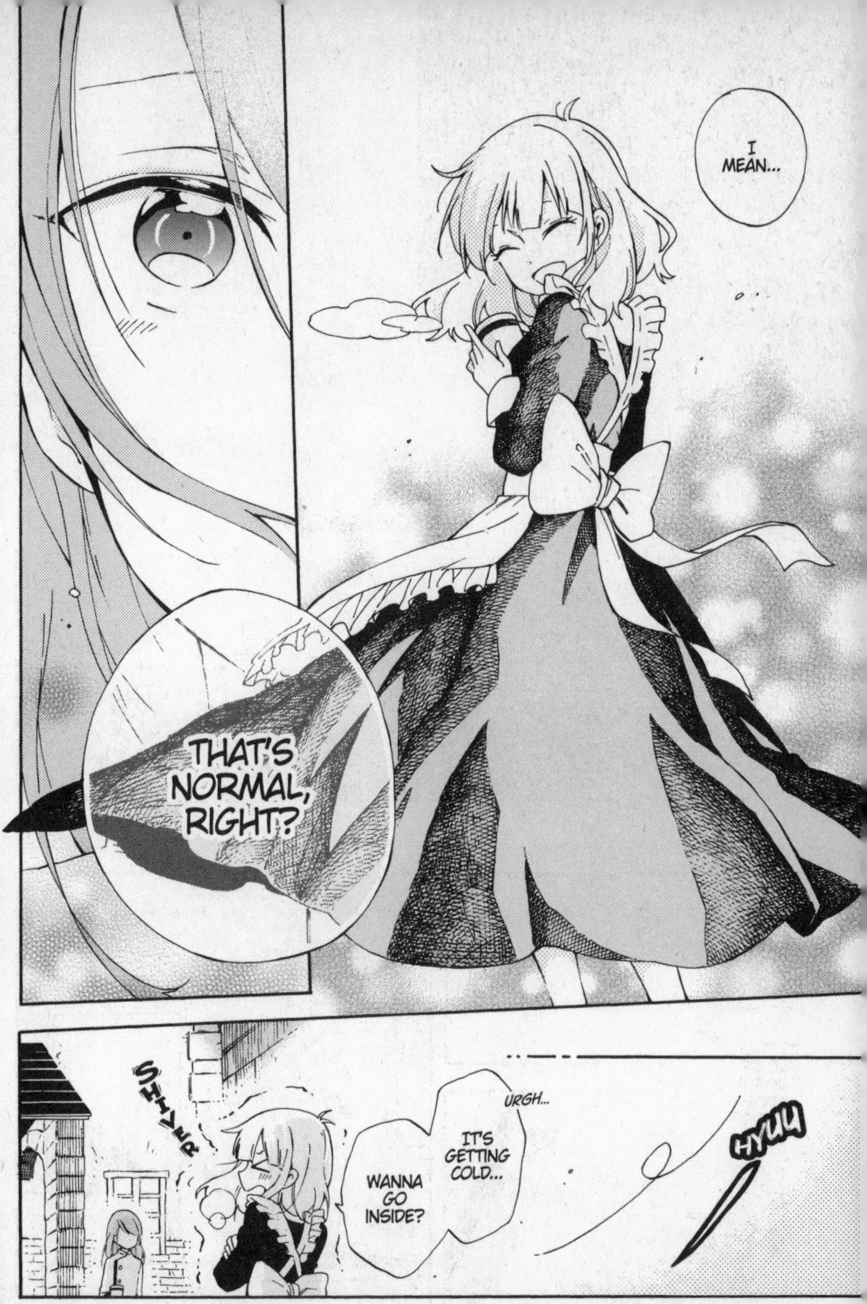
I MEAN...
THAT'S NORMAL, RIGHT?
HYUU
URGH...
IT'S GETTING COLD...
WANNA GO INSIDE?
SHIVER

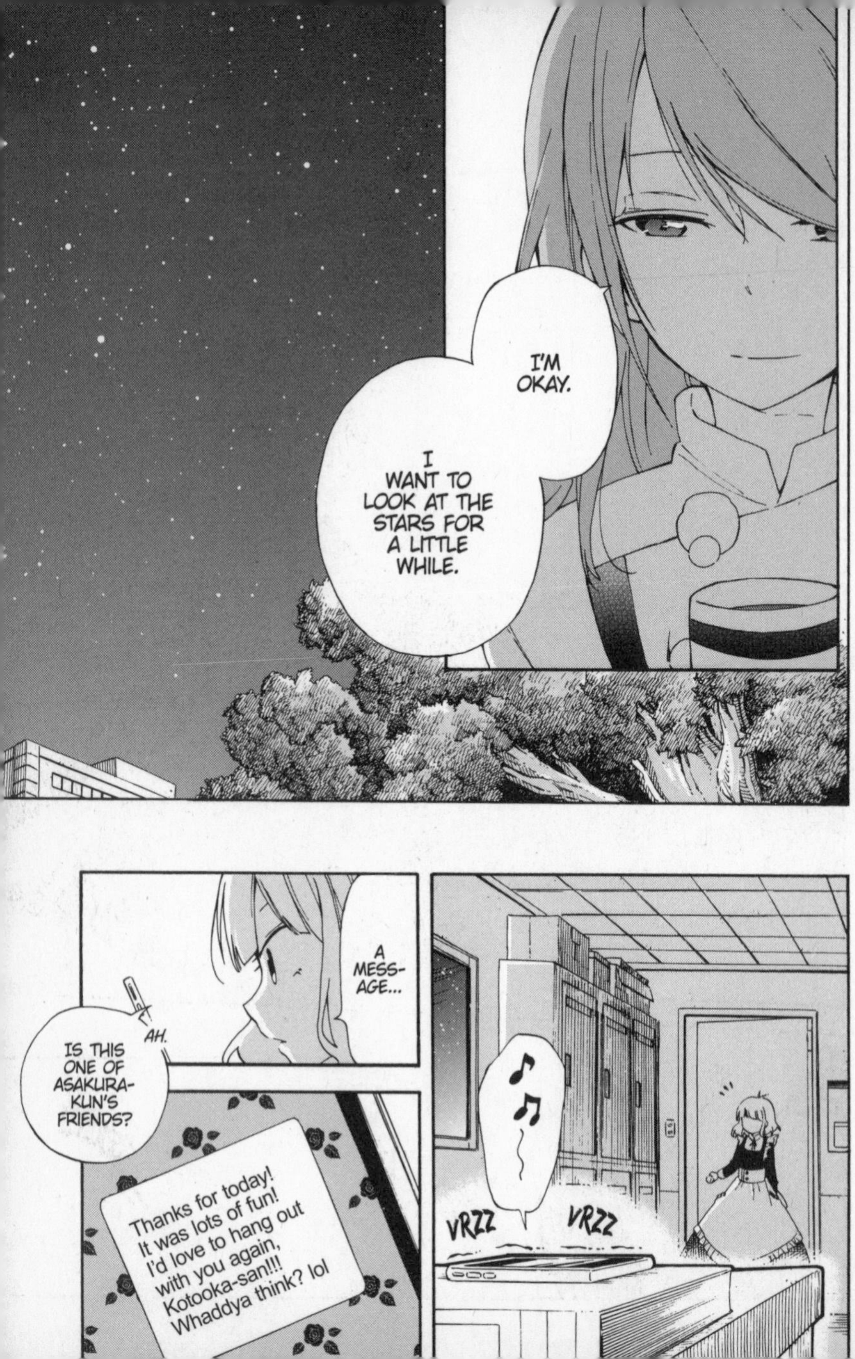
I'M OKAY.
I WANT TO LOOK AT THE STARS FOR A LITTLE WHILE.
VRZZ
VRZZ
A MESS-AGE...
AH.
IS THIS ONE OF ASAKURA-KUN'S FRIENDS?
Thanks for today! It was lots of fun! I'd love to hang out with you again, Kotooka-san!!! Whaddya think? lol

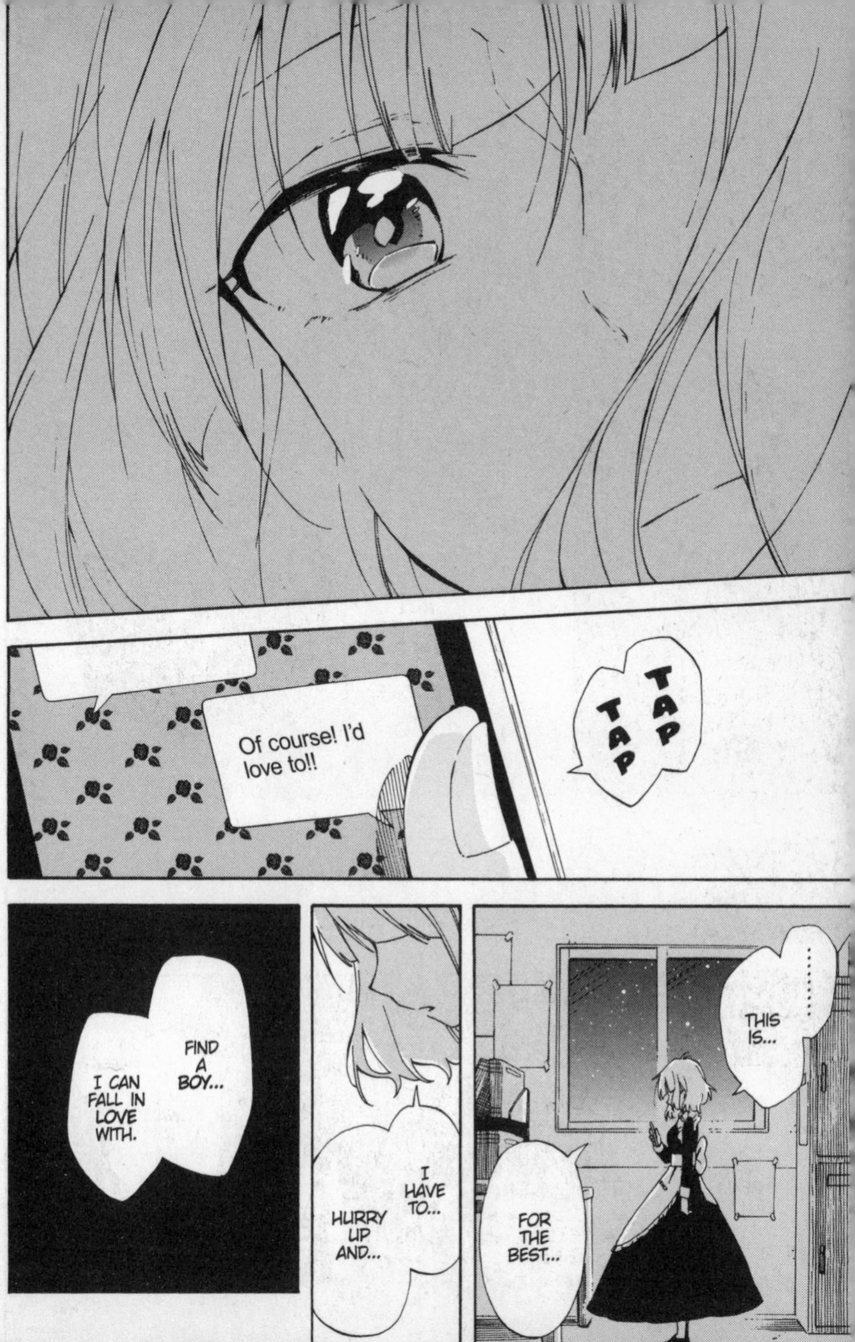
TAP TAP
Of course! I'd love to!!
......
THIS IS...
FOR THE BEST...
I HAVE TO...
HURRY UP AND...
FIND A BOY...
I CAN FALL IN LOVE WITH.

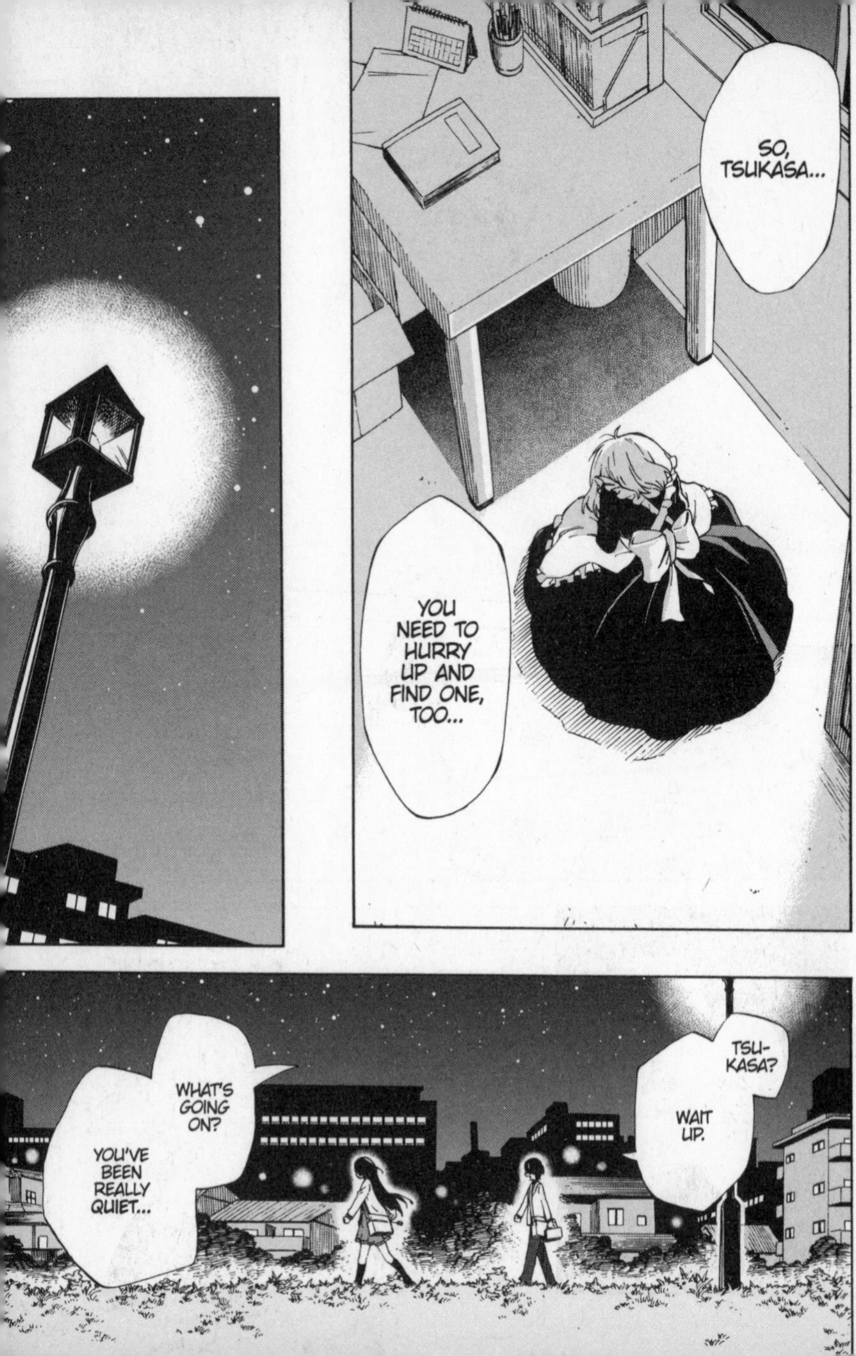
SO, TSUKASA...
YOU NEED TO HURRY UP AND FIND ONE, TOO...
TSU-KASA?
WAIT UP.
WHAT'S GOING ON?
YOU'VE BEEN REALLY QUIET...

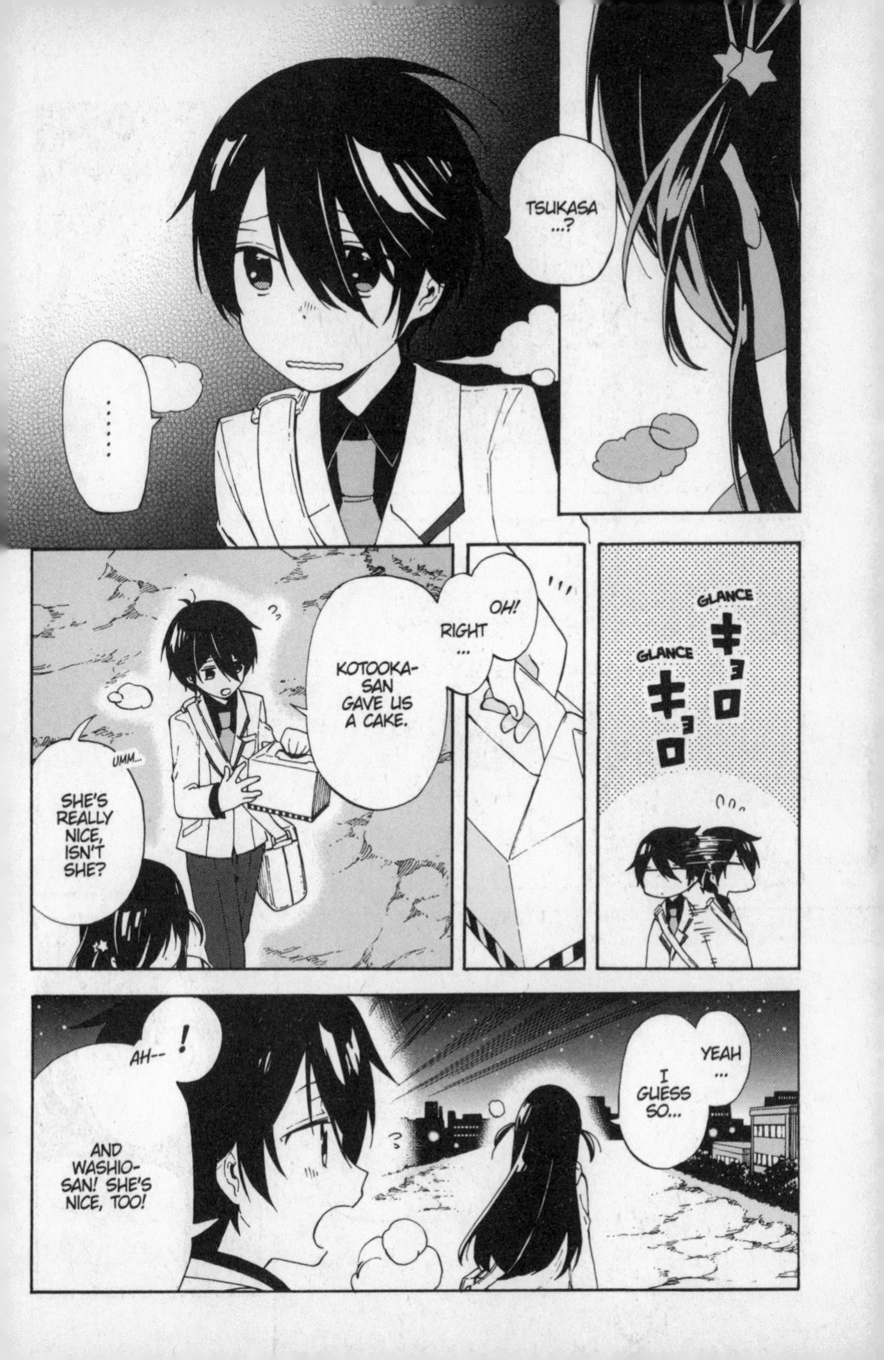
TSUKASA ...?
......
GLANCE
キョロ
GLANCE
キョロ
OH!
RIGHT ...
KOTOOKA-SAN GAVE US A CAKE.
UMM...
SHE'S REALLY NICE, ISN'T SHE?
YEAH ... I GUESS SO...
AH-- !
AND WASHIO-SAN! SHE'S NICE, TOO!

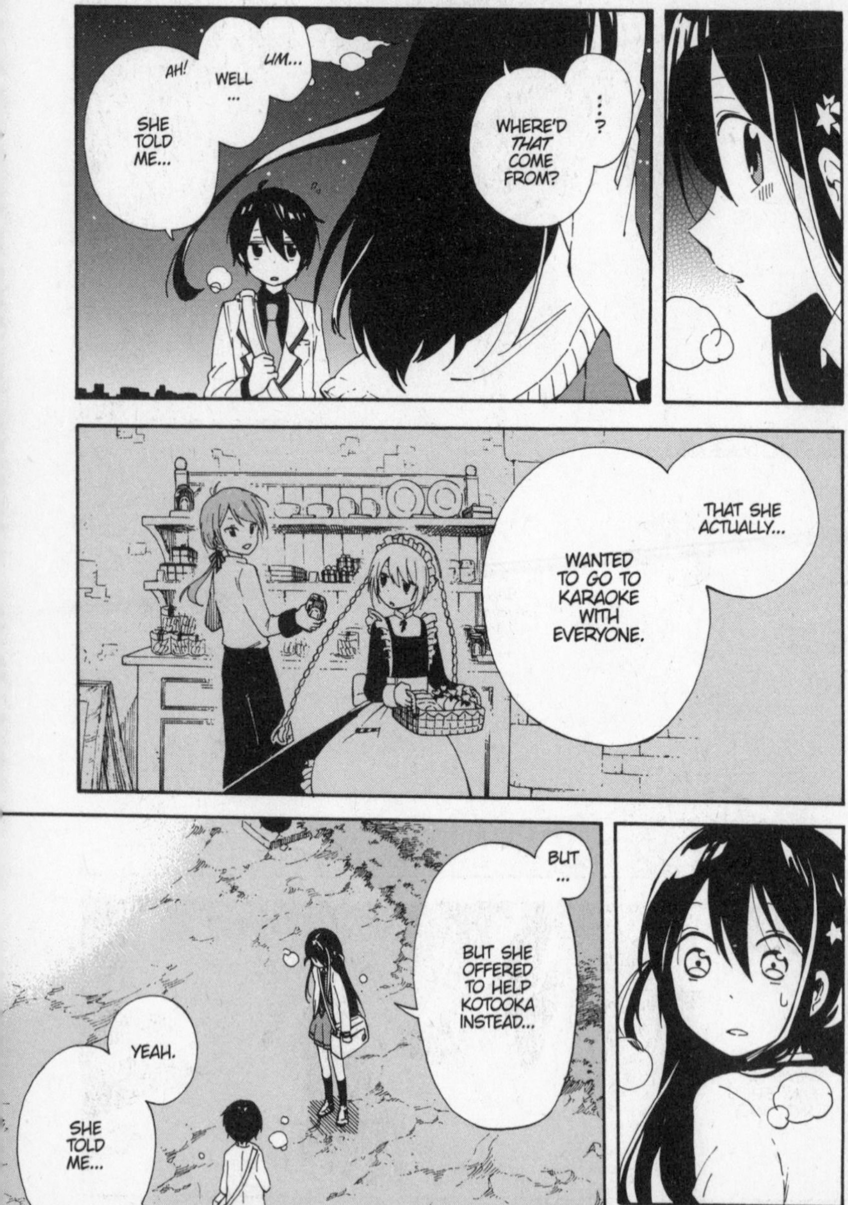
...?
WHERE'D THAT COME FROM?
UM... WELL ... AH! SHE TOLD ME...
THAT SHE ACTUALLY...
WANTED TO GO TO KARAOKE WITH EVERYONE.
BUT ...
BUT SHE OFFERED TO HELP KOTOOKA INSTEAD...
YEAH.
SHE TOLD ME...

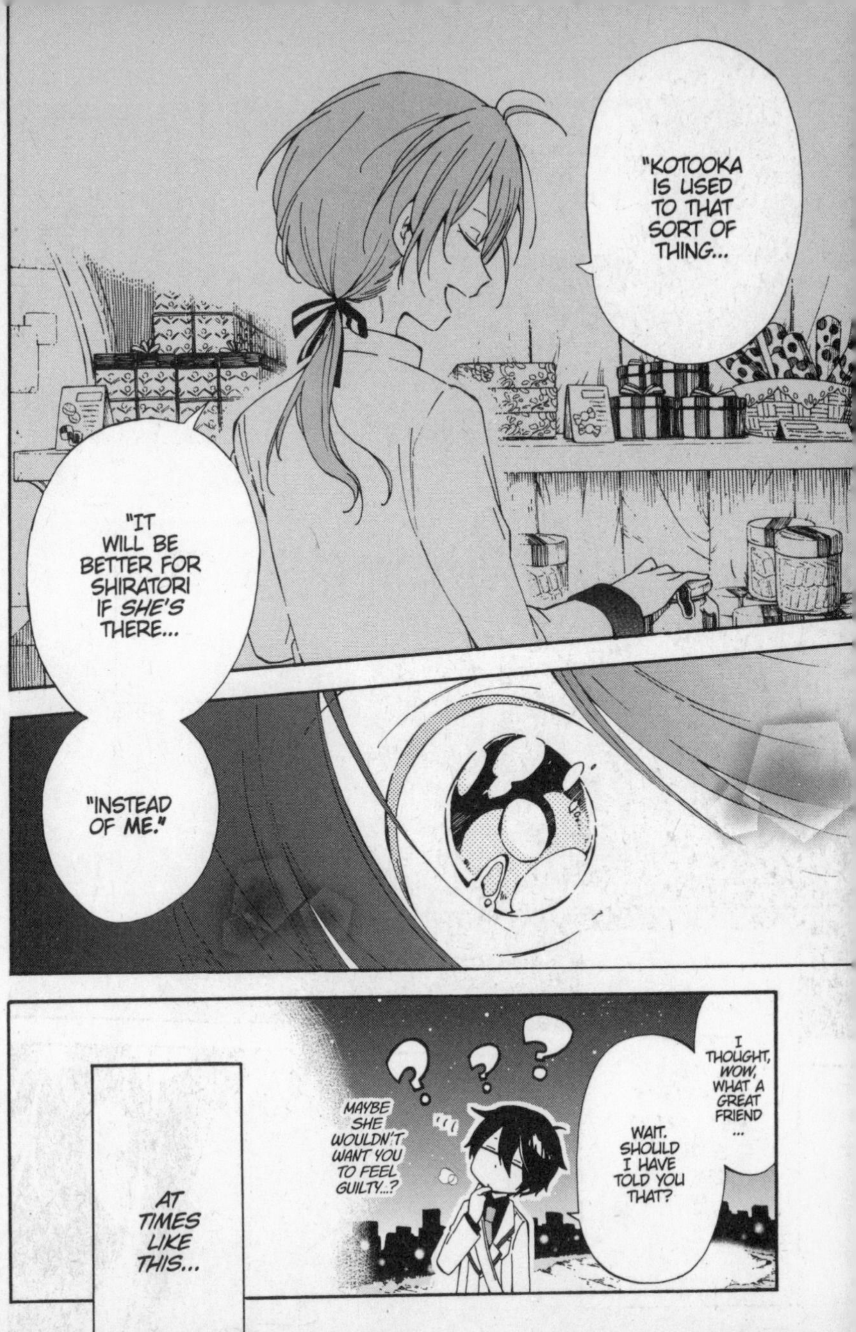
"KOTOOKA IS USED TO THAT SORT OF THING...
"IT WILL BE BETTER FOR SHIRATORI IF *SHE'S* THERE...
"INSTEAD OF ME."
I THOUGHT, *WOW*, WHAT A GREAT FRIEND ...
WAIT. SHOULD I HAVE TOLD YOU THAT?
MAYBE SHE WOULDN'T WANT YOU TO FEEL GUILTY...?
AT TIMES LIKE THIS...

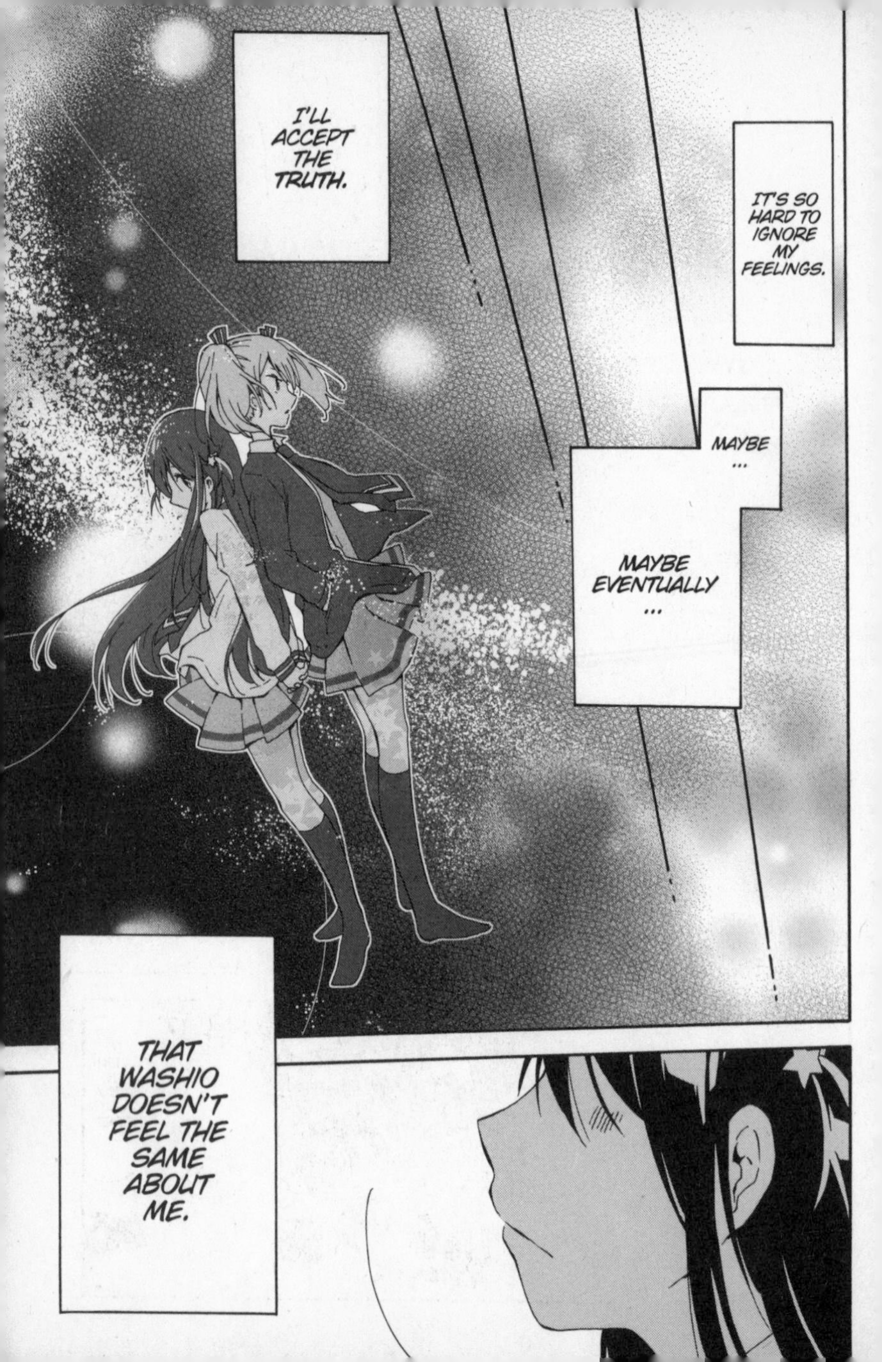
IT'S SO HARD TO IGNORE MY FEELINGS.
MAYBE ...
MAYBE EVENTUALLY ...
I'LL ACCEPT THE TRUTH.
THAT WASHIO DOESN'T FEEL THE SAME ABOUT ME.

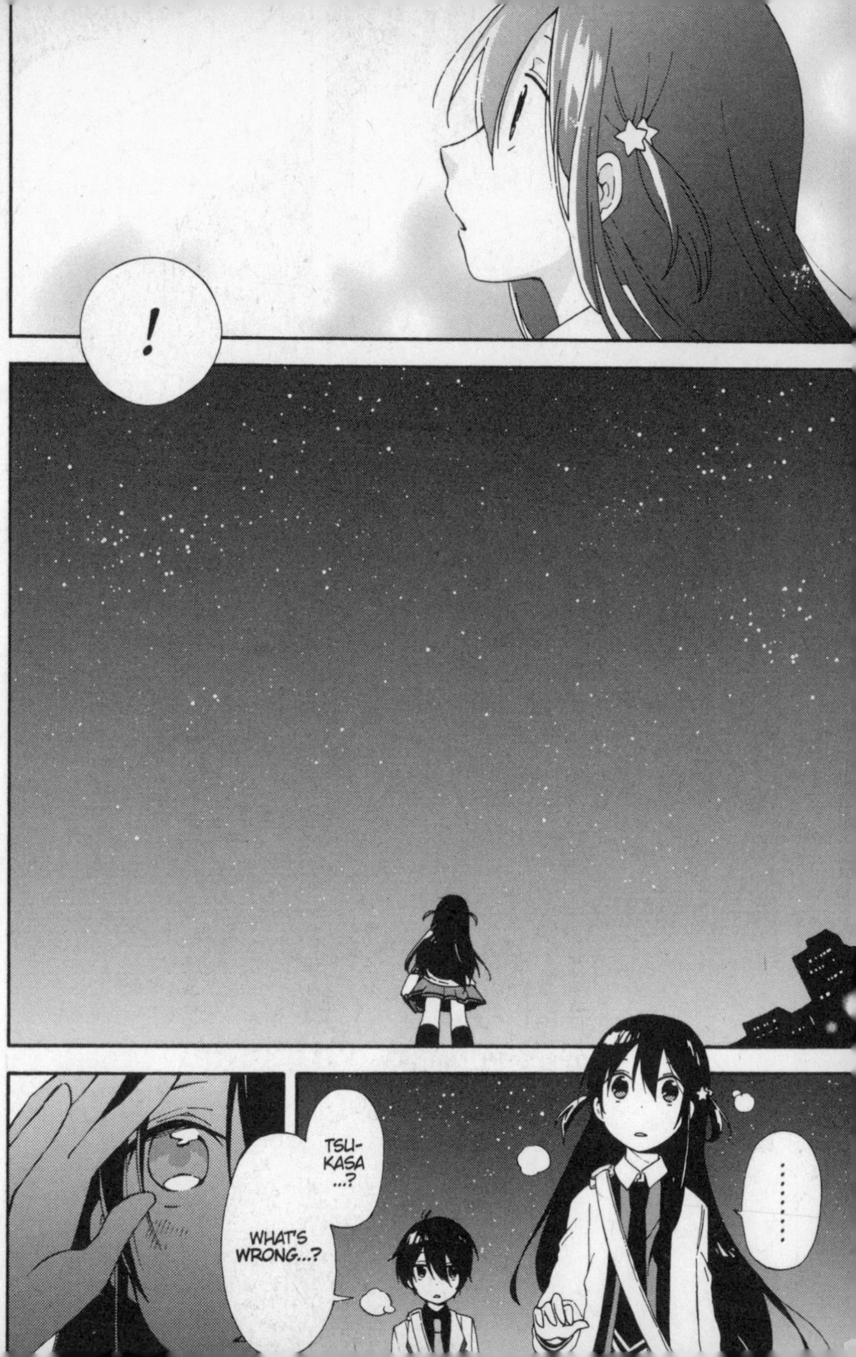
!
......
TSU-KASA...?
WHAT'S WRONG...?

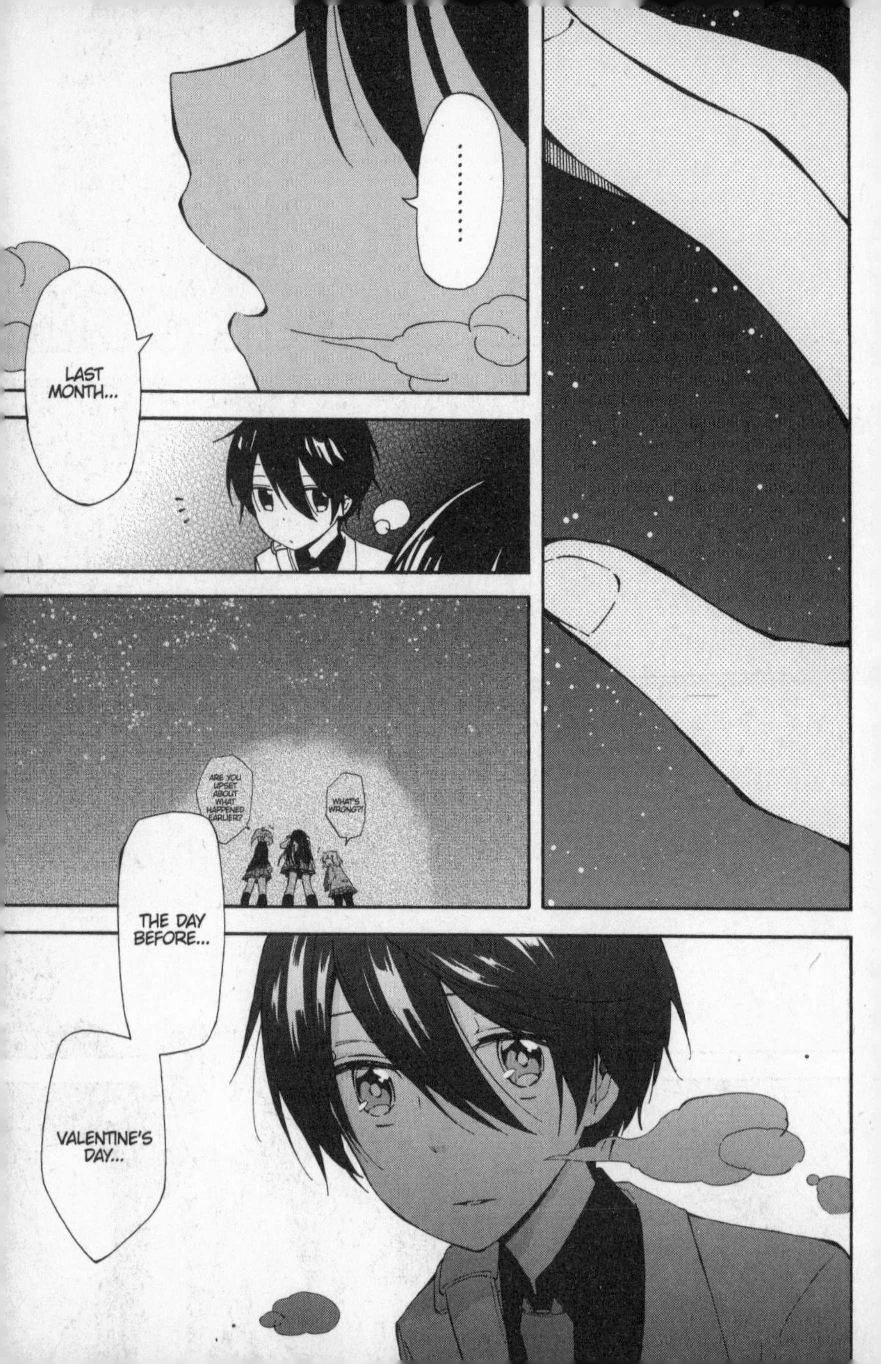
......
LAST MONTH...
WHAT'S WRONG?!
ARE YOU UPSET ABOUT WHAT HAPPENED EARLIER?
THE DAY BEFORE...
VALENTINE'S DAY...

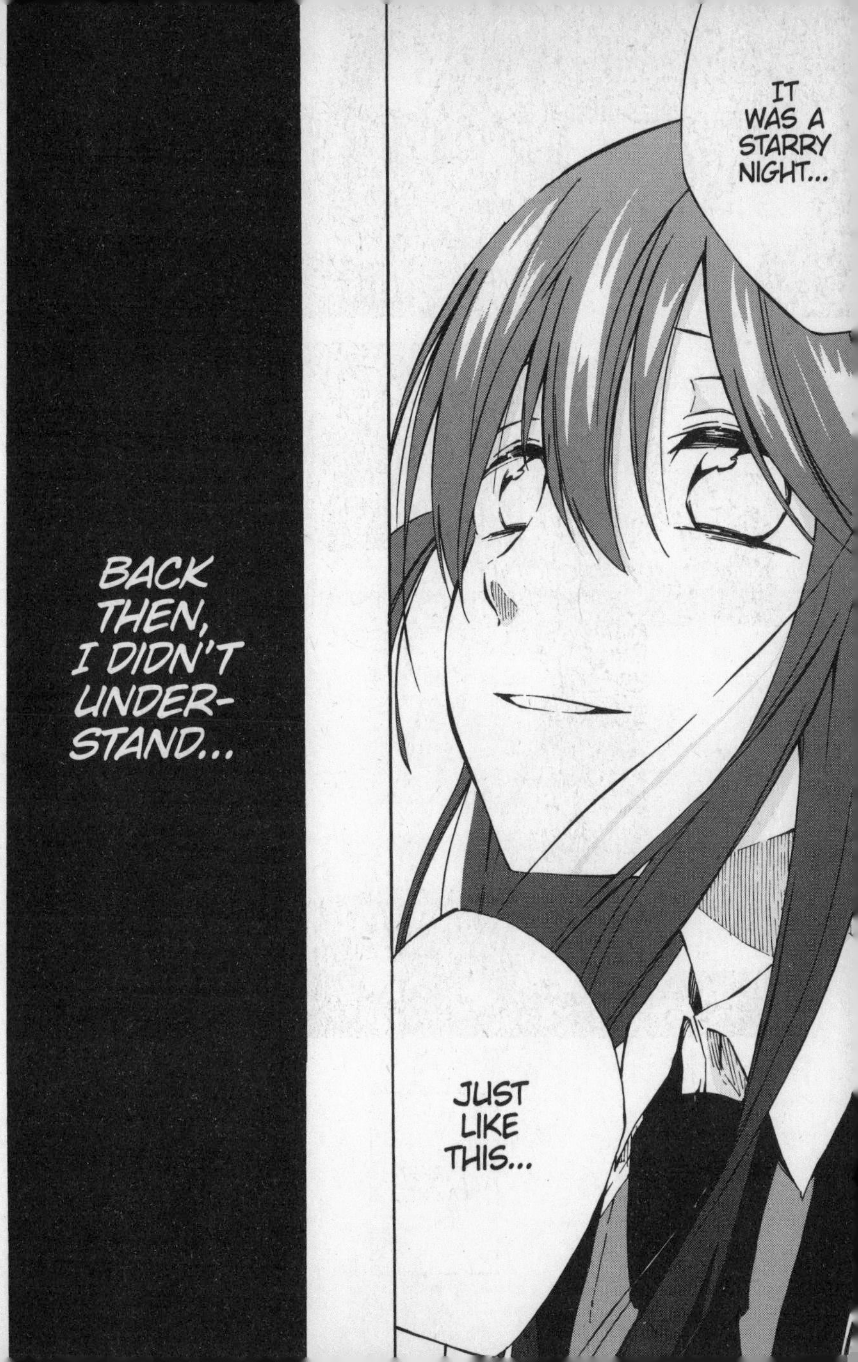
IT WAS A STARRY NIGHT...
JUST LIKE THIS...
BACK THEN, I DIDN'T UNDER-STAND...

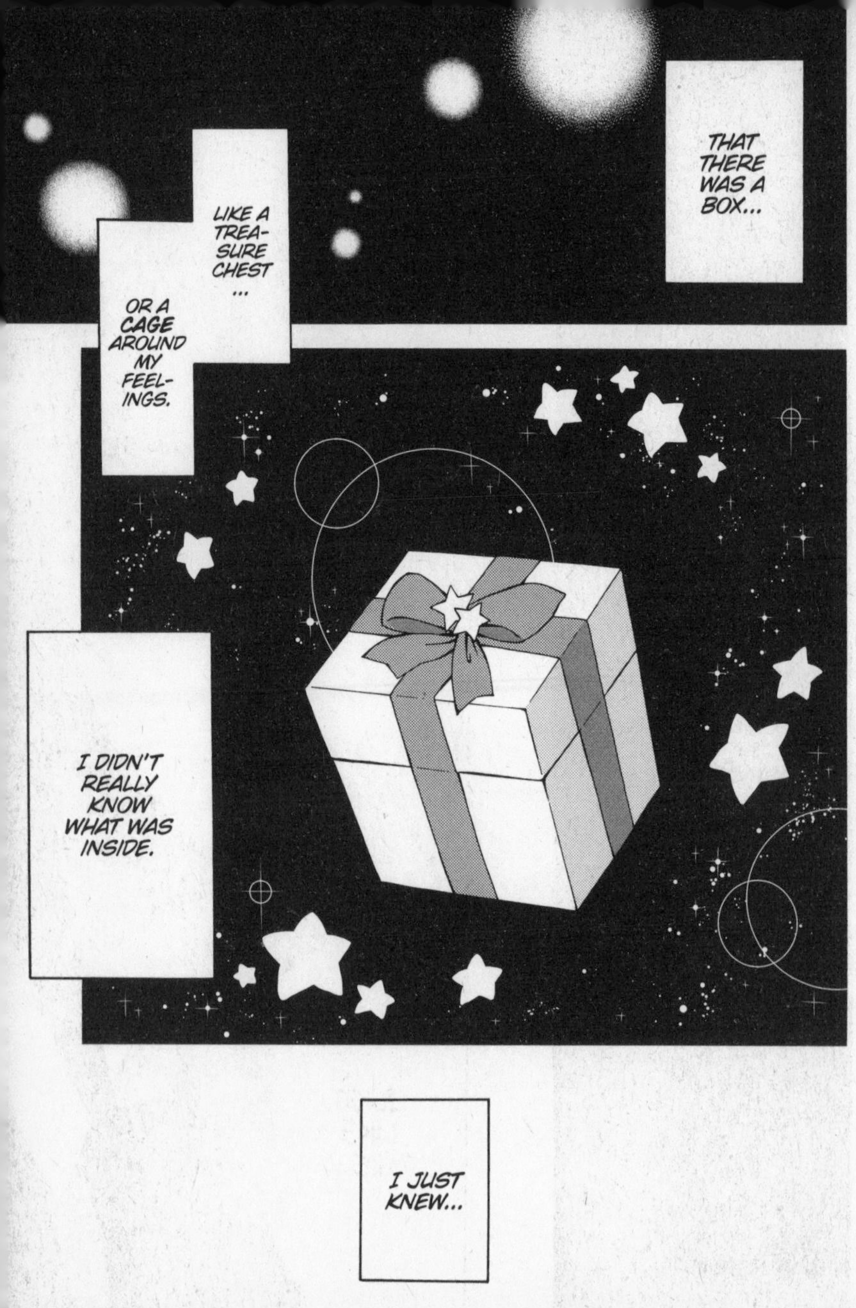
THAT THERE WAS A BOX...
LIKE A TREA-SURE CHEST...
OR A CAGE AROUND MY FEEL-INGS.
I DIDN'T REALLY KNOW WHAT WAS INSIDE.
I JUST KNEW...

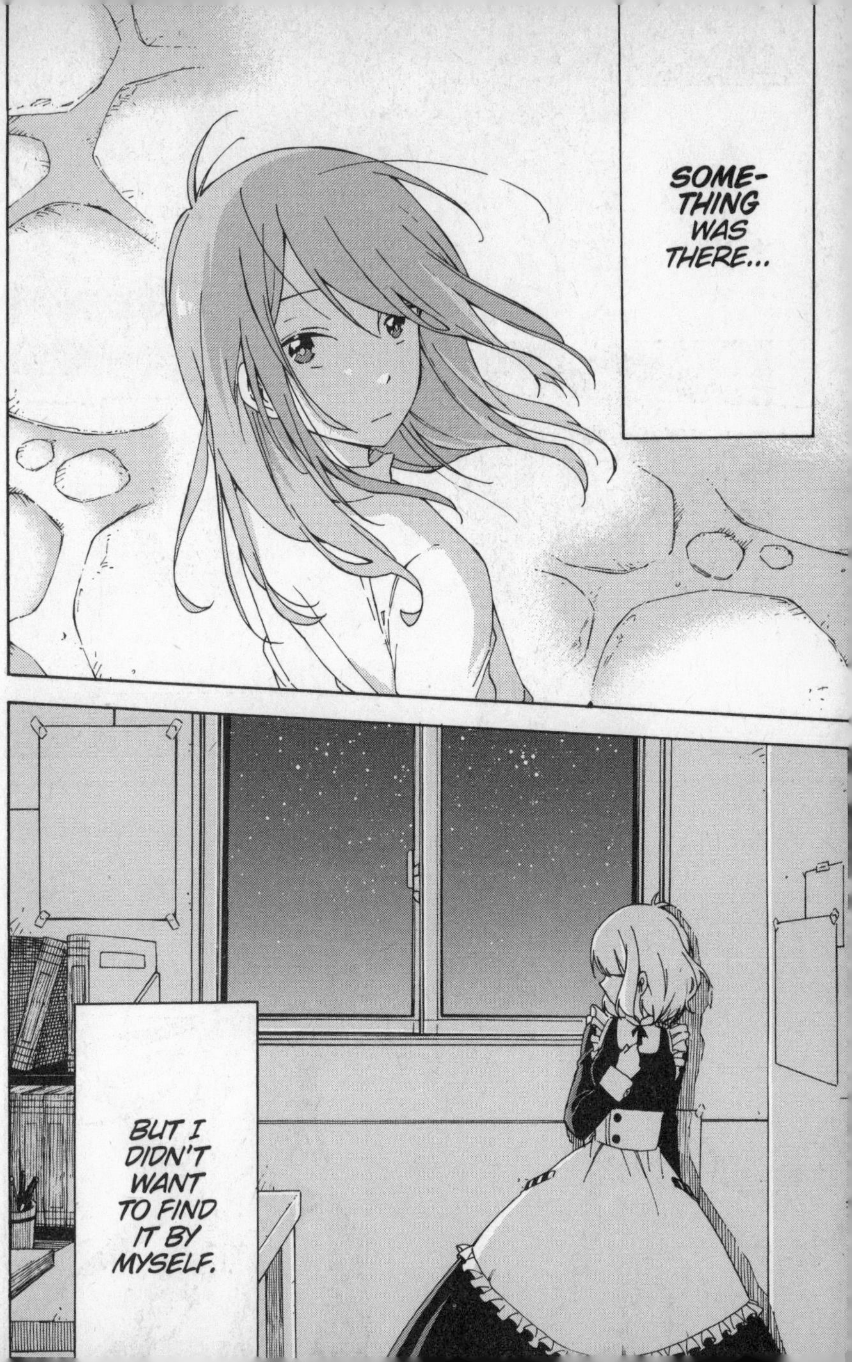
SOMETHING WAS THERE...
BUT I DIDN'T WANT TO FIND IT BY MYSELF.

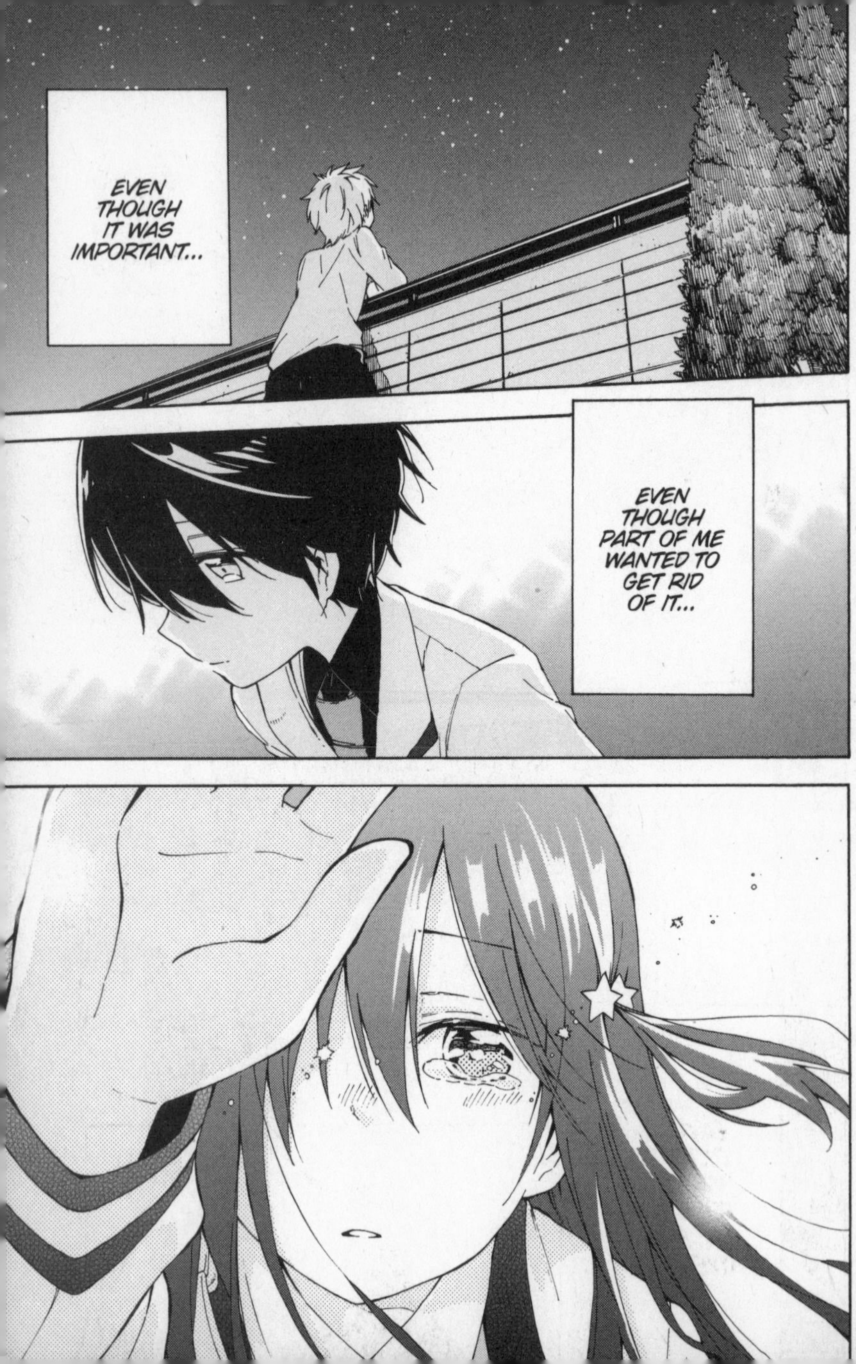
EVEN THOUGH IT WAS IMPORTANT...
EVEN THOUGH PART OF ME WANTED TO GET RID OF IT...

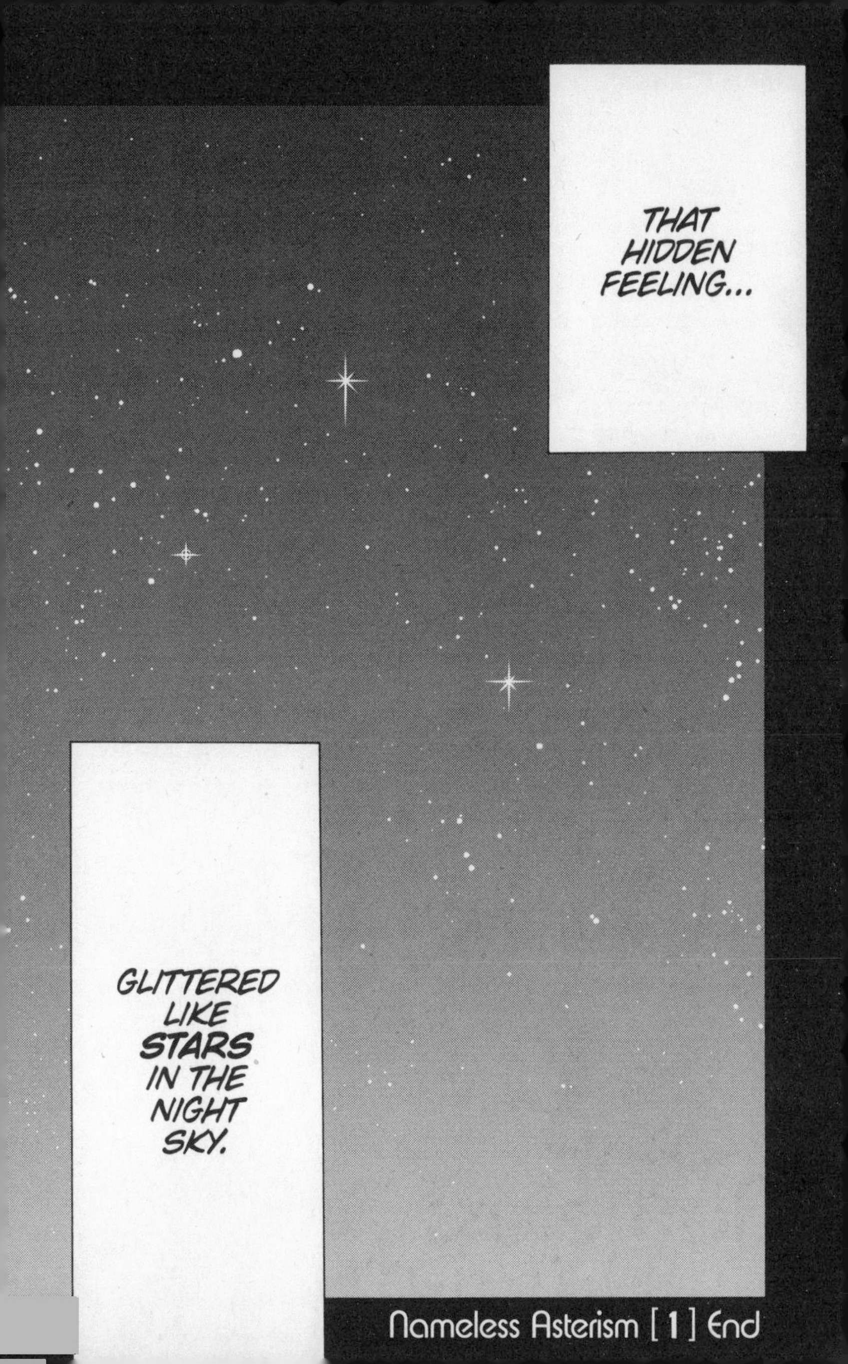
THAT HIDDEN FEELING...
GLITTERED LIKE STARS IN THE NIGHT SKY.
Nameless Asterism [1] End

Nameless Asterism

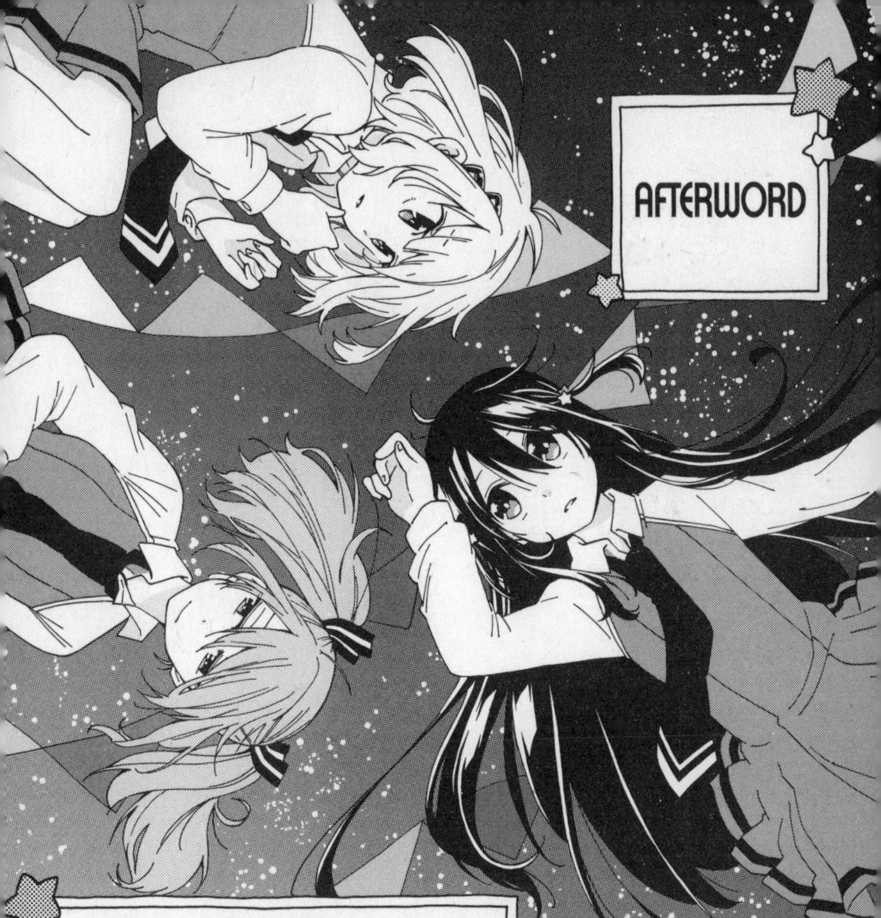

AFTERWORD

Hello. I'm Kina Kobayashi.

Thank you so much for reading the first volume of *Nameless Asterism!!* I'm so happy that my long-time dream of being serialized and published has come true. I have the support of you wonderful readers to thank for that. I'll do my best and hope that you'll enjoy what happens next. Let's meet again in Volume 2!!!

I'm on Twitter. ⇨ @udonkimuchikaki
(Release date information, etc)

Kina Kobayashi

Shiratori Tsukasa

- 149cm
- Blood type O
- Girls' soccer club
- Best subject: gym
- Favorite foods:
  ramen (miso)
  cream puffs
- Least favorite food
  pickled eggplant

SHE USUALLY WEARS A PONYTAIL FOR GYM CLASS, CLUB MEETS, ETC.

POST-JERSEY

Washio Nadeshiko

- 162cm (for now)
- Blood type AB
- Astronomy club
- Best subject: science
- Favorite foods:
  gratin, anything
  matcha-flavored
- Least favorite food
  Sakura Denbu
  (sweetened pink fish flakes)

LIKES
MONOTONE
COLORS.

IN THE BEGINNING,
SHE HAD SHORT HAIR,
BUT AFTER GIVING IT
A LOT OF THOUGHT, I
WENT WITH PIGTAILS.
WHO IS THIS?

ORIGINAL
DESIGN.
↓

Kotooka Mikage

- 153cm
- Blood type B
- Drama Club
- Best subject: home ec.
- Favorite foods:
  yakiniku (grilled meat)
  anything chocolate
- Least favorite food
  raw fish

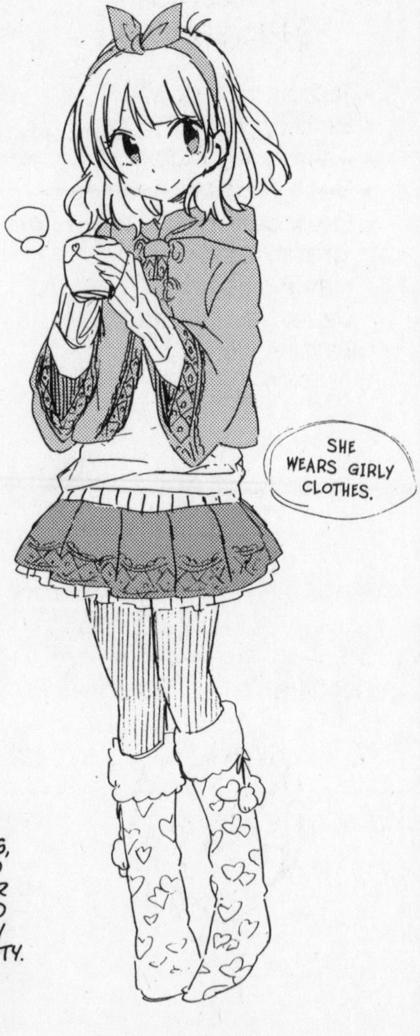
SHE WEARS GIRLY CLOTHES.

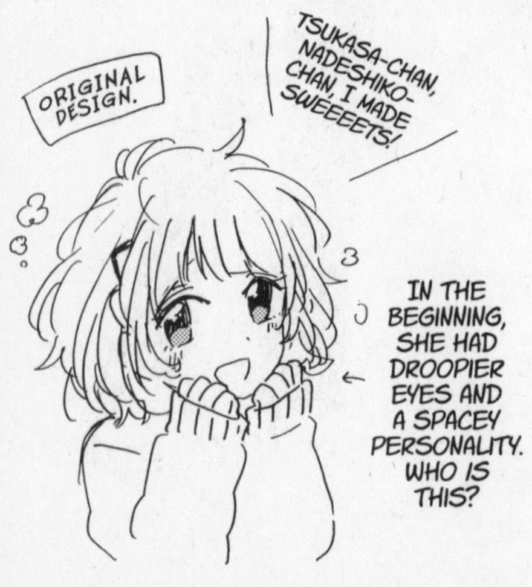
ORIGINAL DESIGN.
TSUKASA-CHAN, NADESHIKO-CHAN, I MADE SWEEEEETS!
IN THE BEGINNING, SHE HAD DROOPIER EYES AND A SPACEY PERSONALITY. WHO IS THIS?

Extra ★ Movie

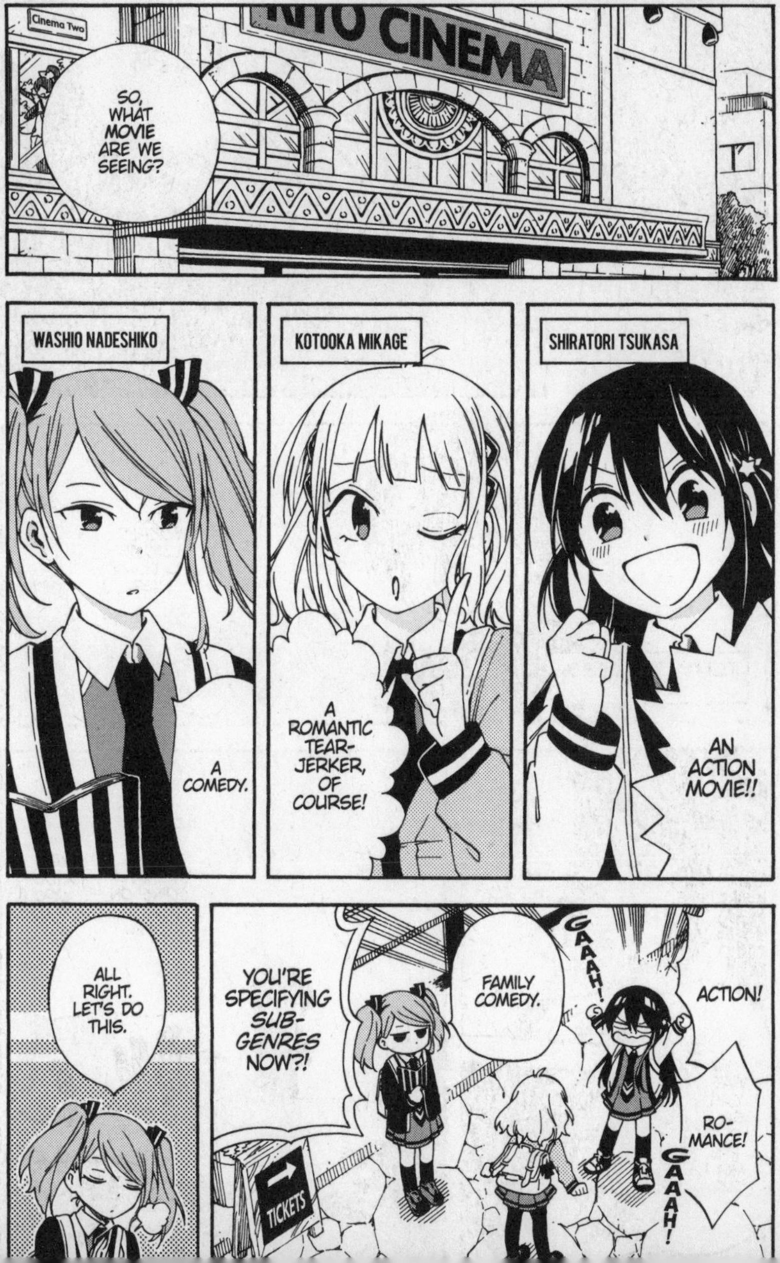

Cinema Two
NTO CINEMA
SO, WHAT MOVIE ARE WE SEEING?
SHIRATORI TSUKASA
AN ACTION MOVIE!!
KOTOOKA MIKAGE
A ROMANTIC TEAR-JERKER, OF COURSE!
WASHIO NADESHIKO
A COMEDY.
ACTION!
GAAAH!
RO-MANCE!
GAAAH!
FAMILY COMEDY.
YOU'RE SPECIFYING SUB-GENRES NOW?!
TICKETS
ALL RIGHT. LET'S DO THIS.

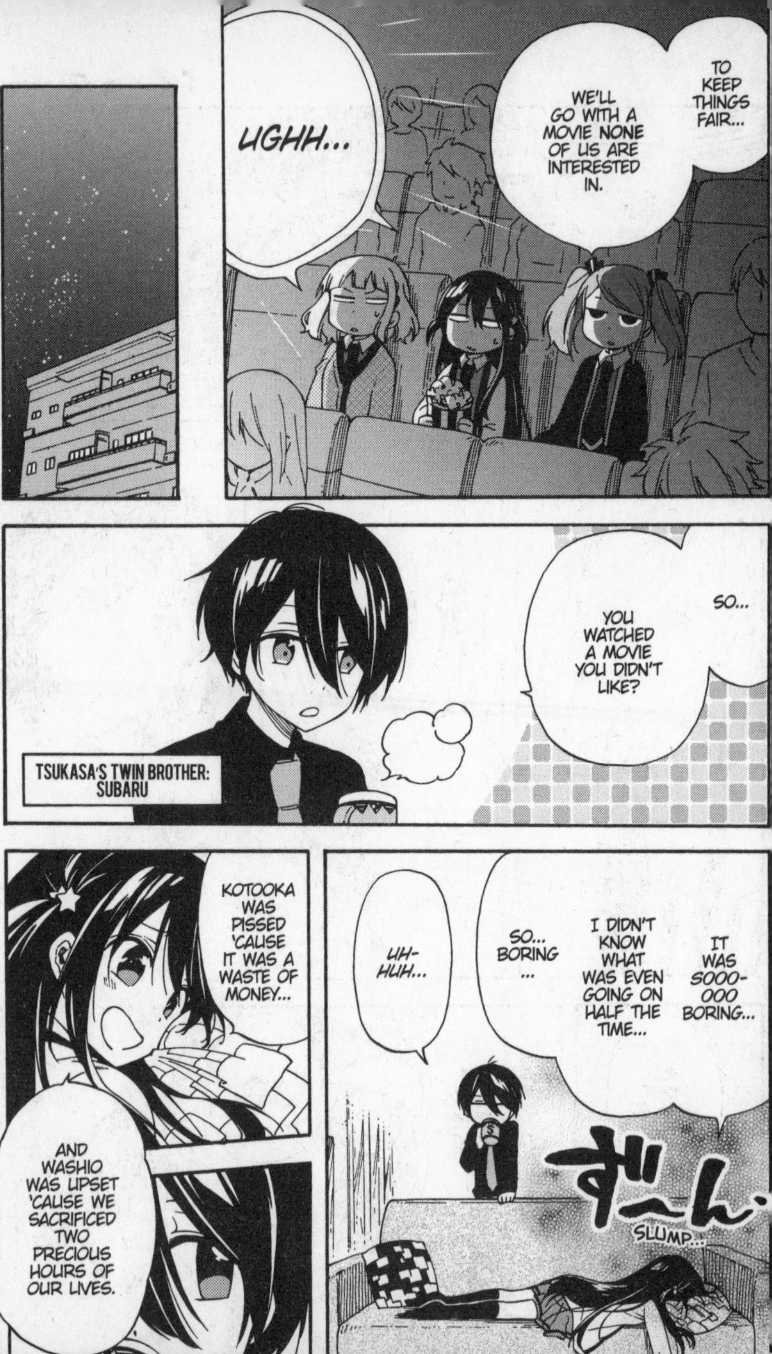
TO KEEP THINGS FAIR...
WE'LL GO WITH A MOVIE NONE OF US ARE INTERESTED IN.
UGHH...
SO...
YOU WATCHED A MOVIE YOU DIDN'T LIKE?
TSUKASA'S TWIN BROTHER: SUBARU
IT WAS SOOOOOO BORING...
I DIDN'T KNOW WHAT WAS EVEN GOING ON HALF THE TIME...
SO... BORING ...
UH-HUH...
ずーん
SLUMP...
KOTOOKA WAS PISSED 'CAUSE IT WAS A WASTE OF MONEY...
AND WASHIO WAS UPSET 'CAUSE WE SACRIFICED TWO PRECIOUS HOURS OF OUR LIVES.

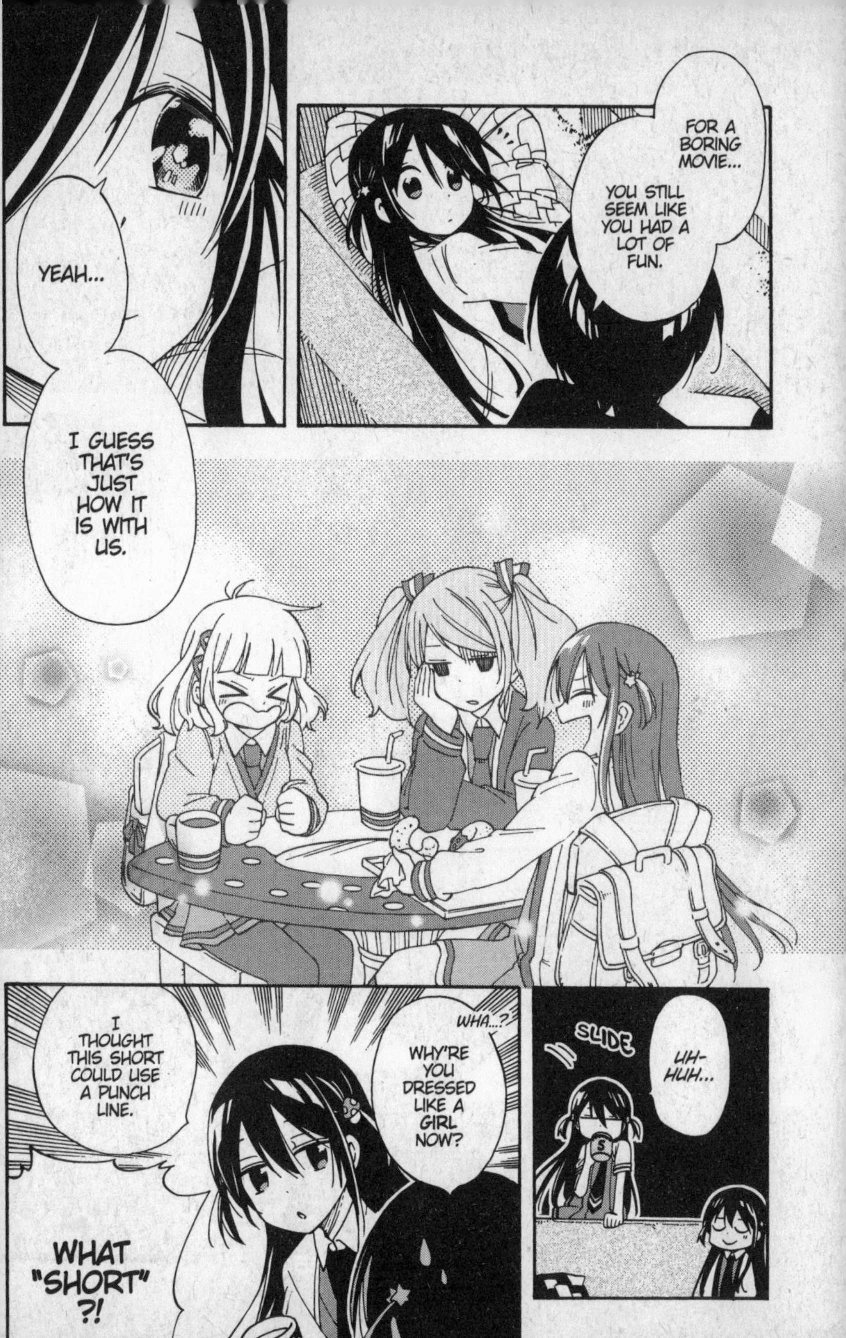
FOR A BORING MOVIE...
YOU STILL SEEM LIKE YOU HAD A LOT OF FUN.
YEAH...
I GUESS THAT'S JUST HOW IT IS WITH US.
SLIDE
UH-HUH...
WHA...?
WHY'RE YOU DRESSED LIKE A GIRL NOW?
I THOUGHT THIS SHORT COULD USE A PUNCH LINE.
WHAT "SHORT" ?!